PEAK
HUMAN

Also by Johan Norberg

The Capitalist Manifesto: Why the Global Free Market Will Save the World

Open: How Collaboration and Curiosity Shaped Humankind

Progress: Ten Reasons to Look Forward to the Future

PEAK HUMAN
HUMAN

What We
Can Learn
from the
Rise and Fall
of Golden Ages

JOHAN
NORBERG

Atlantic Books
London

First published in hardback in Great Britain in 2025 by Atlantic Books, an imprint of Atlantic Books Ltd.

Copyright © Johan Norberg, 2025

The moral right of Johan Norberg to be identified as the author of this work has been asserted by him in accordance with the Copyright, Designs and Patents Act of 1988.

All rights reserved. No part of this publication may be reproduced, stored in a retrieval system, or transmitted in any form or by any means, electronic, mechanical, photocopying, recording, or otherwise, without the prior permission of both the copyright owner and the above publisher of this book.

No part of this book may be used in any manner in the learning, training or development of generative artificial intelligence technologies (including but not limited to machine learning models and large language models (LLMs)), whether by data scraping, data mining or use in any way to create or form a part of data sets or in any other way.

Every effort has been made to trace or contact all copyright holders. The publishers will be pleased to make good any omissions or rectify any mistakes brought to their attention at the earliest opportunity.

Maps designed by Jeff Edwards

10 9 8 7 6 5 4

A CIP catalogue record for this book is available from the British Library.

Hardback ISBN: 978 1 83895 729 2
Trade Paperback ISBN: 978 1 80546 387 0
E-book ISBN: 978 1 83895 730 8

Printed in Great Britain by CPI Group (UK) Ltd, Croydon CR0 4YY

Atlantic Books
An imprint of Atlantic Books Ltd
Ormond House
26–27 Boswell Street
London
WC1N 3JZ

www.atlantic-books.co.uk

Product safety EU representative: Authorised Rep Compliance Ltd., Ground Floor, 71 Lower Baggot Street, Dublin, D02 P593, Ireland. www.arccompliance.com

To my father, who made me realize that the only thing new in the world is history that we have yet to learn

CONTENTS

Introduction   1

1   Athens: Democrats, Dreamers and Other Deviants   11

2   Rome: Melting Pot of Marble   73

3   The Abbasid Caliphate: At the Crossroads of the Universe   127

4   Song China: On the Threshold of Modernity   173

5   Renaissance Italy: The Rebirth of Law, Literature and Libertas   219

6   The Dutch Republic: Trade, Toleration and Other Treasures of the Shore   283

7   The Anglosphere: Industry, Individualism and Impertinence   341

Conclusion: Further Rise or Inevitable Decline?   431

Acknowledgements   446

Notes   448

Index   479

INTRODUCTION

A society that has ceased to concern itself with the progress of the past will soon lose belief in its capacity to progress in the future.
JOEL MOKYR[1]

To every nation a term; when their term comes they shall not put it back by a single hour nor put it forward.
THE QURAN, 7:34

The feeling will be familiar to many who have visited the great cities of history: I had come to Athens for the first time and made a pilgrimage to its democratic Assembly, Plato's Academy and Aristotle's Lyceum. And it left me with a sense of profound sadness. Here were the scenes of some of the most extraordinary moments in human history, and all that was left was rubble, garbage and dog waste. Instead of bustling creativity, there was silence, interrupted only by the odd intoxicated passer-by.

To be sure, I also experienced spectacular beauty in Athens, like the grand monuments on the Acropolis. But even that was a museum to bygone glory. This used to be the place around which the world revolved, and now it's a collection of patched-together columns, stone blocks and shards with plaques telling us that it used to be impressive.

This must be what Shelley – a great admirer of ancient Greece – reflected upon when he wrote about the crumbled monument to Ozymandias, king of kings, 'Look on my works, ye Mighty, and despair! / Nothing beside remains. ... / The lone and level sands stretch far away.'

This encounter with the transience of great civilizations set my mind racing. What made it possible for them to rise so spectacularly, and how could they decline so thoroughly that they left little trace? It forced me to consider whether travellers will one day visit our proud landmarks and plazas and think about how our civilization lost its way and became so sluggish and stationary.

This is a precarious time to write about history's golden ages. Ours is an era of authoritarian and populist revival, with savage dictators trying to extinguish neighbouring democracies, when the fear of inevitable decline seems more prevalent than belief in progress. This may invite speculation that my motive resembles that of the American legal scholar Harold Berman when he wrote his great history of the rise of Western law: it is said that a drowning man may see his whole life flash before him, perhaps in an unconscious effort to find something within his own experiences to escape his impending doom.[2]

I wouldn't go that far. We are not yet drowning. But drawing on historical human experience can be a useful way to avoid ending up in a bad situation: it might even help us to keep our vessels seaworthy. It is said that we should study history to avoid repeating its mistakes, and that is all very well. But our ancestors were not just capable of mistakes.

Human history is a long list of depravations and horrors, but it is also the source of the knowledge, institutions and technologies that have set most of humanity free from such horrors for the first time. The historical record shows what mankind is capable of, in terms of exploration, imagination and innovation. This in itself is an important reason to study it, to broaden our mental horizon of what is possible.

This book is about seven of the world's great civilizations: ancient Athens, the Roman Republic and early empire, the Abbasid Caliphate, Song China, Renaissance Italy, the Dutch Republic and the Anglosphere. Why did I pick those? Because each of them exemplifies, in my understanding, what I think of as a golden age: a period with a large number of innovations that revolutionize many fields and sectors in a short period of time. A golden age is associated with a culture of optimism, which encourages people to explore new knowledge, experiment with new methods and technologies, and exchange the results with others. Its characteristics are cultural creativity, scientific discoveries, technological achievements and economic growth that stand out compared with what came before and after it, and compared with other contemporary cultures. Its result is a high average standard of living, which is usually the envy of others, often also of their heirs.

This could have been a much longer book, exploring many other cultures, because golden ages are not dependent on geography, ethnicity or religion, but on what we make of these circumstances. And these cultures just happen to excel in the era in which they, for some reason or another, begin to interpret or emphasize a particular part of their beliefs and traditions to make it more open to surprises – unconventional ideas and methods imported by merchants and migrants, dreamed up by eccentrics at home or stumbled upon by someone fortunate.

There are certain important preconditions for this progress, and you will find them making cameos in every ensuing chapter. The basic raw materials are a wide variety of ideas and methods to learn from and to combine in new ways. Therefore it takes a certain population density to create progress, and urban conglomerations are often particularly creative. Being open to the contributions of other civilizations is the quickest way of making use of more brains, which is the reason why these golden ages often appear at the crossroads of other cultures, and in every instance benefited greatly from the inspiration brought about by international trade, travel and migration. They were often maritime cultures, always on the lookout for new discoveries. Distance is the 'number one enemy of civilization', as the French historian Fernand Braudel understood so well.

To make use of these raw materials, it takes a relatively inclusive society. Citizens have to be free to experiment and innovate, without being subjected to the whims of feudal lords, centralized governments or ravaging armies. This takes peace, rule of law and secure property rights.

And, most importantly, there has to be an absence of orthodoxies imposed from the top about what to believe, think and say, how to live and what to do. If we limit the realm of the acceptable to what we already know and are comfortable with, we will be stuck with it, and deserve the inevitable stagnation. If we want more knowledge, wealth and technological capacity, we have to cut misfits and troublemakers some slack.

This book will look at how institutions that were built for discovery, innovation and adaptation had profound effects on science, culture, economy and warfare.

It is not easy to sustain such institutions for a long time. The most depressing aspect of studying golden ages is that they don't last. You don't have to wait 2,300 years to go back to Athens. There are many stories about people visiting centres of progress just decades later and finding that it's all over. It's the same place, the same traditions and the same people, but that irreplaceable spark has gone.

The California historian Jack Goldstone calls these episodes of temporary growth 'efflorescences'.[3] It is really another word for an anti-crisis: just as a crisis is a sudden and unexpected downturn in indicators of human wellbeing, an efflorescence is a sharp, unexpected upturn.

Goldstone argues that most societies have experienced such efflorescences, and that these usually set new patterns for thought, political organization and economic life for many generations. This is a corrective to the common notion that humankind has a long history of stagnation and then suddenly experiences progress. History is full of growth and progress; it is just that they were always periodic and efflorescent rather than self-sustaining and accelerating. In other words: they don't last. That is why the subsequent silver, bronze and iron ages so often think of themselves as golden ages.

It is as if history has a Great Status Quo Filter (similar to a hypothesis about the Fermi paradox on why we have not encountered alien life despite the likelihood that it exists). Civilizations in every era have tried to break away from the shackles of oppression and scarcity, but increasingly they faced opposite forces, and sooner or later these dragged them back to earth. Elites who have benefited enough from the innovation that elevated them want to kick away the ladder behind them, groups threatened by change try to fossilize culture into an orthodoxy, and aggressive neighbours are attracted to the wealth of the achievers and try to kill the goose to steal its golden eggs.

Why would intellectual, economic and political elites accept a system that keeps delivering surprises and innovations? Yes, it might provide their society with more resources, but at the risk of upending a status quo that made them powerful to begin with. Often such institutions came about by accident or as a result of revolutionary upheaval, or they emerged unintentionally because they happened to provide important solutions in difficult situations or had to be accepted to provide necessary resources and technologies at a time of fierce competition against rivals.

But, sooner or later, most elites regain their composure, begin to reimpose orthodoxies and stamp out the potential for unpredictability. The great economic historian Joel Mokyr calls this Cardwell's Law, after the technology historian D. S. L. Cardwell, who observed that most societies have remained technologically creative for only a short period.[4]

The perceived self-interest of incumbents who have much to lose from change goes a long way to explaining why episodes of creativity and growth are terminated. But such groups are always there, always eager to stop the future in its tracks. Why do their reactions prevail in some places and moments but not in others? Many factors are at play, and they will all figure prominently in this book. But there is one psychological factor that reinforces all of them.

'What is civilization's worst enemy?' asked the art historian Kenneth Clark, and he answered: 'first of all fear – fear of war, fear of invasion, fear of plague and famine, that make it simply not worthwhile constructing things, or planting trees or even planting next year's crop. And fear of the supernatural, which means that you daren't question anything or change anything.'[5]

We humans have two basic settings: we are traders and we are tribalists. Early humans prospered (relatively) because they ventured out to explore, experiment and exchange, and to discover new places, partners and knowledge. But sometimes they only survived their adventures because they were also acutely sensitive to risks, and instantly reacted to a potential threat by fighting or fleeing back to the familiar, their cave and their tribe. We need both the adventurous and risk-sensitive aspects of our personality, but since *Homo sapiens* emerged over hundreds of thousands of years in a world more dangerous than today's, our 'spider sense' had to be over-sensitive to threats.

Therefore it often misfires and is easily manipulated by those who want to divide and conquer.

As I documented in my book *Open: The Story of Human Progress*, this anxious aspect has remained a central part of our nature, even after we left the savannah for a safer world. When we feel threatened as a community by, say, neighbouring armies, pandemics, recessions or conflicts, there is often a societal fight-or-flight instinct, causing us to hunt for scapegoats and flee behind physical and intellectual walls, even though complex threats might call for learning and creativity rather than simply avoidance or attack.

Again and again, we see civilizations prosper when they embrace trade and experiments, but decline when they lose cultural self-confidence. When under threat, we often seek stability and predictability, shutting out that which is different and unpredictable. Unfortunately, this often makes the fear of disaster self-fulfilling, since those barriers limit access to other possibilities and restrict the adaptation and innovation that could have helped us deal with the threat. The problem with paralysing fear is that it has a tendency to paralyse.

I wouldn't go so far as to say that we have nothing to fear but fear itself. That sounds a bit like underestimating armed raiders and bubonic plague. But it is certainly true that an insular, suppressive angst deprives us of the tools we need to take them on. Outsiders can kill and destroy, but they can't kill curiosity and creativity. Only we can do that to ourselves.

History often repeats because human nature does. All of the golden ages ended, except one – the one that we are in now. 'History', said the American journalist Norman Cousins, 'is a vast early warning system.' Where does that leave our civilization? Let me hold my thoughts about that back until we have looked at the other episodes. But I can reveal this much: we still know how to swim, but it doesn't happen automatically; it takes a conscious effort. For that reason, repeating history's swimming lessons once in a while is helpful.

If you want to situate my argument in the context of current culture wars, I object to both the relativist idea that all cultures are equal *and* to the idea that there is a hierarchy of two opposing and clashing cultures – civilization versus barbarians (often associated with European Judeo-Christian culture vs the rest).

Some cultures are better than others. Denying that is, as pointed out by the physicist David Deutsch, 'denying that the future state of one's own culture can be better than the present'.[6] Then chattel slavery and human rights are equally good (or bad). Some cultures are better than others because they provide institutions for positive-sum games instead of zero-sum, and their eras create liberties and opportunities rather than oppression and destruction, as we shall see in this book.

But, no, we are not talking here about the inherent traits of two opposite and clashing civilizations. Among the seven golden ages featured here, we meet pagans, Muslims, Confucians, Catholics, Calvinists, Anglicans and secular civilizations. Those who were seen as barbarians in one era became world leaders in science and technology in the next, and then roles reversed again. They just happened to excel in an era in which the culture was most open to the contributions of other civilizations, and so gained access to more brains.

This is why both the nationalist right and woke left are hopelessly unhistorical in their crusades against cultural hotchpotch. Civilizations are not monoliths with inherent traits, but complex, growing things defined by how they engage with, adopt and adapt (appropriate, if you like) what they find elsewhere. It's the connections and combinations that make them what they are.

If you come away from this book with the impression that there were seven civilized civilizations and the rest were barbarians, I have not done my job. The battle between freedom and coercion, and between reason and superstition, is not a clash of civilizations. It is a clash *within* every civilization, and at some level within each one of us. Every culture, country and government is capable of decency and creativity, and of ignorance and jaw-dropping barbarianism. That is why 'golden' should be understood as much in relationship to what you could otherwise have been, as a comparison with others. It is of course not just down to sheer will, but you and I have it within ourselves to make our particular place on earth decent and creative rather than the opposite.

By the way, I should emphasize that the question 'golden ages for whom?' is not just overly sensitive sloganeering. All of the civilizations I describe in this book practised slavery, all of them denied women basic rights and all took great delight in exterminating neighbouring populations, to the last man, woman and child.

Whenever I am tempted to look back at these ages and dream about how amazing it would have been to be alive then, to debate philosophy in the Athenian Lyceum or Baghdad's House of Wisdom, to discuss political strategy with Cicero or the Song emperor, or to be present at the creation of the Pantheon, *The Last Supper* or the printing press, I remind myself that I wouldn't have come near those places. I would have been a destitute peasant, struggling desperately to keep my family safe from hunger and raiders for another season.

If I was one of the lucky ones, that is. As the classicist Mary Beard has remarked, when people say they admire the Roman Empire, they always assume they would have been the emperor or a senator (a few hundred people), never the enslaved masses in mines, plantations and other people's households (a few million).

Recorded history is the work of a tiny literate elite, and for most people, in most eras, life was nasty, brutish and short. In fact, that goes for the small elite too. No matter how powerful they were, everything could be lost in an instant if they had the misfortune to displease a capricious ruler, and even he had little chance against, say, a bacterial infection or a barbarian invasion. Remember, every time history books record that a city was 'sacked', it means that thousands of civilians were raped, mutilated and disembowelled. This also tells us something about what mankind is capable of.

That our ancestors got through this is testament to their greatness. Some ten thousand generations suffered horrors and hunger, and then suddenly, in the past ten generations, everything changed, to the extent that many of us today have started seeing peace, democratic liberties and a full stomach as a natural state. History is more than a crime scene. It is also the place where ideas were developed that helped humanity to identify that something is a crime, and how to grow out of it. If we discard all the achievements of those who came before us because they weren't sufficiently enlightened and decent (they weren't), we will eventually lose the capacity to discern what is enlightened and decent. Because that very language and moral sense emerged out of their struggles.

So, if you discover something inspiring and useful there, in the overgrown ruins of the past, that can be salvaged to help ensure that our civilization does not just become one in the long list of Goldstone's temporary efflorescenses, let's fight for it, shall we? As Goethe once told us, you cannot inherit a tradition from your parents; you have to earn it.

Johan Norberg

1

ATHENS

Democrats, Dreamers and Other Deviants

In the history of mankind Greece will eternally remain the place where mankind experienced its fairest youth and bridal beauty.

JOHANN GOTTFRIED HERDER[1]

The period which intervened between the birth of Pericles [495 BC] and the death of Aristotle [322 BC], is undoubtedly... the most memorable in the history of the world.

PERCY BYSSHE SHELLEY, 1815[2]

[H]ad there been no Socrates, no Plato, and no Aristotle, there would have been no philosophy for the next two thousand years, nor in all probability then.

JOHN STUART MILL, 1843[3]

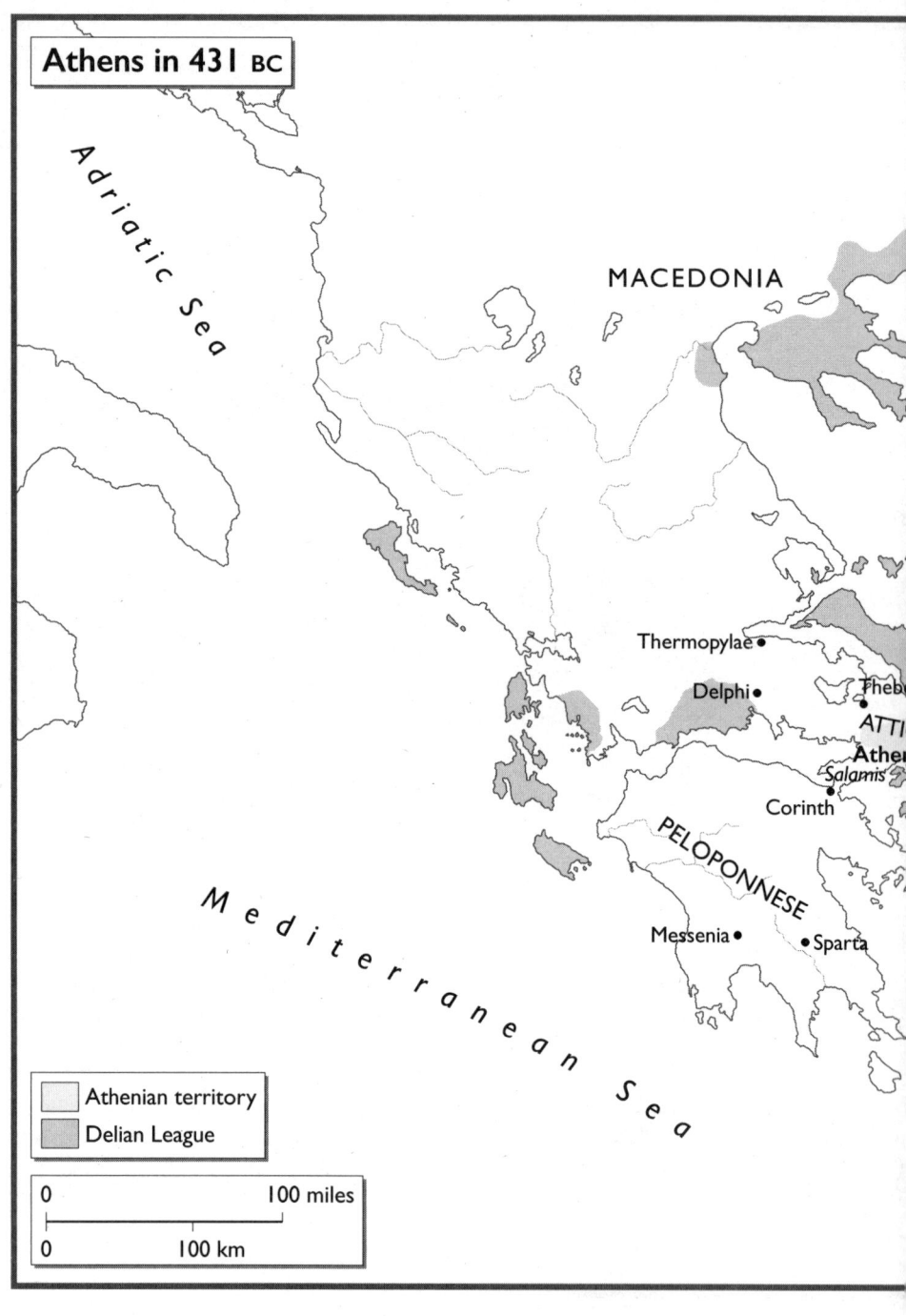

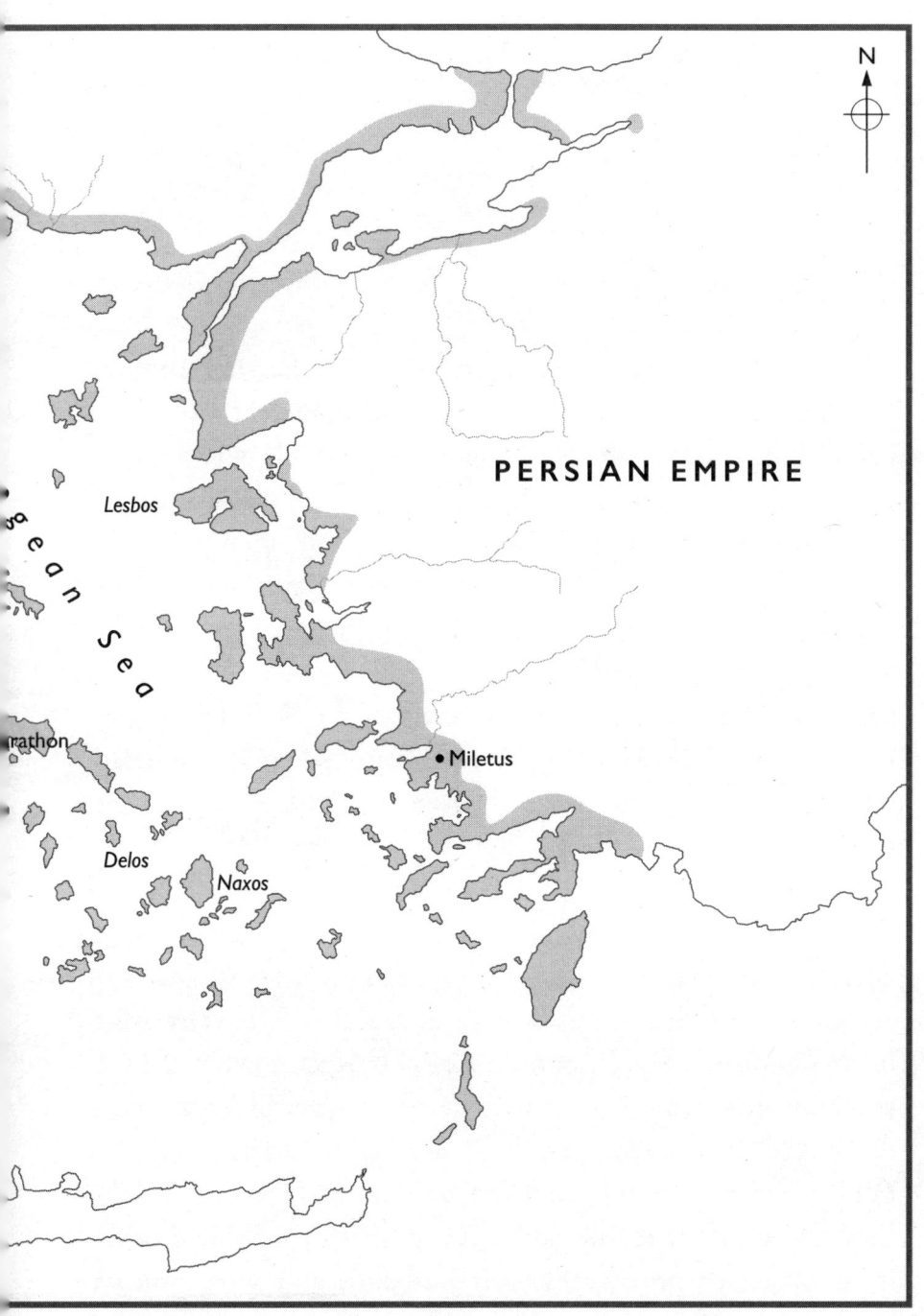

To some, this is the story of the origin of Western civilization:

In 480 BC, the mighty, despotic Persian Empire invaded Greece to destroy the fiercely independent city-states before they could create their golden age, which would go on to inspire the Roman Empire and then the whole of Europe. According to Herodotus, 2.5 million men from all over Xerxes' vast Persian Empire made the ground shake and drank many a river dry. Supported by a fleet of 1,200 ships, they were set to destroy the Greek enlightenment in its infancy. A moment, according to Hegel, when 'the interest of the World's History hung trembling in the balance': a world united under one Lord versus separate states animated by free individuality 'stood front to front in array of battle'.[4]

But then, miraculously, the advance of the largest army the world had ever seen was halted at the narrow pass of Thermopylae near the coast – by no more than 300 Spartans and some allies. Sparta was the admired, authoritarian city-state in the south-eastern Peloponnesian peninsula, governed by a strict hierarchy and a regimented lifestyle, where the landowners devoted all their time to training and exercise. They were the bravest in their fighting, almost always won, and if they didn't, they would rather die in battle. Return with your shield or *on* it, as Spartan women told their husbands and sons. Shields were heavy, and to throw a shield away in order to run from the enemy was a disgrace worse than death.

Under the command of King Leonidas, the 300 Spartans, prepared for a suicide mission, held the hundreds of thousands of Persians back. When ordered to put down their weapons, the Spartans famously replied 'come and take them'. Xerxes threw his best men from three continents at the Spartan soldiers but failed to break through. But, at the end of the second day of brutal battle, the Greeks were betrayed. Someone showed the Persians that there was a mountain path that could take them behind the Greek lines. The Spartans told their allies to escape but preferred to fight to the very end themselves. They came out from behind their defences and fought and fell, one after the other, but not before having taken thousands of invaders with them to Hades.

King Leonidas and his men died at the hot gates of Thermopylae, but they had delayed the Persians, and given others time to mobilize. More than that, the Spartans had, through their noble sacrifice, given the Greeks the inspiration to fight back. In the end, the Greeks united and defeated the Persian army, and so Leonidas's sacrifice was not a defeat but the beginning of victory. It gave the Greeks their freedom and made possible a remarkable era of cultural flourishing and scientific discovery in Athens and other cities, which would go on to create Western civilization and the modern world.

It's an amazing story, and one of the episodes that first made me fascinated with history and antiquity. Unfortunately, it is also almost all hogwash.

The Spartan losers

The Persian invasion did indeed happen, and the whole of Greece was almost subjected to Xerxes' rule. The number of

2.5 million men is a gross exaggeration, but even if modern estimates of around 250,000 invaders is closer to the truth, it was still the biggest invading force the world had ever seen. However, the Spartans did not defeat the Persian army, and they were not defenders of freedom, not in Greece and not even in their own city. They were infamous for being a small oligarchy that, unlike most Greeks, enthusiastically enslaved other Greeks, whole neighbouring populations in fact. The lifestyle of the Spartan landowning elite was made possible by the enslavement of the neighbouring helot population, which was forced to farm the land for them. In ensuing wars, when Spartans failed to defeat Athenians and Corinthians on their own, they were happy to invite Persia back to function as their local enforcers in subjecting fellow Greeks.

About the only good thing that can be said of the Spartans was that the separation of boys and men into the harsh military-style 'agoge' school from the age of seven to thirty (the rite of passage was not the killing of a wolf as in the movies, but sneaking up on and murdering an unarmed slave) gave women a relatively strong position in society, as rulers of the households.

The Spartans were not the invincible soldiers of propaganda. They were good infantrymen who trained more than others, but they were not much better than the average Greek army. One attempt to assess 126 Spartan military engagements estimates that they clearly won only fifty of them, five were stalemates and seventy-one were defeats.[5] And if the Spartans lost or were at risk of defeat, they often fled just like anybody else – leaving their shields behind rather than returning on them, as it were.

The classicist Bret Devereaux argues that the Spartans were uninventive in warfare and mostly tried the same things over and over. They never mastered logistics and did not experiment with new tactics, combined arms or naval operations. Judging

Sparta by how well it achieved its strategic objectives, Devereaux writes:

> Sparta's armies are a comprehensive failure. The Spartan was no super-soldier and Spartan training was not excellent. Indeed, far from making him a super-soldier, the agoge made the Spartans inflexible, arrogant and uncreative, and those flaws led directly to Sparta's decline in power. … The horror of the Spartan system, the nastiness of the agoge, the oppression of the helots, the regimentation of daily life, it was all for nothing. Worse yet, it created a Spartan leadership class that seemed incapable of thinking its way around even basic problems.[6]

At Thermopylae, the Spartans were not 300 but probably more than five thousand with other Greek allies. Sparta decided not to risk their main army far from the hometown and blamed their small number on two ongoing festivals that forced the bulk to stay at home. However, they were joined by several thousand from other cities who had not found a convenient excuse not to fight. Even during their doomed last stand, when the main force had left, the 300 Spartans had the company of Thespian and Theban forces, and the Spartans ordered their slaves to remain, so they were in total more like two thousand men, with Spartans being the smallest contingent.

Neither did their sacrifice inspire the Greeks to unite and fight against the Persians, because they already had – the decision to fight at Thermopylae was a joint one at a congress of allied Greek city-states, and while that battle was underway, a united Greek fleet was fighting Persians ships outside Thermopylae, to stop them from outflanking the soldiers. That was on the urging of the Athenians, since the Spartan commander of the fleet, Eurybiades, wanted to retreat to the Peloponnese and rely on land forces, since he moaned that Persians were invincible by sea – 'not perhaps the best qualification for a Greek admiral' comments one historian.[7] The Athenians had to bribe him to stay.

And, crucially, the battle of Thermopylae was not some sort of great success in disguise, as later mythology would have it. On the contrary, it was a fiasco that almost doomed the whole war effort. Thermopylae was cleverly chosen by the Greeks as the place where the Persians' superior numbers could be offset. The pass was so narrow that at most two chariots could pass by each other. With more than five thousand well-trained and heavily armoured soldiers defending the pass, the position was nearly impregnable, no matter how many Persians lined up to take their turn. Man-for-man, the light-armed Persians could be defeated, and with such a large Greek force, they could constantly rotate out the wounded and exhausted off the line so that there were always fresh and alert soldiers at the front.

And a little persistence was all it would have taken. Xerxes had gathered perhaps a quarter of a million hungry and thirsty men, who lived off the land and were far from home. If the defenders could hold Thermopylae for just a few more days, the invaders would run out of supplies and be forced to retreat. At the Battle of the Persian Gate 150 years later, even fewer Persian soldiers held a similar narrow pass against Alexander the Great's invading army for a month.

The Greeks could have blocked the mountain trail that led around the pass, which the Persians with their famous and feared intelligence capabilities were bound to learn about. But, in an epic miscalculation, King Leonidas stationed less experienced men to guard it, and according to Herodotus they also lacked a clear understanding of their strategic objective. The massive Persian elite force just marched past them (or eliminated them quickly), encircled the defenders of Thermopylae and massacred them. The impregnable pass was overrun in less than three days, and Xerxes' army could quickly proceed to destroy resistant cities – then the road lay open to sack and burn Athens. The legendary Spartans had been 'little more than a speed-bump under the wheels of the Persian war machine', assesses Myke Cole, who has reconstructed the battle in detail in a popular history of the Spartans as soldiers.[8] 'Come and take them', roared the Spartans, raising their spears and swords menacingly, and the Persians swiftly proceeded to do just that.

The Spartans are the most overrated warriors in ancient history; they just had very good PR – partly because the Athenians who wrote about them were aristocrats. They deplored the vulgar democracy of their own city and envied Sparta's totalitarianism, which gave power to a tiny elite.

But in a perfect illustration of our broader historical theme – that openness and innovation tend to beat brute force – what defeated the Persian invaders and saved Greece was not Spartan bravery and muscle, but Athenian intelligence and imagination. As we shall see, through improvisation and innovation, and a lot of trickery and deceit, the Athenians managed to defeat the mighty Persians not just once, but twice. It was an astonishing success that would give the young democracy cultural self-confidence to deepen its freedoms, and unleash a cultural and philosophical golden age that changed the course of history. But not before their city had been burned to the ground and their temples destroyed.

Rocking the Athenian boat

Greece was different. The Hellenic tip of the Balkan peninsula in south-eastern Europe was close to older and more sophisticated civilizations like Egypt and the Mesopotamian cities, the exceptional pioneers of settled agriculture, a formalized economy with contracts and money, the written language, a written legal code and many sciences and other aspects of human civilization.

Greece was also on a Mediterranean ocean that had been culturally and economically integrated by Phoenician traders. Greek cities and thinkers built on these accomplishments, adapting an alphabet from the Phoenicians sometime in the eighth century BC, and picking up sciences, arts and skills from Mesopotamia and Egypt. But the Greeks also learned from each other because, unlike their neighbours, they were not subjected to one imperial ruler.

Greeks sometimes say that when God (perhaps not the *God*, but one of the gods in the ancients' sprawling pantheon) made Europe, he threw all the rocks into Greece. Settlements separated by rocky hills, mountain ranges and stretches of water were not easily unified. Instead, Greece was made up of more than a thousand fiercely self-governing city-states, *poleis* (from which we take the word 'politics'). A *polis* usually emerged around an easily defended acropolis (*acro*, high), close to the sea and therefore trade and transport. These city-states were always competing in wars and games, but they were also observing and imitating one another. They were never complete strangers: they shared language, Homer's heroic epics, and Zeus, Hera and the other gods. Each of the cities bordered on one thousand small laboratories of innovation in law, economics and thought. A 'supermarket of constitutions' where anyone can 'pick out whatever pleases him', wrote Plato.[9]

As seafarers, constantly exploring and trading, they could not help being exposed to new ways and methods. Perhaps this experience of differences and access to options explains the Greeks' peculiar habit of not seeing their rulers as gods, or even as exceptionally well connected to them. Egyptian and Mesopotamian rulers had presented themselves as divine or as rulers on behalf of gods, which meant that opposition to their commands was restricted to the remarkably brave. The Greeks found it odd that only Persian priests could preside over a sacrifice, since any Greek, even women and slaves, could sacrifice to the gods.

This individualism was reinforced by another strange custom. Many Greeks became independent property-owning farmers, rather than serfs and subjects. We don't know exactly how this came about, but it happened after the Late Bronze Age collapse around 1200 BC, when the old Greek palace cultures perished in a calamity of natural disasters and invaders with new, deadlier weapons. The population declined during the dark ages, and the governing aristocrats had to hand more power and land to the farm workers who were left. After a while, a group of farmers had secured property rights to their plots, which they could pass on to their children. This gave them an interest in developing the land and cultivating vines, fruit and olive trees that would take a longer time to bear fruit.

According to the American classicist Victor Davis Hanson, this was the group that changed the world, through their independent position, but also their contribution to war-making.[10] The Greek world developed a special form of infantry, the phalanx, made up of what became known as hoplites. The men stood tightly packed, shoulder to shoulder, in an almost impenetrable formation, eight or more rows deep. Protected by the shields that gave them their name, the *hoplon*, they attacked the enemy with spears and, if these broke, short swords. It was tremendously effective. Before the invention of stirrups, charging cavalry would often just be knocked backwards by the array of spears.

Who could become a hoplite? They did not use a warhorse, so you did not have to be an aristocrat, but you had to be able to afford bronze armour, so you could not be poor. According to Hanson, the hoplites were the middling sort, those who had some independent property but not great wealth; in other words, they were the independent yeoman farmers.

Since they doubled as soldiers defending the *polis*, these hoplite farmers began to see themselves entitled to some share of the power. In some *poleis*, they met formally to listen to important information and sometimes debates between the ruling nobles on crucial decisions. It is not surprising that some of them dared think that they should be allowed to make their own voices heard. Eventually, after public pressure, negotiations, coups and possibly some of the world's first bourgeois revolutions, they took a share of the power in certain places. Among all the things these hoplite farmers cultivated, public participation in government and constitutional rule were the most important. They even pioneered the idea that civilians should set policy for the military.

Trade further diluted the control of the aristocracy. After 750, there were waves of Greek colonization to relieve the burden of growing populations, first towards Sicily and southern Italy, and then the shores of the Black Sea. This stimulated trade over the whole region and created new relatively wealthy groups of merchants, manufacturers and mercenaries. The brand-new Ionian innovation of coinage facilitated transactions and undermined aristocratic gift exchange networks. At the same time, trade exposed the Greeks to other cultures, and spurred innovation in metalwork, vase-painting and poetry.

All these circumstances explain what has sometimes been described as a certain Hellenistic personality – open, curious and flexible. And, among the Greeks, Athens by the Aegean Sea, the most populous *polis*, seemed to embody this spirit par exellence. The Athenians had to become especially outwards-oriented, partly because they had few alternatives. Attica, the land around Athens, had relatively poor soil. Plato described it as a skeleton of a body wasted by disease. The grain harvests were not sufficient for the population, but the land could produce olive oil and wine, so Athenians developed extended trade links early on to import grain from the Black Sea in exchange for their goods. An increasingly impressive merchant fleet, built with imported timber, made the eventual decision to become a sea power natural.

New groups of relatively wealthy farmers and merchants started to upset the old status quo. At the same time, many poor farmers suffered and ended up in slavery because they couldn't pay their debts to large landowners. Other peasants were in a form of bondage, forced to pay a portion of their production to a lord. It was a turbulent period with squabbling and plotting between aristocratic clans and threats of civil disorder and revolution. In an attempt to get to the bottom of the issues that threatened to tear Athens apart, one man, Solon (630–560 BC), was appointed with supreme power as lawgiver in the 590s BC.

Solon is probably the first real living person that we know of in Greek history, from the writings of others and from his own texts, which included many poems. Eventually, Solon became an almost mythical founding father, and all sorts of legislation and stories were attributed to him. He seems to have come from a noble family, but perhaps because of its poverty he became a merchant and travelled widely, comparing different societies and constitutions. His ambition was to create a moderate constitution, balancing the different classes and giving everyone a stake in the system.

He did not try to achieve democracy, but what the Greeks called *isonomia*, certainty of being governed equally according to laws, regardless of being noble or poor. Central to his project was the protection of liberties and property of even the lowest classes. Solon abolished feudal relationships on the land and banned the practice of debt slavery. Debts weren't cancelled in general, but those that mortgaged human beings were. Peasants who had been enslaved were liberated, and it was even said that Solon searched for Athenians who had been sold abroad and brought them back as free men.

It did not remove slavery, though. Like every other *polis*, Athens had a large slave population, usually taken in war or purchased from abroad. It might have been as many as 100,000 in the mid-fifth century. Most of the slaves were owned privately and worked in households or in agriculture, but they also worked in industry and the most unlucky ones were forced to work in the state-owned mines of Laurion, where naked and branded slaves dug silver for a city that prided itself on its liberty. Slavery was taken for granted in the ancient world, unchallenged even by the most advanced and radical thinkers. Freed or escaped slaves also took slaves.

The precise details of Solon's reforms are not known for certain, but they extended legal protection to all Athenian citizens and helped to protect the class of small landowners. He replaced the hereditary monopoly on public offices with a set of property requirements. The highest offices were restricted to the wealthiest, but lower ones were opened up to everybody but the poorest, the landless workers. However, even they got a seat in the assembly, which elected magistrates and held them to account.

Simultaneously, Solon encouraged the monetization of the economy and international trade. Foreign merchants were encouraged to settle in Athens and could even become citizens, which was unique at the time. The export of a cash crop like olive oil was stimulated, while at the same time the export of grain was banned for food security purposes.

The changes left aristocrat clans in overall charge, though, and they continued to feud. In the mid-500s BC, the general Pisistratus established himself as tyrant of Athens, the traditional name for a usurper who governs unrestrained by the law. He has been seen as a fairly benevolent despot who courted the middle and lower classes to secure his position, but the rule of his son, Hippias, degenerated into a paranoid purge of anyone who was seen as an enemy.

It was the struggle against the tyrant that gave birth to history's first democracy, but it happened in a most surprising way and it was dependent on some of the most unlikely champions – exiled Athenian aristocrats and Spartan soldiers.

The democratic revolution

The powerful Alcmaeonid family were at times collaborators with the despot Pisistratus, but at other times they fought with and betrayed him. Eventually they found themselves in exile, from where they plotted their return. Cleisthenes (570–508 BC), a prominent Alcmaeonid, knew that the Spartans might be interested in destabilizing a rival city like Athens. But how could he convince the Spartans to invade and depose the tyrant? Always playing the long game, Cleisthenes had supported the priests of Delphi with a costly refurbishment after an earthquake. After such lavish patronage, Spartans who visited the Oracle of Delphi for advice started to hear the same reply to all their queries: *First, free the Athenians.*

The combination of having a chance to turn Athens into a Spartan client state *and* have divine sanction to do it proved irresistible, and so the Spartan king Cleomenes sent a military expedition to the city in 510 BC. It was defeated, but they then sent another larger one, which succeeded in removing the Athenian despot. That was the easy bit. Much more difficult was furnishing a compromise between the Spartan interest in creating a puppet state and the Athenian aristocrats' ambition to rule. At first, the rival Isagoras, allied with the Spartans, took the offensive and tried to hand power back to the aristocrats. But times had changed. Despite the tyranny, trade had continued to grow and arenas for public participation had continued to function on issues where the ruler had not made up his mind. When the tyrant was gone, people thought the time had come for them to rule, not Spartans or oligarchs.

Cleisthenes knew that Athens had changed and saw his chance. Apparently, he and his groups had spent the exile engaged in some very serious thinking about how Athens could become a more stable place, where their clan did not always run the risk of exile or death when they lost a power struggle. The answer was completely unprecedented: he turned to the *demos*, the people, with a radical set of proposals to give them *kratos*, power. He invited all free men to design the future of the state and was met with a surge of public enthusiasm.

This so angered the Spartans that they returned to dismantle the democracy before it could get going, and to exile Cleisthenes and hundreds of anti-Spartan families. The Spartan king Cleomenes installed himself on the Acropolis with his men and Isagoras to draw up a new oligarchic constitution. But the Athenian people did not leave the Spartan king and his stooge to conspire in peace. Incredibly, they rose up violently in defence of their new freedoms, marched to the Acropolis and blockaded it for two days. By the third day, King Cleomenes was hungry and filthy, and surrendered in exchange for free passage to the border. The Spartans had been defeated not by an army, but by democratic rioters, who went on to slaughter Isagoras's allies.

Cleisthenes returned triumphantly, and the city exploded in revolutionary fervour. Now was the time to create a new constitution, where the people took matters into their own hands. The changes were bold and complex, and implementation seemed extra urgent, since they knew that the humiliated Spartans would soon return in force, and other cities might also exploit the power vacuum. They had to act forcefully and instantly, and they did.

The Assembly of citizens, made up of all men who were not slaves or foreigners, was given supreme power over all issues. Everyone was allowed to meet at the hill of the Assembly, and thousands of people usually did in a typical proceeding. Every Assembly began with the words 'Who wishes to speak?' Anyone could take the floor and argue, and the will of the majority decided any issue. Executive positions were opened to most citizens, even though some property requirements remained for the highest magistrates.

To make sure that the Assembly would not be taken over by a small clique that had conspired in advance, a Council of 500 was instituted, which set the agenda for the Assembly and sometimes prepared specific proposals. Members of the Council were selected by lot, served for a year and could only serve twice during their lifetime. This meant that almost every Athenian would serve at some point.

But this was not all. Cleisthenes decided that he had to break the old aristocratic tribal allegiances entirely in order to make the democracy work. Therefore he divided Athens into more than a hundred districts, *demes*, which would govern themselves; these became the new basis of citizenship rather than membership of a family. To the great surprise of Athenians, from now on, they would take their names from these districts. Instead of having a personal name and your father's name, you would now have your personal name and the name of your *deme*.

Furthermore, each of these *demes* was split into thirds, and out of these ten new tribes were formed, replacing the old hereditary tribes. Each of the ten tribes consisted of a share of urban, rural and coastal neighbourhoods. This meant that every person suddenly had multiple loyalties, and that there was a social and geographical mix in every tribe. Large landowners, urban artisans and poor dockworkers met in one and the same tribe. These tribes had the task of recruiting and organizing one hoplite regiment and a squadron of cavalry, and they elected their commander. They were also the source of members for the Council – fifty members were selected from every tribe. Fifty of the 500 served as the steering committee of the Council on a rotating basis.

Another institution was established that seems strange and cruel to modern observers: ostracism. Every year, the Assembly was asked if it wanted to exile someone from Athens, and if the answer was yes, a new vote was held two months later. Then people scratched the name of the person that they wanted to exile on a shard of pottery – an ostracon. If 6,000 people were present, the person who got the most votes had to leave the city for ten years. This was in fact a safety valve, to make it possible to remove a strongman or potential tyrant, without bloodshed. The ostracized person was not deprived of his property, and after ten years he could return to his old life and status.

Was this a democracy? Not by our modern standards, of course. The fact that women and slaves were entirely excluded from any kind of political influence means that the majority of Athenians did not count in this democracy. However, these groups were not included anywhere at this time. What

Athenians (and everybody else) marvelled at was the fact that so many were included, not that so many were excluded. Suddenly even the poorest and least literate citizens could find themselves preparing issues of war, peace and public administration in the Council for nobles and generals. In the Assembly anyone could speak (if they dared), and when they voted, they each had one vote.

The judiciary was also handed to popular courts. There were no judges or lawyers, just two litigants arguing with each other. A jury of 501 or more, with the power to convict and decide the sentence, were chosen by lot from a group of 6,000 citizens who had volunteered to serve.

If the ancient Athenians were to judge us by their standards, they would probably say that we are the ones who don't have a democracy, since we don't meet in person to decide everything via direct democracy. The fact that we allow representatives to govern us, and can be re-elected again and again, would probably remind them a bit of an oligarchy. Several modern observers, such as Martin Wolf, have argued that some Athenian inventions, like allotted citizens' assemblies, could help our democracies to become more representative and break the power of political tribes and campaigning.[11]

In his play *The Suppliant Women*, Euripides puts democratic ideology into the mouth of the legendary Athenian hero Theseus. When a Theban herald arrives and asks to speak to the 'master' of the city, Theseus replies:

> Your start was wrong, seeking a master here.
> This city is free, and ruled by no one man.
> The people reign, in annual alternations.
> They do not yield the power to the rich;
> The poor man has an equal share in it.[12]

The scale of these changes was absolutely breathtaking, and it is difficult to find any major thinker at the time who thought that this system would work. But the citizen body apparently did. It worked at a frenetic pace to implement wide-ranging changes. All the institutions were in place in time for a coordinated attack on Athens from all sides.

Democrats at war

In the summer of 506 BC, the vengeful Spartans marched with their Peloponnesian allies over the Isthmus, the small land bridge between their peninsula and Attica, while the powerful Thebans were assaulting Athens from the west and a third army attacked from Chalcis on the island of Euboea in the north. The young democracy would be tested in battle for the first time. Standing next to their new tribal comrades, protecting them with their shield, the hoplites marched into battle.

First, the Athenians marched southwards to face the Peloponnesians, but before battle could commence, Sparta's allies began to retreat. Historians cannot agree on a common story. Perhaps they learned about the Spartan plan to install Isagoras as tyrant and found it unjust, or they weren't impressed by friction between the two Spartan kings or perhaps they were simply bribed by Athenians. Whatever the reason, the Spartans now found themselves alone on the south front and rushed back to the Peloponnese without a fight.

The Athenians, ecstatic over what couldn't have been anything but divine intervention, swiftly turned northwards to face the Thebans and won a quick and decisive victory, taking 700 prisoners, according to Herodotus. Later the same day, the Athenians crossed into Euboea and defeated the Chalkidians.

They confiscated the land belonging to its aristocrats and turned it into a colony for some 4,000 Athenian settlers.

The victors must have looked at their tribal partners, standing next to them in the phalanx, in disbelief. Every enemy had been laid to waste, the Spartans had fled, and the last group standing were the free Athenians: citizen soldiers who had fought, not for a tyrant or for aristocrats, but for their own freedom.

Herodotus describes the sense of wonder:

> Thus Athens went from strength to strength, and proved, if proof were needed, how noble a thing equality before the laws is, not in one respect only, but in all; for while they were oppressed under tyrants, they had no better success in war than any of their neighbours, yet, once the yoke was flung off, they proved the finest fighters in the world. This clearly shows that, so long as they were held down by authority, they deliberately shirked their duty in the field, as slaves shirk working for their masters; but when freedom was won, then every man amongst them was interested in his own cause.[13]

The self-confidence these victories inspired saved the revolution. The unprecedented experiment had not just survived, but triumphed. At times, this self-confidence became too big for the city, and the Athenians set out looking for monsters to destroy. In 499–8 BC, when Ionian Greek cities on the opposite side of the Aegean Sea (now Turkey) revolted against their Persian rulers, Athens sent a fleet in a futile attempt to help export its revolution. The revolt was defeated after four years, but the resentment of King Darius of Persia against the Athenians remained. According to legend, he ordered a slave to tell him three times at every dinner, year after year: 'Master, remember the Athenians.'[14]

In 491 BC, Darius sent heralds to Greek cities to demand earth and water, the traditional symbol of submission, and a sign that he planned to conquer the whole of Greece. Most cities quickly folded, but the two largest city-states showed their contempt for Persian demands in the clearest and rudest terms. The Spartans drowned the envoys in a well, telling them that they could look for earth and water there. The Athenians, proud of their commitment to legal procedures, put the envoys on trial instead. But, after conviction, the envoys were executed, nonetheless. At least Sparta came to regret its rash action and eventually sent two Spartan noblemen to the Persian king to be killed as compensation (he politely declined, refusing to absolve Sparta of its guilt). No middle ground could be found, and a Persian invasion force of 600 ships set sail with cavalry and perhaps 25,000 infantry men for what is remembered as the First Persian Invasion of Greece, the one before the more famous invasion referred to in the beginning of this chapter.

The much-dreaded Persian force landed at Marathon, north-east of Athens, in September 490 BC, and an Athenian messenger ran all the way to Sparta to request assistance, only to be turned down. The Spartans were in the middle of a festival (stop me if you've heard this one before) and could not join them until the celebrations were over. The Athenians had to rush out to meet the Persians with a hoplite force that was probably outnumbered by more than two to one. A bloodbath was expected.

A five-day stand-off between the forces ensued until the Athenians noticed that the Persian cavalry was gone, perhaps being loaded on ships to go straight to Athens. This presented a dangerous threat but also an opportunity to attack. The Greeks charged down the hill and smashed into the stunned Persians. To be able to extend their line to match the enemy, the Greeks had to weaken the centre, but this also played to their advantage. The Persians, knowing that no Greek army had ever defeated them in open battle, pushed forward in the middle, but this made it possible for the heavier Athenian wings to push forward and then turn around to encircle them. The Persians fled in panic towards their ships but were pursued and killed. At the end of the battle, more than 6,000 Persians lay dead but fewer than 200 Greeks. It was a stunning victory that sent shock waves around the known world and has ever since been remembered as a battle that saved Greece's independence and so made modern civilization possible. In 1846, John Stuart Mill wrote:

> The battle of Marathon, even as an event in English history, is more important than the battle of Hastings. If the issue of that day had been different, the Britons and the Saxons might still have been wandering in the woods.[15]

But it was not over. The surviving Persian ships were heading for Athens, so the exhausted hoplites had to get up and march quickly towards Athens; they got there just in time to stop the Persians from landing, and so the Persians retreated. This is the march celebrated by the modern Marathon race. There are other origin myths that have conflated this story with the messenger who ran to Sparta, but that is a distance of 225 kilometres. The distance between Marathon and Athens, on the other hand, is around 40 kilometres, close to the Marathon race created at the first modern Olympic Games in 1896.

However, for a real Marathon run you first have to defeat a Persian army in the morning, then run the entire 40-kilometre distance with heavy armour and shields and be prepared to take on a whole fleet in late afternoon. This is what the Athenians did. They proved to the astonishment of the Persians, the whole

Greek world and probably themselves too, that they could defeat even the greatest of empires. A useful skill, it would turn out, since the Persians would soon return.

The Battle of Salamis

And so we're back where we started. In 480 BC, ten years after the Battle of Marathon, Darius's successor Xerxes started the Second Persian Invasion of Greece, the one that made the ground shake and drank many a river dry. The time when the whole world's history lay trembling in the balance. This time, the Persians took no chances. Forces from the whole empire had been assembled, perhaps a quarter of a million men and 600 ships. It was an irresistible force, and indeed, at the supposedly impregnable pass of Thermopylae, the Persians destroyed the Spartan defenders in just two and a half days. The road was open to Attica, where the Persians marched into Athens, killed all defenders, burned the wooden structures then at the Acropolis and destroyed the temples.

This would be a tragedy for any city, but especially terrible for Athenians, who took great pride in the mythical concept of *autochthonous* – they thought that they were indigenous, and that they had not come from anywhere but the soil, and they were not going anywhere either. Only they did. Before the city was destroyed by the Persians, it had been evacuated. The women had left for Troezen in the Peloponnese and all the men to the ships by the island of Salamis just west of Athens. All of this, and the operations that followed, had been planned in advance by the true hero of the Persian Wars, the Athenian Themistocles (524–459 BC), one of the most fascinating characters in the ancient world.

When the historian Tom Holland wrote a beautiful modern account of the war, *Persian Fire*, he explained the different personalities involved by turning to the great epics of Homer, which were essential in forging an ancient Greek identity.[16] If Sparta's Leonidas was Achilles, strong and courageous, yearning for a fight, and dying because he forgot to protect his vulnerable heel, Themistocles seems more like Odysseus, who is also a muscle man, but whose chief strength is his intelligence, schemes and deceits. And where Achilles famously preferred death in battle to a long, happy life, Odysseus only wanted to survive to get home to his wife, Penelope.

Themistocles managed to rise through Athens' political system even though his father seems to have been a greengrocer without political connections and his mother was not even Athenian. He did so by appealing to the lower, previously neglected classes, and he was known to tour markets and taverns to court them. With their help, he became the most prominent politician in the city. He used that position to turn Athens into a sea power, because he knew full well that the Persians, whom he had last met when standing in the weakened centre of the army at Marathon, would soon be back in force.

Themistocles, who incidentally looked a little bit like Churchill if we are to trust a Roman bust after a Greek original, first secured support for a new harbour complex at the port of Piraeus. It was further from the city, but bigger and better protected, just what was needed for a large fleet. Next, he started to argue for the creation of such a fleet, and the discovery of a new rich silver lode in 483 BC made it possible to fund it. Amid opponents clamouring for the silver lode to be divided equally among the Athenians, Themistocles preyed on their competitive drive by arguing that his fleet could be used to defeat Aegina, one of Athens' great rival island-states.

With his plan approved, Athenians imported timber on a colossal scale and in the docks at Piraeus they hurriedly put together a fleet of more than 200 triremes – slim ships with three separate banks of oars, one man per oar. In the front there was a battering ram, often bronze-clad, designed to pierce enemy ships. In effect, the triremes were guided missiles. The Athenians experimented furiously with new designs to improve the speed and manoeuvrability of these ships. Then the men – all the men, because around 40,000 were needed to man such a fleet – started to practise the exhausting art of rowing, for speed and for quick turning. Again and again they practised, because time was quickly running out.

So it was that Athens was at sea when Xerxes invaded. The defeat of Leonidas at Thermopylae was a severe blow, but it was quickly exploited for propaganda purposes. Tom Holland suggests that it was Themistocles himself, the great spin-doctor, who created the myth about the noble sacrifice at Thermopylae, in order to stiffen the spine of reluctant Spartans and other Greeks.[17] If 300 Spartans secured eternal glory by marching bravely into a doomed fight, how cowardly does it make us seem, tens of thousands of us, if we flee to the Peloponnese or surrender? If this theory is correct, Sparta's proudest moment was invented by a trickster Athenian.

The Greek fleet had retreated to Salamis, an island 2 kilometres from Piraeus, from where the exasperated sailors could see smoke rising from the ruins of Athens. Many of the other cities now wanted to retreat to the Peloponnese, build a wall across the Isthmus and make their stand there. For the Athenians it was completely unacceptable to leave Attica to the Persians, and Themistocles also knew that the Greeks would be destroyed by a much larger fleet (mostly Phoenicians and Egyptians) with lighter, faster ships and superior seamanship if they fought on open waters.

Their only chance was to draw them into a constricted area, like the narrows between the island Salamis and the mainland. Themistocles managed to delay the retreat only by threatening to take all Athenian ships, the bulk of the Greek fleet, to Italy with their families and rebuild their city there. But he knew that this was only a temporary respite and that battle had to commence soon before the alliance fell apart. So he pulled off his greatest trick, one of the most successful ruses in military history.

Under the cover of darkness, Themistocles sent a trusted slave, the tutor of his children, to the Persians with the message that Themistocles was fed up with his bickering allies and was willing to betray them. He said that the fleet was preparing a disorganized escape and that the Persians could block their escape and destroy them. This was exactly the kind of betrayal the Persians usually encouraged and rewarded, and the claim of disunity was also so close to the truth as to seem credible. The Persian fleet was ordered to take positions surrounding the strait. Xerxes supposedly seated himself on a gilded throne above the strait to watch the final destruction of the Greeks. The great king had taken the bait.

But perhaps Themistocles had deceived his Peloponnesian allies as well? This was a way to force their hands, prevent their retreat and make sure that the battle took place at Salamis. And who knows? He might even have kept the door open for a real betrayal as well. In the eventuality of a Greek defeat, perhaps his message would give Athenians some claim on Xerxes' mercy. Some of his later behaviour suggests that Themistocles wasn't above medism, as the Greeks called collaboration with the enemy.

The next morning, the Persians, thinking that the Greek fleet was in complete disarray, made the fatal mistake of entering the narrows to mop them up. There were signs that pointed to Greek despair. Some fifty Corinthian triremes seemed to be fleeing north as the Persians entered from the south-east, but then they suddenly turned around back into formation. The other Greek ships had been hidden behind a promontory and, now that the enemy approached, they backed off, closer and closer to the shore. Not in disarray, but with great discipline, and they had every ram pointing at the enemy.

Suddenly, one of them pulled hard on their oars and rammed a Persian ship, and soon all joined in. The Athenians' heavier ships did great damage, and, in the narrowness of the straits, the Persians had no use for their ships' greater speed. The large number of ships created a traffic jam. Formations were lost, oars got entangled and ships crashed into one another. It didn't help that the Persian sailors were exhausted after having rowed all night just to keep their position. Soon the sea was full of shipwrecks and drowned men. It was a calamity for the Persian side. The Greeks had lost forty ships, the Persians more than 200. Xerxes decided to turn back and go home before the Greeks destroyed his bridge over the Hellespont, the narrow strait between Europe and Asia, and cut off his escape. The Ionians in Asia Minor rebelled again, and now the Persians could not stop them.

Even if Xerxes left an army in Greece and the war continued for another year, no single moment has a greater case for being decisive in the war to keep the Greeks independent than the Battle of Salamis in 480 BC. Had the Persian forces won, no fortifications across the Isthmus could have stopped them from landing troops behind the Peloponnesians.

This was Athens' and therefore Themistocles' victory. He was responsible for turning Athens into a sea power at just the right time, he made sure that the Greeks stayed at Salamis, lured the Persians into battle there and led the fleet to its victory.

'Consequently', claims one historian, 'it follows that the efforts of a single individual saved Western civilization in its formative stages.'[18]

On the other hand, Themistocles was a creature of Athens. It is difficult to think of another *polis* that could have given so much responsibility to a half-foreign upstart whose modus operandi was to get the support of the lower classes for constant innovation and change. 'Only a regime as open, innovative, energetic, pragmatic, and meritocratic as democracy could have followed the policy that won at Salamis', writes the historian Barry Strauss.[19]

What Themistocles might have become under another political system was revealed after 470 BC, when the troublemaker who had ostracized so many rivals was ostracized himself. Finally, all the enemies the old schemer had made over the years caught up with him. He set out on a long journey and, in a bizarre turn of events, ended up offering his services to the delighted Persian king Artaxerxes I, son of Xerxes. Themistocles died a few years later, as governor of Magnesia and a loyal servant of his old nemesis.

An open city

'Had Xerxes won at Salamis, we might still be barbarians', wrote Voltaire.[20] This exaggerates the difference in barbarity between Xerxes and the Greeks. The Persians usually left vassal states with their own political systems and had no interest in sabotaging the novel scientific and economic development in subjected Greek states. The crucial consequence of the victory was not that it saved Athens, but that it gave it the confidence to move with greater speed on its new trajectory.

In a pattern that we shall see repeated in many other eras, a military victory created cultural self-confidence, and permitted the victors to deepen the institutions that allowed for innovation and surprises. Their crazy little experiment in democracy had not just survived, it had won in the most desperate circumstances: first against other Greek rivals, then at Marathon and, when all seemed lost, at Salamis, against the Persian Empire. When the citizens returned to Athens and started rebuilding the city, they did it along democratic lines. The more they played up the contrast between free Greeks and Persian serfs, the more they attached themselves to the new democratic ideals. If freedom and innovation had triumphed, that must be what the city was about. The astounding victory in the Persian Wars was the beginning of Athens' golden age.

'And no longer are the tongues of men under guard; for the people have been released, so that their speech is free', declared Aeschylus in his play *The Persians*, which retold the story of the war just seven years after the invasion ended; he might have served in it.[21]

How could the Greeks make sure that the Persians would not return once more? The Greeks around the Aegean, such as the Ionian cities, started to consider some sort of allied fleet. The Spartans, however, were not interested in foreign adventures and told the Ionians to leave for mainland Greece. And, in any case, Athens was now the great power at sea, so the cities asked it to take leadership of an alliance to prevent another invasion, but also to get revenge and spoils of war. Athens needed little convincing, since this would assure them a steady stream of income just for keeping up a navy that it wanted anyway. Member states who did not contribute ships and men had to pay up instead. The alliance was agreed on the island of Delos in 478 BC and the treasury was kept in its temple, so it eventually came to be known as the Delian League. One of its great accomplishments was combatting piracy, making the Aegean and the Black Sea safe for large-scale international trade.

Nothing flatters Athens' transformation after the Battle of Salamis more than the fact that Plato, the great authoritarian of Greek thought, insisted that it made Athenians worse. He complained that the victory was not won by noble warriors on land, but at sea, by 'a motley crowd of ragamuffins', and that this inspired Athens to move to the 'extreme of unfettered liberty'.[22]

The fleet was manned by the poorest section of the population, and just as hoplite farmers had demanded their rights when they defended their country, so did the proletarian oarsmen now. The democratic system was indeed radicalized, especially under the leadership of Pericles (495–429 BC). He was the leading politician in Athens in the fifth century, and his influence was so great that the whole golden age is sometimes named after him. His powerful oratory and strategic nous made the Athenians appoint him general year after year.

Pericles was a descendant of the reformer Cleisthenes and had made a name for himself by sponsoring the staging of *The Persians*, probably to keep the memory of Themistocles' democratic and naval strategy alive. Pericles was a radical democrat, some would say a populist. He opened up all public offices but the highest magistracies to the poorest citizens and replaced elections to most positions with annual appointment by lot, to break the power of families and factions for good. Only generals and other offices that required specialized expertise remained elected.

To make it possible for even the poor to take up such positions without suffering financial hardship, offices became paid. Since there were hundreds of public offices and the term was limited to one year, a large part of the population got experience of running the state. It must have been a powerful spur for even the poor to educate themselves. Suddenly, you could find yourself in one of the state's most powerful positions.

However, Pericles also restricted citizenship to those whose parents were both Athenians. This fitted well with the Athenian myth of being autochthonous, *from nowhere*, but was probably linked to his ambition to make citizenship increasingly rewarding. Even the 500 council members and the juries, which could number even more, were paid by the state now. If you bestow generous benefits on a group, it is often popular to restrict entry into it. But had these rules been in place earlier, Themistocles would not have been allowed to lead Athens, and perhaps the Persians would have conquered the whole of Greece.

Despite discrimination against foreigners, women and slaves, in comparison to every other state, Athens was remarkably free. The most powerful formulation of this freedom comes in Pericles' funeral oration of 431/430 BC, as described by Thucydides. In this speech, Pericles did not just praise the city's dead soldiers, but the ideas that they fought and died for:

> Our constitution is called democracy because power is in the hands not of a minority but of the whole people. When it is a question of settling private disputes, everyone is equal before the law; when it is a question of putting one person before another in positions of public responsibility, what counts is not membership of a particular class, but the actual ability which the man possess.

'Our city is open to the world', Pericles went on to say. Foreigners are allowed to live in Athens and, since the city is based on trade, 'to us it seems just as natural to enjoy foreign goods as our own local products'. In conclusion: 'our city is an education to Greece, and I declare that in my opinion each single one of our citizens, in all the manifold aspects of life, is able to show himself the rightful lord and owner of his own person'.[23]

This openness encouraged a remarkably creative atmosphere and rapid innovation in culture, economics and warfare. Everywhere, people experimented with new ideas and methods in art, rhetoric and production, in competition with one another. Thucydides recounts the story of a Corinthian ally of the Spartans, who warns them that Athens is a very different creature:

> An Athenian is always an innovator, quick to form a resolution and quick at carrying it out. You, on the other hand, are good at keeping things as they are; you never originate an idea, and your action tends to stop short of its aim. ... while you are hanging back, they never hesitate: while you stay at home, they are always abroad; for they think that the farther they go the more they will get, while you think that any movement may endanger what you have already.[24]

Sophocles described this cultural sense of life in his play *Antigone*: 'Wonders are many on the earth, and the greatest of these is man.' Mentioning the invention of language, laws and the conquest of the oceans, the chorus concludes: 'There is nothing beyond his power.'

Unwritten and unfailing laws

A popular interpretation is that ancient Greeks did not know the idea of individual freedom. There might have been democracy, but not liberal democracy. The majority could decide anything without constitutional barriers and protections of individual rights. It is true that there was little division of power and no real checks and balances. The majority was in charge of legislation and even judicial affairs. There are examples of how the Assembly really became a dictatorship of the majority, especially during wartime, as in 406 BC, when generals who had failed to save drowning sailors were sentenced to death in a single vote.

But saying that there was no personal freedom in Athens is inconsistent with the sources. On the contrary, it seems that the Athenians were very protective and proud of such freedoms. Pericles referred to this when he said that 'just as our political life is free and open, so is our day-to-day life in relation with each other. We do not get into a state with our next-door neighbour if he enjoys himself in his own way.' We are, he concluded, 'free and tolerant in our private lives'.[25] During the Peloponnesian War, one general rallied his troops in a desperate battle by reminding them that they fought for Athens, where people 'had liberty to live their own lives in their own way'.[26]

Some of this was no doubt propaganda, to paint a stark contrast between libertarian Athens and totalitarian Sparta, but the critics agreed. Plato complained that, in democracy, each man 'have the license to do what he wants' and 'arrange his life in whatever manner pleases him'.[27] It seems that the Athenian government interfered much less in private morality and lifestyle choices than other polities. Freedom of speech was very broad, not just in the Assembly. One orator pointed out that Athenians were free to praise Sparta's constitution, but Spartans were not free to praise any model but Sparta's. Public religion was taken very seriously, to ensure the ongoing goodwill of the gods, but most of the time there were no obligatory orthodoxies or rituals. The government mostly intervened only when someone publicly derided or violated religious rituals or symbols. It was not mandatory to get involved in politics or jury duty, even though one ran the risk of being considered an 'idiot' (Greek *idiōtēs*, 'a private person') if one did not.

It seems as though a form of governance that involved more people found it natural to respect their respective private spheres. Even though there was no formal constitution, Pericles said that Athenians respected both the written and *unwritten* laws, which made up the body of rules about freedom, property and relationships that were understood as the foundation for the system, and, while not codified, it was seen by most as a limit on what the Assembly could decide.

In the end, the origin of these laws was to be found in nature and was handed down by the gods. This is beautifully elaborated in Sophocles' play *Antigone*, where the titular protagonist disobeys the order of King Creon, and buries her rebel brother according to the sacred rituals. When the king accuses her of breaking the laws, Antigone replies that this was an order that did not come from Zeus, and that even kings are bound by the natural laws:

> Nor did I think your orders were so strong
> that you, a mortal man, could over-run
> the gods' unwritten and unfailing laws.
> Not now, nor yesterday's, they always live,
> and no one knows their origin in time.

The Austrian thinker Friedrich Hayek writes: 'It has often been said that the ancients did not know liberty in the sense of individual liberty. This is true of many places and periods even in ancient Greece, but certainly not of Athens at the time of its greatness.'[28] Hayek even suggested that the Athenian example inspired the development of rule of law in England two thousand years later.

This freedom extended into the economic sphere, as befits a *polis* built on property owners. When a new archon, an important magistrate, was appointed, he took an oath declaring that the property of everyone would be respected during his year in office. There was little regulation of businesses and there were markets in land and labour.

The Athenians had a stable monetary system based on a strong silver currency and some of the first commercial banks, which took deposits and provided credit. The *polis* adhered to a free-trade policy and taxed imports and exports at only a 2 per cent rate. The one major exception in this city dependent on food imports was that no one in Attica was allowed to sell grain to other countries.

In a paper so innovative that it borders on the irreverent, the two economists Andreas Bergh and Carl Hampus Lyttkens tried to quantify the free market in Athens using a modern index of economic freedom produced by the Fraser Institute. Their estimate is that fourth-century Athens would score something like 8.8 on a ten-point scale. Even with a gigantic margin for error, that is astonishing. In the 2023 edition of the index, the highest score is Singapore's, at 8.56. The United States gets 8.14.[29]

Of course, this score should be reduced in proportion to the share of the population made up by women and slaves, who were not covered by these freedoms. Nevertheless, it's impressive. In an era when most people's whole lives were controlled by despots and aristocrats, Athens seemed to be able to develop a system where self-owning men were more economically free than in any country in the world today.

Whatever level of economic freedom Athens enjoyed, it did produce results. Athens became an important trade centre, and the monetized economy created a division of labour that made new goods and services possible. There was also innovation, with new ways of casting bronze and a booming pottery industry that experimented with new styles and became a major export. It was located in Athens' Kerameikos area, from which our word 'ceramics' is derived.

Judging from the limited archaeological record and prices and wages, per capita consumption in Greece seems to have increased 50–100 per cent from 800 to 300 BC. This is very high compared with anything but economies after the Industrial Revolution, especially as the population grew almost ten-fold during this period (though one should remember that the data starts in the Greek dark ages).

This progress was led by the Athenians, who were disproportionally made up of the middling class. Athens was also one of very few pre-modern societies where wages for unskilled workers were far above the subsistence level. The daily wage also increased by more than 60 per cent between the late fifth century BC and 320 BC. It is interesting to note that the peak was reached *after* Athens lost its empire.[30]

Athena, goddess of wisdom and war, was the guardian of the city, and she had offered it the gift of the olive tree. Since it takes many years for olive trees to bear plenty of fruit, the planting of so many olive trees in Athens indicates that people had hope for the future and that they had found ways to feed themselves until then.

This is also the reason why the olive branch became a symbol for peace. If it takes two decades for your trees to bear a substantial harvest, you are extra vulnerable to warfare that might wipe out all your investments in one moment. Therefore olive growers usually insisted on negotiations and reconciliation when city-states were at each other's throats, and the olive came to symbolize both commerce and peace.

That commerce brought Athens unprecedented wealth was not enough to make it widely admired. The economy was changing rapidly, but elite attitudes were still predominantly aristocratic and martial. Leading moralists saw the life of a warrior, artist or philosopher as the most honourable. If there had to be production, it should preferably involve landed wealth. Degrading work like trade and handicrafts could be left to foreigners or slaves. One reason for the hostility towards these activities was that trade had started to undermine social hierarchies, and the elite was penetrated by unworthy men without a lineage stretching back to great warriors or demigods. One of the richest men in Athens was Pasion, a slave who probably came from Syria, and who became one of the most successful bankers.

Plato argued that trade 'breeds shifty and deceitful habits in a man's soul' partly because an open city has a tendency to 'lower itself to copy the wicked customs of its enemies'.[31] In his ideal state, the mercantile community should be segregated from others to avoid the infection of their foreign ideas, and could trade only in simple products at fixed prices.

Aristotle was less hostile and saw the value of economic exchange, but he also feared that the profit-motive could undermine moral codes and had to be strictly controlled. He saw work carried out by an artisan or merchant for money as degrading, especially as it did not leave sufficient leisure time to cultivate virtue. (Plato and Aristotle were men of wealth who had the leisure they wanted. Plato had six slaves, Aristotle had thirteen.)[32]

It is true that the rise of a monetized economy undermined traditional hierarchies. It made it possible for people to break out of their kin group and establish cooperation and exchange with other groups, even strangers. According to the intellectual historian Peter Watson, it also had another long-lasting effect: the emergence of money and markets among the Greeks 'encouraged rational and logical thinking', and by making international trade possible, 'more than anything, helped the spread of ideas around the globe'.[33]

You might even say that all those dishonourable and faithless merchants created Plato and Aristotle.

Periclean Athens

Plato was not an admirer of democracy. But even he admitted that it is probably the fairest of regimes. With its wide variety of individuality and ideas freely expressed, he compared it to a many-coloured cloak decorated in all hues, and so this regime 'would seem to be the most beautiful'.[34]

If you had walked the streets of many-coloured Athens in those days, the chances are that you would have bumped into legends fully engaged in various pursuits. You could have listened to Pericles' speeches in the Assembly; afterwards you might have caught him discussing with philosophers like Anaxagoras and Protagoras or ordering a sculpture by Phidias for the reconstruction of a new, splendid Acropolis.

You could have run into Socrates debating with students like Plato and Xenophon. In another corner of the city, Herodotus was preparing the first work of history. The father of history has often been called the 'father of lies', because he passed on so many tales about myths and monsters. But he probably just loved a good story; don't we all? He was just the first one to record them in a systematic way, from many people in many places. It was an Athenian general, Thucydides, who came to be called the father of scientific history, since he tried to tell the history of the Peloponnesian War in an impartial way without searching for explanations in the interventions of gods.

If you took another route through Athens, you might have come across the world's first dramatists, Aeschylus, Sophocles, Euripides, and if you looked at him in the wrong way, the comedian Aristophanes might call you a dirty word.

'Instead of looking upon discussion as a stumbling-block in the way of action, we think it an indispensable preliminary to any wise action at all,' said Pericles. Athenians had started to chatter freely. Not just because they were allowed to, but because they had something to talk about. After the Persian Wars, they started asking themselves what they had just experienced. Why had they dared to challenge the mightiest empire in the world, at the risk of their lives and their city? It encouraged thought and debate, in taverns, theatres and gatherings of thinkers. What is it to be a citizen, and what is a good life? What demands are imposed on us by the gods, the *polis* and individual honour? Are we at the mercy of fate or is life in our own hands?

Before the great philosophers discussed such questions, popular entertainment did. Drama was invented in Athens and was intimately related to the literacy and quandaries of a citizenry that governed itself. In hymns to the wine and festivity god Dionysus, a chorus had always sung and danced, but at some point a chorus member must have stepped forth, put on a mask and pretended to be one of the characters they sang about. For the first time as far as we know, actors started taking on the role of other people and spoke in the first person, presenting a story from beginning to end. Netflix would not have been the same without it.

Unlike most previous literature in the Near East, the great tragedians did not focus exclusively on the stories of gods, but on the human predicament, societal conflict and moral dilemmas.

Often they staged long debates, and sometimes these could only be resolved by the enlightened ruling of a democratic law court, as in the conclusion of Aeschylus's *Oresteia*. In Aristophanes' comedy *The Frogs*, he let Euripides say that his main achievement was to get the audience to use their brains, to learn to ask: Why is this so? What do we mean by that?

In comedy, Athens was also a pioneer, and here contemporary political issues were often the central plot. The greatest politicians and thinkers were ruthlessly mocked on a regular basis in front of a substantial portion of the Athenian populace. Nothing illustrates the state of free speech in Athens better than the fact that Pericles himself was constantly ridiculed on stage: for his politics, his love life and the shape of his head (apparently the Athenians thought it looked like a squill plant). Such were the dangers involved in going to the world's first theatres. An odd feature of early comedy, possibly inherited from the phallic processions it grew out of, was the moment when the play was interrupted so that the chorus could insult members of the audience.

'Why is this so?' and 'What do we mean by that?' are also the questions posed by the eccentric thinkers who would create the first great era of philosophy. The input came from the outside but was supercharged by Athens' intellectual openness. With the easy availability of so many alternative ways of living and governing, the Athenians understood that more than one way was possible. They even started to see themselves from the outside, realizing that what they considered natural and necessary seemed absurd to foreigners, or even a crime. Herodotus tells the story of a Persian king who summoned Indians and Greeks and asked both of them what price would persuade them to adopt the burial practices of the other group (burn or eat their fathers, respectively); both were horrified and said that nothing could convince them to do it.[35]

Thales of Miletus had opened a new chapter in intellectual history in the early sixth century BC by discussing how the universe and nature worked without resort to the actions of gods and hidden spirits. Now Protagoras of Abdera, who moved to Athens in 433 BC, and the other so-called 'sophists' did the same, but applied it to human nature and society. Sophistry would go down in history as an invective. Plato was the one who shaped the negative perception of the sophists for future generations, claiming that they cared more about money and showing off than about truth. But their challenge of conventional thinking on every level (some of them even seem to have challenged the existence of gods) made Athens the intellectual centre of Greece and created the vibrant environment in which Socrates, Plato and Aristotle started to search for new ways of understanding knowledge, society and humanity.

All these people were thronging the streets of what was rapidly becoming the fairest of cities. Pericles had decided to turn the Acropolis, which had been razed by the Persians, into the most dazzling display of beauty and power in all of Greece. Behind the monumental gate, spectacular temples with decorative sculptures were erected. Supposedly, sailors approaching Athens could see the top of the goddess Athena's helmet and the tip of her spear from afar. Phidias had made this gigantic bronze statue, rising to a height of 9 metres, for the Acropolis.

The colossal Parthenon on Acropolis, with its exquisitely carved Doric columns, is still considered one of history's greatest architectural achievements. It is made up of countless subtle curves and distortions to compensate for optical illusions that would have made the building seem less perfect. For example, there are no straight lines, to counteract the perception that horizontal lines sag, and possibly also to make the building seem more dynamic and alive.

The overwhelming impression must have been greater then than now as the sculptures and motives were originally not white, but many-coloured, decorated in all hues. The white marble we see today is the result of the wear and tear that left us with only the unpainted versions. And sometimes those who restored (or wrecked) the old masterpieces consciously removed the remaining pigments to make them seem purer. One mason who worked on the Elgin marbles said that he had been instructed to make them as white as possible, removing the surface where necessary.[36]

Imperial hubris

Where did Pericles get the funds for his new, spectacular Acropolis? He took money from his alliance partners in the Delian League. Pericles was not just a great democrat, but also a dedicated imperialist. The Athenians had it all, but wanted more. As military victories made them feel increasingly superior, they got themselves entangled in more places. As they came to completely dominate the League, they started taking advantage of its power.

Almost all member states stopped supplying a fleet and instead paid Athens to do it, so they grew weaker as Athens became stronger. Eventually, the Persians were thoroughly defeated, and it made more sense for them to offer the Athenians earth and water than the other way round. Some allies started asking themselves why they should pay for a navy that didn't seem necessary any more, a problem familiar from other defensive alliances in other time periods.

In 470 BC, the island of Naxos tried to leave the League but was forced back in. Athens could make the case that Naxos was trying to freeride on a peace and stability that they didn't contribute to, but they had no such excuse five years later, when a war started with another member island, Thasos. This time it was not related to League issues, but a quarrel over rich gold and silver mines controlled by Thasos. After a two-year-long siege Athens took control of the mines. For the first time it used League resources to achieve its own ambitions against another member state. Soon allies were forced to bring major judicial cases to Athenian courts. When the League treasury was moved from Delos to the Parthenon in 454 BC, it was just belated confirmation that the League had stopped being an alliance of independent states and had turned into an Athenian Empire.

Athens was at the height of its powers. Perhaps it should have been a matter of concern. That is the moment in Greek myth when you are most at risk of *hubris*, the fatal belief that you can break the limits, perhaps even defy the gods. Athens' imperial ambitions started to alienate Greek states that had previously looked upon the city as its protector. By interfering in more regions, it also earned the suspicion of other big powers, like Sparta. Eventually this would lead to a monumental and devastating clash with Sparta, known as the Peloponnesian War (431–404 BC), made famous by Thucydides' great work of that name. He had been an Athenian general but was exiled after having failed to save Amphipolis and so spent the rest of his life travelling around Greece to collect stories about the war.

This war has great relevance for our times because of what has been called the 'Thucydides trap'. This is the idea that war broke out because Sparta feared Athens' growing power; it has been used to argue that there is a great risk of war when rising powers threaten an old hegemon, as when Germany challenged Britain before the First World War, and today, when China's rise is worrying the old hegemon, the USA.

This is a risk. But who knows what might have happened if Athens had just enjoyed its growing powers peacefully instead of provoking Sparta's allies and constantly interfering with other states militarily and with trade embargoes? In a way it's strange how long the Spartans swallowed their anger. After hostilities broke out between Athens and Corinth over one of Corinth's old colonies, the Corinthians convinced reluctant Spartans to go to war by accusing them of not standing up for their friends. Ironically, because of Athens' heavy-handedness, authoritarian Sparta could pose as a liberator of the Greeks (even though its 'liberation' often consisted in replacing democracies with oligarchies).

In the mid-fourth century, Athenian self-recrimination gave rise to powerful anti-imperialist essays by Xenophon and Isocrates. They argued that Athens had once been given its leading position because of its services, not its coercion, and the latter only turned allies against it. They argued that rule by force was tyrannical, dangerous and costly. As a peaceful commercial centre, Athens would be safe, benefit from trade and attract all the merchants and visitors driven away by the war. They had powerful arguments, but this was written with the benefit of hindsight, after a war that almost destroyed the city-state.

Pericles thought that Athens could be an imperial power and yet stay safe by convincing the Spartans that they could not gain from war. Athens had built long walls around its city and all the way to the port of Piraeus, roughly 6 kilometres away. Since Athens commanded the seas, and Sparta never developed siege warfare, the Athenians could simply retreat behind its walls and rely on trade to feed themselves and on the navy to win the war. It was a rational strategy, but with a fatal flaw: it depended on the enemies also being rational, and not being driven by, say, fear of one's reputation and taunts from Corinthians. Peloponnesian armies entered Attica every summer and burned and plundered, then they marched home, because the Athenian population was safe behind their walls – for a while. There was one enemy that even the great Pericles had neglected: microbes.

In the summer of 430 BC, refugees who had huddled together in the city's badly ventilated huts began to have burning feelings in their heads, felt pain in their chests and started bleeding from throats and tongues. After about a week, those affected started dying and soon there were bodies all over Athens. The close quarters had become a breeding ground for a plague that would kill around a quarter of Athens' population. It did massive damage to the city's fighting capability and social cohesion. In an era when natural disasters were interpreted as a judgement of the gods, it was also a terrible blow to morale. One of the victims of the plague was Pericles himself.

Without Pericles, the Athenian Assembly came under the sway of more volatile characters and his fairly cautious approach and limited war aims were replaced by high-risk strategies. Some were successful, but once in a while these characters gambled everything and lost. Most disastrous was the 415 BC plan to conquer the powerful city of Syracuse in Sicily because of the booty it would bring. The Sicilian expedition was a repudiation of Pericles' warnings against overreach and resulted in the loss of half the fleet and perhaps 40,000 soldiers. It weakened Athens even more than the plague.

However, Athens always bounced back, and could at least count on the reliable inflexibility of their enemies. As Thucydides wrote:

> on this occasion, as on so many others, the Spartans proved to be quite the most remarkably helpful enemies that the Athenians could have had. For Athens, particularly as a naval

power, was enormously helped by the very great difference in the national characters – her speed against their slowness, her enterprise against their lack of initiative.[37]

The real Thucydides trap

The Peloponnesian War turned into a long, dreadful struggle that involved the whole of Greece. Almost every *polis* was thrown into tumult and revolutions as democrats usually sought help from Athens and fought aristocrats and oligarchs who appealed to Sparta. Because of the aggressive tribalism of the different factions 'there was a general deterioration of character throughout the Greek world', wrote Thucydides.

In times of peace, individuals follow high moral standards, he thought, but the fear of destruction and the hope for power, plunder and revenge suddenly made people go to every extreme and beyond it:

> What used to be described as a thoughtless act of aggression was now regarded as courage one would expect to find in a party member; to think of the future and wait was merely another way of saying one was a coward; any idea of moderation was just an attempt to disguise one's unmanly character; ability to understand a question from all sides meant that one was totally unfitted for action. Fanatical enthusiasm was the mark of a real man.[38]

Death came in every shape and form. Terrible things had happened, and would happen in the future, warned Thucydides, as long as human nature remained the same. The Athenians did not escape these ungovernable passions and showed themselves capable of great acts of savagery, often excusing themselves by 'whatabouting' Spartan atrocities.

After a revolt against Athens in Mytilene on the island of Lesbos in 428 BC was crushed, the Athenian Assembly absurdly decided that all Mytilenean men should be executed and the women and children sold as slaves. As a trireme was dispatched to Mytilene with these orders, the Athenians started having second thoughts, especially as many Mytileneans had not been on the side of the rebellious oligarchs. The Assembly met again and decided to overturn the decision taken the previous day. A new ship was sent and, rowing day and night, it managed to arrive at the precise moment the massacre was supposed to start.

There was no remorse in 421 BC though, when Athens ended a revolt in the city of Scione, executed the adult men and sold the women and children into slavery. When Athens did the same thing after having conquered the neutral island of Melos, Thucydides records that the Athenian emissary did not even try to justify the actions, but bluntly declared 'the strong do what they have the power to do and the weak accept what they have to accept'.[39]

No matter how they tried, neither Athens nor Sparta could defeat the other, so, in the end, Sparta turned to Greece's old archenemy for support. In 411 BC, it invited Persia to take back its old Greek possessions in return for gold. With these resources, the Spartans built a large navy and hired mercenaries to man the ships. The Athenians kept winning the battles and destroyed the Spartan navies, but with Persian taps open, the Spartans could rebuild them again and again. Their superior pay even tempted some Athenian oarsmen to defect. The Spartan–Persian alliance was too much for the Athenians, since every victory provided nothing but temporary relief, while just one defeat would be fatal. It finally came in late 405 BC when, in a surprise attack, the Spartans captured 171 Athenian ships on the beach. The Spartans could now close the Hellespont to trade and starve Athens into submission.

Sparta's allies Corinth and Thebes wanted to raze Athens to the ground, but Sparta needed a pliant Athens to counter-balance what they saw as worrying Corinthian and Theban ambitions. Instead, Sparta dissolved Athens' empire and destroyed the long walls and the fortifications built by Piraeus. The democratic system was replaced by a council of thirty Spartan-friendly oligarchs.

This is usually seen as the end of the Peloponnesian War, but there is an epilogue that is almost more interesting. The 'thirty tyrants' led by Critias, a onetime student of Socrates, started a reign of terror and killed 1,500 Athenians without a trial. At first, they came for enemies and democrats, but soon they murdered anyone whose land and money they coveted. This horrified Athenians, and thousands fled the city. Exiles united under the leadership of a navy general and soon these rebels defeated both a Spartan garrison and the oligarchic forces. Just eight months after the imposition of dictatorship, the thirty tyrants were deposed and democracy restored. In many ways, democracy was deepened. The unwritten laws were codified, and pay was introduced for participation in the Assembly, creating a new enthusiasm for direct democracy among the poor.

This tells us something extraordinary about the resilience of Athens. Its culture of democracy and openness gave it deep reservoirs of innovation and energic talent that could be tapped in moments of crisis. For the second time in a century the city had been taken by enemies, and for the second time it bounced back. Just ten years after they were razed, the long walls were being rebuilt. Soon the Athenians even founded a second

Athenian League with perhaps as many as seventy allies in a defensive alliance.

In fact, Athens' democratic system, which was seen as chaotic and impossible by most leading intellectuals, preserved cohesion better than other Greek *poleis*. The system never broke down in factional warfare, the *demos* (the people) did not overthrow the laws or confiscate the property of the rich, and oligarchic plots were rare and did not ultimately triumph. With very brief intermissions, the democratic system remained intact for 180 years.

Even Thucydides, who was not enthusiastic about the popular democracy, admired the disciplined way the Athenians pulled itself together in times of crisis. Writing about the aftermath of the destruction of Sicily, he argued that 'like all democracies, now that they were terrified, they were ready to put everything in order'.[40]

While Athens constantly re-invented itself, Sparta slowly suffocated itself. Xenophobia and a lack of markets that could create new fortunes had consolidated the ruling class. The closed society triumphed and, as a result, it faced a terminal decline. According to Bret Devereaux, there were 8,000 male Spartans with full citizenship rights in 480 BC. This fell to 3,500 by 418 BC, 2,500 in 394 BC and 1,500 in 371 BC.[41] The once-proud Spartan army broke down, not just because of battles and earthquakes, but also under the weight of its own oligarchic policies. After the end of the Peloponnesian War, Sparta had compromised itself by allying itself with Persia, subjugating the cities it had promised to liberate or betraying them to Persia. Aggrieved Greeks were hungry for revenge.

In 376 BC, the Athenian League destroyed a Spartan fleet and pushed them out of the Aegean Sea. In 371 BC, when Sparta felt it had to face the emerging threat of Thebes on land, it had an army of only 700 full-citizen Spartans. The bulk of the force were allies. The Theban army, spearheaded by the Sacred Band, made up of pairs of lovers (supposedly to inspire them to act bravely), inflicted a crushing defeat on the Spartans at Leuctra. Sparta's subject cities on the Peloponnese used this opportunity to rebel and got support from Thebes. The Thebans helped them gain independence and went on to liberate the helots in Messenina. At a single stroke, Sparta had lost a third of its territory and the slave population it had held for 230 years; it suddenly found itself surrounded by heavily fortified hostile states. It was demoted to the rank of second-class powers and never returned from there.

In the end, Sparta left us only with stories of their soldiers, and it is still a popular name for football teams and fraternities. But the totalitarian city's want of creativity meant that it left us no literature, no poetry, no art, no architecture and no innovative body of thought. The era of the Spartans was a dark age rather than a golden one. What a sombre contrast to restlessly innovative Athens, which gave us the idea of democracy, the science of history, rhetoric, comedy and tragedy, and achievements in sculpture and architecture that we still marvel at today. And, of course, that beautiful study of fundamental questions named after *philos* (love) and *sophia* (wisdom).

The birth of philosophy

The golden age, as usually defined, was over after the Peloponnesian War. But just when it seemed like the fireworks were over and Athens had exhausted its ability to surprise, this city provided what is arguably its biggest contribution to the world, which would put philosophy, religion and science on new trajectories for more than two thousand years. It originated with three of the most original thinkers ever, in the most exceptional teacher–student sequence in history: Socrates, who taught Plato, who taught Aristotle.

In a Greek world where traditions and hierarchies rapidly gave way, and the power of the old gods and myths were on the decline, the Greeks searched for a new beginning, to understand man, society and the universe. In an era when all that was solid seemed to melt into air, they tried to provide new foundations on which to build knowledge and suggest explanations.

Cicero thought that Socrates (470–399 BC) 'was the first who brought down philosophy from the heavens, placed it in the cities, introduced it into families, and obliged it to examine into life and morals, good and evil'.[42]

This is to write the sophists out of history, but it is a good description of the achievement of this son of a stonemason who served as a hoplite during the Peloponnesian War. Socrates thought that there must be universal standards about right and wrong and good and evil, even though he did not pretend to know them – if he was wiser than others it was only because he knew what he did not know. He was convinced, however, that it started with knowing oneself. Therefore, he walked around the town, asking Athenians questions to make them question themselves and what they meant by what they said. This method forced students to reflect and deepen their thinking, and he attracted a group of devoted followers.

In 399 BC, Socrates was sentenced to death by an Athenian jury. It was a complete betrayal of the city's devotion to free speech and has been interpreted as a reaction to Socrates' ideas, but the accusation of corrupting the youth also had a much more specific and political aim. The thirty tyrants had recently been deposed, and their leader, Critias, had been a student of Socrates. The philosopher's famous distrust of the democratic masses made many assume that he had inspired the tyrants. The fact that he did not leave the city during the dictatorship led many Athenians to associate him with it, though there is evidence that he actually resisted some of its orders.

It probably didn't help that Socrates was considered a difficult and ugly man who neglected his personal hygiene and walked around in shabby clothes, pestering people with bizarre questions. During the trial his arrogant behaviour provoked even more people. He was probably convicted by 280 votes to 221. After a conviction, the jury would vote on the sentence. The prosecutor asked for the death penalty, while Socrates first suggested that he should be 'punished' with free meals for the rest of his life, befitting the benefactor of the city that he was, before offering to pay a fine. The incensed jury voted for the death penalty by an even bigger margin than that by which he had been convicted – thereby proving Socrates' accusation that the masses are not always wise. He refused to go into exile, as his friends encouraged, and instead drank a poisonous beverage of hemlock as if it was a draught of wine.

His most famous pupil, Plato (427–348 BC), set about answering the questions Socrates had asked, and, unlike Socrates, he left us many texts, on an incredible range of subjects. Most of them are dialogues where the character of Socrates is used as the advocate of Plato's views. The English philosopher and mathematician Alfred North Whitehead once described the whole European philosophical tradition as a series of footnotes to Plato, referring to the wealth of ideas scattered throughout his work.

Plato thought that everything we experience in the material world consist of copies or imitations of a higher, eternal world of forms or ideas. What makes something beautiful, muddy or a horse is the fact that they are a reflection of the perfect form of beauty, mud or horse, which exists only in the world of ideas.

An important implication is that reality cannot be understood by those who use their senses alone; understanding takes the kind of access to higher insights about reality that only some have. This is why Plato is hostile to democracy and individual freedom. In his ideal state, philosophers are kings or kings are philosophers. Rulers have to control the passions and selfishness of the people with a detailed system of regulations, compulsory education and religion. 'Freedom from control must be uncompromisingly eliminated from the life of all men' was Plato's ideal way of keeping his state safe.[43]

Plato founded a school just outside the city walls of Athens, and named it after the site, devoted to the mythological hero Academus. This 'Academy' attracted pupils from afar, including, crucially, Aristotle (384–322 BC) from Stagira in northern Greece. While Plato was an aristocrat from a wealthy and influential Athenian family, Aristotle was an immigrant and the child of a physician. His perspective was always more practical and common-sensical, criticizing Plato's theory of forms for just contributing 'empty phrases and poetical metaphors' and not really getting to the bottom of the issues.[44] He argued that one had to look at human nature the way it really is, and accept that certain institutions, such as family and property, could not be erased without establishing tyranny.

To Aristotle, what makes a knife or a sailor good is not that it shares in the form of the good, but that it cuts well or sails well. Instead of dreaming up an ideal state, he studied 158 states and concluded that there was no perfect system, but that a mix was needed. To understand the animal kingdom, he investigated life in all its forms in such quantity and detail that Darwin commented that even the leading modern zoologists were mere schoolboys compared with Aristotle. He was not just one of the first great philosophers, but also one of the first great empirical scientists.

Of course, he was wrong in many of his conclusions, but he provided a method for those who would correct him and continue to acquire knowledge: 'credit must be given rather to observation than to theories, and to theories only if what they affirm agrees with the observed facts'.[45]

Aristotle did not just add footnotes to Plato, he built an entire rival system of thought, on metaphysics, epistemology, ethics, psychology, politics and aesthetics, but grounded in empirical observation, organized according to the laws of logic, which in another monumental contribution, Aristotle discovered and defined. After Plato's death, he founded his own school in Athens, the Lyceum.

There was a certain rivalry between Plato and his star pupil even when they were at the Academy together. It is said that Plato complained: 'Aristotle kicked me away just as colts kick away their mother',[46] and in the *Nicomachean Ethics* Aristotle wrote that 'while both are dear, piety requires us to honour truth above our friends'.[47]

The debate between Plato and Aristotle reveals that Athens had become a culture where intellectual innovation was considered a virtue. This was a giant leap in intellectual history. In the texts that have come down to us from other cultures and previously in Greece there are no examples of authors who criticized received wisdom and claimed that they had an original insight. Even when they did, they usually hid it, by pretending that it was an ancient thought that had been forgotten.

The poet Samuel Taylor Coleridge thought that 'Every man is born an Aristotelian or a Platonist', and he couldn't even begin to imagine a third class of individuals.[48] It might overstate the hereditary aspect, but Plato and Aristotle would indeed go on to inspire different strains of thought ever after, in philosophy, religion, science and politics. Here was the inspiration for the other-worldly, mystical, spiritual and utopian on the one hand, and the secular, rational, empirical and golden mean on the other. Christianity, to pick just one example, was one thing in Augustine's Platonic version and a very different thing in Thomas Aquinas's Aristotelian formula.

Other Greek philosophical schools would continue to ponder all these questions, no doubt inspired by the Aristotelian approval of curiosity as a prime mover for thought and science: 'it is owing to their wonder that men both now begin and at first began to philosophize; they wondered originally at the obvious difficulties, then advanced little by little and stated difficulties about the greater matters'.[49]

Epicurus (341–270 BC) provoked as much with his religious scepticism and embracing of pleasure as life's goal as he did by inviting women and slaves to discuss it in his Athenian garden. This Epicureanism was challenged by Zeno of Citium (334–262 BC), who moved from Cyprus to Athens to teach his philosophy of Stoicism. Man must learn wisdom and self-control not just to rid himself of the passions but to be emotionally indifferent to life's gifts and misfortunes. It is often claimed that Stoics were opponents of slavery, but their argument that no one can really be enslaved because their mind decides how to react to it seems more like a way of trivializing it. However, they upheld a lively intellectual culture where it became commonplace to be curious, to challenge old theories and formulate new ones.

The last stand

The epic sequence of teachers and students does not end here. While Plato and Aristotle were debating metaphysics, a new power was rising: Macedonia. Greek cities that had weakened themselves by constant warfare now fell, one by one, to Philip II's terrifying phalanxes, with their innovative 6-metre pikes. The plan was to unite the whole of Greece, before an invasion of Asia could begin. Athens would soon be forced into the Macedonian alliance.

A king with such grand ambitions could only be content with the very best for his son. That is why, in 343 BC, he invited Aristotle to be the teacher for his thirteen-year-old, Alexander, soon to be 'the Great' (356–323 BC). A few years earlier, King Philip had sacked Aristotle's hometown Stagira and sold its inhabitants as slaves. Now, Aristotle agreed to tutor Alexander, in return for Philip rebuilding Stagira and resettling the population there. For three years, Aristotle taught the future conqueror everything from medicine, botany and zoology to ethics, politics and poetry, and he no doubt shared with him some of his racial prejudices against non-Greeks.

Alexander ascended to the throne at twenty years of age, and Aristotle returned to Athens. He had apparently failed to instil the virtue of modesty and moderation in the young king, who now conquered more land in a shorter period than anyone had before him. In rapid succession Persia, Mesopotamia, Egypt and Central Asia fell to him, creating an empire that stretched all the way to India. On his campaigns, Alexander brought a large group of botanists, zoologists and surveyors, who collected specimens and information for further study by Aristotle and others. Alexander spread death and destruction throughout the Mediterranean and Asia, but also a Hellenistic culture that would live long after him.

One of his great achievements was the founding of the city of Alexandria in 331 BC on the Egyptian coast, a city that attracted Greek, Jewish, Arab and African inhabitants of all faiths. The Great Library of Alexandria was not just the most famous library of the ancient world, but a cosmopolitan scientific centre. With this library and climate of tolerance, Hellenistic Egypt began to take over Athens' role as the centre of intellectual innovation and made possible great scholars like the geographer and astronomer Ptolemy.

The year 322 BC marks the end of both democracy and philosophy in Athens. The year before, Alexander suddenly died in Babylon, at just thirty-two years old. According to an unconvincing rumour, Aristotle had been involved in a plot to poison him, disgusted by Alexander's ambition to deify himself.

In this sudden power vacuum, Athenians saw an opportunity to reclaim their lost independence. Anti-Macedonian feelings ran high. Anger against Alexander's former teacher was only to be expected and a trial seems to have been prepared against him on the grounds of impiety. Aristotle fled Athens to his mother's family estate on Euboea, because, in a reference to the death of Socrates, he would not let Athenians 'sin twice against philosophy'. There, the great thinker died of natural causes in March 322 BC.

Meanwhile, the Athenians had rebelled against the Macedonians, but fared badly at sea. Initial gains at land could not change the fact that they simply did not have enough money or hoplites when the Macedonians banded together and reinforced their army. The Athenians were defeated at Crannon in central Thessaly in August 322 BC.

The Macedonian general Antipater forced Athens to surrender the leading anti-Macedonian activists, pay a war indemnity and accept a Macedonian garrison in the port city of Piraeus. But he had one more condition. Understanding that the secret weapon that provided Athens with its restless energy and insubordinate spirit was its democracy, he decided it had to go. Athens had to restrict political rights to men of property above a level that seems to have disenfranchised more than two-thirds of the Assembly. In September 322 BC, after an incredible 180-year run, the world's first democracy came to an end.

The idea, however, would never die. For twenty-five centuries and counting, Athens' strange system of government has continued to confound observers and inspire reformers and revolutionaries. As Pericles had asserted, 'Future ages will wonder at us.'[50]

Summary

It is still mind-boggling to consider the achievements of ancient Athens. Beginning in the sixth century BC, it was the scene of an explosion of creativity that still influences and inspires us. The Athenians, and the outsiders they attracted, got the historical ball rolling in so many areas, from philosophy and politics to theatre and architecture – and the recording of history itself.

It was made possible by a very unusual openness to innovation and surprises from abroad and from within. New ideas constantly washed over Athens. It was located at the crossroads between Mesopotamia, Egypt and other Mediterranean cultures, and it was just one of a multitude of Greek city-states from which to learn and compete with.

'Our city is open to the world', as Pericles said. The city embraced openness through international trade, first by necessity, and then by choice, when it realized that trade created prosperity. Merchants travelled between regions, observing alternatives and spreading ideas, thereby constantly challenging traditions and orthodoxies. Athens built a system of alliances and cleared the sea-lanes of pirates, turning itself into an important maritime power.

There was also inclusion within democracy and the breaking down of old tribal allegiances. It did not extend to women and slaves but gave a chance for even the poorest free men to yield real power. The broad base of potential leaders made it possible to find talents like Themistocles, when this was needed. 'Who wishes to speak?' was the first question at every Assembly, because anyone could.

Debates also raged on theatre stages and city squares. More people and more ideas were constantly tested in debate, in Assemblies, theatre stages and town squares. It was uncomfortable to many, just as partisan bickering and offensive speech is today, but it was the key to breaking down orthodoxies and to putting more ideas and knowledge into the public sphere.

In combination, this created the first culture we know of that considered intellectual innovation a virtue, and looked inwards and examined itself. Thinkers like Aristotle declared that one had to choose truth over friends and teachers. That is unusual historically. Life close to subsistence level is hard with not much margin for error, so most historical societies that came up with a way of sustaining themselves tried to stick to the original recipe and considered innovators troublemakers. Athens' openness, and the wealth it created, expanded mental horizons. It was suddenly possible to experiment with novel ways of thinking.

Rule of law and a high degree of economic freedom made Athenians extend this to other areas too. They were free to specialize and experiment with sculpture, ceramics, architecture, farming and finance, forcing others to innovate to keep up. The result was a city teeming with eccentric ideas, novel business models and lots of unorthodox artists. It made Athens the richest and most beautiful of cities, the envy of the whole Greek world.

As the Corinthian observer pointed out: 'An Athenian is always an innovator', and this is what set him apart from the

Spartans, who are 'good at keeping things as they are', and therefore closed and stagnant, leaving no legacy for the modern world except misleading tales of martial bravery.

Why did Athens choose this unusual path? An important cause was confidence. The unpredictability of openness and innovation often seems intimidating, but after military victories against both other Greek cities and the Persian Empire, it had proof of concept. The Athenians could clearly see that freedom gave them capacities that enticed them more than its uncertainty scared them. So they extended those liberties and doubled down on democracy and trade.

Sadly, the loss of this confidence undermined the open, exploratory mindset. The suffering during the long Peloponnesian War led to a deterioration of character over the whole of Greece, observed Thucydides. Even the Athenians lost their devotion to principles, to long-term thinking and to looking at questions from all sides. Fanatical tribalism was suddenly the mark of a real man.

Searching for scapegoats for their plight, Athenian democrats even decided to execute the wisest of them all, Socrates, and eventually chased Aristotle out of the city. Facing existential threats, the city that invented intellectual innovation suddenly considered it a capital offence.

The kind of savagery caused by war, fear and zero-sum thinking would be repeated in the future, warned Thucydides, since human beings remain the same. Indeed, this is a pattern that we will see repeated over many golden eras. It is not history that repeats itself, but human nature.

2

ROME

Melting Pot of Marble

The entire history of the world is linked up with this city, and I reckon my second life, a very rebirth, from the day when I entered Rome.

JOHANN WOLFGANG VON GOETHE, 1786[1]

All of Western life and institutions today are traceable to the Romans and their world. We are all Roman children for better or worse.

IGGY POP, 1995[2]

If a man were called to fix the period in the history of the world during which the condition of the human race was most happy and prosperous, he would, without hesitation, name that which elapsed from the death of Domitian [AD 96] to the accession of Commodus [AD 180].

EDWARD GIBBON, 1776[3]

How often do you do it?

According to a viral TikTok claim, women were shocked to find out how often men think about ancient Rome. Originally, this was a Swedish meme that took off internationally in August 2023, when a Roman reenactor called Gaius Flavius published a question on Instagram: 'Ladies, many of you do not realise how often men think about the Roman Empire. Ask your husband/boyfriend/father/brother – you will be surprised by the answers!'

'Every day,' said one. 'Three times a day,' said another, 'There is so much to think about.' Some suggested it's because men are more interested in abstractions and history than in personal relations, others that it was because of the 'masculinity polycrisis'.

I got in touch with Gaius Flavius and, to my surprise, it turned out that I actually knew him from a series of lectures we arranged a few years ago. His real name is Artur Hulu and he said that his experience is that men are obsessed with Rome, often from their respective individual perspectives; engineers think about Roman engineering, lawyers about Roman law, doctors about Latin medical terms, scientists ponder the effect the Roman Warm Period in Europe had on its expansion, and history buffs think about emperors and battles. Rome has had such an influence on our world that it's possible for all of us to think about it without thinking about the same things. Normal people probably think mostly about *Life of Brian* and the Judean People's Front.

'How often do you think about it yourself?' I asked Hulu. 'I thought about it once, and never stopped,' he replied, and added that of course many great scholars of Roman history are women. But he insisted that it's more common to come across men with this particular obsession. Polling bears him out. The research company Novus asked Swedes how many thought of ancient Rome every day; the results showed that 5 per cent of men did but only 1 per cent of women. It's only one in every twenty men. But, still, that's in a country that was never part of the empire, and *every day*.[4]

Slightly fewer Americans think about Rome every day, according to another poll, but 9 per cent think about it every week (13 per cent of men). In addition, 49 per cent of US adults say that the Roman Empire had a positive impact on the world, compared with only 15 per cent who say it had a negative impact: a net approval rating that present-day US politicians could only dream about.[5]

I think there is good reason for people to think even more often about it, considering what the Romans have done for us: its cultural importance to Europe, our legal systems, the urban grid, our architectural styles. Also the word and idea of a 'republic' and a 'senate'. Our Latin alphabet and languages like French, Italian, Spanish, Portuguese and Romanian. The Christian Church in both its Catholic and Orthodox forms. And the calendar. Is it January or March when you read this? The Romans named them after their gods of transitions and of war. July or August? Julius Caesar and his successor Augustus.

Yes, there is much to think about. Rome's technological achievements, concrete and aqueducts, and buildings that still stand to this day, like the Colosseum and the Pantheon. Its efficient legions and brutal warfare (cue masculinity polycrisis). And another reason that we think about Rome is that, due to a treasure trove of literary sources, we know more about it than about any other ancient society.

But one of the most convincing explanations for Rome's continued grip over our imagination is its fall – 'the greatest, perhaps, and most awful scene, in the history of mankind', as Edward Gibbon characterized it in the last volume of his monumental late-eighteenth-century work on the subject.[6] This vast Roman Empire stretched from Scotland to the Sahara, from Portugal to Armenia, and turned the Mediterranean into an inland sea. At its peak, Rome probably governed four-fifths of all Europeans and a fifth of humanity, providing them with living standards that it would take us a thousand years to equal. The combination of its geographical reach, internal unity and control for such a duration has never been achieved since.

And yet suddenly it all crumbled and Rome fell to barbarian invaders, leaving in its wake ruins and a dark age of destitution and superstition. Rome, a metropolis of a million relatively prosperous people declined to perhaps some 50,000 inhabitants, scavenging for food and quarrying material from the ruins. This was not just a transformation, despite how much historians search for continuity; it was a collapse that can legitimately be described as the end of civilization, or at least its very long interruption.

The fall of Rome is the West's *memento mori*. A reminder that we are also mortal and that, no matter how safe, rich and powerful we are, one day the barbarian might be at our gates, killing and pillaging. The founders of the United States of America wanted to recreate a Roman Republic that wouldn't fall and, ever since, Americans have not stopped fearing that they live in the decline-and-fall phase.

The end never ceases to fascinate us. In 1984, the German historian Alexander Demandt collected a list of explanations that had been given for Rome's decline and fall. He found 210 reasons, including barbarian invasions, environmental destruction, lead poisoning, moral decay, Christianity, immigration, sadness, capitalism, communism and gout. Just as we perceive our own obsessions in the rise of Rome, we also do in its fall. The Republican Speaker of the US House of Representatives, Mike Johnson, recently argued that the empire collapsed because of 'rampant homosexual behaviour'.

However, it's not the first empire to fall and it will not be the last. Sooner or later, they all do. Rome lasted for more than a thousand years, and as an empire for almost half a millennium, and that is even if you don't count the much longer-lasting eastern part of the empire. As suggested even by Gibbon, who in many ways initiated our obsession with Rome's fall, the real question is not why Rome fell, but why it lasted so long.

When Rome did not fall

The history of Rome could very well have ended on 2 August 216 BC, near the village of Cannae in south-east Italy. The Roman army, perhaps 80,000 men in total, confronted Hannibal, the brilliant commander of their stubborn nemesis Carthage, a powerful, maritime offshoot of Phoenicia. Hannibal's smaller forces, which had famously crossed the Alps with their war elephants two years earlier, managed to surround and attack the Roman legions from both flanks simultaneously. In one afternoon, the Romans were wiped out, in Polybius's telling almost to the last man.

It was one of the deadliest days in human history, destroying the bulk of Rome's army. Panic gripped the city, which even resorted to human sacrifice to the gods. In less than two years, Rome had lost around one-fifth of its population of male adult citizens. Anyone in their right mind would have embraced

Hannibal's proposal for peace negotiations, especially in the light of other disastrous defeats around the same time.

The Romans didn't. The Senate even prohibited use of the word 'peace' and ordered full mobilization, and 'full' was not just a word. Rome lowered the draft age and enlisted new groups to fight another day. Unbelievably, the almost defeated Romans were soon able to command around a quarter of a million men, fighting on several fronts at once. (Alexander the Great invaded Persia with fewer than 50,000 soldiers.) Every time the Romans lost, they raised more legions. They fought on for another fourteen years, until finally defeating Hannibal.

The city of Rome could achieve this because of its extensive network of allies, its *socii*. These were subject peoples, required to send troops when asked. Powerful states usually subjected other territories, of course, and forced them to pay up and deliver manpower, but they did this as occupiers, extracting resources by force. That is costly to administer, and dangerous, since armed serfs might very well rebel. Rome had another system, one that the historian Bret Devereaux has called 'willing compliance', even though 'willing' comes with heavy qualifications.[7] If a city revolted, the Roman army would destroy it. But they had come up with a more successful formula for imperial expansion, partly by accident.

Around 500 BC, the Roman Republic had already established itself as one of the strongest cities in central Italy. This power could be used to build patron–client relationships with smaller cities. In exchange for protection from each other and from outside forces, they provided manpower when needed to sustain and expand Roman power, and then they also got to share the loot from the campaigns. It gave the new subjects a stake in the system and made them more willing to supply the army with men kitted with expensive iron and bronze.

By leading alliances of cities against common enemies, such as the Volsci and later the Gauls, Rome acted like Athens had when it built its maritime empire – cooperation when possible, conquest when pressed. By 264 BC, Rome had signed no fewer than 150 treaties with polities across the Italian peninsula.[8]

Tim Cornell has compared the Roman model to 'a criminal operation which compensates its victims by enrolling them in the gang and inviting them to share the proceeds of future robberies'.[9] And it was so successful because there was honour among thieves. The Romans proved again and again that they kept their word and sacrificed blood and resources whenever an ally was threatened. Rome was the big bully that you would do best to have on your side.

The military of other empires was usually funded by having the army conquer, occupy and tax an area. It was a great self-perpetuating system so long as they were successful in war, but once they met a defeat it could quickly unravel. The army was gone, and so was the ability to tax regions to raise a new one. (This is a more likely reason why Greeks often sued for peace after a defeat than the suggestion that they were gentlemen knowing when they had been beaten. They just had to keep some of the army intact or crumble completely.)

Carthage was reliant on mercenaries and faced the regular threat that they would turn against it every time it ran out of funds to pay them. Rome's system was superior since it could rely on a multitude of allies who armed and provided their own soldiers. Since Rome was a republic, it could also have many armies in play simultaneously, led by any one senator, instead of having just one army led by a king who feared making anyone else a powerful commander. So, whenever Rome lost an army, they sent a new one. As inspirational speakers love to misquote whichever boxer is most famous for the moment: it's not about how many times you get knocked down, it's about how many times you get back up.

Rome's eventual expansion beyond Italy was a bit different, based more on outright conquest, and the old tax-and-spend system. But, still, a pattern had been set for a more decentralized empire: if a city surrendered and agreed to pay up, the elites were allowed to stay in place, with their fortunes, traditions and religions intact. Often local gods were incorporated into the Roman pantheon, sometimes being treated as an aspect of a Roman deity. The vetting process was not exactly rigorous. When the Romans invaded a city in southern Galatia in AD 67, they publicly praised 'whichever' gods protected the city.[10]

All of this made conquest easier and tempted many to surrender without a fight, and then Rome could also outsource the raising of taxes to local leaders. Because of this system, Roman history did not end on that grisly summer day in 216 BC. Instead, that day and its aftermath can be said to illustrate what turned Rome into such an unparalleled power.

Sparta, with its restrictive entry into the elite, died a little every time it lost a battle. Athens, though a much more open power than Sparta, embraced the myth of an 'autochthonous' population. Athenians didn't come from anywhere: they sprang from the soil and this limited their ability to incorporate outsiders and benefit from new blood. Rome's strength was that its foundational story was the complete opposite. All Romans came from somewhere else.

A city of refuges

According to Virgil's epic poem *Aeneid*, the story of Rome is the sequel to Homer's *Iliad*. After Troy had been sacked by Achilles,

Odysseus and the other Greeks, the Trojan hero Aeneas and other refugees fled to Italy, where they were destined to found a new civilization that would rule the world. In 753 BC, this was at last done by Romulus and Remus, the twin children of a woman descended from Aeneas and the god Mars. Seeing them as a threat to his rule, the king made sure that the twins were abandoned to die, but as souvenir sculptures, buttons and t-shirts in present-day Rome helpfully remind us, they were in fact brought up and nurtured by a loving she-wolf.

After having killed his brother in a spat over which hill to build their new city on, Romulus became Rome's first king and populated the city by erecting a temple on the Capitoline Hill to the vagabond god Asylaeus and inviting refugees from everywhere to his asylum. The grand Roman Empire was thus originally founded by foreigners, outcasts, debtors, servants, escaped slaves, pirates and even murderers (one must assume that Romulus sensed an affinity).

If you have seen Mel Brooks' western *Blazing Saddles* and remember Hedley Lamarr's invitation to all the 'rustlers, cut throats, murderers, bounty hunters, desperados, mugs, pugs, thugs, nitwits, halfwits, dimwits' you get the idea. Nine hundred years later, the Roman satirical poet Juvenal told noble Romans: 'Whoever your earliest ancestor was, he was either a shepherd or something I'd rather not mention.'[11] But they weren't necessarily ashamed of it. Even noble Roman families talked about their immigrant background.

It turned out that the sexes were not equally represented in this group and that Rome had accidentally become a colony of bachelors. Therefore, the Romans staged games in order to draw people in from neighbouring cities and kidnap their women. The abduction of the Sabine women naturally resulted in war, but if we are so gullible as to trust the myth, the brawl was magically resolved when the women proposed that the two peoples join peacefully and build a new polity.

First we make our legends and then our legends make us. The Athenians came from nowhere, the Spartans were not going anywhere and did not let anyone in, but Romans came from everywhere and anywhere and kept expanding by constantly absorbing new groups, peoples and ethnicities into its own system and giving them an opportunity to rise through the ranks if their ability allowed them. In the mid-second century, the Greek orator Aelius Aristides summarized Rome's success formula: 'In your empire all paths are open to all. No one worthy of rule or trust remains an alien.' Just as the sea received the rivers, 'this city receives those who flow in from all the earth'.[12]

In some circles it's popular to blame Rome's fall on immigration, and certainly on that fatal day in AD 476 when the last western Roman emperor was deposed, it was Germans who were responsible. But as Quintus Cicero, the brother of the great philosopher, wrote in a letter to him: the city of Rome was formed from a meeting of nations. If immigrants helped topple the Roman Empire, it's also true that immigrants founded it and made sure it lasted longer than most other political entities in history. All empires fall, few survive this long.

One way of attracting outsiders was through the institution of citizenship. A Roman citizen had the protection of the law, could own property, engage in commerce and marry another Roman. In most cases, they could also vote in elections and stand for office. The Roman way of gradually extending citizenship stands in sharp contrast to the Greeks. Remember, Aristotle could not become a citizen of Athens.

Foreigners could receive citizenship for special services to Rome, and (eventually) after having served in auxiliary troops for twenty-five years. This was a clever way to get experienced and well-trained soldiers to devote their lives to service. Step by step, citizenship was also extended to entire populations, breaking the link between citizenship and ethnicity. During the Social War (91–88 BC), when many cities revolted, Rome responded by granting citizenship to all loyal Italians. Under Caesar, this was extended to Cisalpine Gaul in northern Italy, and emperor Vespasian gave it to Hispania. In 212 BC, emperor Caracalla declared that every non-slave throughout the whole empire was a Roman citizen, regardless of background and ethnicity. By the end of the second century, more than half of the senators came from the provinces. The word 'Roman' had shifted its meaning from membership in a city to a common nationality, remarked Aristides. Much like 'American' today.

In AD 48, the emperor Claudius gave a speech in the Senate, arguing for political rights for the defeated Gauls, even letting them be admitted to the Senate. He did so by emphasizing the uniquely open character of Rome:

> What else was the downfall of Sparta and Athens, than that they held the conquered in contempt as foreigners? But our founder Romulus' wisdom made him on several occasions both fight against and naturalize a people on the same day![13]

Furthermore, the Gauls were now so well integrated that they no longer wore trousers, added Claudius. The Romans did not embrace foreigners because they were liberals. This was a society that considered the subjugation of other peoples a great virtue. Anyone who did not surrender, or who rebelled, was annihilated. Rome was a society that took spectacular joy in the suffering of others in gladiatorial arenas. So the Romans did not embrace tolerance because they were enlightened; they did it in order to beat everybody else and take their stuff. They wanted to integrate people to benefit from them.

Indeed, Claudius's argument for welcoming the Gauls was 'let them also bring their gold and riches instead of holding them apart', and perhaps Caracalla's reform was just the consequence of the infamous spendthrift desperately needing a larger tax base. However, the Romans knew that, by integrating local manpower, ideas and technologies into their own system, they could make use of more talent and more knowledge, and so became more powerful. The Greek historian Polybius pointed out that the Roman superpower was that they were unusually willing to replace their own customs with better practice from elsewhere.[14]

This was strategic tolerance. Openness was a weapon for the Romans: the organization of their legions was inherited from Etruscans, they took their protective metal-ring armour from the Gauls, their oblong shields (according to legend) from the Sabines, their spears from the Samnites, and the 'Spanish sword' (*gladius hispaniensis*) was exactly what it said on the tin. When the Romans decided to build a massive fleet, they took the entire design from a Carthaginian shipwreck. Rome even experimented with war elephants for a while after having confronted Hannibal's. 'They learned from their enemies, copied tactics and equipment, and adapted to fight each enemy in turn', writes the military historian Adrian Goldsworthy.[15]

Of course, all cultures borrow, but some identify with their traditional ways to such an extent that imports and renewal become needlessly difficult (as in the case of Sparta). By turning imitation and adaptation into its foremost tradition, Rome gradually embraced more groups and methods and so accelerated the process. In Claudius's speech above, he also reminded the senators that every high tradition was once new, and therefore it is not wrong to innovate, because if it is successful, it will also set a precedent and become tradition.

As the French Enlightenment thinker Montesquieu explained:

> the main reason for the Romans becoming masters of the world was that, having fought successively against all peoples, they always gave up their own practices as soon as they found better ones.[16]

The Romans even gave up their own emperors as soon as they found better ones. Many of them were born far from Rome. Hadrian, born close to Seville in Spain, was mocked for speaking Latin with a strange rustic dialect. Antoninus Pius had roots in Gaul, Macrinus came from a Berber family and Septimius Severus was of Punic ancestry and born in present-day Libya.

Rome, captive

It was only natural for a people based on the absorption of anything useful or beautiful to become mesmerized by Greek culture. Traders had spread the Greek alphabet, on which the Romans based theirs, and its customs and religious beliefs for centuries. Slowly but steadily, Greece's Zeus was transformed into Rome's Jupiter, Hera turned into Juno, Poseidon became Neptune, Athena became Minerva, and Aphrodite Venus. Apollo even got to stay on as Apollo.

As Rome took control of old Greek territories, this trickle turned into a flood. When the Roman general Marcellus sacked Syracuse in 212 BC and brought home the loot, he himself claimed that he taught Romans to respect and adore the wondrous works of the Greeks:

> Before this time the Romans were unaware even of the existence of such elegant and fine things, and they had no taste for graceful and delicate art like this. ... Marcellus greatly pleased the masses in Rome because he adorned the capital with Greek works that were graceful, charming and imitated the forms of nature.[17]

This was the start of the Greek craze in Rome. Everything Hellenistic was suddenly wildly fashionable. Over the next 150 years, renewed conflicts would provide Rome with a never-ending stream of art, books and people from the Greek world, so there was always something new to marvel at. Romans displayed Greek pieces of art, and soon the first marble temple in the city was built. Decorative bronzes from Corinth became highly sought after, and by the mid-first century, every Roman of rank craved a set of Greek statues for his country villa.

Many Greeks came to Rome as slaves, and it must have been a bewildering experience for Romans to find that their slaves were better educated than they were. Rich households increasingly bought or hired Greek doctors and teachers, who spread their culture to the next generation. Greek sculptors were employed to make copies of classical pieces.

When the Roman general Sulla sacked Athens in 86 BC, he took the library of Apellicon of Teos, a rich book collector, back with him. It contained the only remaining known copies of the works of Aristotle, worm-eaten and sodden with damp. In Rome, the philosopher Andronicus of Rhodes edited and arranged them into the first collected edition of Aristotle's works. The texts of Aristotle that have survived to our time are based on these. Andronicus thought that the texts dealing with the fundamental structure of reality came after (*meta*) the ones on physics, and so gave us the word metaphysics.

Philosophy had been all the rage since 155 BC, when a group of Athenian philosophers arrived in Rome and performed for large crowds, especially the young, who were seduced by the new ideas. Educated Romans started reading Plato and Aristotle, and debated whether the Stoics or the Epicureans were right. One of the most important works in the Stoic tradition was written by an emperor, Marcus Aurelius.

Athens was always recognized as a special place because of its long intellectual tradition, and it was a popular location to go to study. Emperor Augustus renovated the city, and even more was done by Hadrian, who loved the city. Hadrian supplied Athens with an aqueduct and a library, and, at great cost, he finished the temple of Olympian Zeus, which had been begun by the tyrant Pisistratus 600 years earlier.

Upper-class education in Rome was soon based on a Greek curriculum, and after the enslaved educator Livius Andronicus adapted a Greek play into Latin, with actors in a Greek setting wearing Greek dresses, Romans also took up theatre. The elite comfortably switched between speaking Roman and Greek. Caesar's last words were probably spoken in Greek, '*Kai su teknon*', 'you too, my son'. It was Shakespeare who translated it into '*Et tu Brute?*' since his audience understood Latin better.[18]

The martial Romans also admired Alexander; in fact they were the ones who began to call him 'the Great'. Many imitated his hairstyle and went clean shaven like him. Emperor Augustus even showed his respect by visiting Alexander's tomb in the city of Alexandria and placing a diadem on his mummified head (and, in the process, accidentally broke off his nose).

Some Romans worried that Greek cultural imperialism undermined traditional morality. They were especially suspicious of the drunkenness and sexual depravity at unofficial Bacchanalian festivals, based on the Athenian festival for Dionysus, god of wine and insanity. The historian Polybius tells us that the debauchery among young men had spread so far 'that many of them were willing to pay a talent for a male prostitute and 300 drachmas for a jar of Photic pickled fish!'[19]

The senator Cato the Elder warned that Greek culture would ruin Romans and make them lose their empire. But the fact that even he studied Greek rhetoric and memorized Thucydides and Demosthenes in order to make his conservative case shows that attempts to freeze Roman culture in time were impossible. The meeting between the curious Romans and the sophisticated Greek tradition was already in the process of creating a new Graeco-Roman hybrid culture. As the leading Roman poet Horace memorably wrote in one of his epistles, 'Greece, the captive, took her savage victor captive.'

Res publica

Like the Athenians, the Romans had a set of institutions that facilitated constant change and adaptation. Politically, it was the republican institutions, with their exchange of ideas and constant change of consuls and praetors. Economically, it was a market economy with a relatively free exchange of goods and competition between different farmers, artisans and merchants.

The Roman Republic, before it transformed into an empire, admired the goddess of liberty, Libertas, who was usually portrayed with the soft felt cap worn by freed slaves. The origin of the republican institutions was the revolution against Rome's seventh king, Tarquin the Proud, in 509 BC. Like his *Star Wars* namesake, Tarquin was a tyrant who summarily executed enemies and forced the people to work on his big vanity projects. When the Romans threw him out, they established a new system with popularly elected consuls, who led both the civil government and the armies. Power was now divided and temporary. There were two consuls and they held office for just one year. Their power was balanced by the aristocratic Senate, which came to control finances, administration and much of foreign policy, and assemblies which passed legislation.

Rome became a *res publica*, a public matter, held in common by the people, not by any one ruler. One important implication was that all free men should have the right to vote to elect those who served on the legislative assemblies, just as in Athens. However, unlike in Athens, votes did not have equal weight. Romans voted in units according to their wealth (traditionally based on classes' contribution to the military), and, despite being smaller in number, the richest class had much more influence than the rest of the population. It was a plutocratic republic rather than a democratic one. Furthermore, as votes had to be cast in the city of Rome, it benefited the rich, who could afford the journey and the time off to go there. And, in any case, most of the real power was invested in the Senate and the executives.

Soon after the founding of the republic, there was another rebellion. The plebeians, the commoners, attacked the hereditary privileges of the patrician elite. In a long process that took more than two centuries, called the Conflict of the Orders, plebeians won almost all the rights of patricians, and almost all major offices opened up to them, even the consulship. One of the most spectacular incidents was the threat of a strike. The plebeians threatened to walk out of Rome if they did not get equal rights, and since they did the actual work it would stop the motor of the city.

The plebeians succeeded in bringing about a new legal foundation for the republic around 450 BC, called the Twelve Tables. It is said that the ten men appointed with crafting the new laws first travelled to Greece to study their laws, including Solon's Athenian constitution. It mostly codified the rules that were already understood to be in force (including the right to infanticide and that a son whose father has sold him three times is free from parental authority). The innovation is that the Twelve Tables declared that rules made for good and steadfast citizens apply to everyone, introducing an idea of rule of law.

The ninth table is most explicit in proclaiming equality before the law: 'No privileges, or statutes, shall be enacted in favour of private persons, to the injury of others contrary to the law common to all citizens, and which individuals, no matter of what rank, have a right to make use of.'[20]

By the end of the long Conflict of the Orders, the patricians did not retain many more privileges than the exclusive right to wear fancy red sandals with a high heel.

Of course this devotion to liberty did not mean liberty for everyone. Rome was a slave society, and foreign conquests brought thousands of new slaves into the city every year. In the mid-second century as much as 20 per cent of the Italian population was probably owned by somebody else, who had the right to kill, torture and rape them at will. A slave's testimony was never accepted in court unless the slave had been tortured first. Under Nero's reign, a proposal that slaves should be forced to wear a uniform was rejected as this would make it obvious to the slaves how many they were, and a revolt would stand a chance of success.

The divide between the free and slaves was less absolute than in many other slave societies, though. Slaves in mines, mills and fields were ruthlessly exploited until they perished, but urban slaves often received an education, which was banned 2,000 years later in the American south. Slaves often got positive incentives to perform tasks and they could receive property from the owner. This 'peculium' was protected by law, even from the slave owner (slaves could even have their own slaves). Sometimes this property was used by the slaves to buy their freedom.

Slaves were in fact often freed, sometimes because they paid up, sometimes out of the goodwill of their masters, and sometimes because owners did not want to pay for old slaves who could no longer work. In any case it created an unusual opportunity for social mobility that some outsiders credit as responsible for Rome's success. Often slaves ran their owners' business and bought their freedom from a previously agreed share of the profits. It has been estimated that around 10 per cent of adult slaves were freed over a five-year period in the early empire, compared with no more than 0.2 per cent in the American south in the 1850s.[21]

Unlike in the Greek cities, freed men also became citizens. Some became successful businessmen, others worked in civil service. In AD 193, Pertinax, the son of a freed man, even became emperor. Setting slaves free was so common that it has been estimated that in the second century AD, most Romans had slaves among their ancestors.[22]

Some desperately poor mothers left their children on dung or rubbish heaps, to be raised as slaves by others. In Egypt, some of these children were given the unfortunate name Kopros, *dung*. A few of them did so well that, after they gained their freedom, they passed it on as a proud family name to successive generations.

There was another way in which Rome was more inclusive than Athens and most other ancient societies. Roman women were treated as second-class citizens and did not have the right to vote or stand for political office but, according to Mary Beard, they actually had some rights that British women did not have until the 1870s.[23] They did not fall entirely under their husband's legal authority and they did not take his name. They could make contracts and go to court to sue and be sued. When her father died, an adult woman could own property, buy, sell, inherit and write a will. Augustus freed women who had given birth to three children from the need to have a guardian. Even though women had to sit in the back rows of theatres and arenas, they were not meant to be invisible in public, as they were in Athens. They often dined with the men, which outraged prudish Greek visitors, who only found it acceptable to dine with female entertainers and prostitutes.

The greatest proponent of the Roman idea of *libertas* was the statesman and lawyer Marcus Tullius Cicero (106–143 BC), who loved Greek culture so much that he travelled to Athens to study philosophy, and Rhodes to study rhetoric. He took the ideal of equal liberty further than the Greeks had. In opposition to Plato and Aristotle, he argued that in rational faculties humans were more alike than unlike. He did not go so far as to reject slavery, but at least he rejected the idea that there are natural slaves. By nature, no one has the right to rule over anybody, and even people who had sold themselves into slavery had to be treated well.

On this basis, Cicero developed what Michael Hawley calls a 'natural law republicanism', which is a precursor to liberalism. Cicero thought that every individual had a natural right to love and preserve himself, and you may never harm him unless he has done something wrong. This meant that no one was allowed to deprive others of bodily security, personal freedom and private property. The two ways of dealing with others are speech and force, and force is adequate only for beasts. Cicero also acted according to this conviction as a lawyer in famous cases against mighty officials who had abused the defenceless.

Liberty, he wrote, 'does not consist in having a just master, but in having none'.[24] Governments are set up to protect these rights and must govern according to laws, not the will of men. He even argued that if a ruler violates the law, tyrannicide is allowed.

Cicero was not an Athenian democrat and did not trust the poor and uneducated. Democracy would be rule by the mob, and the mob would ignore the rule of law, confiscate property and probably raise a tyrant to power. He similarly feared the uncontrollable passions of a monarch. Like Aristotle (whose prose he called 'a flowing river of gold'), he preferred a mixture of democracy, aristocracy and monarchy, where assemblies, the senate and consuls checked and balanced each other.

In other ways Cicero's republicanism is astonishingly modern, as when he rejects Plato's and Aristotle's conviction that the government should train people in virtue. He makes the case that every individual must find the good life themselves, because it is not the same for all, and there is no guarantee that the rulers will be superior to citizens in virtue and wisdom. The real mark of liberty is therefore, 'to live just as one pleases'.[25]

Of course, Cicero was not representative of the Roman Republic. Many of its leaders had no qualms about destroying entire populations who had done no harm, with the sole aim of acquiring fame and fortune. But Cicero's refinement of a certain libertarian aspect of Roman ideology also says something about what it was about, and sometimes served as a corrective to the abuses. Since Cicero would be read and memorized by students and scholars for two millennia as the very archetype of

Latin eloquence, he also went on to have a lasting influence on future generations. He'll make guest appearances in subsequent golden ages, but his lasting influence was not enough to save his beloved republic.

The death of the republic

The republic was incredibly successful, and its economy benefited from a warmer climate that boosted agriculture, but it was also deeply unstable. In 146 BC, Rome managed finally to defeat Carthage and, in the same year, beat the Achaean League at Corinth and so concluded its conquest of mainland Greece. It was a moment of triumph and the beginning of hegemony, but quite similar to Americans winning the Cold War: when the Romans lost their common enemy, they began to turn on each other. Internal unity began to unravel. Class divisions and partisan conflicts brewed, and in a huge urban metropolis without even a small police force, conflicts quickly turned violent.

The populist aristocrat Tiberius Gracchus was killed by a mob of senators in 133 BC, after having provoked their ire with land reforms. The career of his brother, Gaius Gracchus, ended in even worse bloodshed a decade later. In 88 BC, hostilities descended into outright civil war, followed by a bloody reign of the victor, the traditionalist Sulla, who had a large part of Rome's elite executed.

A common interpretation was that the republic's conquest by decentralization was too successful for its own good. The city-state woke up one day to find that it had acquired an empire. Athens was very big by Greek standards, but it never had more than perhaps 300,000 inhabitants. In Italy alone, there were around 2 million Romans including their allies. Soon Rome also had overseas territories, and how does a consul rule an empire for a year if it takes a substantial part of that year just to travel from one part of it to the other? Rome came to depend on powerful individuals instead of institutions, and they had ambitions of their own. As Mary Beard asserts, 'The empire created the emperors – not the other way around.'[26]

The republic's institutions were too small and the loot too big for Rome's massive egos to stick to the rules. A political career was costly, so senators happily accepted bribes, and provincial governors used their terms ruthlessly to extract resources from the people. Some tried too hard to impress during their short term in power and began to overstep their authority.

Every senator wanted desperately to win a battle and kill 5,000 enemies, which would give him the much sought-after privilege to celebrate the triumph in Rome, in a glorious public procession where he was treated like a god for a day (which is why he supposedly had to be stalked by a slave reminding him that he too was a mortal). Some would go to any lengths for glory, abandoning frontiers to find an army to attack or provoking neighbours to break a peace treaty. One consul started peace negotiations with the enemy when he feared that he would be replaced by someone who would claim credit for an ensuing victory in battle, only to restart the war the moment he had been assured that he would remain in command.

Having several armies simultaneously under competing commanders might have been a recipe for military prowess, but in due course it also became one for civil war. As the army grew bigger, it started recruiting from the whole population, not just from wealthy families. These new soldiers were more dependent on booty and retirement benefits, preferably land from which they could sustain their families after service. The rewards became dependent on the success of their campaigns and the goodwill of their generals. It made soldiers more loyal to them than to the republic. There were worrying signs that they were prepared to follow their generals anywhere, perhaps even across the Rubicon, the river that marked Italy's northern boundary.

The man who finally broke the system was of course the ambitious and ruthless Julius Caesar (100–44 BC). But he was just one of many potential autocrats who fought for wealth and glory in an increasingly deadly rivalry. To keep his power and wealth, Caesar committed so many crimes that he, like some modern counterparts, became desperate to stay in command, since the office came with immunity from prosecution. But after his successful (and often illegal) campaign in Gaul, the Senate ordered him to step down from his command. Pushed into a corner by his own previous actions, Caesar defied the senators and instead took one of his legions across the Rubicon, the boundary of Caesar's legitimate command.

By crossing this fairly unremarkable river in 49 BC, Caesar set in motion events that would destroy the republic and unleash two decades of unimaginable bloodshed all over the Roman world. By the end of it, almost all the republic's political, military and intellectual leaders had been viciously killed.

It started with a four-year civil war all over the realm between the forces of Caesar and those of Pompey, a one-time ally and another would-be despot, who had joined forces with the Senate only because they now had a common enemy. Whichever side won, it would mean the end of Roman freedom, feared Cicero. In the end, Caesar won, declaring himself dictator for life, which gave the temporary office of 'dictator in an emergency' a bad name for two millennia.

However, he had not won all hearts and minds. Caesar's sworn enemy was the senator Cato the Younger (95–46 BC), so designated as not to be confused with his great-grandfather, Cato the Elder, of anti-Greek and 'Carthage must be destroyed' fame. Cato was as famous for his austere life as he was for his dedication to the ideals of republicanism. He had consistently opposed generals who wanted to amass power. At one point he had even proposed that Caesar should not be celebrated for his conquest of Gaul, but instead turned over to the enemy, to be tried for unprovoked aggression against women and children.

After a series of retreats, Cato found himself in command of the city of Utica on the coast of what is now Tunisia. There he learned of the defeat of one of the last loyal armies and understood that the city would soon fall. He evacuated Romans from Utica but stayed behind, discussing Stoic philosophy over dinner with his friends. His prospects were not necessarily bleak. Caesar was happy to grant pardons to defeated enemies, but to Cato that would have been an unacceptable humiliation, implying that Caesar was his master, with the right to decide who gets to live or die. He would not give a tyrant that satisfaction. After dinner, Cato stabbed himself with his sword. His friends intervened and a doctor sewed up his wound, but Cato, Stoic to his last breath, pushed the doctor away and, in Plutarch's excessively graphic version of the story, pulled out his own bowels through the wound and died.

It was the end of Cato the man, but the birth of Cato the legend. His heroic defiance would go on to inspire opposition to tyranny for the next two millennia, not least during the American Revolution. One who was deeply influenced by Cato's example was his nephew Brutus, who even wrote a pamphlet celebrating him. Together with around twenty other senators, Brutus stabbed Caesar to death on 15 March 44 BC. This regicide, committed to terminate Caesar's royal ambitions and restore the republic to its full glory, ended up destroying it forever. History is a long series of unintended consequences.

The plotters lacked a serious plan for how to pacify Rome after the assassination, and created an opening for Mark Antony, Caesar's loyal lieutenant, to turn people against them. Soon different armies marched on each other and a new player emerged, Octavian, who was the adopted son of Caesar and the inheritor of his wealth. He was young and inexperienced, but with his fortune he raised an army that could tip the scales. At first Octavian fought Mark Antony, but soon he joined with him to defeat Caesar's assassins.

Under their brutal regime, all enemies were hunted down and a large number of senators and aristocrats were murdered so that they could take their property. One of the victims was Cicero, who had earned Mark Antony's wrath because of his persistent letters and speeches about why all forces should unite to fight this dangerous despot. Octavian apparently argued against killing Cicero, but the new allies had to trade some friends, relatives and associates to secure the inclusion of their own opponents on the kill list.

Cicero's head and hands were cut off and displayed publicly in the central Forum of the city, symbolizing the end of the man who had spoken and written more forcefully and eloquently than anybody else. It is said that Mark Antony's wife Fulvia took out her hairpin and jabbed Cicero's tongue with it repeatedly. Just as Athens once had, Rome executed its most prominent philosopher.

Predictably, Octavian and Mark Antony soon fell out with each other and, after having been defeated in another war, Antony committed suicide with his wife Cleopatra in Alexandria, Egypt. Octavian was the last man standing, and in 27 BC took power under his chosen name Augustus (63

BC–AD 14). He also called himself Imperator, 'commander', and took the name of his adoptive father, as did all his successors: 'Caesar' would eventually become 'Kaiser' in German and 'Tsar' in several Slavic languages.

The old Rome was gone and most old Romans were dead. The most ruthless warlord, Augustus, had secured total power. But then came the most extraordinary second act in political history.

Pax Romana

This was the moment that the Roman Republic morphed into the Roman Empire, with political control vested in one man, just as the Star Wars Republic was reorganized into a Galactic Empire after a cataclysmic civil war. With total power and his enemies disposed of, Augustus, at the age of only thirty-two, could easily have allowed this empire to sink into an abyss of depravity, chaos and corruption. There was some of that, of course, but for reasons that historians still debate, Augustus, who ruled for forty years, turned out to be a fairly competent statesman who established relative peace and economic development.

Perhaps Augustus had picked up some sensible ideas along the way, after all. Plutarch tells the story of how Augustus one day came across one of his grandsons reading a book by the executed Cicero. The terrified boy tried to hide the book in his gown, but Augustus took the book, read for a while and then returned it to the boy, saying: 'A learned man, my child, a learned man and a lover of his country.'[27]

Or perhaps it was just that Rome (and Augustus) was exhausted by civil war and had to look for ways of establishing peace. Like a Machiavellian Prince, Augustus cut off heads to attain power but then wielded that power in a gentler way, through masterful propaganda, for example. Virgil was assigned to write the *Aeneid* celebrating Rome's mythological past and imperial present. Just as Pericles had given Athens a new, striking and costly image, Augustus now filled Rome with proud new monuments, leading him to boast that he found Rome a city of bricks and left it a city of marble. In two centuries the Romans quarried more marble than has been quarried in the world since antiquity, making it look like a magnificent Greek city.[28] You dress for the job you want.

Augustus also flooded the empire with his own public image. There may have been as many as 50,000 statues of Augustus, guaranteeing that he stayed forever young and beautiful, despite having bad teeth and messy hair, according to the gossip Suetonius. (A modern reconstruction based on the statues reportedly gave the impression that the emperor was 'as hot as Daniel Craig'.)[29]

Augustus undermined popular elections but made peace with the old senatorial class by pretending that the old republican institutions were intact and by giving them administrative duties and legislative powers. It created some balance of powers, but was also safe for the emperor, because everyone knew who was ultimately in charge. This mutual understanding is reflected in the story of a treason trial when a senator asked emperor Tiberius to cast his vote first, because otherwise 'I might find that I have voted the wrong way by mistake'.[30] Or, as a much later senator, famous for his oratory, answered when asked why he let an emperor correct his use of a word publicly: surely everyone must 'acknowledge that the man who controls thirty legions is the most learned of all'.[31]

One of Augustus's most successful efforts was the monopolization of the use of force, and under him the city finally got a police force in the city. The rivalry between war lords was ended when Augustus made himself the commander-in-chief of all the armed forces and began appointing major officers. He also introduced retirement benefits for soldiers to end their dependence on a particular commander. Soon no more triumphs were staged for generals outside the family. Ironically, the empire became less militarized than the republic had been.

Augustus descended from Volsci, a non-Latin Italian city that had often been at war with Rome, and he now integrated more wealthy non-Romans into the elite. Even though Rome lost many liberties, some provinces got more breathing space without governors who wanted to take as much as possible during their short stint in power. For these provinces, with an emperor in lasting charge, Rome turned from being a roving bandit to being a stationary bandit, with an interest in the long-term prosperity of its victims. That is, after all, the only way to get more tax revenue in the long run. Tiberius, the second emperor, warned his governors not to be ruthless in their tax collection: 'it is the duty of a good shepherd to shear his sheep not skin them'.

Augustus was also lucky, coming to power during what is known as the Roman Warm Period, a very humid time, when agricultural output and therefore population were boosted in southern Europe and the Near East. After Rome's conquest of Egypt and parts of Germania and the Balkans, and the pacification of Spain, the empire was immense. The only way in which it could function was by not trying to direct all of these territories from Rome. As long as the provinces were loyal, at peace and paid their taxes, everyday administration was left to local elites. The emperor was the final arbiter of everything and replied to letters about specific concerns or conflicts, but he rarely tried to plan ahead and interfere in the details. In fact, the Romans complained if the provinces wrote too often and asked for guidance. This meant that if the Romans had a crazy emperor, who made a horse a senator (which Caligula might have done) and killed their mothers (which Nero probably did), it did not necessarily affect citizens' lives too much. The whole Roman bureaucracy was probably made up of just a few hundred officials and their slaves, for an empire of perhaps 50 million people.

This was the start of the period sometimes known as 'Pax Romana', the Roman peace. It was a period without long, devastating civil wars, and subjected territories were forced to solve conflicts through the means of the law instead of arms. Augustus consciously portrayed himself as a guardian of that peace. An ancient tradition held that the doors to the temple of Janus were to be closed in times of peace. In all of Roman history until then, they had only been closed twice. During Augustus's long rule, he ordered them closed three times.

In 13 BC, the Senate commissioned an 'Altar of Augustan Peace' in central Rome, which celebrated the end of war and the coming of progress and abundance. Olive branches, familiar from Athens' peace-loving olive growers, figure prominently on the monument. Such was the confidence in peace that few Roman cities were walled for defence, something that would not be repeated elsewhere in Europe until after explosives had made walls obsolete.

This does not mean that Rome was not at war. The relative tranquillity was based on superior fire power. Often the Romans made a desert and called it peace. The first two times the gates of Janus were closed, they were re-opened within a year. The third time, news of war actually arrived even before they had been closed as ordered.[32] There were constant battles on the frontiers of the growing empire, but at least the armies mostly stayed there.

Soon the most expansionist phase was over, especially after Germanic tribes spectacularly defeated three Roman legions in the Battle of the Teutoburg Forest in AD 9, making the Rhine the de facto border of the empire. Augustus's stepson and successor Tiberius called an end to imperial expansion, only temporarily restarted by Claudius's invasion of Britannia in AD 43.

The empire was relatively stable, and safe for trade and mobility. In the late republic, the Mediterranean had been freed from pirates (who had been offered new land in compensation) and now the Alps were cleared from raiders who robbed travellers. The fact that many bought land far from the place where they lived shows that there was a high degree of trust in the law and property rights. Important Republican ideals were back in vogue. Cicero wrote: 'Poor men of humble birth sail across the seas to shores they have never seen before, where they find themselves among strangers', confident that one single fact will be their defence against all sorts of calamity: 'I am a Roman citizen.'[33]

Empire of globalization

It was said that Romulus originally decided to place Rome by the river Tiber, which led straight to the sea, to be able to import necessities and export surpluses. Peace, law and infrastructure combined with this initial wise decision to usher in a golden era of globalization. Hadrian's Wall was an exception. During the golden age, the Romans rarely built walls, and even Hadrian's Wall had a gateway at roughly every Roman mile, through which economic exchange and travel took place.

Economies of scale in the Roman Empire enabled access to much more varied sorts of goods at cheaper prices. The archaeologist Andrew Wilson writes: 'Pottery, glassware, bricks, coins, plate, and humble metal objects such as nails were produced in enormous quantities to standard shapes and sizes, and widely traded around the Roman Mediterranean and northern Europe and even beyond the frontiers of the empire, reaching India and the Sahara.'[34]

Wilson suspects that a perceived lack of originality and innovation in Roman sculpture compared to the Greeks might not be the result of a lack of imagination, but the clever use of mass manufacturing to compensate for a lack of artists to meet booming demand.

Bigger ships with better sails and massive port facilities enabled the shipment of wool from Asia Minor and fermented fish sauce from Spain. Spices and metalwork became major export industries, as did Gallic wine – it has been estimated that the city of Rome consumed 1.5 million hectolitres of wine each year.[35] Trade in olive oil was so massive that there is to this day a small mountain in central Rome, Monte Testaccio, made up of fragments of the countless amphorae discarded there after the oil had been unloaded and decanted at the port.

If goods had to be transported by land, there was a dense network of roads, originally for military purposes, which were funded with tolls at city gates and bridges. There were 400,000 kilometres of road, of which over 80,000 kilometres were stone-paved, and many of these roads really did lead to Rome. In the Forum there was a Golden Milestone, where all roads were considered to begin, and all distances were measured in relation to.

The Greek orator Aristides declared that to see all the products of the world, one had two alternatives – to visit the entire world or to visit just the city of Rome:

For whatever is grown and made among each people cannot fail to be here at all times and in abundance. And here the merchant vessels come carrying these many products from all regions in every season and even at every equinox, so that the city appears a kind of common emporium of the world.[36]

Through ports on the Red Sea, Roman merchants and sailors used the monsoon winds to build a vast network of trade, stretching from the Mediterranean to Arabia and Ethiopia, all the way to India and Sri Lanka, where they established permanent settlements. The Romans sent wares and coins and in return received silks, cottons, scents and spices, especially pepper, which they could not get enough of. The fashion for silk among rich and noble Roman families helped to firmly establish the Silk Routes, some 6,000 kilometres of roads, paths and trading stretching from the Mediterranean all the way to China.

In a large but fairly ordinary house in Pompeii buried under volcano ash, an ivory statuette from India has been found, possibly representing an Indian goddess of fertility. Archaeologists have found massive quantities of Roman goods at sites in Scandinavia and the Baltic states and are only beginning to uncover the extent of these ancient networks.

An important consequence of the empire was that knowledge, talent and innovations from one part of it rapidly spread to the others, spurring the imitation and learning that was always a part of Roman tradition. Farmers made use of new reapers, better screw presses and salting vats. Even archaeological sites in distant and poor parts of the empire reveal new styles of tools and jewellery. Mining and metallurgy improved, giving all regions easier access to metal, much of which was used for armour and weapons. The Romans picked up watermill technology from the Greeks and developed it further to power grain mills and industrial mills. In some places, like Barbegal in southern France, they built huge complexes of watermills that could produce enough flour for a large town.

Rome was not built in a day, but it was built extraordinarily quickly, because it mastered the art of building in synthetic stone: concrete. Through many experiments in many places, the Romans came up with the best ratio between different materials to produce a durable mix, and could source raw material from distant places; the best limestone, the best volcanic ash and lots of timber for fuel and scaffolding. In this way, the Romans could quickly construct housing, temples and deep-water harbours. They built aqueducts that still stand today and light, vaulted roofing that needed fewer columns for support, such as in the Pantheon, still the world's largest unreinforced dome.

Rome was an urban empire, especially in the richer and more commercial eastern part, with metropolises like Alexandria, Antioch and Ephesus. Even where there weren't cities to begin with, the Romans founded them as administrative centres. The local elites that led the town councils were expected to use their own money to fund the impressive building projects that we now associate with Roman times: the temples, baths, aqueducts and amphitheatres, as well as religious festivals and games. Urban economies and its possibilities drew migrants from afar.

City life created opportunities and growth but, in the absence of the germ theory of disease and modern public sanitation, also rampant disease. Rome had a complex system of sewers and public latrines, and the aqueducts that brought millions of gallons of fresh water to the city every day were marvels of engineering. Yet there were limits to what could be done with the state of knowledge and technology of that time. Most houses were not connected to sewers, and even though people were supposed to bring their garbage outside the city walls this became impractical as the city grew to a million people. The waste disposal system was limited to a law against hurting bystanders by dumping garbage out of buildings.

The Romans were the masters of the world, but after defecating they still wiped themselves with a sea sponge on a stick that was shared with others. As the historian Kyle Harper has observed, in fierce competition with legions and barbarians, the deadliest force in Roman times was probably diarrhoea.[37]

Peak wealth

In the words of the Russian historian Michael Rostovtzeff, the early empire was 'a time of almost complete freedom for trade and of splendid opportunities for private initiative'.[38] This might be taking it too far, but unlike other monarchs, the Roman emperors did not nationalize industries and did not conflate society's wealth with their own. Instead they contented themselves with amassing their own (huge) private fortunes within a system of relatively free markets for labour and products, where prices were free to move in response to supply and demand. The empire had a high degree of economic freedom (with the usual obvious exception of slavery).

The economic historian Peter Temin writes: 'From an economic point of view, the important characteristic of the early Roman Empire was the relatively large role played by market forces, certainly as compared to the medieval economy that would follow.'[39] Goods and resources were traded freely, and Temin's reading of the evidence is that the late republic and early empire had markets in land and for urban buildings, which created incentives to improve building techniques.

Workers who were not enslaved mostly had the freedom to move between employers and negotiate their wages. One labour contract suggests that the worker had more freedom to quit than many European workers in the nineteenth century.[40]

There were also advanced money markets and banks that provided credit. Interest rates were probably regulated at 12 per cent per year, but alternative rates did exist. Merchant and shippers could borrow at a higher interest rate than usual to compensate for payment being conditional on a safe return – an early form of insurance.

During the early empire, the tax system was also changed in a way that encouraged growth. Previously, revenue was often raised by 'tax farmers', wealthy Romans who bid for the right to tax an area for a particular period. They had an incentive to take as much as possible during their period in charge, often by taxing incomes as much as they could get away with. Augustus replaced this system with a wealth tax of 1 per cent and a poll tax on each adult. This changed the incentive for provinces. After previously having seen most of a rise in income disappear into the pockets of Romans far away, they now faced a zero marginal tax rate. Any added production and extra profit were now theirs to keep, and so it suddenly paid to trade, invest and innovate.

This did not stop the government from intervening in some markets, often to buy the loyalty of the people. The Roman government supplied citizens in the city under a certain income threshold with grain. At first it was a temporary measure to deal with food insecurity, but like so many other temporary government programmes through history, it became permanent. The government bought giant grain supplies on the market, and commissioned hundreds of merchant ships to supply perhaps 200,000 Romans with this grain dole. Emperors often complained about the size and cost of the programme – yet still kept expanding it, from subsidized grain to free grain to free bread (and free circuses to keep citizens happy). Eventually, the growing size of the welfare-dependent population and the higher taxes to pay for it would hurt the economy's productive forces. The Romans could conquer the world, but not even they were capable of entitlement reform.

However, trade and competition led to economic specialization, technical innovation and, for a long time, real economic growth. In most previous societies, as populations grew, they ran up against a resource limit and faced diminishing living standards and often hunger. The opposite happened in Rome. Robust productivity growth increased wages even for unskilled workers and standards rose, at least until the late second century AD.

Archaeological evidence reveals a much stronger economic expansion than can be explained by population growth, in everything from building activity to meat consumption. The number of Roman shipwrecks increased after around 500 BC, and then rose to unprecedented levels in the late republic and early empire. This indicates that long-distance maritime trade was larger than ever before and much larger than it would be for the next 1,500 years. Atmospheric pollution conserved in ice cores from Greenland reveal a peak of metal extraction around the same time, indicating that the money supply (and environmental problems) increased sharply.[41]

The economic historian Peter Temin estimates that the gross domestic product (GDP) per capita in the early Roman Empire was not surpassed by the United Kingdom, France and Germany for almost one and a half millennia. This was reflected in an extraordinary urbanization rate. The early Roman Empire was probably around 10 per cent urbanized, and the Italian peninsula 30 per cent.[42] These are remarkable numbers. In

1700, the percentage of urbanization for Italy and Spain was 20, and for England, France and Germany it was 10.

Rome managed to create an overall standard of living that was probably higher than anything that came before it and would not be surpassed for another one and a half millennia. The economic historian Joel Mokyr notes that 'The Rome of 100 A.D. had better paved streets, sewage disposal, water supply, and fire protection than the capitals of civilized Europe in 1800.'[43]

The long decline

This again forces us to think about what Gibbon described as 'the greatest, perhaps, and most awful, scene in the history of mankind'. How could all of this just end? For some time, it has been fashionable to say it never did. The odd feature of the barbarians who sacked Rome repeatedly in the fifth century was that they didn't want to destroy it; they wanted to be a part of it. They didn't want to tear down the throne; they wanted to claim it. In AD 395, the western and eastern administrative regions of the empire became separate entities, so even if the empire fell in the west, it survived in the east.

In a reaction against older history books' razor-sharp demarcations of different eras, rises and falls, modern historians hold that the empire had been invaded, split and reunited several times, and that the invading Christianized Germanic tribes maintained many Roman traditions and rituals. It was a gradual process, rather than history just turning a page one day. There is some truth to that, but not enough.

The Roman Empire really did fall. Not necessarily on the day in 410 when Rome was sacked by Visigoths, or in 476 when the last Western Roman emperor was overthrown by Germanic troops; but, over a longer period, the archaeological evidence of a complete collapse, whether you look at peasants, kings or saints, is overwhelming.[44]

The number of literates plummeted. Entire industries and commercial networks unravelled. Suddenly, very few coins seem to have been in circulation. The sophisticated material culture all but disappeared, and the quality, quantity and diversity of goods like pottery deteriorated. With very few exceptions, stone and brick buildings were replaced by ones made of wood. The art of mixing concrete and building with it was lost. Roof tiles started disappearing. Where (at least) the Roman elite could walk on marble and mosaic floors, soon everyone's flooring was beaten earth. Even the churches became smaller, leading one scholar to quip that even God would have been cramped.

In the mid-sixth century, the grain trade had crumbled and the aqueducts had been cut. Agriculture could no longer produce enough food, meat consumption became rare and even the cattle shrank in size. Rome almost disappeared. The city was abandoned by at least 90 per cent of its population. The main harbours became unusable, and roads dangerous. After a while, only noblemen had surnames, since 'so few inhabitants ever left the village in which they were born, there was in any case no need'.[45] People huddled together in the safety of their villages and married neighbours. Some even developed local dialects that were incomprehensible to people only a few villages away. An era of globalization had gone in sharp, sudden reverse.

Despite the heroic efforts of revisionist historians, there is no doubt that the age between around AD 400 and 1000 was pitch dark, even if Rome didn't fall in one day. By sifting through the available archaeological evidence, we find another kind of continuity, one of decline. Previously mentioned indicators of shipwrecks, metal extraction, construction and meat consumption, which had reached such dizzying heights during the late republic and early empire, began to decline soon after, before collapsing in the fifth century. In some areas there were partial recoveries, but the overall pattern is clear, Rome started to decline a long time before it fell, just as Gibbon once suggested. According to Ian Morris's ambitious attempt to measure the world's social development in the West and the East over 15,000 years, the fall of the Roman Empire was the biggest social regression in history. However, the index also indicates that this regression began as early as the late second century.[46]

So what started the decline? Perhaps it was just difficult to uphold such complex institutions over such a large territory over the long term. Innovation in warfare slowed down as there was no more low-hanging fruit, while simultaneously neighbours borrowed Rome's absorption technique, ideas and technological capabilities and therefore became more of a threat to it. The climate optimum was also drawing to a close, creating more difficult challenges for farming.

Over the centuries, the empire also suffered from events that set difficult trends in motion. The most devastating ones were related to the fact that the cities were so crowded while also being connected to the disease pools of the rest of the known world. In AD 165, the empire was ravaged by the Antonine Plague, the first disease event worthy of the label pandemic. It was probably smallpox, brought home by soldiers on campaign. It may have killed around a tenth of the population, and twice that level in the most affected areas. Even with this conservative estimate, the deaths of 7–8 million people made the Antonine Plague the worst mortality event in history at that point.[47]

It was followed by severe economic disruptions, inflation and famine. The army was wrecked by the disease, and it is said that emperor Marcus Aurelius had to recruit slaves and gladiators to fight off barbarian invaders. He spent his last years fighting in the north, in a surprisingly long and exhausting war. His death in AD 180 is often considered the end of the Pax Romana. His son, Commodus (of *Gladiator* fame), was the first successor who had been reared from the cradle to become emperor, and he is not a good showcase for the biological principle of succession. He really did fight in the gladiatorial arena himself, and not in a very honourable way. His bizarre and increasingly tyrannical rule was cut short in 192, when he was killed in his bath. Civil war returned to Rome as many different men claimed the title for themselves; AD 193 is remembered as the Year of the Five Emperors.

However, the fifth emperor of that turbulent year, Septimius Severus of Libyan origin, managed to restore stability to the empire, and, with one brief exception, his dynasty would rule until 235. By relying more on the army that had given him power, and giving it more money and authority, he regained control. Inflation was reduced, the economy revived and the population started to grow again. Severus continued Marcus's policy of integrating provincials into the upper ranks, and this inflow of talent gave new energy to the empire. His son, Caracalla, went one further, by giving citizenship to all free citizens of the empire. It was a legal milestone, with far-reaching implications. 'A little later, we find women on the fringes of the Syrian desert asserting their rights to property ownership' by invoking Roman law, writes the historian Kyle Harper.[48]

Rome had survived its first serious crisis with most institutions intact, even though the army's increasing power was a harbinger of worse things to come. It would not be as lucky in the next pandemic. In 249, the Plague of Cyprian started to make its way across the whole empire. It seems to have been a pandemic influenza or a viral haemorrhagic fever and, while there are no reliable estimates of total numbers of deaths, it was said that 5,000 people died in the city of Rome every day at its peak.

The pandemic did not just break human bodies, but during a period of succession crises and buckling frontiers, it almost broke the whole empire, its economy and its relative tolerance. This was the 'crisis of the third century'. A re-energized Persian Empire attacked in the east and Germanic tribes in the north. Several provinces declared independence. In 260, an invasion force almost reached Rome. Many regions and towns were laid to waste. Between 235 and 284, the Roman Senate recognized 26 emperors, most of them killed by enemies, the Praetorian guard or their own troops. Usurpers usually gave their soldiers a bonus when they captured the throne, thereby unintentionally inspiring other soldiers to revolt in turn in the name of their own commander.

Unable to collect sufficient taxes, the Romans started debasing the currency – the silver was mixed with an increasing share of metals of inferior value, and soon there was no silver left in the coins. A century of galloping inflation followed, which destroyed banks and credit markets and undermined all forms of trade. The Austrian economist Ludwig von Mises thought that the combination of Rome's debasement and price controls was a more destructive enemy than the invaders, since it 'completely paralyzed both the production and the marketing of the vital foodstuffs and disintegrated society's economic organization'.[49] The division of labour broke down and, to avoid starvation, those in the many deserted cities began to grow food for themselves. Large estates made themselves self-sufficient. Instead of acting as producers and consumers in an extensive and integrated market, they turned themselves into landlords receiving rents from tenants and sharecroppers.

The new emperors rose from frontier armies, and rarely if ever saw Rome. By the end of the third century, some of them managed to end the chaos by a series of military victories. Two military strongmen, Diocletian and Constantine, would rule for almost the whole period from 284 to 337. They put the pieces of the empire back together, but the new form would hardly have been recognizable to previous generations. What was left of republican traditions was swept away by an open military dictatorship. Senators in the high command were replaced by professional soldiers, and while Constantine restored the Senate, he filled it with his own favourites, ending its role as a balancing force. Rome was no longer an empire with an army, but an army with an empire.

The emperor became a more imposing figure, adopting more elaborate ceremony. He started wearing a crown and ruled from distant palaces, Diocletian from Split in Croatia and Constantine from his new Greek capital in the east, Constantinople. Where previous emperors had pretended to be senators, and could be approached by anyone, the new emperors pretended to be gods, demanding that all prostrated themselves before them. It was more... Byzantine, to anticipate events by a few years.

These new emperors were eager interventionists. Provinces lost independence as they were reorganized into smaller units that could be ruled more directly. The number of state bureaucrats, which had numbered just a few hundred in the early empire, swelled to perhaps 35,000. You could trace the regression in the cities.[50] City walls were now built, even around Rome, reflecting a new sense of insecurity. As local elites lost power and resources to the imperial bureaucracy, they reduced their investments in the urban environment. In Britain cities start to decline in the 360s, almost a century before the Anglo-Saxon invasions.

The new rulers' ambition was to fix social relations and bind whole classes to their professions, a first step away from the market-oriented ancient world to the feudalism of the Middle Ages. Tenant farmers and sharecroppers were banned from leaving the land they had farmed, so that landlords could pay the higher taxes that the emperors now needed to pay their troops. Whole towns could be collectively punished if someone did not pay up. Similarly, sons of soldiers and veterans were forced to follow in their fathers' footsteps, making it a heritable status. If someone cut off a finger to escape the draft, he was burned.

The last days

In this fearful climate, the old toleration that had defined Rome in so many ways began to crumble, and superstitions ran wild. The new rulers wanted religious unity and blamed the pandemic on a small eccentric sect known as Christians. It must have been their refusal to sacrifice to the gods that had provoked the wrath of the gods. For the first time, emperors forced people to partake in sacrifice in 249. Christians were soon systematically persecuted, most fiercely under the rule of Diocletian. Those who surrendered the scriptures to the authorities became known by their fellow Christians as *traditores*, 'the ones who handed over', from which we get the word 'traitor'. The persecutions seemed only to have encouraged the spread of their religion, however, until emperor Constantine converted to Christianity in 313. Soon it was the turn of pagans to be persecuted (and any Christians who did not believe in the 'right' way).

The most notorious symbol of the new interventionism was Diocletian's price edict of 301, which blamed inflation on greedy businessmen and fixed the price of more than

1,000 products – from sandals to lions. The price controls were a spectacular fiasco that only led to shortages and black-market activity, despite the threat of the death penalty. Since Diocletian continued to debase the currency, inflation continued unabated.

It was not all straight downhill from there, though. Constantine again allowed gold to circulate at the market price, thereby restoring the currency on a gold standard. The stabilization of the monetary system brought markets back to life. Banks became active again, and Mediterranean trade could once again flourish. This started a partial economic and cultural recovery, and gave many Romans the sense that the empire had been saved. But it was at a lower level than before, with weaker cities and much smaller margins for failure.

This background is important to the eventual 'real' fall of Rome. A more centralized system became dependent on the imperial bureaucracy and lost the capacity to adapt locally to changing circumstances. The eventual breakdown of the Roman state in the western part of the empire therefore left the provinces without the administration and resources to deal with invaders and chaos. Unfortunately, as Bret Devereaux points out, this is the centralized system the rulers of fifth-century break-away kingdoms tried to emulate, 'leading to a precipitous decline in state capacity'.[51]

This final chapter started with 'armed climate refugees on horseback' around 375.[52] Nomadic Huns from the steppe invaded Europe in the late fourth century, escaping a catastrophic drought. With their overwhelming cavalry, they quickly conquered large parts of the continent. The Huns pushed Germanic tribes off their traditional lands and in wave after wave these tribes entered Roman territory, sometimes as refugees and allies (helping Romans to fight off the Huns), sometimes as raiders and conquerors. Finally, Romans faced the reckoning for their crime of trying to possess their fellow human beings: when the barbarians amassed at the gates, the Roman slave population rose up and joined them.

The first to fall was the empire of ideas. Under pressure from decline and invasions, the Roman mind shed its worldly, practical philosophy. No one was more important in this transition than the theologian Augustine of Hippo (354–430). Inspired by Plato and the neo-Platonist Plotinus, he developed an idea of an all-powerful God who judges our every thought.

Augustine was the church father who developed the idea of original sin: the whole of humanity is condemned since the sin of Adam and Eve is transmitted to every new generation by sexual intercourse. In sharp contrast to the traditional pagan view, Augustine saw the individual as hopelessly weak and her senses clouded. To save souls, he advocated religious persecution. It was better with 'short-lived fires of the furnace for the few', so as not to 'abandon all to the eternal fires of hell'.[53] While he did not condone the execution of heretics, he endorsed religious compulsion.

After the sack of Rome in 410, Augustine wrote *The City of God*, to refute the claim that the empire was falling because it had just become Christian. According to Augustine, the real cause of decline was Rome's long-lasting moral corruption (prompting the question why God would wait a thousand years to mete out his punishment). But he also argued that it didn't really matter. The earthly city would always be one of decay and disaster, the triumph for the chosen ones comes instead in the city of God, in heaven after death. Therefore the Aristotelian curiosity about this world was nothing but a malady, 'the lust of the eyes', just as bad as the lust of the flesh. The potential for scientific and technological progress here on earth was removed from the intellectual vocabulary and would not return as a dominant theme in Europe for 800 years.

After a century of constant pressure, the Roman military defences had been completely worn down. On 4 September 476, the last emperor of the Western Roman Empire, Romulus Augustus, just a child, was deposed by the Germanic general Odoacer, who declared himself king of Italy. After a thousand years of conquest, growth and glory, Rome had fallen. But, to be fair, much of its world had vanished a long time before that. Much like a Hemingway bankruptcy, the Roman Empire fell in two ways: gradually and then suddenly.

Sic transit gloria mundi

Odoacer did not consider himself a barbarian usurper; he represented himself as the client of the real emperor, in Constantinople. In the Eastern Roman Empire, no one thought that the empire had fallen, for now. The emperor Constantine had founded this city in the rich eastern provinces because of its location, easily defended and along important trade routes. For another thousand years, until the invasion of the Ottoman Turks in 1453, emperors here would consider themselves the true heirs to the Roman Empire. But it bore little resemblance to classical Rome.

In the sixth century, Byzantium (the ancient Greek name for the city of Constantinople) tried to reclaim the western half of the empire, and with naval power it managed to reconquer large parts of North Africa and Italy. But the most lasting effect of this destructive war was that the aqueducts into Rome were destroyed, and so the city could no longer sustain a major population until the modern era.

The Byzantines were soon driven out of most of Italy and became entangled in a long and devastating war with the Sasanian Empire of Persia, while at the same time experiencing a severe plague. The two empires fought themselves to exhaustion, leaving a void that was exploited to the fullest extent by an upstart rival, the Muslim Arabs. The Prophet Muhammad had united the Arabs under his new faith, and after his death in 632, his successors now moved into the territory of the weakened superpowers. The speed was astounding. In just a few decades, they conquered Mesopotamia and Persia and took Syria, Egypt and North Africa from the Byzantines.

Constantinople itself survived several sieges, but the city and its hinterland was the only part of the old Eastern Roman Empire that remained intact for the whole period. The population of Constantinople was in decline and, when the walls of the city were destroyed by an earthquake in 740, they could not afford to rebuild it. A guidebook of 760 describes the city, before it started a slow recovery, as 'abandoned and ruined'. The empire fell both in the west and in the east.

What remained also lost its connections to ancient Rome. Soon after the end of the empire, Western Europe forgot the Greek language. When a copyist came upon a Greek word in a text, he started writing *Graecum est – non legitur*: 'it is Greek, it cannot be read'. Eventually, this would give rise to the idiom 'it's all Greek to me' for anything impossible to understand. So, ironically, the Greeks, who had mocked the 'barbarians' for speaking in a nonsensical way that sounded like 'bar... bar...' to the Greeks' ears, soon found their own language had become the very symbol of incomprehensibility.

At the same time, the Byzantine Greeks tried hard to forget their ancient texts, which supposedly stirred only dissent and division. Since these were written on easily perishable papyrus, all the Byzantines had to do to make them go away was not to copy them again, but, for safety, they were often burned. The teaching of pagan philosophy was banned and, after nine hundred years, Plato's Academy in Athens was closed. In 532, the seven last philosophers of the Academy left to seek refuge with the Persian king.

Philastrius, the bishop of Brescia in northern Italy, condemned the whole tradition since the time of Thales of explaining events with reference to natural causes rather than divine intervention: 'There is a certain heresy concerning earthquakes that they come not from God's command but, it is thought, from the very nature of the elements.' John Chrysostom, archbishop of Constantinople, commanded: 'Restrain our own reasoning, and empty our mind of secular learning, in order to provide a mind swept clear for the reception of divine words.'[54]

Pagans and Jews were now forcibly baptized. Christians of other denominations than the orthodox, such as the Nestorians, fled. One clause in a peace treaty with Persia was that its officials would help to track down dissident Byzantine priests and bishops who had escaped there. A group of bishops, asked by the emperor about their opinion on the trinity, wisely dodged the question, declaring that they 'avoid difficult questions beyond human grasp. Clever theologians soon become heretics.'[55] Montesquieu, who believed that the Romans conquered the world by learning from it, thought that this intolerance was the beginning of the end:

> Just as the old Romans strengthened their empire by permitting every kind of religion in it, so was it subsequently reduced to nothing by amputating, one after the other, the sects which were not dominant.[56]

In his work on ideas and innovations, the intellectual historian Peter Watson writes that for three centuries, from the middle of the sixth century to the middle of the ninth century, there is no record of the classics and hardly any education. There are very few manuscripts of any kind from this period and many old ones disappeared. Some survived in single copies, from which all later copies are derived. Watson calls it 'a near-death experience for the book'.[57] This is why we call it the Dark Ages.

Constantinople still had a Senate, but it was a ceremonial building more than a function, and after a fire it was rebuilt on a smaller scale. When a commentator in the eighth century tried to explain the name, he guessed that it must have been built by a man called 'Senatus'.[58] The break with the past that geographic barriers and the rise of Christianity entailed was so complete that the monuments of the old emperors and their battles would eventually not even be recognized. They came to be seen by the Byzantines as prophecies from ancient necromancers about the end of the world.[59]

Summary

Rome was the city of seven hills that conquered much of the known world. Just like the Athenians, Romans built their power on openness to ideas and influences from abroad, not through the traditional method of extensive foreign trade, but via an unparalleled system of absorption. Rome constantly integrated manpower, ideas and technologies from elsewhere into their military, economy and institutions, thereby giving them access to more talent and capacity than anybody else. Romans were famous for abandoning their traditions and methods the moment they found something better elsewhere – not the least from the Greeks.

Rome developed a founding myth that made it exceptionally hospitable to strategic tolerance. It was a city of immigrants, made up of people from everywhere, and the very word 'Roman' changed its meaning from signalling an ethnic identity to a political identity. Rome constantly integrated foreigners and outsiders, and they could become wealthy merchants, powerful senators and even emperors. This stands in contrast with Greek cities, which had more restrictive access to its citizenry and especially elite. One result was that Rome achieved a growing population and could field bigger armies and raise new ones every time it was beaten.

This remained the case even after the republic gave way to the empire. Augustus's actions after his victory in the civil war had many similarities with Athens after the victory over the Persians. He formed a confident and outward-facing Roman identity with the help of propaganda and huge building projects. He established an era of relative peace, making sea-lanes and roads safe for merchants and migrants, based on rule of law and a relatively free market economy. The Pax Romana made it possible for discoveries, inventions and goods that appeared anywhere in the empire to travel quickly to all the other corners of it. It boosted competition and creativity to great heights.

Rome was less democratic than Athens, and after the fall of the republic, not at all. But in other ways it was actually more inclusive. Women had substantially more rights than Greek women, and slaves were set free at an astonishing rate. More people were allowed to exchange ideas, goods and services in Rome than anywhere else, based on a system of law and economic freedom. The Italian peninsula had an urbanization rate higher than that of western Europe in 1700. Millions mingled and mixed in melting pots of marble.

All of this made Rome last longer than other empires. But not forever. In the third century, it suffered a series of blows that will be familiar from Athens' experience. The empire was overstretched on many fronts, a major epidemic shook the economy and the ability to feed the people, and wars became more destructive. Rome had survived calamities before, but this time it reacted to the crisis by abandoning the whole culture of openness and constant innovation that had made it successful. Emperors became more authoritarian and centralized their control of the provinces, abandoning institutions that had helped them to adapt to changing circumstances, and making them more vulnerable to shocks.

In this fearful climate, they also searched for a new orthodoxy to instil unity. Pagan emperors started persecuting Christians, and then Christian emperors persecuted pagans. Intellectual elites replaced worldly, practical Greek philosophies with mystical theories of man's original sin and hopeless weakness. A city that conquered the world by learning from and integrating every new group, started amputating them, one after another, until nothing much remained, barely even the city itself.

However, in an extraordinary turning of the tables, among the Muslim troops that attacked the last remnants of the last Roman Empire, Byzantium, in the eighth century, there was a startling link to the past. They claimed that the Byzantines were unworthy of their Greek and Roman heritage, and that the true successor of the openness and rationality of the ancients was none other than themselves, and the Abbasid Caliphate they fought for.

3

THE ABBASID CALIPHATE

At the Crossroads of the Universe

For four or five centuries, Islam was the most brilliant civilization.

FERNAND BRAUDEL[1]

After the fall of [the Romans] the empire of the Califfs seems to have been the first state under which the world enjoyed that degree of tranquillity which the cultivation of the sciences requires. ... their mild, just, and religious government diffused over their vast empire revived the curiosity of mankind.

ADAM SMITH[2]

The Graeco-Arabic translation movement of Baghdad constitutes a truly epoch-making stage, by any standard, in the course of human history. It is equal in significance to, and belongs to the same narrative as, I would claim, that of Pericles' Athens, the Italian Renaissance, or the scientific revolution of the sixteenth and seventeenth centuries.

DIMITRI GUTAS[3]

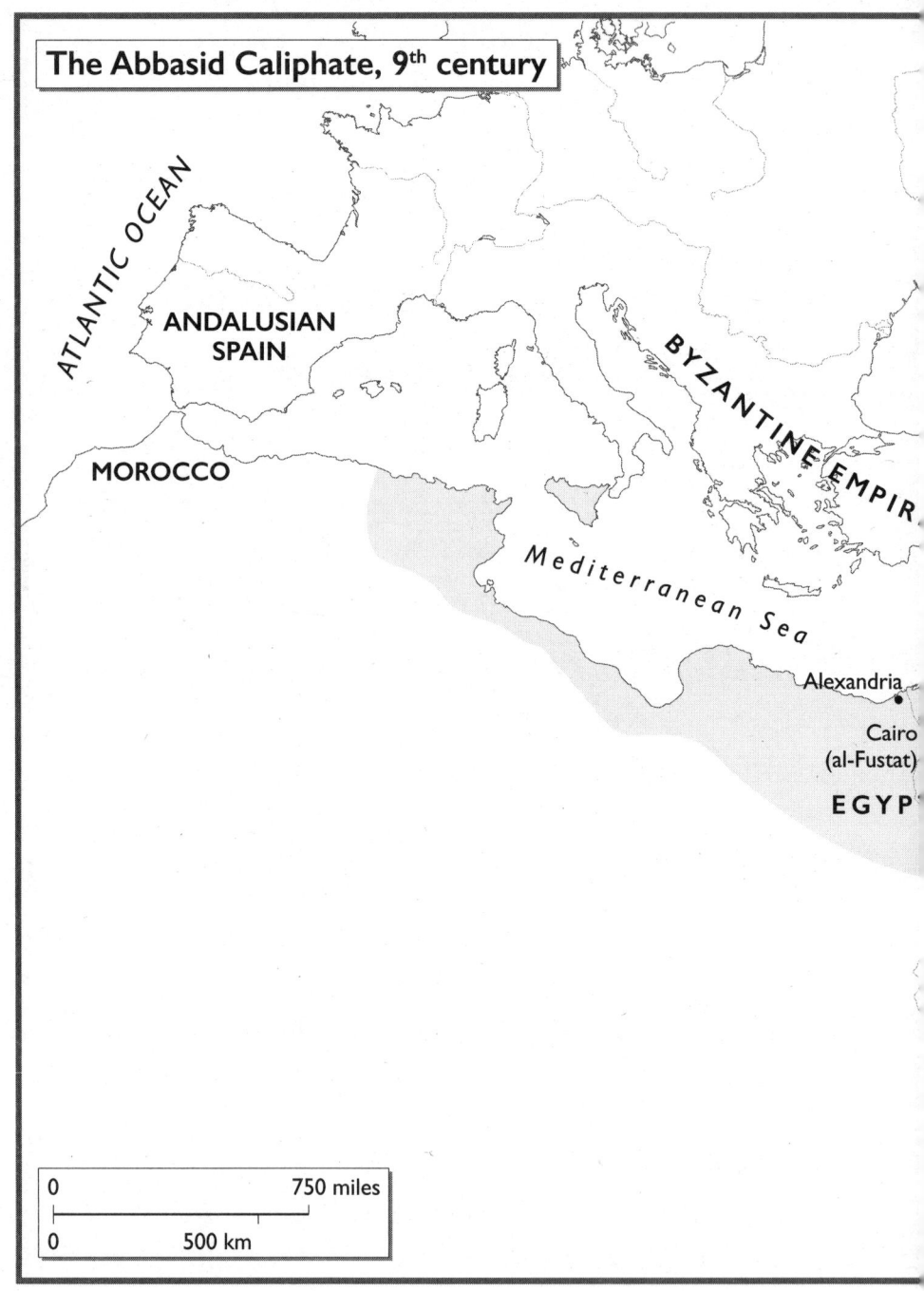

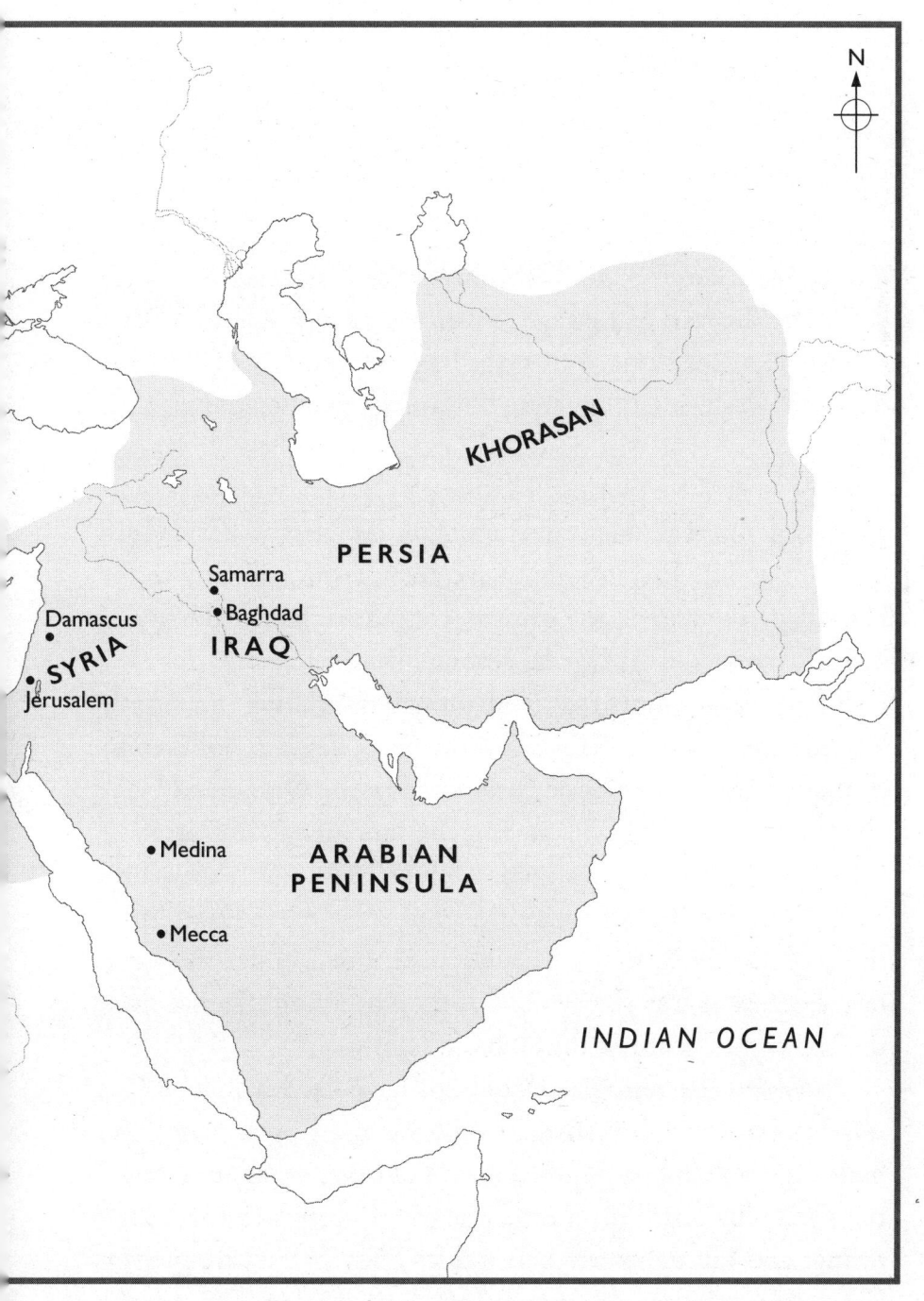

In 2014, Islamic State, ISIS, raised the black flag in Iraq to declare the start of a savage terrorist campaign against infidels and fellow Muslims. Across the flag the Arab text of 'No God but God' was printed in white, but in ragged letters, to give the impression that it was designed before Photoshop. It was an attempt to evoke a glorious Islamic past, an era when a powerful, prosperous caliphate ruled much of the known world. ISIS are not the only Jihadists that have taken a special liking to the black flag. They are in the company of the Afghani Taliban and several chapters of Al Qaeda, among others.

There are accounts that Muhammad used black as a signalling colour on the battlefield, but the black flag was not used by the early Caliphate, it is not promoted in the Quran and black is not a holy colour in Islam. But the fundamentalist terrorists are right that there was a golden era of Islam when the world looked towards it with admiration and envy, when the caliphs, the supreme leaders of a Muslim state, ruled under the black flag, because it was the symbol of the governing dynasty from the late eighth century, the Abbasid family.

However, the terrorists would not have liked it much. This was the era when the Islamic world was most open to science, trade and mobility, and most tolerant of other ethnicities, traditions and religions. This was the age when Muslim rulers did not torture and kill dissenters and infidels, but learned from them and exchanged ideas, insights and goods with them. This was the moment when Arab culture built on the achievement of other cultures to unleash a creative era of science and philosophy that would go on to inspire medieval Christianity and the Renaissance.

The great Catholic historian of liberty, Lord Acton, wrote:

> Western Europe lay under the grasp of masters, the ablest of whom could not write their names. The faculty of reasoning, of accurate observation, became extinct for 500 years, and even the sciences most needful for society, medicine and geometry, fell into decay, until the teachers of the West went to school at the feet of Arabian masters.[4]

We don't have to go further than the letter A to observe our intellectual debt to the Arab world: Arabic numerals, algebra, algorithm, arithmetic, average. Or for that matter: Averroes and Avicenna, two thinkers who had such an influence on the medieval Christian world that they were given these Latinized names, and whom Dante, when writing *The Divine Comedy*, did not leave among the heretics in the *Inferno*, but in *Limbo*, together with virtuous pagans like Aristotle, Socrates and Cicero. Averroes, specifically, was so important to the revival of European philosophy that Raphael included him among the intellectual giants in the fresco *The School of Athens*, with Aristotle and Plato in centre stage.

In fact, Arabs accused the Byzantines not just of being infidels, but also of having ruined the Greek and Roman legacy. The real successors of the ancient Greeks, claimed the early ninth-century Abbasid caliph al-Mamun, were the Muslims, who embraced ancient philosophy and developed it further, while books were being burned in Constantinople. The Byzantines might speak Greek, but they did not *think* Greek.

The pagans in Greece and the early Roman Empire had embraced a spirit of rationality and developed science and philosophy, wrote the historian al-Masudi, 'until the religion of Christianity appeared among the Byzantines; they then effaced the signs of philosophy, eliminated its traces, destroyed its paths, and they changed and corrupted what the ancient Greeks had set forth'.[5] The ninth-century philosopher al-Kindi even invented a genealogy according to which Ion, the mythological ancestor of many Greeks including the Athenians, was the brother of Qahtan, the ancestor of the Arabs. With this creative rewriting of history, embracing Greek science was just a way of repatriating it to its original owners.

The caliph al-Mamun himself was said to have been inspired by a dream, which was used to explain his project to translate Greek texts. It exists in several versions, but in all of them, the caliph suddenly faces a man with a powerful charisma. 'Who are you?' he asks, and the man, of reddish-white complexion with a high forehead, bald head and dark blue eyes, answers: 'I am Aristotle'. In the earliest versions al-Mamun asks him what is good or right, and Aristotle answers that this is not down to tradition and orthodoxy, but to individual intellect. In a later account, Aristotle is a more explicit campaigner for the caliph's project and urges him to search for new ideas because 'knowledge has no boundaries; wisdom has no race or nationality. To block out ideas is to block out the kingdom of God.'[6]

This was part self-flattering propaganda, but propaganda built on some real foundations. The Caliphate devoted massive resources to translating ancient texts into Arabic and contributed their own ideas and observations to them. Science was flourishing in the Muslim regions, and philosophical debate was lively and daring.

Sometimes this interpretation was even supported by Byzantines themselves. The Byzantine monk Michael Psellus was one of the great intellectuals of the eleventh century and an advisor to the emperor. He often despaired about how Constantinople had lost its connections to its own past (something he accidentally exemplified himself when, in his histories, he confused Cicero, the defender of the republic, with Caesar, its destroyer).

Psellus observed that there had been a reversal of roles when the Arabs embraced the ancients at the same moment that the Byzantines forgot them: 'The barbarians inherited the spiritual wealth of Ancient Greece, when its legitimate inheritors should have been its successors. There was a reversal of roles, so that now the Greeks became barbarians and the barbarians became Greeks.'

The rise of Islam

Imagine that, out of the blue, tiny Iceland took advantage of Europe's weakness after the Second World War, and in short succession conquered Britain, France and Germany and established a vast empire. This is the comparison the Scottish historian William Dalrymple uses to make us understand how unexpected and shocking the Arab conquest was.[7]

The Muslim calendar begins in 622, when the founder of Islam, the Prophet Muhammad (570–632), migrated to Medina (in today's western Saudi Arabia) to escape persecution in Mecca. Just thirty years later, Muslim Arabs had brought the world's two exhausted superpowers, the Byzantines and the Persian Sasanians, to their knees. Persia and the Levant, the richest and most important parts of the Eastern Roman Empire, were absorbed into what would become a huge Muslim empire, stretching from Algeria to Afghanistan. It seemed like the Arabs came out of nowhere to create one of the biggest, richest and most intellectually dynamic empires.

The 'Iceland' of our story was made up of independent Arab tribes, nomadic Bedouins and sedentary farmers in oasis towns in western Arabia. They were famously mobile and used to fighting for honour or loot. 'All the customary activities of the Arabs lead to travel and movement', wrote the historian Ibn Khaldun of his fellow Arabs.[8] But they had also established merchant cities on the prosperous caravan routes that ran alongside the Red Sea. Originally these routes were established by camel trains bringing huge quantities of incense from Yemen to Mediterranean cultures that needed them for rituals and to hide the stench of cramped cities without decent sanitation.

One reason for the speed of their military campaign was that Arab commanders emulated the Roman tactic of sparing the lives, property and religious practices of those who surrendered. Landowners, farmers and merchants were allowed to go about their businesses, and expropriation was usually reserved for state-owned land.[9] This offer was attractive to Christian communities that had been persecuted by the Byzantines for dissenting theories about the proportion of human and divine in Christ. One cleric wrote enthusiastically that the invaders did not just avoid hurting Christians, 'but even commend our religion, show honour to the priests and monasteries and saints of our Lord'.[10]

Under Muslim rule, Christians and Jews (also Sabians and, according to some interpretations, Zoroastrians), as 'People of the Book', were free to define their religion, practise it and govern their communities according to their own rules, as long as they paid a special poll tax and accepted some legal limitations. Supposedly, this tax was compensation for their exemption from military service.

Bernard Lewis, a historian of Oriental studies often seen as one of the great intellectual critics of Islamic societies, concedes that while the freedom granted by classical Islam compares unfavourably to modern Western democracies, 'it offered vastly more freedom than any of its predecessors, its contemporaries and most of its successors'.[11] Sometimes even polytheists were tolerated, although polytheism was against the letter of the law. Only atheists were beyond the pale, but mostly only when their non-belief was made public and caused a scandal.

There were many examples of locals who did not just refuse to fight the Arab invaders, but actively assisted them. Jewish populations often aided the conquests and at the important Battle of the Masts in 655, when Arabs took control of the western Mediterranean from the Byzantines, their navy was made up mostly of experienced Christian seamen. In the 680s, a Mesopotamian monk wrote that, among the conquerors, there were 'not a few Christians, some belonging to the heretics and some from us'.[12]

In just a few decades, the Arabs had become the inheritors of several of the world's oldest and most impressive cultures, Rome, Syria–Palestine, Egypt, Babylon and Persia, and stretching into Central Asia and bordering India. Their new empire was populated by a sprawling array of different ethnic and religious groups. There were Muslims, Zoroastrians, Jews and Christians, and they spoke Arabic, Persian, Aramaic and Greek. Importantly, the Euphrates river, the ancient border between the East and West, was now open for trade and travel (the new fiercely contested border between empires was in the Mediterranean, ruining old cities like Alexandria). It resulted in an explosion of intellectual and economic innovation. Agriculture benefited quickly, as landowners imported new crops from India and Africa and adapted new methods including sophisticated irrigation systems. Landowners and peasants profited, and the diet of people improved.

Instead of trying to impose their own orthodoxy on these diverse groups, the conquering Arabs learned from their traditions and built on their achievements. They minted imitations of Byzantine coins in Syria and Persian coins in Iraq. The octagonal Dome of the Rock in Jerusalem and its mosaics were inspired by Byzantine churches. Baghdad seemed inspired by the classic Persian citadel. The Roman bathhouses, which had almost become extinct in Western Europe, became central to the new lifestyle. The Barmakids, an originally Buddhist family from what is now Afghanistan, became important patrons of the arts and providers of influential viziers (first ministers). The translation of Persian, Indian and Greek texts would soon contribute to an exceptional Islamic Enlightenment. But it was forged in fire and brimstone.

The Abbasid revolution

The Umayyad dynasty, which took over the Caliphate after the death of Muhammad in 632, tried to centralize control to Damascus. Many groups used to self-governance felt that a small group of Arabs were trying to monopolize power and resources. This brewing discontent was exploited by a rebel movement that talked about Islam as a universalist creed with equality for all groups and ethnicities that embraced the new religion.

The actions and sayings of Muhammad are clearly in opposition to privileges by birth, descent and race: only merit and piety should decide rank and status. This was of course honoured more in the breach than in the observance by secular rulers and aristocracies, but it could serve as a rallying cry for oppressed groups, merging religious observance with political grievances.

These groups turned to another family that could symbolize the return to a pure faith, since they were the descendants of Muhammad's uncle, Abbas (566–653). Their agents were particularly successful in the Persian region of Khorasan, an area now divided between Iran, Turkmenistan and Afghanistan. Here the Caliphate seemed both too distant – Damascus was a twenty-day ride to the west – and too intrusive. Arab settlers and converted locals resented high-handed and corrupt Umayyad governors who taxed them harshly.

It was here in the summer of 747 that a mysterious commander calling himself Abu Muslim (father of Muslim) raised the black flag of the Abbasids for the first time. He was probably a Persian and might have been a former slave. He was by all accounts a talented and brutal general. His local troops, hardened by many years of frontier battles, drove the Umayyads out, and then went on the offensive.

After an impressive series of victories, Abu Muslim's men met the much larger Umayyad army for a decisive battle on the river Zab in northern Iraq in February 750. The Abbasids knelt and pointed their lances towards the enemy. The overconfident Umayyad cavalry charged against them, but the shield wall held and the attackers were destroyed. It caused panic among the Umayyads and their army disintegrated. Retreating soldiers were cut down by pursuers, and others drowned in the river. The last Umayyad caliph fled all the way to Egypt before he was found and killed. In another part of Iraq, the city of Kufa, rebels organized a coup. The new caliph, who took the name al-Saffah (721–754), appeared from a safe house, and natives and soldiers swore their allegiance. So began the Abbasid Caliphate.

The Abbasid family had not fought in the war and, apart from their ancestry, they did not have much of a reputation. Perhaps this goes some way to explaining the ruthlessness with which they now consolidated their power. The name taken by their first ruler is a not-so-subtle hint about this: al-Saffah means 'the Blood-Shedder'.

It is said that the Abbasids did not manage to capture every Umayyad family member, so they invited more than eighty of them to a banquet under the pretence that there was a chance of reconciliation. However, at a signal from al-Saffah, his thugs entered the room and clubbed his guests to death. Then carpets were supposedly rolled over the moaning victims, so that the Abbasids could continue to enjoy their meal.

The story is unlikely to be true, at least not in every respect, but the caliph would probably not have minded that such Game-of-Thrones tales were told about him. Fear was a powerful motivator. We do know that at least one Umayyad prince got away, the 19-year-old Abd al-Rahman. He dodged the regime's assassins and escaped through North Africa to Muslim Spain, Al-Andalus, where he set up an independent state that would last for three centuries.

It was not only enemies and rebels that were executed. Whenever the loyalty of allies was doubted, they met a quick and bloody end. The second caliph, al-Mansur (714–775), who would rule for twenty-one years, even decided to kill the hero of the revolution, Abu Muslim. He feared his power and popularity in Khorasan, had his throat cut and bribed his commanders to stay calm. Mansur's cruelty was so infamous that Justin Marozzi wrote of him: 'The caliph's executions were so numerous, in fact, that there are instances when the historian wonders how he found the time to attend to other affairs of state.'[13]

But Mansur did find the time. Like Augustus in Rome, he was not just a brutal executioner but also an impressive statesman. He moved the capital of the Caliphate to a newly built city in Mesopotamia, closer to the heartland of Abbasid power. He called it Madinat as-Salam, the City of Peace, since he intended to create his own Pax Islamica. The city would become famous under the name of the original settlement, Baghdad. The centre of the city had a circular layout, which might have been an attempt to emulate a perfect circle in honour of the geometric teachings of Euclid, whom Mansur admired. It would become the biggest city on the planet, with lavish palaces, magnificent mosques and vibrant bazaars as well as bookstores, schools and hospitals. The markets were crowded with people, and the river filled with gondolas. According to some estimates, a million people populated the Abbasid capital at that time.

It was a wonder of the world, but nothing is left of it today. Unlike Athens and Rome, Baghdad did not have major stone quarries, so sun-dried mud bricks were mostly used for construction, which left the city vulnerable to the wear and tear of time, nature, fire and invasions.

Baghdad was an extremely cosmopolitan city, described by the geographer Yaqubi as 'the crossroads of the universe'. Immigrants came from the whole empire, first to build the city, then to benefit from its location and thriving economy. Here were Arabs and Persians, but also Armenians, Turks, Kurds and Indians. Muslims lived alongside Jews, Christians and Zoroastrians. Just as Rome had once been, Baghdad became even more international by the many slaves who were bought or kidnapped from India, Africa, Eastern Europe or the Iberian Peninsula, many of whom were later set free by the owners and became integrated. There was already a set of international scholars active in the Near East who went where the environment was most hospitable. Baghdad became a powerful magnet for them.

Therefore it is a simplification when I talk about this as the Arab or Islamic world. In the histories of this period, an

'Arab thinker' might speak Persian or Syriac, and 'Islamic science' might have been conducted by a Jewish or Christian scholar. Arabic was the language of administration and science, and Islamic law governed relations, but it was the blend that made this culture so dynamic. As the Arabist and Hellenist scholar Dimitri Gutas writes, 'what is called classical Islamic civilization is the result of the fermentation of all the divergent ingredients which their various backgrounds, beliefs, practices, and values provided.'[14] It was 'a cosmopolitan utopia of sorts', argues Peter Frankopan.[15]

This was the world of *One Thousand and One Nights*, a place of mystery and wonder, where adventure and hazard could wait around every corner. *The Arabian Nights*, as it is often called, is a collection of Middle Eastern folktales, many set in Baghdad. Sometimes they feature the caliph al-Rashid (763/766–809), Mansur's grandson, when he wanders the streets at night in the company of his friend and advisor Jafar al-Barmaki, of the influential Barmakid family, the important sponsors of science and translations.

A fascinating aspect of these tales is how often the hero is a merchant involved in a daring adventure in order to acquire wealth. In Western fiction the protagonist often fights for honour, justice or the princess and half the kingdom, but rarely for economic gain. However, as Nima Sanandaji writes, 'Many Iranian, Arab and Kurdish folktales feature characters that enrich themselves and benefit society by working hard, trading and investing.'[16] The independent story of Sinbad the Sailor, which was added to *One Thousand and One Nights* at a late stage, is one example. It tells the story of seven magical voyages of a Baghdad merchant who defies shipwrecks, monsters and cannibals to do business and restore the family fortune.

It's a typical tale from the crossroads. Baghdad, a city on the river Tigris and close to the Euphrates, had many benefits over landlocked Damascus. The caliph said that the city was built here to make sure that trade flowed smoothly and prices stayed low. Grain could come from the north, dates and rice from the south, and luxury goods from the Far East. 'This is the Tigris; there is no obstacle between us and China: everything on the sea can come to us on it.'[17]

The new empire was a vast free-trade area, governed by a system of beliefs and rules understood by all: just like in Rome, a citizen could expect the same treatment and rights wherever he travelled. The principles of free trade were also extended to cover external trade, so the same taxes applied to both. Islamic coins from this era have been found in central Europe, England, Scandinavia and even Iceland. But of most interest were the richer parts of the world, Central Asia, India and China. Exceptionally, the three important routes to Asia – the Red Sea, the Persian Gulf and the Silk Route – were now under control of the same empire, and this enabled an integrated logistical system under a Pax Islamica. A triangular lateen sail adopted from the North African Christian Copts helped to connect the waterways, allowing vessels to tack into the wind.

It was as close to a global market that humanity had hitherto achieved. In his history of world trade, William Bernstein writes:

Within a few centuries of the Prophet's death, his followers had knitted almost the entirety of the known world into a vast emporium in which African gold, ivory, and ostrich feathers could be exchanged for Scandinavian furs, Baltic amber, Chinese silks, Indian pepper, and Persian metal crafts.[18]

A Chinese visitor couldn't believe his eyes: 'everything produced from the earth is there. Carts carry countless goods to markets, where everything is available and cheap.'[19] It resembled trade under the Pax Romana, with the difference that the Muslim common market was much bigger, and private capital and individual adventurers played a larger role than in Rome.

Merchants more powerful than viziers

Just as in Athens and Rome, the foundation for all of this trade was a market-based system back home, with a high degree of freedom for people to make their own economic decisions. Land was mostly the property of individuals, who had the right to sell, mortgage, will, cultivate or rent it. In *The Encyclopaedia of Islamic Economics*, the system is summarized: 'The Abbasid economic system was generally a market and profit oriented economy largely based upon private property, private initiative and free market exchange.'[20]

Prices were free to move according to changes in supply and demand, helping to steer trade and investments to the areas where it was most in demand. This was an important aspect, an implication based on the story that Muhammad had opposed calls to impose price controls when food prices spiked. Regulation of prices was a traditional and popular policy, but Muhammad rejected it, saying that 'Allah is the one who fixes prices.'[21]

Even though Athens and Rome were also market-based economies, they mostly still saw commerce as a necessary evil, best left to slaves, freed men and foreigners. Even thinkers with a sophisticated understanding of the value of exchange found it degrading. Aristotle thought that trade for profit was vulgar, and

Cicero found it embarrassing for a gentleman to sell his labour. And Jesus said that it was easier for a camel to go through the eye of a needle than for a rich man to enter into the kingdom of God.

Islamic culture was different. Alone among the world religions, Islam was founded by a merchant. In one hadith (the collection of sayings and actions of the Prophet), Muhammad says that, 'The truthful, trustworthy merchant is with the Prophets, the truthful, and the martyrs.' The Quran is filled with the vocabulary of the marketplace and encourages 'trade by mutual consent'. Islamic religious law busied itself with protecting merchants and their interests.

Extensive trade and economic flourishing created a very rich and esteemed class of businessmen. In his history of the era, Shelomo D. Goitein went so far as to talk about a 'bourgeois revolution' in the region. (And with that, incidentally, came etiquette books on how to eat properly, for readers who wanted to show that they deserved to climb socially.) He quotes a tenth-century writer who claimed that '[m]erchants are more powerful than viziers', since a bill of exchange was more happily accepted than an allocation of income from taxes.[22]

Prosperity was not limited to the elite. Records of clothes taxes reveal that many people wore silk and cotton. In 892, there were over a hundred bookshops in Baghdad, which would not have been possible if only the privileged bought books.[23] The wealth also filled the coffers of the caliphs, who used much of it on the military, palaces and harems, the isolated domestic space reserved for the women of the house, wives and enslaved concubines. But the caliphs also spent lavishly on science and libraries.

The great exception to economic freedom was of course slavery. In Islam it was illegal to enslave fellow believers, so slaves were usually brought from far away, after conquests, kidnappings or purchases. Often Christians enslaved each other to sell to the booming Arab region (until the Christian Church imitated the Muslim ban); other slaves came from the trans-Saharan slave trade. It has been estimated that around 10 million slaves were brought to the Muslim world, perhaps more.

However, unlike in many ancient states and the modern colonial system, the slave was granted certain legal rights and the owner had certain obligations. Slaves were a commodity, and could be bought, sold, sexually exploited or killed, but they were not seen as cattle or things. Astonishingly, marriages between slaves (if allowed by the owner) were legally protected in the same way as other marriages. If the owner did not treat a slave humanely, a judge could order the slave to be sold or even freed. Setting a slave free was seen as a meritorious act.

These detailed regulations meant that slaves were mostly better treated than in classical antiquity and in North and South America in the 1800s, but it also meant that slavery was officially authorized and harder to extinguish than in most other places. Legal slavery was not abolished in Saudi Arabia until 1962 and remained in Mauritania until 1981.

There is a parallel with the position of women. 'The Muslim woman had property rights unparalleled in the modern West until comparatively recent times', writes Bernard Lewis.[24] Women were allowed to start businesses, sign contracts and did not have to give their pre-marriage property or earnings from work and business to their husbands. They also had inheritance rights, though not equal to men. And there is no stipulation in the Quran for women to wear a face-veil.

However, when there is a subordination of women to men, even though less radical than elsewhere, and it has a theological sanction, it is much more difficult to change it. And so it is that the same property and inheritance rights that were at first the most progressive, can eventually appear as the most reactionary, relative to the changes in other places. One reason why the Caliphate did not continue to evolve was that its legal institutions could not adapt as easily.

In his book *The Long Divergence*, the economist Timur Kuran documents that something similar can be said in the economic realm. The Islamic world had sophisticated economic institutions and contract laws. However, these did not change when the needs changed, for example to embrace changes in economic relations, so they blocked innovations in civil society and commercial enterprises. For example, economic partnerships ended with the death of a partner in order to protect inheritors, preventing the development of more complex forms of corporations such as those that would appear in the West.[25]

But the stagnation that these fixed institutions would eventually lead to could not have been foreseen at that time. For now, Muslims were the masters of the universe.

Houses of wisdom

The Abbasid market produced not only economic wealth, but also intellectual wealth. The prosperity of the Caliphate, the diverse traditions it inherited and the challenges it faced combined to initiate an energetic hunt for new texts and thoughts that could be translated into Arabic. This would have enormous historical repercussions. As an Andalusian historian of the eleventh century wrote, 'people's ambitions revived from their indifference and their minds awoke from their sleep'.[26]

This translation movement has sometimes been described as a purely conservationist effort, with the Arabs in the roles of passive transmitters of old traditions. However, the evidence suggests that translations started for practical purposes and that the intellectuals did not just admire, but grappled with, developed and challenged the ideas that they translated. They often produced two or three translations of the same book, as more accurate versions became available. First, they translated books, then they wrote books using these ideas, and often they also wrote books explaining where these ideas were wrong.

One starting point was the new ruling family's need for legitimacy. Persian rulers claimed that they could discern their right to rule in the stars, and when the Abbasids inherited such claims, they searched for knowledge about astrology. (This was a long-lasting obsession in many cultures – in the 1340s, scholars at the University of Paris explained the Black Death with a malign conjunction of Mars, Saturn and Jupiter.) One of its beneficial consequences was an interest in the related fields of astronomy and mathematics. A group of Indian scholars who understood the stars' movement and could predict eclipses were invited to the caliph Mansur's court in Baghdad. He ordered translations of the scientific texts in Sanskrit that they brought, which would jumpstart Arab study of astronomy and arithmetic.

The new bureaucracy also had to master many subjects to be able to administer the empire and Islamic law. The secretaries had to understand timekeeping, engineering for construction and irrigation, and mathematics for accounting and surveying. Algebra became an important tool to work out the complexities of inheritance laws. Every civilization has similar needs, of course, but in a new empire with nomadic traditions, there was little previous and tacit knowledge about such subjects. It had to be learned through formal procedures and the use of plenty of books. 'We have all the words, but they have all the ideas', as one translator said about the Persians.[27]

Eventually, the translation movement became self-perpetuating. The original commissions and funding came from the Abbasids, courtiers and officials, but in due course all economically and politically important groups, regardless of ethnicity and religion, became involved. Support came from generals, merchants and landowners, Muslims, Christians, Jews, Zoroastrians and pagans. Soon translators and scholars commissioned translations themselves, because they came across problems in their work that they had to solve with the help of other texts. What do you do when measurements or cosmological models from different cultures are incompatible? The attempts to apply and debate the new ideas generated theoretical questions about the nature of knowledge, and these could only be addressed by translating more philosophical texts.

This is how the Arab world became captivated by Greek philosophy, especially Aristotle, whose logic could be used to organize knowledge and to argue rationally. Aristotelianism helped scholars of the period to set down rules to sort fable and fabrication from empirical facts, and to analyse everything from everyday experiences to the most complex movement of the heavens.

After two centuries, almost every single secular Greek book available except fiction and history had been translated into Arabic. Dissident Christians who had escaped the reach of Byzantium were an important early conduit. They had access to many of the Greek texts in Syriac translations. At first books were translated into Arabic from Syriac, until Greek versions became available, and then they were translated again, directly from Greek. The seventh Abbasid caliph, al-Mamun (786–833), who took power from his brother in a civil war and was said to have been inspired by his dream of Aristotle, turned this Greek–Arabic translation project into a central pillar of his long reign, 813–33.

All of this was facilitated by a revolutionary invention from the East. Abbasid troops defeated the Tang Chinese in Kazakhstan in 751, and, according to legend, they learned from Chinese war prisoners how to make a new material to write on, made from linen and hemp fibres – paper. It was both cheaper and more durable than the papyrus traditionally used, and much more so than the animal skins Europeans called parchment. Soon public and private libraries were filled with paper books. When an Islamic school was founded in Baghdad in 1234, it was said to have received an endowment of 80,000 books from the caliph's personal library.[28] This background allowed people to take seriously the story that the author al-Jahiz died in his own library when one of many large piles of books fell and crushed him.

The undeniable proof that there was a lively intellectual atmosphere was that not all the books published were dignified tomes on elevated subjects. Many were written for humour, satire and pure entertainment, and some were contrarian and scandalous. The book titles of one author included 'The Boasting of the Comb over the Mirror', 'The War of Bread and Olives', 'Adultery and its Enjoyment', 'Stories about Slave-boys' and 'Masturbation'. One author wrote an essay about the superiority of speech to silence, and also another essay that argued the opposite. One poet was famous for his rejection of conventional wisdom, praising envy, spite and solitude; he famously compared a rose to the anus of a defecating mule.[29]

Science and philosophy became necessary tools to understand and improve the world, but also indicators of status and lucrative careers. The wealthy sons of a former highwayman were said to pay the equivalent of more than $40,000 for a full-time translator. This type of demand created a class of independent private translators, unaffiliated with institutions, and they started to search the world for texts. Legend has it that, as a condition to make peace with Byzantium after a battle, the caliph demanded a number of Greek manuscripts, one of them the astronomer Ptolemy's important *Almagest*.[30]

Even though the story has probably been slightly exaggerated, it captures the obsession of this era. Books were one of the most important treasures after a war. One translator wrote of his search for one of the works of the Roman Greek physician Galen: 'I travelled in its search in northern Mesopotamia, all of Syria, Palestine, and Egypt until I reached Alexandria. I found nothing except about half of it, in disorder and incomplete, in Damascus.'[31]

The idea that motivated the project was that knowledge had no borders. This was ground-breaking. There was no 'Christian science', 'Muslim science' or 'Persian science'; there was only science itself, a search for observable facts and a rational methodology by which we discover causal links between them. And then it doesn't matter where the person who did the observing came from or what the faith of the person who documented the link was. As Frederick Starr writes about what he calls Central Asia's Golden Age: 'the best thinkers of the region showed themselves remarkably open to the unfamiliar and the inconvenient and ready to deal with it'.[32]

The Arab thinker al-Kindi (801–873) personified the spirit of the age. He was one of the great minds of the era, and wrote more than 250 books, of which more than thirty were devoted to geometry and more than twenty each to medicine and philosophy. In an oft-quoted passage Kindi explained his method: 'We ought not to be ashamed of appreciating the truth and of acquiring it wherever it comes from, even if it comes from races distant and nations different from us.'[33]

This spirit was not limited to the intellectual innovators. Al-Kindi's more traditionalist contemporary, Ibn Qutayba, said that 'the ways to Him are many and the doors of the good are wide… Knowledge is the stray camel of the believer; it benefits him regardless of where he takes it: it shall not disparage truth should you hear it from polytheists, nor advice should it be derived from those who harbour hatred.'[34]

It barely needs spelling out, but this is of course the exact opposite of what militant Islamists say today, when they demand obedience without question, or reject any knowledge that seems to come from 'infidels'. Classical Islamic civilization would have thought of them as barbarous ignoramuses.

The tenth-century geographer Al-Maqdisi was among the many who took this search for knowledge deeply seriously:

> No royal library remained without my persistent examination of it, no literary works of any sect that I have not scrutinized, no people with whose opinions I have not acquainted myself; there is no group of ascetics with which I did not mingle, no preachers anywhere whose convocations I have not attended. In this way, I attained to the soundness of knowledge I strove for in this science.[35]

One of the most prominent manifestations of this spirit were the salons of debate in the caliph's court. Scholars were invited to present and debate freely their positions on science, philosophy and religion. We have records of debates with rivals, such as a Christian bishop from Syria. When he grew understandably hesitant to answer an especially controversial point, the caliph al-Mamun encouraged him: 'Speak your disclaimer; answer without fear,' he said. 'No one will threaten you with anything; nor should you be distressed personally in regard to anyone. This is the day on which truth is to be made evident.'[36]

Often this translation and research project is understood to have taken place at an establishment called the 'House of Wisdom', which attracted scholars from different regions and religions. It is a great brand, but it has probably been somewhat exaggerated by modern scholars who would love nothing more than tenure at such an institution. House of wisdom was the name of libraries in the previous Persian empire and our limited sources indicate that the Abbasids inherited the model. It was a form of national archival institution, possibly involving research related to astronomy and mathematics, but it was not a centre for translations, an academy or a conference centre, and most important scholars had no affiliation with it. Translations took place in homes all over the empire, there were plenty of libraries, and scholars met and debated in all kinds of salons, including, as we have just seen, the Abbasid court.

In a way, all the attention showered on this single institution takes something away from the broader achievement of the period. Between the eighth and mid-eleventh centuries, it seems that almost three-quarters of Islamic scholars or their families worked in commerce and/or industry.[37] The real House of Wisdom was a pervasive intellectual culture rather than a state institution. Perhaps we should instead, as suggested by Jim Al-Khalili, talk about Baghdad as the City of Wisdom instead.[38]

A scientific revolution

From this fertile soil sprang many new traditions, scientific breakthroughs and ground-breaking philosophy. The philosopher, physician and poet Ibn Sina, famous under his Latinized name Avicenna (980–1037), is often described as the father of early modern medicine. Rejecting the idea that diseases and disorders were the actions of gods or demons, he insisted that they had natural causes. He also had pioneering ideas about preventive medicine and the effect of the environment on health. When his five-volume medical encyclopaedia was eventually translated into Latin, it was used as a guide to medicine for hundreds of years. Building on this and further studies, in the 1240s, Ibn al-Nafis became the first to describe the pulmonary circulation of the blood.

The ninth-century mathematician al-Khwarizmi developed a set of rules to find solutions to linear and quadratic equations and ways of calculating areas and volumes. The title of his book, *Al-Jabr* ('completion'), gave us the word *algebra*, and the Latin version of his name (Algoritmi) gave us 'algorithm'. Helpfully, he also imported the Hindu numeral system with ten digits, including zero, which would later be imported by Europeans as 'Arabic numerals'. Crucially, the Hindu–Arabic system is positional, where the value of a digit depends on its position. This makes all arithmetic calculations (addition, subtraction, multiplication and division) easier than in the Roman system. Avicenna claimed to have learned it as a child by studying with a vegetable seller who used them in his trade.

One of the most important meta-inventions was the experimental method. The father of optics, Ibn al-Haytham (965–1040), rejected the ancient theory that we can see because eyes emit rays of light. He established an experimental laboratory with dark rooms, mirrors and viewing tubes to make repeated experiments to prove that it was the other way round: objects reflect light into the eyes. He was correct, but his method was even more important – testing a hypothesis with experiments based on confirmable and replicable procedures. During a much later scientific revolution, Haytham's insights would frequently be cited by scientists like Galileo, Kepler and Newton.

There was also technological progress. In 807, the caliph Rashid sent an embassy with gifts to Charlemagne, the king of the Franks, confirming their alliance against Andalus. Charlemagne was also a book collector, but there were not as many books available to him. He himself was illiterate. The Abbasids showed off their technological supremacy with an elaborate mechanical water clock made of brass. The stupefied reaction of Charlemagne's court proved the science fiction writer Arthur C. Clarke's dictum that every sufficiently advanced technology is indistinguishable from magic.

As a Kraftwerk fan, I am particularly intrigued by the later musical machines of al-Jazari, especially the boat with four automatic musicians that seems to have performed different rhythms as pegs were moved around, in effect a programmable drum machine.

Astronomy and geography were always important obsessions. The caliphs did not just translate Ptolemy's texts, they also ordered experiments and built observatories to find out if he was right. They understood the heavens better than others and created the most accurate maps yet. A map commissioned by an early ninth-century caliph surpassed the Ptolemaic perception of the Indian Ocean as an inland sea, and showed oceans around the continents, hinting at the possibility of circumnavigating Africa.

In the early eleventh century, the polymath al-Biruni measured the circumference of the earth surprisingly correctly and it led him to assume the existence of a continent somewhere between Europe and Asia. He hypothesized that it was inhabited. Working with a team of scholars, the Persian astronomer Omar Khayyam managed to measure the length of the year as the remarkably accurate 365.2421986 days and devised a solar calendar that was more precise than the Gregorian calendar introduced in Europe 500 years later.

In philosophy, Aristotle reigned supreme, and the debate was mostly about how he should be interpreted and complemented. The most radical theology was Mutazilism, a school that emphasized humanity's free will and the power of reason. The Mutazilites believed that rationality was a tool to understand not just the world and the laws of nature, but even morality, religion and God. When reason and the Quran collided, the latter had to be re-interpreted, or understood in an allegorical way. The Mutazilites argued that this was possible since the Quran was created and not eternal, as other theologians claimed.

This belief in human reason led some of the Mutazila scholars to go so far as to denounce kings and despots. They denied that political power was given by God and called for decentralization and sometimes democratization. A few of them, who have been called 'Mu'tazila anarchists', even thought that an Islamic society and Islamic law could function without any government. Patricia Crone summarizes their argument: '[I]f an imam *were* to turn into a king, by ceasing to govern in accordance with the law, then the Muslims would be legally obliged to fight him and depose him.' 'Since imams kept turning into kings, the best solution was not to set them up in the first place.'[39]

This opposition to authoritarianism makes Mutazilism a highly improbable candidate for a religious inquisition, but the fact that one happened showed that no idea is so good that it cannot be abused. In 827, the caliph al-Mamun turned a certain aspect of their doctrine into state orthodoxy: the createdness of the Quran. In 833, just a few months before his death, Mamun established a form of inquisition, which meant religious scholars could be punished for dissent, giving the lie to his earlier statements about free speech.

The most infamous case of this *mihna* (trial; ordeal) was the imprisonment and torture of the traditionalist scholar Ahmad ibn Hanbal. When Hanbal stated his belief in the uncreatedness of the Quran, he was flogged until he was unconscious. This made a martyr out of Hanbal, whose popularity surged. The Mutazilites were forever tarnished by the brutal policy they were associated with, even though they were probably not directly responsible.

Partly as a result of this backlash, and the fact that the idea that governments control religion had now been legitimized, Mutazila scholars would soon be the ones who were flogged. The tenth Abbasid caliph, al-Mutawakkil (822–861), otherwise famous for heavy drinking and wasteful spending, tried to style himself as the guardian of orthodoxy. In the 840s, he replaced the intolerance of the rationalist camp with the reverse. He had no patience for inquiry and debate but emphasized submission and tradition. Even translators of texts that could be seen as rationalist were jailed. He also became increasingly intolerant of Christians, Jews and interpretations of Islam that differed from his own. This was a sign of worse to come.

As the Muslim liberal Mustafa Akyol writes: 'The *mihna* was certainly wrong, unwise and disastrous. However it lasted for only sixteen years. Soon after that, things turned upside down – and not for a short period, but forever.'[40] If the Arabs had bothered to translate Greek tragedies and not just science and philosophy, they would have recognized the haunting concept that you often meet your destiny on the road you took to avoid it.

Twilight of the Abbasids

Mamun's inquisition and Mutawakkil's counter-repression revealed the weakness of a culture of openness and creativity dependent on enlightened despots. If one man changed his mind, everything could change. Unlike in Athens, power was not in the hands of the people, and unlike in Rome there was not even a nominal Senate that could restrain the ruler. This did not mean that the caliph was above the law. According to Islam, no sovereign could be above the Sharia. There are stories about caliphs who did not get their way and did not feel that they could punish someone without good legal cause. Islamic law applied to the ruler as well. But you reminded him of that at your own peril.

With such concentration of power, anything could happen to anyone. In *One Thousand and One Nights* and for most of their real lives, the caliph Rashid and his advisor Jafar were the very symbol of a warm and constructive friendship. One day, Rashid suddenly had Jafar killed, cut up his corpse and displayed the parts on the bridges of Baghdad. Perhaps he suspected him of disloyalty or of sleeping with his sister. No one knows. Unlike Socrates and Cicero, Jafar did not even get to hear the charges against him.

The fight over who got to wield this power created more permanent damage to the empire. In 861, the intolerant caliph Mutawakkil was killed by his own Turkish guards, and a decade of chaos ensued, known as 'Anarchy at Samarra'. A previous caliph, al-Mutasim (796–842), had relocated to Samarra in central Iraq in 836. He had to find space for his new army of Turkish slave soldiers, who weren't popular in Baghdad and stoked tensions there. But the guards hired to protect the caliphs soon became their masters. After all, if these 'mamluks' were invincible, why should they stay slaves? In many ways this period of anarchy is reminiscent of Rome's 'crisis of the third century'. A succession of four caliphs, puppets of different army factions, rose to power only to be toppled shortly thereafter, often by the very troops that had first anointed them.

This weakness of the centre stoked rebellions all over the empire. The situation was worsened by climate change. A shift towards warmer and drier conditions in the ninth century threatened towns and agriculture, and salinization destroyed the soil. At times, food riots were reported. Constant war and the loss of both land and territory led to a drop in tax revenue just as costs for troops surged. Soon secessionist forces began to tear the Caliphate into pieces. In 869, a major slave rebellion broke out in Iraq when enslaved Bantu peoples who had been captured in south-east Africa for hard work on plantations rose up. It took fourteen years and tens of thousands of lives before the Abbasids regained control.

A Turkish mamluk who had been made governor of Egypt took advantage of the chaos to break Egypt and Syria away from the empire. In the early tenth century, the Fatimid dynasty took control of North Africa and eventually marched into Egypt. Then even the heartland was threatened. In the 930s, the Persian Buyids conquered much of Iran and set their eyes on Iraq. In 945, they invaded Baghdad.

The Buyid dynasty actually supported the Abbasid caliphs and left them in power. But it was now more of a nominal court without real control of its formal possessions. The empire ended, but the intellectual atmosphere did not. On the contrary, for a while, scholars and philosophers even benefited from the greater pluralism of patrons competing for influence and power. Even in Byzantium, there was a return of scholarly activity, and the Greek secular manuscripts that the Arabs had given a new lease of life were now copied there again.

The value the Buyids placed on learning is illustrated by a lovely anecdote about Sahib ibn Abbad, writer and grand vizier, who was said to bring his 100,000–200,000 books on his journeys, carried by 400 camels trained to walk in alphabetical order. Sadly, it is not true, but it is based on some reality. Ibn Abbad was once asked by another Persian dynasty to join their service, and he replied that his private library prevented him, since it would take 400 camels to transport it.

Unfortunately, the economic foundation for this culture was slowly being undermined by a turn towards a feudalistic system. As state revenue declined and the wage bill became unaffordable, Abbasid rulers instead started rewarding services with *iqtas*, the right to tax or extract revenue directly from certain lands.

In this way, land that had previously been the private property of civilians came to be dominated by military officials. The soldier did not own the land, though, so he was mostly interested in short-term revenue. If the land or the farmers were ruined, he would just turn to the state for another source of compensation. This militarization of the economy substantially weakened agriculture, entrepreneurship and the whole merchant class, but in the short term it was inexpensive for the rulers and lucrative for the military, so it was expanded and imitated by subsequent dynasties.

This was an unintended blow to intellectual culture, since merchants had been important patrons and customers. That was just the start, though. Next came an intentional attack, much broader and more direct. The immediate cause was rivalry within Islam. The Fatimids and Buyids were Shia Muslims, holding that Muhammad had designated his son-in-law Ali as his successor. So were the Hamdanids, who controlled the northern parts of Syria and Iraq, and the Qarmatians, who had established themselves in the eastern Arabian Peninsula.

The caliphs in Baghdad, in contrast, were Sunnis, believing that Muhammad had left no successor. The Abbasids felt vulnerable as Shia powers rose all around them, but they also knew that this religious rivalry could be exploited in the great game of power and territory. This clash was further complicated by divisions within each camp. In his attempt at the first objective history of religions, al-Shahrastani listed seventy-three different Muslim sects. Brutal attempts to repress this incredible diversity would have devastating effects for the Arab enlightenment.

The caliphs started pushing back by trying to end the theological debates and unite all Sunnis around a single orthodoxy, reversing the policy of openness they had usually been associated with. A step in this direction was the Qadiri Creed of 1017, which ordered Mutazila scholars and other nonconformists to renounce their ideas on pain of first torture and exile, and eventually death. The major turning point came when the Caliphate found a powerful ally in their cause.

The counter-enlightenment

In the early eleventh century, a new Turkish Sunni dynasty made rapid progress through Central Asia, took control of Iran and extended into Anatolia. The Abbasids quickly recognized the potential for an alliance with this Seljuk Empire. By embracing the Seljuks, they could push out the Shia Buyids and return Baghdad to Sunni traditions. The caliph al-Qaim married a Seljuk princess and, on his invitation, they invaded Baghdad in 1055.

The strongman of the Seljuk state, the capable vizier Nizam al-Mulk (1017–1092), who argued for strong hierarchies and against social mobility, systematized the feudalization of the economy to reward and maintain the large army. Still, the Seljuks were uncertain about their control of hearts and minds amidst intensified religious strife and rivalry, and Nizam responded with an elaborate plan to end the intellectual openness of the Muslim world.

In 1065, he began establishing madrasas (schools) where the most conservative version of Islam was to be taught to the future elites of society. These 'Nizamiyyas', named after him, were usually funded with donations from rulers and officials and their families, but functioned like state schools. Unlike other schools, these were not places where knowledge was pursued, but where a doctrine was defined and promulgated, to arm students against Shiites, Sunni dissenters and secular philosophers. Doctrinal purity and rote learning took the place of inquiry and research. No established church with its own hierarchy ever came about, but it is reasonable to talk about the imposition of an orthodoxy.

This was a watershed moment, establishing what the political scientist Ahmet Kuru has described as the first 'state–ulema alliance' between rulers and orthodox Islamic scholars, sidelining intellectuals and merchants.[41] Some see such an alliance as a defining part of Islam, but it was only in the eleventh century, more than 400 years after the death of the Prophet, that it was created.

Until then, Islamic scholars had not been appointed by the government or any religious institution. Many of them, even traditionalists, warned explicitly against taking money from the rulers since it would create dependence on them. An important figure in early Muslim jurisprudence declared that 'the profession of the honest merchant, or indeed any trade, pleases God more than Government service'.[42] Most Islamic scholars or their families made a living by producing or selling textiles, food, books, leather, jewellery, perfumes and other goods. Others worked as teachers, translators or bankers. The new Nizamiyyan madrasas changed this. Now scholars were hired, paid by and subjected to the rulers, and they had to stick to the official line. Sometimes it is said that religion took over the Muslim states, but it is just as correct to say that states took over, controlled and supervised religion.

In 1091, the leadership of the prominent Baghdad madrasa was handed over to a man who would, despite his own sophistication, ultimately undermine the reputation of philosophy in Islamic culture, the 33-year-old theologian and writer al-Ghazali (1058–1111). During his time, the Baghdad branch had some 3,000 students, making it the world's biggest educational institution, rivalled by Nizamiyyas in only a few other cities.

In *The Incoherence of the Philosophers* and other works, Ghazali appreciated some aspects of philosophy, such as logic, but he still condemned the Muslim philosophers for becoming 'infidels' by accepting the metaphysical views of the Greeks. He also denied cause and effect and famously argued that fire does not make cotton burn: we observe fire and then we observe the cotton on fire, but nowhere do we see the act of ignition, because this is an act of God. But we know from miracles that God can do anything, so if he felt differently one day, the cotton would not burn.

This theory of perpetual miracles undermined the enlightenment project. It meant that there were no natural laws that could be discovered by scientists and exploited for technology. Instead we have only the habits of God, and they can be understood by studying religious texts and obeying tradition. Ghazali was a complex thinker, and he did see a role for science so long as it was subordinate to religion, but his ideas were used to let faith shove philosophy and science aside.

Ghazali's teachings were wildly popular for several reasons. He used rationality in a clever way to attack the rationalist camp, but he was not above personal attacks. Avicenna's habit of drinking was used to discredit the religious beliefs of the philosophers. Ghazali attracted the conservatives who were shocked by thinkers who used reason to examine even religion. His attack on philosophers also attracted many young who were exhausted by studying the sometimes difficult writings of scientists and philosophers. Now they could just study religion and feel superior to shallow infidel philosophers.

Most importantly, rulers found Ghazali's message incredibly useful. Ghazali wrote that 'the state and religion are twins. Religion is the foundation while the state is the guard. That which has no foundation will certainly crumble and that which has no guard is lost.' This statist view has sometimes been falsely attributed to Muhammad, but Ghazali lifted it from a story about the non-Muslim founder of the Sasanian Empire.[43]

As we saw, Mutazila scholars were often sceptical of political power, and Avicenna had even written that the citizens had a right to kill a despot. Ghazali, on the other hand, provided legitimacy for autocratic rule. In the legal and theological traditions that he now synthesized, there were explicit statements that a ruler had to be obeyed even if he was unjust, wicked and had grabbed power by force.

Ghazali's reversal of Thales' secularization of nature (explained by natural causes rather than divine intervention) was similar to what the early Christians had preached in Rome and, just like Augustine had before him, Ghazali asked why philosophers and scientists so often disagreed with one another if their methods could really explain the world. This might have seemed like a self-defeating argument when, outside his door, people were killing each other over different interpretations of the faith. Under strain from domestic threats and Christian military Crusaders, the Fatimids in Cairo had become more intolerant of Sunnis and Christians. In their turn, the Seljuks persecuted their Ismaili branch of Shia Islam, which provoked some of these to launch a terrorist campaign, involving suicide attacks on leading Sunnis and Seljuks. It was claimed that they had been emboldened in their deadly task by the use of hashish, which eventually gave us the word 'assassin'.

For Ghazali, however, this religious civil war was a reason to enforce one belief and one interpretation at the tip of a sword. Again, just like Augustine, he declared that dangerous ideas and books had to be banned to save people from themselves. They both justified compulsion in religion by likening adults to children. Augustine wrote that sinners had to be stopped, just like 'one who pulls a boy's hair in order to prevent him from provoking serpents by clapping his hands at them', while Ghazali thought that it was just like 'the boy is barred from the bank of the river so that he does not fall in'.[44]

But Ghazali went further, in effect arguing that some people should be pushed into the river. He wrote that those who strayed from the correct interpretation of Sunni Islam – not just the philosophers but also the whole community of Ismaili Shiis – were apostates and should be punished by death. Their doctrinal offences were so grave that others 'may spill his blood and take his property'.[45]

This was not just a theoretical exercise: alarmingly, Ghazali had a 'naughty' list. The authorities were delighted to achieve religious justification for a policy they already pursued. Mobs from the Baghdad madrasa no doubt felt like they had an official sanction when they rioted in the streets, physically attacking dissidents and driving women into their homes. Many of the remaining Zoroastrians gave up and fled to the north-west coast of India where they became known as parsis.[46]

The Nizamiyyas became incredibly influential and were imitated in Egypt, Syria and throughout the Islamic world. Versions of the ulema–state alliance were also established in the succeeding Muslim polities: the Ottoman, Safavid and Mughal empires. Just at the moment that the militarization of the economy made it more difficult for scholars to attract funding, and independent thinking could be punished by death, along came an opportunity to gain paid employment so long as you left your critical faculties at the door. It was a simple choice for most. This is the moment when houses of wisdom were replaced by barracks of orthodoxy.

The scanty remains

Scientists continued to be active in many places, and great achievements are on record even centuries later. Many rulers, even the Seljuk, supported some philosophers and scientists, but increasingly these pivoted towards safe areas of research. Astronomy and medicine remained popular fields since rulers always wanted to understand their fate and stay in good health. However, support for other sciences was often replaced by subsidies for the arts. This ensured that successive Muslim empires radiated sophistication and glorious architecture, but they did not have the same dynamic spirit of exploration and interest in unfamiliar cultures. Eventually, just as happened after the fall of the Roman Empire, many of the important manuscripts were neglected, forgotten and crumbled physically.

Sensing that his world was about to come to an end, the great Persian polymath al-Biruni complained: 'it is quite impossible that a new science or that any new kind of research should arise in our days. What we have of sciences is nothing but the scanty remains of bygone better times.'[47]

A quantitative analysis shows that the number of published books on scientific topics began to decline, and the moment this happened in a specific region is correlated with the time when state madrasas were established. In Baghdad and the eastern Islamic world during the golden age, 12 per cent of the books published were on scientific topics. After 1100, this dropped abruptly to 3 per cent.[48]

In a final parallel with Augustine's experience in Rome, Ghazali's followers had to see their empire fall apart just as it had come around to his orthodox faith. Once again feudalization of the economy and internal divisions, stoked by repression, were compounded by barbarian invasions. The Seljuk Empire began to fracture in the late eleventh century. At the same time, the first European Crusaders invaded the Middle East and the Christian 'Reconquista' of Spain celebrated its first victories. In 1085, the important city of Toledo fell to the Christians. In July 1099, Crusaders broke through the walls of Jerusalem, and during the next few days they went from door to door to slaughter the civilian Muslim and Jewish populations.

Cities can be rebuilt and repopulated, but a lasting effect of these conflicts was that it further diminished the openness of Muslim society. Cultures that used to turn outwards for ideas and inspiration now saw marauding armies coming from those directions. Interestingly, contemporary Arabs did not view this so much as a religious conflict as the Crusaders did – that aspect was emphasized much later by nationalists and Islamists. A more common interpretation was that this was just another vicious invasion force with another faith, which you fought, endured and sometimes allied with against Islamic rivals. However, as Ahmet Kuru writes, the invasions 'led many Muslims to seek safety from both the military state, as a possible protector against the invaders, and the ulema, as a provider of meaning to depressive conditions of invasions and massacres'.[49]

This civilization would leave an intellectual time capsule to succeeding generations, however. Do you remember the Umayyad prince who got away from the banquet of blood, the 19-year-old Abd al-Rahman? In one of those ironic twists that history delights in providing us, it might be said that he saved the spirit of the original Abbasid revolution for posterity. When he escaped the Abbasid assassins and established an independent Islamic polity in Spain, Al-Andalus, he created a separate lifeline for philosophy and science.

This region of Spain alternated between periods of tolerance and persecution, peace and calamity, and eventually disintegrated into a number of smaller kingdoms, that could be picked off by North African and then Christian armies. But Al-Andalus shared a broader cultural atmosphere with the whole Arab world, and some of the rulers tried hard to show that the Abbasids were not the only ones who loved knowledge. At times, extraordinary thoughts could be entertained.

The most brilliant Andalusian mind was Ibn Rushd, more famous under his Latinized name, Averroes (1126–1198). Sometime around 1169, the caliph gave him an assignment to explain Aristotle, which would result in an incredible body of work over three decades. Averroes wrote commentaries on almost all of Aristotle's texts – a short summary for beginners, a middle version that explained it and a long version that developed it with original thoughts, making Aristotelianism and Islam compatible. He also wrote at least sixty-seven other books, using rational philosophy to explain nature, medicine, law and theology.

Averroes also thoroughly refuted Ghazali's *The Incoherence of the Philosophers* with his own mischievously titled *The Incoherence of the Incoherence*. He explained that Ghazali's rejection of a real world governed by natural laws implied a denial of knowledge. It turned God into a tyrannical prince who acted arbitrarily, and therefore was a radical form of relativism, with neither facts nor values.

In some areas, Averroes was revolutionary. Both Averroes' enemy Ghazali and his hero Aristotle were united in their belief that men are superior and that women exist to obey. Averroes objected that there is no difference in intellectual capacity between the sexes, and women should have the same right as men to marry and divorce of their own free will. It might seem as though women were less capable, but that was only because they were stopped from developing their talents. If they were allowed freedom, women could become philosophers, soldiers, judges or even rulers. Discriminating against women was unjust and impoverished the state, he argued.[50]

Averroes' work was an incredible achievement, and it would go on to electrify the European mind and inspire Renaissance ideals. In Europe he would become known as 'the Commentator', while Aristotle became 'the Philosopher'. This is why we have Averroes' texts preserved in Hebrew and Latin translations, but not all of them in the original Arabic. He was too late to save his own civilization. Fear and repression had already destroyed the demand for rational philosophy and science. The caliph's successor turned against Averroes, probably to rally conservative clerics against invading Christians. By the end of his life, Averroes was condemned as a heretic and he was banished to a small town. He was restored to favour a few years later, but by then his philosophical books had been burned.

Soon an even more calamitous army would appear from the east. In the late twelfth century, a young Mongol boy lost his father and was abandoned by his tribe in the mountains, but through his ingenious and brave mother, and a brilliant combination of charisma, diplomacy and brutality, he survived, defeated his enemies and unified the Mongol tribes. Under his taken name Genghis Khan (1162–1227), he initiated one of history's most successful and destructive military campaigns.

The Mongols, able to stand up in stirrups and shoot their arrows while galloping, quickly conquered Central Asia and annihilated the old, rich cities that resisted. Oasis communities and urban centres had made the deserts bloom by building dams, canals and underground channels, and they built walls to stop the spread of deserts. The invaders demolished these irrigation projects and turned farmland into pastures. Agricultural production crumbled.

In January 1258, a Mongol army under Genghis's grandson Hulegu broke through the walls of Baghdad. The accomplishments of generations – palaces, mosques and perhaps thirty-six libraries – were destroyed in days, and the Mongols reportedly sank under the weight of all the gold, silver and fabrics looted. Since both Hulegu's mother and favourite wife were Nestorian Christians, he allowed Christians to hide in a church, but everyone else remaining in the city was mercilessly killed: 800,000 people in a manner of days, according to some sources. It was said that the water of Tigris turned black from the ink of all the books thrown into it, and red from all the people slaughtered.

Since the Mongols considered it bad luck to spill royal blood, they rolled the last Abbasid caliph in carpets and let horses trample him to death. It was reported that Hulagu had to move his camp upwind, to avoid the stench from the destroyed city. The 'crossroads of the universe' was reduced to rubble and ruins.

However, as we have seen, internal forces had already done everything they could to tear down this remarkable civilization from within. That had the most lasting effect. Muslims, after all, defeated the Crusaders, and soon they converted the Mongol invaders to Islam and rebuilt powerful empires. But they did not regain their openness and curiosity. Writing before the Mongol invasions, one of Ghazali's disciples claimed triumphantly that the punishments and exile of '[t]hose who meddle in philosophy' would be so successful 'that their fire will die out and all traces of it, and of them, will be obliterated'.[51]

The great thinkers had already been purged and their books burned. In the end, there were no scientists and no wealth and organizational capacity left to rebuild the sophisticated irrigation systems that had been destroyed. The reaction prevailed, and the deserts triumphed. As Shelley might have put it, around the decayed ruins, 'the lone and level sands stretched far away'.

Summary

The Abbasid Caliphate is a fascinating corrective against the idea that some faiths are doomed to intolerance and superstition. While many present-day Islamic states are oppressive and underdeveloped, the Caliphate was the world's richest and most advanced culture while Europe was still in its dark ages. It is not the religion itself that decides the outcome, but how it is interpreted and what is emphasized. In eighth-century Baghdad, it was interpreted as the way to peace, openness and progress.

By now, this is a familiar golden-age scenario. Confident after having won a major war, the Abbasid dynasty decided to go all-in on international exchange and intellectual openness. Where Athens had the Delian League and Rome had Pax

Romana, the Abbasids built the City of Peace and established a Pax Islamica, with a system of law and economic freedom that gave citizens liberties and protections across a vast empire stretching from North Africa to Afghanistan. They created an integrated economic area even bigger than Rome's and did not just practise free enterprise and free trade as the Athenians and Romans had done, but also embraced a culture where entrepreneurship and trade was seen as noble. Women had rights to property and business activities that Western women only achieved in modern times. The result was a bustling, urbanized civilization and broad economic progress.

Just as Athens benefited from its location close to old civilizations, so did the Abbasids, and they consciously built their new capital there, at the crossroads of the universe. It was a cosmopolitan utopia of sorts, where faiths, languages and ideas mixed and interacted. When the regime needed new capacities to administer its new empire, it could find them in the treasure trove of philosophy, science and economics bestowed upon it by the ancient cultures it had conquered.

Therefore, the Abbasids developed a tolerant policy that actively encouraged participation by people of different ethnicities and religions, and translated and developed texts from all cultures. The combination of, and clash between, different traditions and ideas led to a flowering of art, science and technology, just as it had done in other golden ages. The scientific accomplishments were extraordinary and inspired many succeeding cultures, not least the European ones.

But, just like in other golden ages, the Arabs began to question their openness when they felt their power slipping away. Where Athens and Rome had been ravaged by plagues, Baghdad suffered from political instability, revolts and a drier climate. Separatists broke away parts of the empire, and the lack of tax revenue started a process that was similar to what we saw in Rome: rulers began to undermine private property with a more feudal system. Military officials started to push out independent farmers. The role of merchants and private capital was compromised.

Abbasid rulers reacted most destructively when this separatism was combined with religious divisions. They felt that they had to stamp out other interpretations of Islam, and also learned that a fight for the one true interpretation could be used to mobilize supporters. In alliance with the Seljuk Turks, the Abbasid state took control of religion and debate, and sabotaged its own tradition of tolerance and science. Religious oppression only caused more conflict, and so created more demand for the repression they thought would be conducive to stability. The traditions of science and philosophy rapidly decayed.

The end of free markets and intellectual openness impoverished societies and left them with smaller margins for failure. When new waves of invaders destroyed the dams and irrigation canals, the Arabs were in the same position as the late Romans when their aqueducts were cut: they lacked the capacity to rebuild the amazing technologies previous generations seemed to have erected so effortlessly, and started to think about the now-terminated era as a golden age.

Eventually, things went so far that many started to think of Muslim societies as hopelessly despotic and superstitious, just as the Abbasids had once thought of Christians. Yet failure is not a fate but a choice.

Around the time the Abbasids began to lose power over their empire, a new dynasty in China would prove this, making its country richer, more culturally advanced and technologically capable than anything that had come before it. According to one story, Muhammed once encouraged his followers to: 'Search for knowledge, even if you have to go as far as China.' So, as the Muslim world saw its golden age slipping away, and Europe started to forget that it ever had one, that is where we have to go next.

4

SONG CHINA

On the Threshold of Modernity

The Chinese…, when we were unable even to read, knew everything essentially useful of which we boast at the present day.

VOLTAIRE, 1764[1]

China has been long one of the richest, that is, one of the most fertile, best cultivated, most industrious, and most populous countries in world.

ADAM SMITH, 1776[2]

In the key areas of economy, government, social structure, and intellectual life and scientific investigation Song China was as close to modernity as eighteenth century Europe.

STEPHEN DAVIES[3]

What are we to make of China's meteoric rise after opening up the economy in the late 1970s? A slew of commentators urged us not to act so surprised. This was not an anomaly, they said; the stagnation until then was. After a hiatus, China was on its way back to its traditional position as a world-leading economy with pre-eminence in culture and technology. It was more rare for us to hear about which era all these commentators were thinking of when talking about China's past superiority, and what made that possible.

As a clue, I would point the reader to a unique handscroll painting that gives us a sense of a vibrant, energetic Chinese city in the early twelfth century: *Along the River During the Qingming Festival*. It is often called 'China's *Mona Lisa*', but has also been more accurately described, by Bob Jones of the 'Why We Love the Song Dynasty' podcast, as a combination of the Bayeux Tapestry and *Where's Wally?* Measuring 5.25 metres long (25.5 cm high), the detailed scroll depicts an urban centre and a rural area with a river running through it; it features 30 buildings, 28 boats, 814 humans and 60 animals. There are also irrigated fields, farmhouses and goat herders.

It is a dizzyingly free market. People are loading, buying and selling wine, grain, cookware, medicine, furniture, fabrics and musical instruments. There are doctors, barbers, monks, millers, metalworkers and carpenters. There are multi-storey restaurants, food stalls and even food delivery drivers. There are actors, jugglers, servants, scholars, monks and fortune-tellers.

Modern technologies, exotic goods, foreign visitors and local merchants. It is everything, everywhere, all at once.

All the transportation that this advanced, globalized economy needs is well represented in the painting: a caravan of camels, and goods carried on boats, wagons, wheelbarrows, backpacks and donkeys. Most famously, in the centre of the painting, there is a bridge, crowded with vendors. A boat is struggling in the currents and seems to be seconds away from crashing into either the bridge or a nearby boat.

Even though there are beggars depicted too, these are mainly prosperous people by historical standards. The most prosperous in the history of the world until then, in fact. Estimated incomes, in relation to the price of rice and silver, were twice as high during the Song dynasty in 1080 as they would be in 1400. They would not be exceeded for at least 800 years.[4]

In 1620, the English philosopher Francis Bacon wrote that there were three great inventions unknown to the ancients that have 'changed the whole face and stage of things throughout the world': gunpowder, the compass and printing. According to Bacon, 'no empire, no sect, no star, seems to have exerted greater power and influence in human affairs than these three mechanical discoveries'.[5] Karl Marx, in 1861, insisted that 'these are the three major inventions that foretell the arrival of bourgeois society',[6] since they blew up the knight class, opened the world market and created the scientific renaissance.

But these three inventions, which Bacon called 'recent' and of 'obscure' origins, were already in use a thousand years ago by the Chinese along the river during the Qingming festival. The Chinese printed books, navigated with a magnetic compass and, when they had to fight, they did it with gunpowder.

Back then, China was 'the most intellectually sophisticated country in the world, and the most technologically advanced', writes Peter Watson in his work on ideas and innovations in history, and adds 'China's pre-eminence was probably greater during the Song dynasty (960–1279) than at any other time'.[7]

James Needham, who devoted his life to studying the history of technology in China, writes in the first of his many volumes: 'Whenever one follows up any specific piece of scientific or technological history in Chinese literature, it is always at the Song dynasty that one finds the major focal point.'[8] This goes for hydraulic engineering, shipbuilding, bridge-building, architecture, chemical science, gunpowder, medicine, mathematics, botany and horticulture. What the Song Chinese didn't invent themselves, they were often the first to describe and teach, because of their highly literate culture. This was the society that came close to initiating modern science and unleashing an industrial revolution.

This was very different, however, from what Arab traders saw when they arrived in China in the middle of the ninth century. At that time, the cosmopolitan Tang dynasty was in place and facing a crisis of economic hardship and rebellions. Foreigners, who used to be warmly welcomed, were now being scapegoated. In 836, a decree banned Chinese from having relations with 'people of colour' (non-Chinese). Buddhism, which had spread rapidly throughout the country for hundreds of years, was banned in the 840s. More than 4,600 monasteries and temples were demolished or converted, which made it possible for the regime to melt down sculptures of precious metals and tax the monks and their slaves.

An increasingly heavy burden of taxes and forced labour service created desperation in the countryside. Peasants starved, sold their children into slavery and resorted to banditry to survive. One bandit leader managed to unite many diverse groups and, in May 879, they captured the trading centre of

Guangzhou; a massacre of tens of thousands of Arab, Persian and Indian merchant families ensued.

China was soon falling apart as different warlords and nomad raiders took whatever they could, during a long, chaotic period of unrest and war known as the Five Dynasties and Ten Kingdoms. The beginning of its end came when the emperor of one of these short-lived dynasties died in 959 and left his six-year-old son in charge.

The coup at Chen Bridge

Night had fallen over the camp by Chen Bridge in early 960, but the officers who had been sent by their child emperor to fight against a rumoured invader were sleepless and restless. There had been rumours of strange signs in the heavens and there was mutiny in the air. Their commander, Zhao Kuangyin (927–976), lay sleeping, apparently after a heavy drinking bout. However, he hastily awoke as some of his men entered his tent with drawn swords. What he saw next stunned him: the soldiers held out a yellow robe, the traditional colour of emperors. Walking out to the gathered men, he was confronted by their fervent calls that they could not take orders from a child, and wanted him, a military hero, to usurp the throne.

Some are born emperors, some achieve empire, and some have it thrust upon them. Or so the story goes. Apparently, the loyal Zhao was furious with his troops, but not so furious (or loyal) as to decline the demand. Even though the sources talk about a spontaneous uprising and a reluctant usurper, all signs point to a carefully orchestrated coup. The rumoured invasion suddenly dematerialized as Zhao began marching back towards the capital, Kaifeng, suggesting that it might have been a ploy to assemble the army. It seemed a little too convenient that the appropriate yellow robe was available in the camp just as the troops turned against their ruler. Zhao accepted the nomination on condition that the soldiers swore allegiance to him personally, and the troops left the unseated emperor unharmed and did not loot Kaifeng.

This was a marked break with previous invaders in this chaotic era, and a clever move, since it both protected the city's wealth and secured the loyalty of a large part of the population. Without a fight, court officials bowed to their new master. A new dynasty was born, named after the army Zhao had commanded in Song Prefecture. Zhao himself would go down in history under his posthumous temple name, Taizu of Song, Progenitor of Song. The dynasty soon adopted the element of fire and the corresponding colour of red as its symbol. In portraits of Song emperors, they often wear red dress.

Having taken power by force, Taizu understood something important about the power of the military. He was determined to break the warlordism that had ruined China over the past eighty years. Therefore he launched a programme to strengthen the civil principle (*wen*) over the military (*wu*), an important ideal in Confucianism, the ethical school that builds on the ancient philosopher Confucius (551–479 BC), which the dynasty wholeheartedly embraced. It would give the Song Empire some unique characteristics.

With enemies out of the way, Taizu's main threat were his friends. His own co-conspirators commanded the armies and had already shown that they were prepared to depose their emperor and elevate one of their own. If they united against him, he did not have sufficient power to resist. So, on 20 August 961, he is said to have invited them all to a drinking party. I know what you may be thinking but, no, Taizu did not have his potential rivals clubbed to death and carpets rolled over them while he kept on partying. Instead – with tears in his eyes according to some accounts – he talked about his fear for the future of China and of the horrors of civil war. He warned that their own positions might be used by plotting subordinates who wanted to advance in the hierarchy. His generals, moved by his words, asked what they could do to allay his anxiety.

Ah, good question! The emperor, of course, had a plan. He said that they could have long and prosperous lives if they gave up their commands and retreated to comfortable mansions to serve as local governors. If they did, they would be invited to become a part of the new dynasty by marrying into the imperial family. And, apparently, his surprised and drunken guests all emphasized strongly that they had no interest in power or war. Did they perhaps fear thugs behind the curtains if they declined? History doesn't tell. But, the next day, they all asked to be relieved of their posts.

It was a stroke of genius. Over a cup of wine, Taizu had neutralized a potential threat while at the same time extending his power over his territories with new, powerful family members as regional governors. In this way a remarkable demilitarization of Chinese institutions was introduced. Taizu retired many old generals and appointed new ones from other sections of the army, breaking up old power relationships. The moment a commander grew too strong in a province, he was recalled to the capital. At the same time, as a sign of his devotion to learning, Taizu urged his generals to read more. In the eleventh century, a Song historian wrote admiringly: 'The emperor Taizu accorded with the hearts of men, troops did not bloody swords, markets were not changed into execution grounds.'[9]

This was clearly hyperbole: lots of swords were bloodied. For the next sixteen years, Taizu fought to subdue the independent kingdoms that had formed in central and southern China. This region had been spared most of the fighting during the previous war, production had not been as disrupted as in other parts of China, and an influx of refugees had increased the population. This wealth made them hostile to outside intervention but also turned the region into a taxman's dream, enticing the Song emperor. In these decades, the Song army was, according to the historian Peter Lorge, 'one of the great military machines in history'.[10]

Taizu's special way of making war facilitated the conquest, reminding us of the strategic tolerance of the Romans and Arabs. He did not just spare the lives and wealth of those who surrendered, he even gave deposed rulers a comfortable, if closely supervised, life in the capital. One of the preparations for a military campaign was the construction of a large mansion for the soon-to-be-dethroned enemy. Some wars ended before they began in earnest, with a negotiated surrender.

Taizu's soldiers were ordered to follow his highy unusual rules of conduct: 'do not loot the countryside, do not abuse the civilian population, avoid loss of life whenever possible'.[11] When soldiers were nonetheless given a free rein to ignore these rules after the invasion of Shu in 975, the generals who allowed it were beheaded, and the one subordinate commander who restrained his men, Cao Bin, was rapidly elevated and soon commanded the whole Song army. Taizu acted out of strategic moderation, not squeamish compassion. When one rogue commander was found to have been especially cruel, Taizu had his whole clan executed.

Peace through superior financial power

The new regime set about erecting a government that was more rule-bound than the arbitrary rule of previous dynasties. Taizu created a council of ministers that both made policy and administered the country, and the chief councillor increasingly took on the role of prime minister. In place of hereditary military governors, a professional civilian bureaucracy was constructed. At first, the new officials were selected based on connections, but a growing empire needed more of them, and the second emperor, Taizu's brother Taizong (939–997), needed men in government without ties to his late brother. Therefore he massively expanded the existing nationwide examination system in Confucian classics, history, law and mathematics.

This established a certain meritocracy. As the examination system became the way to get a government job, even people from a humble background had at least a nominal chance to rise through the ranks. The importance of this cannot be exaggerated. The cost of equivalent study in private academies was high and only 1–10 per cent passed the exams even to make it to the next-level examinations in the capital. In the early thirteenth century, there was just one degree-holding administrator per 75,000 people being administered.[12]

An eleventh-century report of a scholar who returned to his home in a horse-drawn carriage after a successful examination reveals how unusual this education system was (and why modern academics envy it even more than they envy the Abbasid House of Wisdom):

> people would gather on both sides of the road to watch and sigh. Ordinary men and stupid women rush forward in excitement and humble themselves by prostrating themselves in the dust stirred up by the carriage and the horses.[13]

Many hundreds of years later, the examination system came to be seen as a reason for China's stagnation since it relied heavily on memorizing the classics, but it helped to create a powerful class of scholar–officials and make China a literate civilization. It meant that power and prestige came from education and examination, not as a birthright, so the elite was constantly rejuvenated with able outsiders. The system went to great lengths to ensure social mobility. Candidates' names were even hidden so that examiners could not identify who the student's father was, and two examiners had to read each paper.

The story about one of these scholars, Lu Mengzheng, though blending fact with fiction, became a source of inspiration for generations. It was said that he had lost his parents and, as a poor student, he had to eat melons left behind by traders to get by. But he studied hard and eventually got top grades in the imperial exam. He went on to become prime minister under emperor Taizong. One version of the story has Lu returning to the place where he once gathered fruit and building a pavilion there as a source of encouragement to others.

One of Taizu's unconventional policy reforms was to refrain from killing officials who disagreed with him. Those who flattered the emperor were still closest to the ruler's heart, but retaining those who challenged him ended the institutionalized promotion of yes men, and made it possible for 'friends with arguments' to broaden the emperor's knowledge base with inconvenient news and contrary opinions. There are many examples of heated debates in the court, about things like peace or war, private or public ownership. In general, the emperor preferred to punish misconduct with the loss of rank or exile rather than death.

If this makes it sound like a refined form of government based on the rule of law, that would not be entirely inaccurate, at least compared with previous and contemporary cultures. There are instances when the emperor wanted to be more lenient to favourites who had done something wrong but was reminded by his advisors that the law applied to them as well. However, there was still one individual at the top, with a mandate from heaven and not his people, and he could impose his will on his subjects by means of the sword if he chose to.

Some rulers certainly took liberties. There were persistent rumours that emperor Taizong took power by killing his brother Taizu, and it is at least likely that he had Taizu's two sons and his own younger half-brother murdered after he assumed power.

Another aspect of Song geopolitics has strengthened the impression of a process of demilitarization: the dynasty paid dearly to avoid war with dangerous rivals. The various steppe kingdoms in the north of China proved themselves too powerful to be defeated, and their desire to raid and loot neighbours always posed a threat. In 1005, to end an invasion by the Liao dynasty, the third Song emperor, Taizong's son Zhenzong (968–1022), bribed the invaders to leave and remain peaceful by offering them annual deliveries of silk and silver. Much of that money was recaptured by the empire since the end of hostilities allowed borders to be opened for trade.

Achieving peace in this way meant that the China of the previous Tang dynasty was not completely reunified. Song China was limited to slightly less than 3 million square kilometres, much smaller than today's China, but substantially bigger than the whole of Western Europe. This quest for peace has been interpreted as a weakness by some contemporaries and many later historians, who are used to thinking about power as aggressive and expansionary. It is true that, eventually, the Song dynasty met a gruesome, blood-soaked end after an invasion from the north, but that was after 319 years and eighteen Song emperors. Few imperial dynasties survived that long: neither the Tang, Ming nor Qing did. The Song emperors ruled for an average of eighteen years each, compared with an average of eight years for other Chinese dynasties.[14]

Like every other civilization, China had a slave population, often war prisoners and those who had to repay debts with their freedom. If the Song relied less on slavery than other Chinese dynasties, as is often suggested, it is probably mostly because its policy of peace meant that the country received fewer slaves taken in war.

The fact that the Song dynasty was based on peaceful co-existence provided the space for the economy and culture to flourish. A border that had regularly been crossed in both directions by different armies now remained peaceful for more than a hundred years. However, it was not that the alternative was a promising road not taken. It was only after having failed repeatedly to invade the north that the Song settled on this policy. When at times the peace faction lost ground at court and the Song did charge northwards, as in the 1081 attack on Western Xia and the 1206 attack on the Jin, they soon came to regret it.

As the military strategist Sun Tzu explained in the fifth century BC, the greatest skill is not to win one hundred battles, but to subdue the enemy without a fight.

Why there are so many Chinese

What really made Song China different was that it had a voluntary army. It did not have a feudal system, where aristocrats were given control of land and peasants in return for military service, and it relied much less than others on conscripting soldiers. The original explanation was probably that the only way to enlist troops during the chaos and migrations of the civil war era was to pay them well. But it would have huge implications for the future development of China.

If you are not dependent on services in kind, you don't have to control people and where they live. On the other hand, you do need lots of cash to buy such services from volunteers. In early Tang China, married couples were assigned a specific bit of land where they had to stay and pay taxes and perform labour services. People were only allowed to leave when the government wanted to populate a new area.

Song China did not need such controls and could loosen restrictions on internal migration. But it did more than that: it actively encouraged mobility and commerce, since it now depended on taxes from trade and urban consumption. Extraordinarily, the Song state granted many peasants private property rights to their land, including the right to bequeath, sell and lease it. Instead of forcibly relocating peasants to new territories as earlier and later rulers did, they were given a positive incentive to move: families who farmed uncultivated lands were awarded a permanent right to it.

Before the Song dynasty, Chinese tenants had become tied to the soil, and often, when manorial lords sold their land, tenants were included in the contract. In 1027, a decree tried to stop this practice: '*Henceforth*, tenants shall no longer need a permit from their masters if they are to move.'[15] However, we know that the letter of the law was often ignored. In some regions, large landed interests took over local administration, and fugitive tenants were forced to return. Courts had to repeat calls for tenants to 'be allowed to do as they please'.

There were serfs and there were tenants, bound to the land, but despite heavy pressure from large landowners, this did not develop into a feudal system. Manorial justice was not recognized by the law, and the estates were not run by a privileged military class. Land was bought and sold, and money transactions replaced many demands for shares of the harvest.

The share of farmers who owned and managed their own land increased despite population growth, and was around 60–70 per cent, even though the average farm was small. In the more commercial regions only 10–20 per cent of the rural population lacked land, which would have seemed unbelievable to contemporary Europeans. Going through all the numbers and comparing different regions, the Chinese economist William Guanglin Liu concludes: 'the relative decline in the poorest population was associated with the development of the market economy'.[16]

Property rights and the opportunity to sell at markets encouraged farmers to replace traditional practices with more productive ones. They took to terrace farming and made more extensive use of manure, river mud and lime as fertilizers. Complex forms of water control were developed with the introduction of dams, sluice-gates and waterwheels to raise water to let it flow to irrigation networks.

This period also saw the introduction of new crops that gave a higher yield or ripened earlier, like new strains of rice from what is now central Vietnam, which gave two harvests a year. Farmers began to experiment with drought-resistant varieties, red rice to reclaim saline land, fragrant rice to perfume dishes and rice especially suited for brewing. As they could now safely buy the rice or grain they needed at market prices, many farmers started to specialize in cash crops to sell, such as tea, sugar cane, mulberry and indigo.

With trade and better transportation, the surplus in one area could fill the empty stomachs in another. A common saying was that 'if [the fertile regions of] Su-chou and Hu-chou have a good harvest then the whole empire has a sufficiency', but soon it could be added that because of 'the new cultivation, reed-swamps and thickets being opened up each year and the dyked fields spreading ever wider, even if they do not enjoy a good harvest they still obtain enough to sustain them for several years'.[17]

We often associate China with rice and tea, but the Chinese had traditionally eaten wheat and millet, and had drunk wine. Tea was a drink for royals and nobles until Song farmers transformed tea cultivation from wild plants to controlled farming. It was not nature or tradition, but trade and productivity, that turned rice and tea into staples of the Chinese household. 'Both townsfolk and countrymen, whether in the fields or away from them, seek only for profit from morn till night', observed the suspicious official Ssu-ma Kunag in the late eleventh century.[18]

The government helped to develop agriculture by publishing books on new methods and crops. In less-developed regions, pictures were placed on the walls of government offices to illustrate ways of using the land more productively. Land under cultivation increased but, more importantly, the Chinese got much more from the land they used, as the innovations spread over the country. Agricultural output more than doubled in the Song era, feeding the population explosion. With the possible exception of India, China now had the world's most advanced agriculture and, in many areas, agricultural yields would not be surpassed until the twentieth century. 'It was thus that the foundations of China's enormous present population were laid', writes Mark Elvin, a leading scholar of its history.[19]

The agricultural improvements meant that a smaller proportion of the growing population was needed to feed the country. Some farmers lost their incomes, and many sold their land and moved to town. This set the stage for another radical transformation of Chinese society, an urban revolution, which would make China the world's most urbanized country.

Tearing down the walls

The capital of Kaifeng was the hub of inland water transportation, so it was natural for the Song to build an economy based on a lively river trade. China has impressive rivers like the Yellow River and the Yangtze, but these mostly run from the west to the east. With a massive expansion of canals, the Song Chinese linked the rivers into a single transport network that connected the large population in the north with the even larger population in the south. Transportation became much smoother through the invention of the pound lock, a chamber with gates at both ends, that made it possible to control the water level inside.

There were great improvements in shipping, with better construction and design for larger tonnage, higher speeds and enhanced manoeuvrability. New business organizations and ownership structures were created, and commercial bookkeeping and contracts were drawn up to launch even more ships. The resourcefulness was impressive. When the government began to requisition some merchant and fishing boats for official purposes, groups of shipmasters insured themselves against the threat of ruin by jointly paying for ships and offering some of them to officials.

All these developments reduced transportation costs and made it possible to feed growing cities. Thousands of barges constantly delivered food and other goods, and removed waste and refuse. Shipping brokers stood ready to buy and store cargo in warehouses, quickly turning round ships. Passenger ships up to 90 metres long ferried hundreds of people, accommodating them on two decks.

'All the economies of scale and advantages of specialization that Adam Smith was later to describe began to assert themselves', writes the American historian William H. McNeill.[20]

The river links integrated interior cities and provinces with coastal regions, and therefore it was only a small step further for China to start engaging in international trade. Chinese ships borrowed from Persian, Arab and South East Asian designs, and after 1090, they used a magnetic compass, with a needle pointing to the south, making it possible to navigate safely even in the darkness and cloudy nights.

Laws were passed to protect shipwrecked foreigners, which encouraged more ships to venture to Chinese shores. An ordinance of 1146 describes this success story: 'The profits of maritime trade contribute much to the national income. We ought to continue the old system by which people of faraway countries are encouraged to come and abundantly circulate goods and wealth.'[21]

Trade on such a large scale was made possible by the invention of paper money, at least 600 years before Europeans did. It was first created by private traders. They used to carry around strings of copper coins with a hole in them, but these were heavy and dangerous on long trips, so they started writing promissory notes and exchange bills on paper. The government soon recognized the benefits of this system and backed it up with use of force: on the notes produced by the government, the wording stated that counterfeiters would be beheaded.

Some fifty major urban centres emerged. The capital, Kaifeng, grew from 890,000 people in the 980s to 1.3 million in the 1100s, at a time when Paris had around 50,000 inhabitants and London fewer than 20,000. Traditionalists complained that the city's constant expansion meant that it no longer looked like a perfect square, but more like a 'crouching cow'.[22] But it was a very productive cow. Tax revenue came to surpass the Tang era by perhaps five- or seven-fold. By the late eleventh century, roughly two-thirds of revenue came from taxing non-agricultural sectors, especially in the form of excise taxes.[23]

As emperor Gaozong put it: 'Profits from maritime commerce are very great. If properly managed they can amount to millions [of strings of coins]. Is this not better than taxing the people?'[24]

The growing cities were populated with masses of landless migrants who took up jobs in service sectors or in the manufacturing of paper, silk, textiles and charcoal. Eastern cities rapidly spilled over the city walls and expanded into the surrounding countryside. Crowded cities set the stage for an unparalleled exchange of ideas, goods, services and influenza viruses.

Many urban workers produced metal products like nails, pans and needles, because, hundreds of years ahead of Europe, the Chinese had become masters of casting iron in a fully liquid form. A heat source was needed for the furnaces, and northern China had been deforested during the Tang dynasty, so these industries had to find an alternative source of fuel – fossil fuels. They had come across large coal deposits and learned to use coal as a fuel to produce pig iron. Coal was mined on a large scale for furnaces that produced high-quality iron and even steel. This provided farmers with better tools, merchants with coins, ships with nails, soldiers with armour and the salt industry with pans and vats.

How could the Chinese state make urbanization work on this scale? Because it didn't plan for it. Cities were spontaneously deregulated by the inhabitants themselves. Until this period, cities had been administrative areas, and urban life had been strictly regimented. Chang'an, the magnificent capital of

Tang China, typified the ideal city. Emperors had magnificent gardens and recreational places, but ordinary people were not given access to any public squares in case they used them for gatherings deemed potentially dangerous.

The city was divided into wards separated by walls of rammed earth, 3 metres high and heavily guarded. Residential areas were segregated according to class, so commoners and merchants did not mingle with aristocrats and officials. At sunset, drums were beaten 800 times and the gates were closed. Mounted soldiers policed the streets and captured anyone out after dark. In the morning, the sound of the drums could be heard again, and gates were opened. At noon, the only two markets that were legal, the western and the eastern markets, were opened, and then closed again at sunset.

Despite harsh measures, it was difficult to keep urbanites down. Residents often broke holes in the walls and built illegal gates, to trade informally or participate in all-night musical performances at religious shrines. Others built unauthorized shops and stalls. When Kaifeng took over as capital, such exceptions became the rule. The new line of Song emperors encouraged private initiative and market transactions to rebuild the city and began to loosen the restrictions on markets and mobility. A radical makeover of Chinese cities ensued.

People demolished the walls that had separated them and started to move about and mix freely. Instead of being assigned a particular area, people could settle and build homes wherever they could afford to. The old principle that commercial activity took place only in an officially designated place was abandoned and markets started to appear inside residential areas. Many people turned their street frontages into shops. The stern regulations of opening and closing times were neglected, and emperor Taizu extended the curfew to one o'clock in the morning. In the next century, it was scrapped entirely.

For the first time, markets and recreational activities could go on all night, creating the buoyant 24-hour Song city, as seen along the river in the *Qingming Festival* scroll. Everywhere, bathhouses, restaurants, teahouses, theatres, temples and brothels sprung up, as well as workshops, stalls, markets and shops, with all basic necessities and a wide selection of foreign luxuries.

A 1088 document describes international traders who bring a wide variety of overseas goods: 'Although these are without exception prohibited yet such is the eagerness of petty persons for profits that they will scale the mountains and sail the seas, devising a hundred clever schemes, so that it is quite impossible to prevent some inflow of these articles.'[25]

In his history of this era, Dieter Kuhn writes: 'Song Society enjoyed a degree of early laissez-faire liberalism that distinguished it from contemporary societies.'[26] But, interestingly, this was not based on an elaborate plan from the top. It came from the citizens on the ground. And often the government fought hard to retain control. For a long time and in most provinces, it held lucrative monopolies on wine, tea and most controversially on salt. This government policy was attacked in a famous poem by the influential official Su Shi, for which he would later be exiled.

Unlike in the Arab culture, merchants and markets were not highly esteemed. Much like the ancient Greeks, Confucius had claimed that the mind of superior men was filled with righteousness, whereas the mind of the mean man was filled with profits. 'Most of the foolish populace give priority to business activities and wealth', grumbled one writer. One of his contemporaries agreed that the best life was obviously that of a Confucian scholar, but if that was unachievable, becoming a merchant or artisan was at least no more disgraceful than becoming a spirit-medium, a Buddhist or a Taoist, and better than becoming a beggar or a thief.[27]

The reason why Song society became so thoroughly commercialized was simply that this is how the Chinese behaved from the moment the controls were slightly loosened, and free markets created a tremendous increase in economic activity and wealth. This of course benefited the emperor and the scholar–officials as well. In 977, emperor Taizong banned officials from using agents in commercial activities, but this had little effect since the practice was so enticing. 'Great ships sail only for profit', as the poet Li Qingzhao observed.[28]

Ten thousand things

Song China was a relatively inclusive society, with more people from more places free to try to enter civil service, test ideas, build businesses and trade. But these were primarily men. In the 5.2 metres length of the famous handscroll painting of the Qingming festival, we find no more than about twenty women, and women of high status were not seen outdoors unless accompanied by men. This was probably the ideal of Confucian moralists, who wanted to reduce women to child-bearing servants of their parents-in-law, but the dynamic Song era provided women with other opportunities. Unlike in European cultures, a woman had rights to property and inheritance, and this was kept separate from her husband. If she was divorced or widowed, she could keep her land and possessions and bring them in to a new marriage. In cities, women often went into business and ran shops, restaurants and guesthouses.

On the other hand, by law, men – fathers, grandfathers and husbands – were the rulers of the family, and the woman's place was often supposed to be in the home. Partly as a reaction to female freedoms, the ghastly custom of foot binding took hold in wealthy households and spread through the country. Very young girls had their feet bound with ever tighter bandages (often breaking bones) to keep them small and – according to the perception of the times – beautiful. It made walking painful, if not impossible; women who had been disabled in this way needed help to move about and mostly stayed at home. But it also increased the status of the family, since it showed that the woman did not have to work. The practice would not be banned until 1912.

When it came to intellectual culture, the Song Empire was much more progressive. Just like the Abbasid caliphs, the Song emperors commissioned texts that promoted their ideology and worldview. Taizong and his successors had Confucian classics printed and initiated historical works. In 984, a group of scholars finished a massive encyclopaedia with 5,363 sections about everything from the military, dynasties and barbarians to anatomy, flora and fauna. It is said that it took the emperor a whole year to read the manuscript and come up with suggested edits.

This was a literary culture where books were mass produced. Since the ninth century, the Chinese had carved words and illustrations into wooden blocks that were inked and pressed against paper. The printing of older works on science and technology spurred an interest to mastering and surpassing those achievements.

In the 1040s, the first movable type was invented, supposedly by the blacksmith and alchemist Bi Sheng. Since it was common practice to attribute all inventions to the emperor's court, no matter who came up with them, we should probably take it seriously when an invention is attributed to a commoner. Instead of having each block consisting of an entire page of text, he used ceramic types fastened on an iron plate with glue. By reheating, these could be removed and fastened again in a new pattern for the next page. Ceramic types were fragile, but their use inspired further experiments, until wooden movable type was developed in the late thirteenth century.

This climate of innovation did not stop scholars from despairing that the printing press was the end of culture. Some worried that the quality of books and of scholarship would decline. Zhu Xi (1130–1200), the great philosopher of neo-Confucianism, worried that with cheap printed books people would read inattentively and stop learning texts by heart.[29] Ironically, his own system of ideas would be the greatest beneficiary of the new technology, as aspiring civil servants over the whole empire could suddenly afford to buy Confucian classics.

Neo-Confucianism is a Western word for the revival of Chinese philosophy under the Song dynasty. It built on Confucius's worldly thoughts about human relationships and the cultivation of virtue, but added elements from two other important schools of thought, Taoism and Buddhism (while also reacting against them). It rose to prominence as urbanization and commerce began to generate new questions about the relationship between tradition and innovation, faith and reason, social responsibilities and individualism. In this period, Confucianism came to be interpreted in a much more open and individualist way than at other times of Chinese history. People were to be equipped with education to cultivate themselves and understand the world, and not just to become obedient servants of the state.

Zhu Xi's thoughts came to be most influential. In reaction to Buddhism, he downplayed the role of the supernatural in the world of human affairs and developed a more secular metaphysics. He portrayed the universe as good and ordered, and humanity as having the potential to be good, but requiring education and self-cultivation. He described man as a pearl in a bowl of dirty water. The pearl might look lustreless, but remove it from the bowl and it suddenly shines. This left a prominent role for a practical rationality that investigates itself and the natural world. Reality has a permanent existence and it is possible to discover patterns in it; therefore there is a role for scientists and artists who want to explore it.

As another important neo-Confucian, Cheng Hao, argued, the universal principle does not have a separate Platonic existence, but exists in everything that can be experienced with our senses. Therefore it is worth exploring 'the wonderful mystery of principle in ten thousand things'.[30] This kind of thinking was a reflection of the amazing accomplishments of practical merchants and scientists in Song society, while at the same time providing them with ideological legitimacy.

Neo-Confucianism became state ideology, but not orthodoxy. Emperors who espoused Confucian ideals could also be followers of Taoism and Buddhism. Unlike in the late Tang dynasty, dissenting ideas could be expressed and spread. Interestingly, it was only towards the end of the Song dynasty, when it was fighting for its life against invaders, that neo-Confucianism moved towards becoming a state orthodoxy. In the cultural atmosphere of the golden age, artists moved away from the otherworldly and developed a highly sophisticated representational art, with detailed and differentiated paintings of plants, animals, landscapes and street life. At times, the artistic approach could seem almost scientific. Poems were written about less dignified things than previously, such as earthworms and lice.

Scholars studied the world around them systematically. In subjects like chemistry and pharmacology there were sophisticated attempts to adapt theoretical systems to new empirical findings. Some scholars engaged in experiments, and new facts and relationships were used to develop new technologies.

Scientists in this period created a water-powered clock tower, a slowly rotating artificial sky often called the world's first planetarium, a detailed relief map of China, representing the three dimensions of the landscape, and wrote the first systematic treatise on forensic medicine. A husband-and-wife team compiled the *Catalogue of the Inscriptions on Stone and Bronze*, which recorded 2,000 ancient inscriptions. A monumental history of China by Sima Guang was pioneering, not because of its 354 chapters, but because thirty of them were devoted to methodology and how to reach conclusions about facts when sources disagree.

A second chance

Song China in the early twelfth century was unlike anything the world had seen before. China's population had been stable at around 50 million people throughout the first millennium. Song China covered a smaller territory than China had previously, but spectacularly increased its population from perhaps 30 million in 1003 to possibly as many as 110 million in 1120. It was probably twice the whole population of Europe at the time, and close to a third of the whole world's population.

The economy, however, grew even faster. Intensive farming and specialized manufacturing lifted productivity to unprecedented heights. According to one interpretation of tax returns, by the late eleventh century, iron output had increased six-fold, to a level almost as high as the whole of Europe managed to produce in 1700.[31] What we have here is 'modern style intensive growth', concludes Stephen Davies.[32] Not just the extensive growth where we use more resources, but the kind where you get more bang for your workhours and inputs.

Song culture seemed absolutely unstoppable – except possibly by mounted warriors from the north. In the early twelfth century, the Jurchen people in Manchuria (north-east China) rose up in rebellion against the reigning Liao dynasty, which existed in parallel with the Song dynasty and had been pacified by a constant flow of Song money. Their new Jin dynasty, which replaced Liao, didn't stop there but kept pushing southwards. In January 1127 they conquered and sacked the Song capital of Kaifeng. They captured the emperor Qinzong and demoted him to a commoner.

This could very well have been the end of the Song if it wasn't for the emperor's brother, later known as Gaozong (1107–1187), who escaped and declared himself the new emperor. He was constantly on the move to escape capture and, when the city of Yangzhou fell in February 1129, Gaozong galloped to a crossing point on the Yangtze river and made it onto a ferry boat at the last moment. Jin riders were just minutes away from ending the dynasty.

He fled to Hangzhou on the east coast, at the southern terminus of the Grand Canal, which would eventually become the new capital. The Jin armies soon followed him there and occupied the city. The Song court's last resort was the open sea, and they fled in junks. The Jin warriors waited in vain for their return, but when the summer brought heat and rain, they had to turn back north.

Their decision to retreat and then negotiate a peace agreement was considered shameful by many. The unfortunate general Yue Fei, who was poisoned for his desire to keep waging war, is still seen by some Chinese nationalists as a martyr, and is often exploited by Communist Party propaganda. In 2023, his death was the plot of the Chinese blockbuster movie *Full River Dead*. However, this series of events also saved the Song dynasty and allowed it to live on for another 152 years, albeit in a smaller territory. This state is now usually known as 'Southern Song', just as the whole territory it had previously governed, in retrospect, came to be called 'Northern Song'.

In some ways, previous trends towards innovation and individualism were radicalized in this young region, which lacked the long traditions of Kaifeng. A poem by Lu You in 1187 expresses the gloom of some scholar–officials in a city increasingly shaped by markets and masses:

> The Mayor? The governor? We don't even know their names,
> What's it to us who wields power in the palace?
> See what Heaven gives me – luck thin as paper.
> Now I know that merchants are the happiest of men.[33]

Private initiative and investment became even more important now that an entirely new capital had to be built; in a very short time, Hangzhou became the world's largest, richest and liveliest city. There was a scramble to build as fast and high as possible for a city that more than doubled in population in just a few decades. In 1270, there were probably over a million people in a city that previously had only 200,000. Arab travellers say that they saw residential homes of three to five storeys and only small alleyways in between.

The city quickly filled up with shops and stalls and soon there were twenty-three entertainment districts, crowded with singers, dancers, poets, storytellers, puppet players, comedians, acrobats, jugglers and boxers. The writer Wu Zimu declared it 'the hub of the universe', where there was demand for everything and every demand was met. 'Vegetables from the east, water from the west, wood from the south and rice from the north', was a popular local free-trade saying.[34]

For the first time, the Song also built a permanent navy to protect this trade and its borders. Now the sea and the river were to be its Great Wall (referring to China's ancient wall against northern invaders). 'The age was one of continual innovation', writes Joseph Needham,[35] exemplified by the new treadmill-operated paddle-wheel crafts. The Song had used gunpowder in creative and deadly ways for a long time. In the early twelfth century they came up with the first gun, by exploding gunpowder in a tube, initially made of wood and bamboo, and eventually made of metal. The Song navy then used ship-mounted catapults that threw gunpowder bombs. Using this technology it could defeat an invading Jin navy on the Yangtzee in 1161, even though it was five times larger.

Southern Song lost access to the rich coal deposits of the north. The south was not as well endowed, but ingenious industrialists found ways to make use of the cheaper and dirtier coal that was abundant there. Soon iron production was back on track, and they also discovered a method to extract copper from the dirty by-products of ironworking.

Cities continued to expand and their populations continued to grow. The city T'ing-chou in Fukien, which had built its walls in the middle of the eleventh century, soon found that it had only three of its quarters (*fang*) inside these walls, and twenty-three outside them. Cities broke through walls and markets through regulations, with creative culture following through the cracks. Dieter Kuhn writes 'the laissez-faire attitude that can be observed in economic matters pervaded all areas of private life, from preferences in house building and fashion to matters of hygiene, amusement and charity'.[36] A spectacular diversity of ideas and styles started to proliferate, as people experimented with religion, music, art, ceramics and food.

Intellectuals complained that people started building in eccentric styles and adopted the foppish fashion of sitting on chairs instead of on woven bamboo. One of them was particularly upset with the kind of young men who 'wrap themselves in strange turbans and bizarre garments... to the point where everyone else is heartily weary of watching it. There is no longer the pure simplicity of former times.'[37]

Building codes, dress regulations and traditions had a hard time keeping up. Sumptuary laws on personal expenditure were apparently systematically disregarded by the lower classes: 'These days the families of artisans and merchants trail white silks and brocades, and adorn themselves with jades and pearls. In nine cases out of ten, if one looks a person over from head to foot, one will find that he is breaking the law.'[38]

The Song gentleman was expected to master painting, calligraphy, Chinese chess and the lute, but there were no limits to people's pastimes as they grew richer and more experimental. Associations thrived as urbanites found new interests and organized themselves with other like-minded people into specialized associations. Patricia Ebrey has found a 1235 document that mentions Hangzhou associations such as the West Lake Poetry Society, Tea Society, Physical Fitness Club, Luminous Society, Occult Club, Young Girl's Chorus, Plants and Fruits Club, Exotic Foods Club, Horse Lover's Club, Antique Collectors' Club, Refined Music Society and various sports clubs.[39]

We should not let the Monty Python-esque character of names like the Society for Vigorous Debates and the Society of Painted Leather for the Friends of Shadow Plays deceive us. This represented an explosion of civil society, where voluntary interest-based associations started to compete with those based on kin and class.

In urban Chinese culture, there was 'a new emphasis on the importance of self-discovery and the self-improvement of the individual'. It was as if citizens could suddenly decide what to think and how to think, an interesting tension arose between social duties and commitments to the self. Among some, there appeared to be 'a desire to mold the individual personality like a work of art'.[40] It sounds oddly similar to popular descriptions of the Italian Renaissance, and one is tempted to think about what could have become of this emerging cultural tendency if it had been allowed to continue unhindered.

The same goes for many of the economic and technological developments. Thousands of Chinese merchant vessels were plying the oceans, with stern-post rudders for more control, making use of Chinese inventions like the compass, capstan, anchor and drop-keel. Their hulls were divided in separate watertight compartments in a way European hulls wouldn't be for 600 years. Stunned visitors described ships with four decks and four masts, rigging twelve sails.

A 1178 account described the awe-inspiring spectacle: 'The ships which sail the southern sea and south of it are like giant houses. When their sails are spread they are like great clouds in the sky. Their rudders are several tens of feet long. A single ship carries several hundred men, and has in its stores a year's supply of grain.'[41] If the Chinese had wanted to, they could have sailed around the world.

Another intriguing development was the new textile machines, possibly first invented to deal with a shortage of cloth. Spindle-wheels, silk-reeling frames and pedal-powered looms made it possible to produce fashionable textile products in large quantities. A very large mechanical spinning device for silk had been invented in the twelfth century, and it was later adapted for hemp thread. Muscle, animal or water was used to drive thirty-two spindles that could produce almost 60 kilograms of thread in 24 hours. It seems to have been widely in use, especially in areas close to running water.

A poem by Wang Chen expresses admiration of the technology:

> There is one driving-belt for wheels both great and small;
> When one wheel turns, the others all turn with it.
> The rovings are transmitted evenly from the
>   bobbin-rollers.
> The threads wind by themselves onto the reeling-frame.

While some of the poetic ambiance might be lost in translation, it is obvious that this was an expression of a culture with a sense of wonder for automation and progress.

> It takes a spinner many days to spin a hundred catties
>   [roughly 70 kilograms],
> But with water power it may be done with supernatural
>   speed.[42]

The similarity between this device and an early eighteenth-century European machine for retwisting flax thread 'is so striking that suspicions of an ultimate Chinese origin for it... are almost irresistible', writes Mark Elvin. The idea is fairly close in design to Richard Arkwright's water frame, which has been credited as an important stage in Britain's Industrial Revolution; it just lacked the rollers to straighten the fibres out.

Elvin thinks that 'if the line of advance which it represented had been followed a little further then medieval China would have had a true industrial revolution in the production of textiles over four hundred years before the West.'[43]

It is a mind-boggling thought. The obstacle in the way of further progress in textile automation was not a lack of scientific knowledge. Further tinkering and trial and error should have been able to come up with the fairly modest changes needed to make such machines more efficient. Rather, the obstacle 'must have lain in a weakening of those economic and intellectual forces which make for invention and innovation'.[44]

And it wasn't even a very subtle obstacle that leaves historians guessing. It was the horsemen of the apocalypse. Thousands upon thousands of them.

The Mongol horde

In 1200, Song China had the world's richest and most integrated and monetized economy, with a merchant navy that had the potential to discover the world, an industrial development that Western Europe would not be able to match for 400 years, a restless civil society and an emerging scientific and philosophical enlightenment. An alien visiting planet earth would no doubt have concluded that this was the place to watch.

But China's joyful curiosity and spectacular line of progress was not allowed to develop further, because it had to focus on its immediate survival. Its unprecedented wealth once again attracted the attention of nomad raiders, this time the most persistent and destructive of them all, the Mongols.

In 1227, Genghis Khan ordered his troops to attack the Jin, and at first the Song thought they had discovered an ally against the old enemy that had deprived them of northern China. But, as soon as the Jin were defeated, in 1234, the Mongols turned their attention to the richest part of China and started invading the Song region of Sichuan. Because of the terrain, resources and technology of the Song empire, this would be the most difficult of all Mongol conquests. Thirty years later, the frontiers had barely shifted. The war lasted almost half a century. Six Mongol emperors died without seeing their troops enter Hangzhou.

However, the Mongols persisted and defeated surrounding kingdoms to be able to attack from all sides. Just as other golden ages had done when they faced an existential threat, China now abandoned its tradition of intellectual openness to create an official state orthodoxy. In 1241, Emperor Lizong posthumously ennobled the most important neo-Confucian thinkers. The five great sages thereby secured a place in Confucian temples, and ceremonies and sacrifices were held in their honour, attended by teachers and students.

What made the Mongols such formidable enemies was their absorption of technology from those whose territories they invaded, as the Romans had done with great success. They could use manpower, resources and innovations from all their conquered Eurasian territories, and for decades they had been zealous students of the Song Chinese themselves, via trade and osmosis, but also from defectors and war captives.

In this way they had gained gunpowder weapons and the secrets of iron production. Their feared horsemen were now armoured, and their arrow tips were no longer made of horn and bone, but of iron. The rivers still functioned as a barrier, and the Song navy was vastly superior. Their paddle-wheeled boats, powered by windlasses or treadmills, were fast and could easily outrun and outmanoeuvre the rafts and inflated skins used by the Mongols. But this changed when a Song commander who had defected suggested that the Mongols could create their own navy, based on Chinese models.

Nevertheless, by 1268, the Mongol offensive was stuck outside China's strongest fortresses, the twin cities of Xiangyang and Fancheng. Unable to break the walls, Kublai Khan, Genghis's grandson, sent for two Muslim experts in siege machines from Mosul, Iraq, where the Mongols had just ended the Abbasid dynasty. The pair built powerful counterweight trebuchets that were more accurate and had a longer range than anything in the east. When these weapons, called 'Muslim trebuchets' by Chinese historians, were first used in 1273, it is said that the noise shook heaven and earth. Buildings, walls and turrets were pulverized by heavy rocks. After years of resistance, the twin cities fell in days and the road lay open to the south.

In cities that resisted, the population was massacred, so as the Mongols approached Hangzhou in early 1276, terrified Chinese defected in great numbers. In February, the Grand Empress Dowager brought the five-year-old emperor with her to the Mongol camp to capitulate. By all accounts they were treated well. The emperor's brothers had escaped though, and some Song loyalists fought on in what was to be their last rear-guard action. Eventually, the invaders caught up with the seven-year-old emperor Bing and his troops at Yamen in Guangdong. There the Mongol fleet, commanded by a Chinese and a Tangut, destroyed the last remnants of the Song navy on 19 March 1279.

The Song loyalists had been mocked for centuries for choosing retreat and negotiations when cornered instead of sacrificing their lives. Now, when all hope was lost, in a final act of defiance, many officials, families and concubines committed suicide by throwing themselves into the sea. The chief councillor of Bing of Song, the last emperor of this long and proud dynasty, embraced the small boy and hurled them both into the sea, choosing death over defeat.

One of the Mongols' captives was an earlier chief councillor, Wen Tianxiang. Conscious of his status and competence, Kublai Khan offered him a place in his service, but Wen declined. He declared that he was loyal to the Song and could never serve its subjugator. After four years of imprisonment, torture and temptations, Wen maintained his refusal to serve the new rulers. In January 1283, Wen was taken to a crowded marketplace in the new Mongol capital, now called Beijing, to be executed. His last recorded words were: 'I have completed my service.'[45]

As the great Song writer Li Qingzhao had urged her compatriots in one of her most famous poems: 'In life, we should be heroes among men, after death, we should be heroes among ghosts.'

The Ming counter-revolution

The Mongols wrought havoc with cities and farmland, and the population declined sharply. But Kublai Khan had no ambition to destroy China, with all its wealth, culture and technology. He wanted to rule it. He preserved many of its old policies, and Mongol China was quickly sinicized. Combined with trade and ideas from all over conquered Eurasia, now reconnected via the Silk Road, the new Mongol dynasty could maintain a rich and advanced civilization.

But, no matter how much Kublai Khan enjoyed the prosperity that came from demilitarized rule and free markets, a warlord in the habit of commanding people and taking what he wants could not be expected to maintain such institutions in the long run. They were often unintentionally undermined.

Increasingly, government appointments were given to Mongols and became hereditary, and self-owning farmers were pushed out by military farms. The government began to rely more on poll taxes and compulsory labour, and increasingly restricted overseas trade.

The growth of major cities stopped and sometimes reversed itself around the early fourteenth century, further diminishing economic prospects. Ironically, the gender preferences that many traditionalist Confucians had tried to push through in vain were now realized by invading nomads, who disdained the rights women had acquired in an urban civilization and began to dismantle their rights to independence and property.

Intellectual horizons that had been constantly expanding were now confined within more sharply defined constraints. Thinkers and artists stopped exploring the world and turned inwards. The art historian Max Loehr has commented that, around 1300, the meaning of art changed profoundly in China. The Song dynasty had been an era of magnificent representational art, the last word in 'objective and highly differentiated images of the visible world', described by Loehr as 'an almost scientific character'. But, after the Song era, the objective world was discarded and replaced with an 'expressionistic, or intellectualized art that was no longer concerned with the image of nature or external reality'.[46]

This was still just a managed decline. The collapse came later. A series of epidemics and natural disasters in a civilization with smaller margins created famine and stoked rebellions in the 1340s. The initiative was seized by a group called the Red Turbans, who wanted to throw out the Mongol barbarians and restore what they thought of as traditional Chinese culture. In 1368, one of their warlords founded the Ming dynasty, which would launch a sweeping anti-modern revolution, marking the beginning of the end of China's long-standing international superiority.

Ming rulers wanted stability after two decades of chaos, and Chinese isolation after rule by Mongols. They also blamed the Mongol invasions on Song openness, which is ironic given that few cultures managed to hold Mongol armies back as long as the Song had. Their first act set the standard. When Ming troops came upon wondrous mechanical gadgets in the Mongol palace, elaborate waterwheel clocks, dragon-fountains with balls dancing on jets, dragon-headed mechanical boats, dragons spouting perfumed mist and a tiger robot, their first emperor ordered the troops to smash them to pieces with hammers and axes.[47]

The Ming wanted a stable society where relations and hierarchies were static, so they did all the things the Song dynasty had done, but in reverse. According to the economist William Guanglin Liu, the Ming dynasty established a pre-industrial 'command economy', where market mechanisms were replaced by coercive top-down controls. 'People were required to provide services according to status, and their duties would be transferred to the succeeding generation when the seniors passed away.'[48] Millions of Chinese were forced to build the new Ming cities, renovate the Grand Canal and serve the grain shipments to cities.

Free movement was ended. Peasants and artisans were confined to their registered places and were no longer allowed to travel within the country without a government permit. In their first century of rule, perhaps as many as 11 million people, more than a sixth of the population, were forcibly located to areas in the north and south-west that had been devastated.

Around 1400, ordinary people were forbidden to use gold or silver, and the value of paper money collapsed, since the emperor funded the army via money printing, causing hyperinflation.

But the government itself did not think it needed a monetized economy, since it used forced labour for public projects and took up taxes in kind. On markets, people used cloth, grain, rice and cowrie shells as money when they could not access smuggled silver. But not much of the commercial economy remained in any case. The size of urban markets and long-distance trade shrank by more than 90 per cent between 1077 and 1381.[49]

The Ming emperors feared that overseas trade would create centrifugal coastal powers that were difficult to control, so, step by step, international trade was banned. When 'the ignorant people' of the coast nonetheless stayed 'in communication with the outer barbarians' (as a decree formulated it), they simply prohibited the use of foreign perfumes and goods in 1394, to reduce the incentive for smuggling.[50] Foreign trade was made punishable by death, and eventually even coastal trade was banned, resulting in the expression 'there was not an inch of planking on the seas'.

All international trade was monopolized with massive official tribute missions. Exploiting Song advances in shipbuilding, between 1405 and 1433, the Ming sent a gigantic fleet on seven voyages to create a system of tributary states around the Indian Ocean. According to some estimates, the flagship was 135 metres long (in comparison, Columbus's 1492 ship *Santa Maria* measured some 20 metres).

But even government-led exploration was too much in this isolationist climate. In 1433, the emperor ordered an end to the voyages, and three years later, the construction of seagoing ships was banned. And so the world's leading naval power abandoned the oceans, just as Europeans a world away were discovering them. The greatest armada the world had ever seen was left to rot, and the Chinese soon lost the knowledge to build such large ships.

Where Song China was diverse and experimental, Ming society turned into a live-action roleplay set in the imagined good old days. The emperor decreed that all clothes and hairstyles should revert to the standards of the Tang, 500 years earlier. In 1392, men were banned from shaving their head to leave a strand of hair, as this was associated with the Mongol style. If an offender was discovered, the barber and his customer would be castrated, and the family of the offender would be exiled. Merchants and commoners who wore leather boots, transgressing the distinction between the upper and lower classes, were beheaded in public.[51]

The art scholar Max Loehr observes a new influence on art in this period. While artists after Song abandoned the search for objective representation, at least they explored subjective expressions. During the Ming era, art explored art. The artists reproduced styles of the past and engaged in allusion and commentary instead of innovation. Where Song artists tried to make representations of the world, the accomplished painters of the Ming era tried to make representations of previous representations. In effect, they dabbled more in art history than art.[52]

A few generations later, the influential writer Wang Yangming (1472–1529) even overturned the neo-Confucian emphasis on the natural world and its patterns. To him, only the mind was real, and knowledge of the good came from intuition, not instruction. Reality did not exist independent of the mind, and therefore empirical study lost the significant position it had during the Song. Since no sensory experience could challenge such a complex metaphysics, nothing was really puzzling or challenging, and therefore all the empirical anomalies that troubled European scientists at that time, forcing them to investigate and develop better instruments, could safely be ignored.

Wang's undermining of science and philosophy had a similar impact to Augustine's in Christianity and Ghazali's in Islam.

His School of Mind pushed out the investigation of ten thousand things. 'The consequences of this philosophy for Chinese science were disastrous', argues Mark Elvin.[53]

The whole traditionalist counter-revolution was a cataclysm for China, bringing an astonishing era of progress to a dreary end. Eventually, the Ming court could not even adjust its calendar since the occupants of the now hereditary posts at the directorate of astronomy didn't know how to do it.

According to Liu, China's estimated real income per capita dropped by half between 1080 and 1400.[54] At the same time, taxes as a share of income almost doubled and farmers had to contribute involuntary labour. In the records of two merchant brothers Liu has found evidence of six farmers who were forced to sell their land to them in 1401 to raise money to travel to the assigned state depots (often in the capital) to leave the grain the government demanded of them in taxes.[55]

In the mid-sixteenth century, a compiler of a new gazetteer lamented what had become of a once-rich coastal city:

> The times have changed and human circumstances altered, so as to be totally different from how they were in the past. Ever since the prohibition of maritime trade, walls were built where the official troops stand guard, sources of profit are cut off, and all traces of the past [prosperity] have disappeared. People see nothing out of the ordinary, nor do they admire foreign objects. Their only occupations were farming, fishing, and woodcutting, and for women, nothing more than domestic chores.[56]

Writing in 1859, John Stuart Mill used the example of this now desperately poor country as a warning. Despite all its talent and its rich history, China had become stationary, and this fate could befall any nation, Mill thought. The problem he identified was that China had succeeded in the effort, shared by collectivists in Europe, in 'making a people all alike, all governing their thoughts and conduct by the same maxims and rules; and these are the fruits'.[57]

Summary

No classic civilization came as close to unleashing an industrial revolution and creating the modern world as Song China. Its achievements in technology, production and urbanization would not be equalled by Europe for half a millennium.

Similar to previous golden ages, it started with a major military victory that allowed the ruler to secure peace and stimulate trade. Taizu demilitarized the government and established a system of rule of law and property rights. Combined with the relative meritocracy of the civil service, this allowed people from new backgrounds to contribute their ideas and talents to Chinese society. One result was a wide variety of experiments and competition in the economy, but also in art, music, religion and fashion. China became a wildly innovative society.

In China, it seems to have been the decision to build a professional army paid by taxes instead of relying on services in kind that set this fascinating sequence of changes in motion. The dynasty abolished restrictions of movement and encouraged commerce, monetization and mobility to secure tax revenue. Liberated farmers adopted new crops and technologies that boosted productivity, feeding a population that more than doubled over a short period.

In turn, this led to massive waves of urbanization. China had cities of a million people at a time when London had fewer than

20,000 inhabitants. The Chinese started to tear down the walls and regulations that had kept urban life static. Crowded cities became dynamic centres of commerce and intellectual life where methods and fashions constantly developed and changed. Just as in previous golden ages, economic development was followed by, and further inspired by, a culture of learning and philosophical flourishing, where thinkers began to examine traditions and relationships and debate better ways.

All of this gave Huangzhou, capital of Southern Song, a reputation as 'the hub of the universe', just as Baghdad had been called 'the crossroads of the universe'. 'Merchants are happier than mayors', concluded one poem, reminding us of the observer of the Abbasid era who thought that merchants were more powerful than viziers. Revolutions in ironmaking, textile machines and ocean traffic seemed to point the way to an age of discovery, industry and prosperity.

However, there was a sudden weakening of the intellectual forces that create experiments and innovations. It began as Song China had to fight for its survival against Mongol invaders. Society responded to these threats with a turn towards intellectual orthodoxy in a similar way to what happened in Athens, Rome and Baghdad. A new, reactionary mentality stifled innovation in art and philosophy. In place of 'ten thousand things', Song China put one single acceptable answer.

After 1368, the Ming dynasty dealt the death blow to the golden age with an ideology that deliberately rejected innovation, trade and mobility. It erected a command economy that replaced markets and mobility with central control and hereditary relationships, similar to the way late Roman emperors and Abbasid caliphs undermined their economies. International trade was prohibited.

China's new rulers promised stability after all the uncertainty and unpredictability – and instead delivered 500 years of stagnation. This turned the world's most advanced civilization into a poor and weak country, attacked and humiliated by previously insignificant European powers in the nineteenth century. China would return to the global stage only in the late twentieth century when Deng Xiaoping once again opened up its economy under a slogan that sounds oddly like a Song era motto: 'reform and opening up'.

5

RENAISSANCE ITALY

The Rebirth of Law, Literature and Libertas

[T]wo things, two little things, which belong to that age more than to any of its predecessors: the discovery of the world and the discovery of man.

JULES MICHELET, WHO COINED THE WORD 'RENAISSANCE', 1855[1]

It is but in our own day that men dare boast that they see the dawn of better things… Now, indeed, may every thoughtful spirit thank God that it has been permitted to him to be born in this new age, so full of hope and promise, which already rejoices in a greater array of nobly-gifted souls than the world has seen in the thousand years that have preceded it.

MATTEO PALMIERI, 1436[2]

Just to think that in 1505 an idler on the Piazza della Signoria [in Florence] could have in a matter of days bumped into Leonardo da Vinci, Raphael, Michelangelo, and Botticelli; such an efflorescence of creative talent may be never again repeated in any city.

VACLAV SMIL[3]

In the origin stories of modern Europe, the Italian Renaissance between the fourteenth and sixteenth centuries holds a privileged position. It is often seen as the very evidence of a natural continuity between the Judeo-Christian heritage and Graeco-Roman culture that sets Europe apart and, according to some, makes it superior. Apparently, the epoch and its aesthetics hold a particular appeal for the nationalist Right. In 2021, a collaboration between nationalist populist parties from Italy, Hungary and Poland promised a new 'European Renaissance' that would make Europe great and Christian again.

Therefore it is ironic that the Italian Renaissance in fact emerged in opposition to the traditional Christian elite, and that much of the inspiration for it was provided by the Chinese, the Arabs and a pagan Graeco-Roman culture that the Christian Church had tried to extinguish. Merchants from north Italian cities came across these cultures on their travels, and one reason why Europe was so open to these influences was a palpable sense of inferiority. Poor, uneducated Europeans realized that they had everything to gain from the ideas and methods of more advanced civilizations. As the Spanish priest Hugo of Santalla wrote: 'it befits us to imitate the Arabs especially, for they are as it were our teachers and the pioneers'.[4]

A major influence were the stories of astonishing wealth and technology in the Far East. In 1274, Marco Polo, a young Venetian merchant and explorer, reached China after a long journey with his father and uncle. Kublai Khan took a great liking to him and used him as a foreign emissary throughout South East Asia. After seventeen years in Asia, Marco Polo returned to Europe. Venice was at war with Genoa at the time, and Marco Polo was imprisoned by the Genoese. He started sharing his stories with a fellow inmate, who wrote them down and turned them into one of the few international bestsellers before the printing press. All over Europe, readers marvelled at his descriptions of a magical empire with vast transport networks, money made of paper, and 'black stones' that they dug up and burned instead of firewood. Even in decline after the end of the Song dynasty, China seemed so incredibly advanced and prosperous that many assumed that Marco Polo had made it all up (and not just the parts he did in fact make up – like Christians moving mountains with a prayer, and reporting himself as at a battle that actually took place before he left Italy).

Visiting the old Song capital of Hangzhou, apparently fifteen times bigger than his native Venice, the thrilled Marco Polo described it as 'the greatest city which may be found in the world, where so many pleasures may be found that one fancies oneself in paradise'. And the Yangtzee had 'a great number of vessels, and more wealth and merchandize than on all the rivers and all the seas of Christendom put together!' Markets were 'so well provided with every amenity that it is a veritable marvel'.

The stories told by Marco Polo and other adventurers, and the exquisite silk, spices and porcelain imported, whetted the European appetite to set sail, to trade and to raid, but most of all to imitate. The insight that very large ships with multiple masts had been built, and could stay at sea for extended periods, spurred innovation. Medieval Europe suddenly started building ships with stern-post rudders instead of steering oars, which had offered almost no control in storms on the high seas. Europeans soon also fitted their vessels with three masts, to be able to deal with adverse winds, basically building the kinds of ship that were needed to go on journeys of discovery.

With the extremely limited knowledge that Europeans had of the real China and its production methods, these stories mostly showed them that something different, richer and more exciting was possible and could be worth trying. As a modern scholar argues: 'As a place that at once provided material inspiration while at the same time remaining elusive, China engendered an assiduous inquisitiveness: curiosity in the modern sense.'[5]

Arab teachers

An even more stimulating import came from the Arabs, as their ideas began to seep into Christianity. Italian trading ports such as Pisa had acquired huge collections of books captured during the Crusades of the eleventh and twelfth centuries. And Sicily, which had been Byzantine–Greek, then Arabic, and then Latin after the Norman invasion in the late eleventh century, became a multicultural centre, where scholars and books from the Arab world met the European. The Scottish scholar Michael Scot, working as an advisor at the court of Frederick II, the Holy Roman emperor ruling from Sicily, translated the works of the great Muslim philosopher Averroes into Latin, and these texts were distributed to Italian universities. But these influences represented trickles compared with the flood of material from Spain.

When Christian armies began to take Andalusian cities during the Crusades, they marvelled at the wealth, the ordered cityscape and the majestic buildings. But, most importantly, in private and public libraries, they found all the books that they had heard rumours of but were never entirely sure existed:

almost mythical works by Euclid, Galen, Archimedes, Averroes and Aristotle.

The exhilaration of coming across these sources of wisdom was combined with an interest in understanding the 'infidels' in order to convert them. Therefore, in the mid-twelfth century, the visionary Archbishop Raymond of Toledo initiated a European version of the Abbasid translation movement. A multilingual, multifaith team started to translate books from Arabic, Hebrew and Greek into Latin, and eventually into old Spanish when Alfonso X of Castile started sponsoring the movement in the thirteenth century.

The shock waves that these discoveries sent through the Christian community is conveyed by the English philosopher Daniel of Morley, who described how he saw religious scholars in Paris pretending to be very important, but 'because they did not know anything they were no better than marble statues', yet 'when I heard that the doctrine of the Arabs… was all the fashion in Toledo in those days, I hurried there as quickly as I could, so I could hear the wisest philosophers of the world'.

Learn from pagans and Muslims? Of course, argued Daniel, why should knowledge and science be the exclusive preserve of non-Christians? 'Let us then borrow from them and, with God's help and command, rob the pagan philosophers of their wisdom and eloquence. Let us take from the unfaithful so as to enrich ourselves faithfully with the spoils.'[6]

Among the most coveted spoils were Averroes' writings, the Andalusian who had done so much to make Islam and Greek philosophy compatible. His extensive discussions of Aristotle made the ancient philosopher both accessible and attractive. In fact, the first time many of Aristotle's texts became available was through the extracts in Averroes' writings. The breadth and depth of Aristotelian ideas was awe-inspiring. His system for analysing and understanding the natural world, from plants and animals to the movement of the stars, though one and a half millennia old, was so far ahead of anything in Europe as to prove irresistible – or terrifying.

The radical ideas were a sensation and enormously popular among young scholars. The idea that human reason and empirical study were the path to knowledge, and that we are not born to suffer in this world but to attain worldly happiness, set medieval minds aflame. 'Averroists', such as Siger of Brabant and Boethius of Daca at the arts faculty of the new university of Paris, began to use rational methods to question even religious dogma.

But doctrine fought back. The Catholic Church's first instinctive reaction when coming face to face with this philosophy was similar to the Caliphate's last – they found it threatening and tried to vanquish it. One powerful man of the Church attacked the curious and inquisitive for 'tearing out the guts of God's secrets',[7] and Averroists and Aristotelians were persecuted by Church leaders. After having been condemned for heresy and exiled to a monastery, Peter Abelard wrote regretfully: 'I do not wish to be a philosopher if it means conflicting with Paul, nor be an Aristotle if it cuts me off from Christ.'[8]

The long controversy over the legacy of a Dominican priest from Sicily, Thomas Aquinas (1225–1274), who quoted Averroes some 500 times, would eventually convince the Church that it was possible to be an Aristotelian without being cut off from Christ. Aquinas's life's work was to make Aristotelianism compatible with Christianity, just as Averroes had done for Islam. Aquinas put the Renaissance foot in the medieval door, leaving room for curiosity to slip through.

The continent without a shepherd

When new ideas, technologies and businesses models from abroad threatened to upend the status quo, European economic and intellectual elites wanted to stamp it out, like so many other elites in other cultures had. But Europe's blessing was that they were just not very good at it.

China and Byzantium had their emperors, and the Islamic world its state–ulema alliances, but Europe had no dominant power, lamented pope Pius II in 1455: 'Christendom has no head whom all will obey – neither the pope nor the emperor receives his due. For there is no reverence and no obedience... Every city has its own king, and there are as many princes as there are households.' He wondered aloud: 'Who would be the shepherd of such a mixed flock? Who could command their diverse languages? Who would be able to regulate their varied customs?'[9]

No one, it turned out, and that made all the difference. In the fourteenth century, there were probably around a thousand different polities in Europe: principalities, duchies, cities and clerical possessions, separated by mountain ranges, dense forests, rivers, lakes and wetlands, and yet united by the Latin language and Christian faith. It was in a way similar to the ancient Greek world, and the consequences would be similar. Nominally, many European princes and lords were subjected to the Holy Roman Empire, which according to Voltaire's quip was neither holy, Roman, nor an empire. It laid claim to the conquests of Charlemagne, who had been crowned 'Roman Emperor' in AD 800, inventing the fiction that power had been inherited from ancient Rome. But the Holy Roman emperors were elected by mostly German prince-electors, and only ruled a patchwork of self-governing kings, dukes and counts. There was no real capital or administration, so the emperor ruled by holding court in different regions and trying to rally local armies for common causes. Some polities developed their own separate associations, like the north German and Baltic merchant cities that created the Hanseatic League.

And there was of course the pope himself, the Vicar of Christ and the head of the Church, but how many divisions did he lead? At first, he did not even command local churches and their bishops, who were under the authority of local kings and lords. Furthermore, the pope was in a state of constant rivalry with the emperor, who also claimed to be the spiritual leader of Christendom.

This rivalry turned into outright war in the late eleventh century, in a conflict known as the Investiture Controversy, when the pope demanded the right to appoint bishops. But such a simple statement underplays the historic significance of this papal revolution of 1075. It was about nothing less than the authority over all Christians, and whether the emperor had the right to appoint and depose popes, or the pope had the right to appoint and depose emperors.

Weary of constant imperial interference, and in an attempt to protect property that the clergy had gained through gifts, taxes and business (between a third and a fourth of the land of western Europe), the papacy had started a campaign for the 'freedom of the Church'. In 1075, pope Gregory VII (1020–1085) was ready to put a radical programme into effect. Sensationally, the pope suddenly declared his supremacy over the whole Church and the Church's supremacy over secular matters, including kings and emperors. This meant that the Church was no longer just a spiritual power in a decaying world, preparing souls for the Last Judgement, but was prepared to become an independent, worldly power, with a bureaucratic apparatus and authority over secular rulers.

When emperor Henry IV (1050–1106) rejected this power grab by a 'false monk' and declared him overthrown, the pope took the unprecedented step of excommunicating the emperor and releasing all Christians from their oath of allegiance to him. Rebellious German princes used this religious justification to rise up against Henry IV, so he had to patch up his relations with the pope until he had gathered sufficient forces. Famously, he travelled to Canossa in northern Italy, where the pope was staying in the castle of the powerful margravine (the title of a female ruler over an imperial border territory) Matilda of Tuscany. According to legend, the emperor repented by waiting outside the gate for three days, wearing a hair-shirt, barefoot in the snow.

However, this was not the end but the beginning of a long civil war. Popes and emperors ousted each other in turn, and a series of rival 'anti-kings' and 'anti-popes' were appointed, until a compromise was reached in 1122, where both sides renounced their most radical claims and acknowledged the authority of the other. The significant outcome of this constant tug of war was that many subjects could carve out some independence from both powers. Princes and cities played the two authorities off against each other and, to get their loyalty, popes and emperors had to offer something in return. Maastricht built a townhall with two stairways, one for the Bishop of Liège and one for the Duke of Brabant and coined the phrase 'One Lord, oh Lord! Two lords – good!'[10]

Writing in 1877, Lord Acton credited the relative freedom that Western Europeans came to experience to this division between the sacred and the profane:

> To that conflict of four hundred years we owe the rise of civil liberty. If the Church had continued to buttress the thrones of the Kings whom it anointed, or if the

struggle had terminated speedily in an undivided victory, all Europe would have sunk down under a Byzantine or Muscovite despotism. For the aim of both contending parties was absolute authority. But although liberty was not the end for which they strove, it was the means by which the temporal and the spiritual power called the nations to their aid.[11]

The legal revolution

Of immense importance to the future of Europe was the fact that both the papacy and the empire began to write down laws to define and defend their claims, laws that were also used by those who wanted to secure their own independence from them. In their battle for supremacy, the papacy and the empire had both searched the written record for any documents and decrees that could strengthen their case. And some time after 1070, the greatest imaginable reservoir of legal thinking was rediscovered in northern Italy.

In the 530s, the Byzantine emperor Justinian had ordered a massive compilation of Roman legal thinking. The *Digest* consisted of fifty books with extracts from the texts of Roman jurists on a wide variety of legal questions, civil, criminal and constitutional law. This collection of centuries of complex legal analysis, particularly its recognition of individual rights such as rights to life and private property, created a surge of interest in law. Its width and sophistication quickly made it seem like the ideal of law, and the question was only how to interpret and implement it.

Universities were founded at least in part to study Roman law and apply logic to the body of law. What is often seen as the first

European university, the university of Bologna, was started in 1088 when students came together to hire a teacher to educate them in law. The groups of students who travelled from abroad organized themselves in 'nations' to defend their rights, and these nations were collectively called 'universitas', which was a word for corporation from Roman law. Students governed themselves, made their own contracts with teachers, and even fined them if they were not good enough or not punctual. Only later were teachers hired by cities and controlled by bishops, but, even then, what set universities apart from previous forms of education was their relative freedom to express and develop different opinions.

In *Law and Revolution*, Harold Berman's pioneering work on the rediscovery of Justinian law, he cites another expert on medieval law, Fredric William Maitland: 'Maitland called the twelfth century "a legal century." It was more than that: it was *the* legal century, the century in which the Western legal tradition was formed.'[12]

Until then, Western authorities had obviously enforced rules and procedures and punished crimes, but there were no legal systems differentiated from other systems of social control. There was no concept of a systematized body of law where contradictory customs could be reconciled, there were no textbooks on law and no scholars to analyse and interpret them, and no trained jurists who acted as judges, advocates or advisors. The Church had records of decrees from leading bishops and church councils, but they were usually just arranged chronologically, without internal consistency and hierarchy.

Now, in just a few decades, this changed with 'marvellous suddenness', as Maitland phrased it. Under pressure from the papal ambitions and with the *Digest* as a guide, polities all over Western Europe developed autonomous bodies of law to organize their mass of inherited legal materials, and professional judges and practising lawyers emerged. All these new legal systems overlapped. Suddenly there was ecclesiastical law, royal law, feudal law and urban law. Fascinatingly, mercantile law was developed by merchants themselves, who started building a trans-national system of rules and mercantile courts to protect the rights of foreign visitors and merchants. The pluralism of law meant that people lived under several different legal systems and could sometimes appeal to another jurisdiction if they thought they had been wronged. It is another example of how norms and order often emerge from the bottom up rather than being imposed from the top.

This legal revolution had several radical implications. Barons claimed privileges from kings, and citizens demanded rights they were entitled to according to urban charters. Serfs escaped to cities and, after a year and a day, were able to claim their liberty under urban law. Foreign traders demanded protection from arbitrary taxation and harassment under mercantile law. Many laws originally written to defend power were suddenly used to control it. Harold Berman emphasizes the immensity of this unintended consequence: 'In these and other struggles law was invoked against prevailing material facts and conditions; it was turned against the very social structure that had mothered it, so to speak.'[13]

The examples are many. In the *Digest*, scholars found the Roman maxim 'What concerns everyone ought to be considered and approved by everyone.' It was a Roman approach to dealing with testamentary disposition but was now wielded by some scholars as a broad proto-democratic principle, calling for the consent of the governed, something that would eventually give us rallying cries like 'no taxation without representation'. European scholars might have thought that they had simply restated Roman law, but they had in fact used Greek logic to analyse and systematize Roman legal practice into a new, radical constitutional principle that did not exist previously.

It would have appalled Justinian, who preferred the opposite idea, written down in his teaching handbook and not in the collection of Roman law: 'What pleases the prince has the force of law.' The political battles in Europe over the next centuries would revolve around the battle between these two principles.

In an influential attempt to systematize canon law by the Bolognese monk Gratian, *A Concordance of Discordant Canons*, around 1140, the subversive aspect of law is explicitly stated. He claimed that divine law is the will of God as found in revelation, but there is also natural law, which reflects God's will, but can also be found in human reason and conscience. From this, Gratian concluded that 'princes are bound by and shall live according to their laws'. Incredibly, he also argued that it applied to the Church: 'Enactments, whether ecclesiastical or secular, if they are proved to be contrary to natural law, must be totally excluded.'[14]

Building on these principles, legal thinkers such as Azo of Bologna and Marsilius of Pauda argued that political authority, even the emperor's rights, came from the people, so rulers had to be controlled by the law and their powers could be revoked by the people. Some went so far as John of Salisbury and argued that 'To kill a tyrant is not merely lawful, but right and just. For whosoever takes up the sword deserved to perish by the sword.'[15]

The Magna Carta of 1215, which committed King John of England to respect the rights of his subjects, is the most famous statement of the limits of arbitrary rule, but it was far from the only one. The Assizes of Ariano in Sicily in 1140, the Golden Bull of Hungary in 1222 and the Constitutions of Melfi by Emperor Frederick II in 1231 are other documents in which rulers reluctantly admitted that they were bound by law.

What a stroke of good fortune that they found that old book on ancient Roman law before it disintegrated.

The Italian city-states

So there was revival before there was a renaissance. Our deep-rooted perception of the gruesome misery of the Middle Ages was reflected in a line in the 1994 movie *Pulp Fiction*: 'I'm going to get medieval on your ass.' As a historian of ideas, I consider that a fairly accurate reflection of the half millennium after the fall of Rome. But the High Middle Ages, after around 1000, was the beginning of something entirely different.

The early medieval period had been a world of agrarian villages and manors, with very few towns of more than a few thousand inhabitants. But, after 1000, an expansion of trade and a warmer climate increased the population, and people settled in growing towns and cities all over Western Europe. In many of these cities, law and secular learning emerged. Agricultural surplus made specialization possible, fairs and markets became important institutions, and merchants started crossing borders. None were more successful in exploiting this confluence of factors than the increasingly wealthy trading cities of northern Italy – the first to 'shake off that barbarous rust, with which Europe had been covered since the decline of the Roman empire', in Voltaire's words.[16]

The Italian peninsula, hilly with long coastlines and located between northern Europe and the Middle East, was made for seafaring and commerce. In the eleventh and twelfth centuries, cities like Venice, Pisa, Genoa, Florence and Siena gained prosperity and confidence through economic exchange with the Byzantines and Arab states. The wealth they brought in seeped inland, and new cities and suburbs grew rapidly. New middle classes emerged and often began to elect their own magistrates.

Venice had been founded by refugees from the Roman Empire fleeing the barbarian invasions, and as Byzantine power declined, they declared independence. After having mastered the tricky currents of the Adriatic Sea, the Venetians turned their marshy lagoon into a commercial centre. When the pope objected to their economic relationship with Syria and Egypt, they replied: 'We are Venetians first and only then Christians.'[17]

The Crusades established new port cities in the eastern Mediterranean, and Italian merchants were best placed to provide them with supplies. As one Muslim observed, between Christians and Muslims 'the fires of discord burn' but merchants 'come and go without interference'.[18] Some Europeans started to say that 'Trade should be free, and unhindered, even into the gates of Hell.'[19]

Soon other cities emulated Venice's path to autonomy. In 1115, Matilda of Tuscany, the owner of the famous castle of Canossa (the scene of the repentant emperor's barefoot vigil in the snow), died. Uncertainty about the future of her vast possessions in Lombardy, Emilia, Romagna and Tuscany was exploited by these independent-minded cities. 'Practically the entire land is divided among the cities', complained the emperor's nephew on his trip to northern Italy in the 1140s, 'they are so desirous of liberty that they are governed by [elected] consuls rather than rulers'.[20]

Emperor Frederick I Barbarossa repeatedly tried to put an end to this abomination with military force but was pushed back. The Italian cities united as the Lombard League, with the pope as a symbolic leader. After the fifth invasion, they defeated the imperial troops at the Battle of Legnano in 1176. The emperor's princes soured on the whole enterprise and forced him to sign a peace agreement where the Italian cities swore formal allegiance to the Holy Roman Empire in exchange for de facto rights to elect their own councils and enact their own legislations.

This was the start of the golden age of the medieval city, the 'quick forge and working house of thought', as Shakespeare called it. Chinese cities had never developed a separate civic culture and independence. The Chinese countryside was already so commercialized that cities were closely integrated into the whole economy, and the unified imperial structure did not allow for audacious cities to go their own way. Cities in the more fragmented Western Europe were different: islands of refuge and independence in oceans of feudalism and serfdom. Italian cities did not abstain from mostly small-scale wars between themselves, but many political battles were also morphed into legal questions. Instead of always taking up arms, they often solved disputes by consulting the Justinian *Digest*.

In growing cities where at least the upper class and guilds governed themselves, there was a tremendous growth in communal organizations such as universities, confraternities and corporate economic associations. It didn't hurt these new urban ideals that Aristotle's *Politics* appeared in Latin translation in 1265, a treatise where the city-state is seen as the model. Banks – named after the *banki* (benches) they were seated at to do business – sprang up to fund risky international trade, sometimes with 'credit' facilities (from the Latin for 'to trust').

Commerce was facilitated by new financial tools like double-entry bookkeeping, joint stock companies, insurance, bills of exchange and a systematized foreign exchange market. It's no coincidence that, among English words of Italian or Latin origin, many are related to business: bank, bankrupt, carat, career, cartel, cash, credit, mercantile, management and net.

Much of this was influenced by Arab traders. As Fernand Braudel concluded in his history of European commerce, 'anything in Western capitalism of imported origin undoubtedly came from Islam'.[21] Arab traders also inspired Italians to abandon Roman numerals, which had made complex calculations difficult. Leonardo Fibonacci was the son a customs official from Pisa, based in Algeria. He travelled around the Mediterranean and learned the benefits of Hindu-Arabic numerals from its merchants. Fibonacci popularized the system by writing about how it simplified bookkeeping, currency conversion and calculation of interest. In Italian cities, commerce was rapidly being transformed from buccaneering adventure into organized enterprises, based on calculation and long-term planning.

Europe suddenly found itself at the confluence of new ideas from abroad, expanding cities, a wealthier middle class, elements of law and a system of finance. It benefited from all of these – as well as an invaluable absence. I once had the pleasure of hearing the great libertarian theorist Tom G. Palmer summarizing world history in one sentence during a lecture. Out of his virtuoso knowledge of human societies and institutions, he chose, only half-jokingly: 'The lesson from history is: don't get invaded by Mongols.'

Both the Abbasid Caliphate and Song China were devastated by the Mongols, and so was much of the rest of Eurasia. In the early 1240s, Europe's turn came. In December 1241, a siege of Kiev in eastern Europe ended with the city's fall, and the much smaller city of Moscow was burned down. It established Mongol domination over Russia for 250 years, and their armies were free to advance westwards. In quick succession, Mongol armies defeated Poland and Hungary, which were said to have been turned into a barren wasteland. They then marched on to German territories, and soon some troops reached north-east

Italy and the outskirts of Vienna. In one of his many history books, Winston Churchill wrote: 'it had seemed as if all Europe would succumb to a terrible menace'.[22] But then, in September 1242, the Mongols suddenly turned around and rode back home.

It was a miracle. Many Europeans thought that God had answered their prayers. The traditional explanation is that the Mongols had received news that their ruler, Ögedei Khan, Genghis's son, had died, and they now had to assemble in Mongolia to choose who to elect as successor. Other reasons for their sudden retreat have been suggested, from muddy terrain to fierce resistance, and it might simply be that the Mongols were disappointed with the modest loot on a continent that was still very poor compared with the great civilizations of the Middle East and Asia.

But the real reason doesn't matter. What's important is that Western Europe was spared a Mongol conquest, unlike most of the rest of Eurasia, so the new trade links from north Italian cities to the East weren't severed, the farms that had recently become more productive in a warming climate weren't destroyed and the cities that had started growing weren't razed. And it was in the cities that the magic happened.

The Renaissance humanists

In the fourteenth century, the era of the humanists began. The newly empowered cities and an increasingly worldly Church were in need of scholars who could administer secular matters and argue over the newly discovered body of law. This spurred literacy and social mobility. It has been estimated that around half of all Italian city-dwellers were literate. Furthermore, the fragmentation of power and the new fortunes created meant that there was a growing group of potential patrons for scholars, who often moved between cities and between secular authorities and the papal bureaucracy to get funding for their work.

These thinkers, who often came from humble families and mostly started their careers with legal studies, lived in a world that was being radically transformed by pagan philosophy. Aristotelian ideas had been condemned time and again, but always found a new home in the archipelago of independent cities, universities and mobile scholars. In 1323, Thomas Aquinas, the controversial protagonist of a Christian Aristotelianism, was canonized by the pope, and from then on, Christendom increasingly saw the world as a beautiful place that could be understood through reason, logic and the evidence of the senses, and not just a vale of tears where we suffer and die, preparing for afterlife. The European barbarians would, as it were, become Greek.

The 'humanists' of the Renaissance were scholars who were interested in human endeavours, rather than theology and metaphysics. They concerned themselves with the possibilities in this life, its activities and pleasures, rather than life after death. This does not mean that they were proto-atheists – most of them were deeply religious – they were just more interested in the affairs of men than gods. And, when they talked of gods, it often happened to be Apollo. They were not afraid to criticize and even mock the Church, even though some of them were employed by it.

The Italian humanists also had something others didn't to the same extent: they were surrounded by overgrown ruins that were a stark reminder of a lost golden age. Every day, Italians walked past the remnants of buildings made of material they could not reproduce, and constructed in ways they could not comprehend. In once-mighty Rome, the only viable industry seemed to be scavenging for material among old ruins.

For some, these ruins reinforced the Augustinian belief that the world had been in a state of decay since the fall of man. But others instead became obsessed with the idea of restoring and recovering something exceptional that had been lost. The Tuscan poet Francesco Petrarch (1304–1374) mocked successive popes for having abandoned Rome for Avignon in France (for protection and to escape turmoil in Rome), where they spent their days drinking bad wine. He wanted them to return to Rome to signal a rebirth of the city.

Petrarch was a hero of the humanists. He 'restored Apollo to his ancient temple and brought back the Muses, soiled by rusticity, to their pristine beauty', according to a fellow writer.[23] Petrarch did this through his own writings but also through the texts rediscovered by him. His obsession with antiquity led him to travel all over Europe in search of forgotten texts in monasteries and libraries, to make it possible for the world to walk 'in the pure radiance of the past'.[24]

The commercial book market had collapsed after the fall of Rome, but monks were expected to read, and therefore they conserved and copied the few books that remained, many of which had been saved during the reign of Charlemagne. Since Europe had lost access to papyrus and had not yet learned about paper, these books were written on animal skin, parchment. Good parchment was expensive, and the best (from stillborn calves) was a rare luxury, so priceless texts were sometime never copied again and disappeared from the historical record. Sometimes they were washed away with brushes and rags and written over with religious texts.

It was also very time-consuming to copy hundreds of pages by hand. One exhausted scribe ended a book with a cry of relief: 'Here ends the second part of the work of Brother

Thomas Aquinas of the Dominican Order, incredibly long, verbose and tedious for the scribe. Thank God, thank God, and again thank God!'[25]

For all these reasons, it was a race against the clock to find ancient works before they were lost forever, and Petrarch led the search. In June 1345, he made his greatest discovery in the cathedral of Verona, one that would set Renaissance minds ablaze. Among all the books in the library, he suddenly laid his eyes on the only known collection of hundreds of letters of the Roman politician and philosopher Cicero, who was the writer Petrarch said he admired 'as much or even more than all whoever wrote a line in any nation'.[26]

Petrarch thanked God for this amazing discovery and, since the copyists found the text unintelligible, he proceeded to copy the letters himself. Petrarch treasured this large volume so much that he kept it leaning against the doorpost in his library. Unfortunately, it repeatedly fell and struck him above the ankle, creating a wound that never healed. But the impact of these letters on the intellectual climate and the ambition to revive ancient learning was worth it.

Through Cicero's letters, humanists had their first eye-witness account of the late Roman Republic and its fall, and for recently independent republics it was deeply fascinating and created an interest in the study of history itself. But the letters also spurred an interest in individuality. Cicero, whose Latin was always considered the model, had been seen as something of a superhero but, in these letters, he came across as a real human being, with ambitions, emotions and anxieties, and with a very active involvement in society and politics.

As Petrarch observed, the 'disease' of writing is highly contagious, and, from now on, humanists tried to emulate Cicero: his style, his devotion to liberty and his love of learning. One defining characteristic was that they talked about the immense joy they found in reading, writing and understanding. This was something new. Monks read, but that was out of piety and duty. One monastic rule said 'even if he does not want to, he shall be compelled to read' and other rules instructed that those who did not read and those who argued over the text would be punished physically.[27]

The humanist scholars, on the other hand, wrote about how texts stimulated curiosity and debate. At home, by the fire or in taverns, scholars met and discussed philosophy and poetry. This also turned them into better human beings, they claimed. In a way that seems charmingly naïve to a modern reader they often suggested that education would save the world. 'All evil is born from ignorance. Yet writers have illuminated the world, chasing away the darkness', explained Vespasiano da Bisticci, the leading bookseller in Florence.[28]

These writers were becoming accessible now, thanks to the efforts of Vespasiano and others. Around 10.8 million manuscripts were hand-copied in Western Europe in the thousand years between the fall of Rome and 1500. And 4.9 million of those manuscripts, almost half, were produced during the 1400s, 1.4 million of which were produced in Italy.[29]

Uncovering the superior art, sculpture and literature of Greece and Rome, radical humanists began to claim that nothing of value had been created between the fall of the Roman Empire and now. They disparaged the period in between as 'Middle Ages'. They were now in a moment of *rinascita* (rebirth) of ancient theories and art, according to the art historian Giorgio Vasari. It was Jules Michelet's nineteenth-century translation of this concept into French that would eventually be used to describe the whole period between the fourteenth and sixteenth centuries, *Renaissance*.

Most early humanists were surprisingly uninterested in the natural sciences and often belittled fields like medicine, physics and astronomy. However, their questioning of authorities and encouragement of open debate would encourage the next generation of scientists. The only way to move research forward was to challenge one's predecessors, claimed Lorenzo Valla. He pointed out hundreds of errors in the book *In Praise of Florence* published by his mentor Leonardo Bruni. Of more immediate political significance was Valla's proof that the Donation of Constantine, a fourth-century imperial decree that supposedly transferred authority over the Western Roman Empire to the pope, was a forgery.

Ancient heritage sometimes stifled innovative thinking: the Church had a tendency to take radical ideas and fossilize them into new orthodoxies. Instead of borrowing Aristotle's empirical approach, the Church imitated his conclusions (that celestial bodies moved only in uniform circular motion, for example) and turned it into articles of faith. If the rediscovery of the ancients made the Renaissance possible, it was only by being as irreverent to the ancients as the ancients had been to their predecessors that we moved on towards the scientific revolution.

The birth of the individual

Modern writers love to mock Cicero for coming across as ambitious, vain and conceited in the letters he left us. Since other ancients did not open their hearts to us, they appear more dignified.

Renaissance humanists felt differently, however. They were intrigued by Cicero's self-centred approach; it seemed exciting in an age when one was supposed to think of oneself only as a humble part of the 'Great Chain of Being', the hierarchical model of the universe. Some began to imitate Cicero's approach. Petrarch wrote about his own activities, interests and looks, his love of dogs and fear of ocean travel. The word 'ego' figures prominently in his writings. People started writing diaries and more personal autobiographies. In their letters they wrote about how to deal with their patrons and market their books, and documented their feelings when reading, how they laughed and cried and evaluated texts. When nineteenth-century historians talked about the Renaissance as the birth of the individual, this is what they meant.

In his 1860 study *The Civilization of the Renaissance in Italy*, Jacob Burckhardt wrote that: 'Man was conscious of himself only as a member of a race, people, party, family or corporation', but this mask started to slip. 'Italy began to swarm with individuality; the ban laid upon human personality was dissolved; and a thousand figures meet us each in its own special shape and dress.'[30]

Of course this is an exaggeration. Renaissance society remained hierarchical, and all these individualists lived their lives and pursued their goals through their families and communal organizations. But there is no doubt that a larger share of the population experienced greater freedom to form their own destiny through urbanization, education and enterprise, and began to emphasize their individual identity and ambition. Just as in Song China, a new self-assertiveness could be found in the literature, and words like *unique* started to take on a positive meaning.

Some thinkers such as Leon Battista Alberti went so far as to suggest that 'men can do anything with themselves if they will', though his own excellence in everything from church-building and cryptography to music, poetry and ball-playing makes one think that of course *he* would say that.[31] Alberti's motto *Quid Tum*, 'What Next?', symbolizes the restless optimism of one line of Renaissance thinking.

The influential painter and art historian Giorgio Vasari wrote that 'Rivalry and competition, by which a man seeks by great works to conquer and overcome those more distinguished than himself in order to acquire honour and glory, is a praiseworthy thing.'[32] So if you're fed up with the rat race, you are somewhat justified in blaming the Renaissance. On the other hand, the elite had always competed for glory; the difference was that they were now less inclined to do it by taking to horseback and mowing down as many peasants as possible, and more by producing and trading ideas, texts, textiles, pottery and great works of art.

A Venetian fourteenth-century innovation contributed to this individualism: the glass mirror. The old, expensive bronze mirrors did not reflect much light, which is why the Bible uses the mirror as a metaphor for not seeing the whole truth ('For now we see in a mirror, darkly'). Venetian glass mirrors, coated with a mixture of tin and mercury, made it possible for those who could afford them to stare into their own eyes for the first time. They could see their unique characteristics and expressions, and they began to understand how others saw them. A song about mirrors in sixteenth-century Florence expresses the sentiment: 'So a man can take his own measure and say, "I will be a better man than I have been."'[33]

Historians like Ian Mortimer think that the mirror changed our very psychology. People started to think of themselves as unique, not just as part of a group. This is the moment when people began to order portraits of themselves, and artists started making self-portraits. Letters were increasingly filled with expressions of thoughts and feelings, rather than just accounts of activities or formalities and requests.[34]

A simultaneous apocalyptic event contributed to another kind of liberation. In 1347, Genoese traders returning from the Mongol siege of Crimea brought the Black Death to Europe.

The bubonic plague quickly spread over the continent and killed more than a third of Europe's population: according to some estimates, up to 60 per cent of all Europeans. To many it seemed like the end of the world.

It was, at the very least, the end of the old world. The rigid feudal order, where everybody had a particular place inherited from their parents, was severely shaken. A large part of the population was suddenly gone, leaving positions and land open to those who remained. With the workforce decimated, peasants began to demand higher wages and moved to other areas with more opportunities. Feudal lords fought back against these creeping market forces, and in eastern Europe they mostly regained control by using even more brutal methods, but in the more fragmented west, with more independent towns and regions, peasants had better options and bargaining power.

Italian cities had already begun to emancipate serfs within their jurisdiction, to attract workers from the countryside and increase the number of independent taxpayers. Bologna abolished serfdom as early as 1256. The period after the plague saw a series of dramatic uprisings, such as France's Jacquerie of 1358, Florence's Ciompi Revolt of 1378 and England's Peasants' Revolt of 1381. They mostly failed, but they showed worried oligarchs and aristocrats that increased repression might end in disaster, and the whole system began to fracture. By 1450, serfdom had been abolished in large parts of Western Europe.

The capital of the Renaissance

The capital of the Renaissance was Florence, which in the eyes of Voltaire became 'a second Athens'.[35] This major Tuscan city had no pope, no king and it didn't even have a large, prestigious university. It was a self-described republic, restoring the Roman ideal of a government held by the people in common, not by a single ruler. Instead of a spectacular court or dominant intellectual tradition, it had endless debates and controversies. In 1433, two out of every three Florentine males were theoretically eligible for public office.[36] Even though voting was usually rigged by the oligarchs, it created a sense of inclusion and a responsibility to stay informed, close to what Athenians must once have felt. 'Here the whole people are busied with what in the despotic cities is the affair of a single family', wrote Jacob Burckhardt, who called it 'the most modern state in the world'.[37]

This was all the more impressive since such inclusive systems were not easy to uphold in the long run. Venice had been the very model of a republic, with power in the hands of the continually renewed Great Council, but in 1297, the Serrata (Closure) made membership of the council hereditary, thus shutting out minor aristocrats, plebeians and other outsiders.

The most modern state in the world was also soon the richest. Florence had grown wealthy from its textile industry, with raw materials imported from northern Europe, and the resulting products exported everywhere. Because of Florence's position on the river Arno, it had a route to the Mediterranean and the rest of the world. The Datini family traded with 200 cities, from Scotland to the Levant. Banks and trading companies funded such commercial operations and soon generated a prosperous industry in its own right. Burckhardt mentions that in 1422 there were seventy-two exchange offices around the Mercato Nuovo market. A thriving economy stimulated social mobility and boosted the growing middle class.

Florence lost more than half its population to the plague, but its entrepreneurial traditions helped it to bounce back. In 1375, the pope tried to conquer the city, and the chancellor, the Petrarch disciple Coluccio Salutati (1331–1406), responded with a fierce propaganda campaign urging other cities to throw off papal tyranny and defend republican liberties.

Merchants and artisans were natural lovers of liberty, claimed Salutati, who 'desire peace in which to practice their studies and arts, they love equality among citizens and do not glory in the nobility of family or blood'.[38] The distraught pope responded by cancelling all religious services in the city and placing under arrest any Florentines found in papal territories. The Florentines retaliated by taking over religious services and began to confiscate church properties, until the death of the pope ended the war.

When Visconti, the Duke of Milan, attacked Florence, Salutati once again rallied citizens with eloquent pleas to the ideals of liberty and rule of law. Visconti famously said that just one of Salutati's letters caused him more harm than a thousand Florentine horsemen. Visconti died in 1402, and Florence lived on. Soon it took control of Pisa and therefore gained an outlet to the Mediterranean – defending the city-state by ruining another city-state.

This was the moment when everybody's eyes turned towards Florence. In 1397, the Medici family had started an innovative bank that would make them fabulously rich, bankers to the pope and eventually rulers of Florence. At the same time, in another part of the city, the Byzantine scholar Manuel Chrysoloras had started to teach the forgotten language of Greek, making it possible for humanists to read Aristotle and Plato in the original Greek. The language was still so unknown in Italy that the only recent translation of Homer portrayed the goddess Athena, who wore the *aegis* (a goatskin shield), as milking a goat.[39]

Salutati's pupil and successor Leonardo Bruni (1370–1444), who translated Aristotle into Latin and wrote a biography of

Cicero, went even further by arguing that what made Greece and Rome great was their republican liberty. In his history of Florence, Bruni argued that Florence was founded during the late Roman Republic, refuting the claim that Caesar (who was 'hated and scorned in Florence') or Charlemagne had been important to the foundation of the city. The implication was that Florence was an independent republic owing no allegiance to the Holy Roman emperor.

As Pericles had done in a funeral oration for the war dead in Athens, Bruni declared that he lived in the best and most open city: 'There is no place on earth where there is greater justice open equally to everyone. Nowhere else does freedom grow so vigorously, and nowhere else are rich and poor alike treated with such equality.' Bruni argued that even a poor man with intelligence could win glory and position in Florence. He claimed that these protections extended to foreigners as well, turning Florence into a sanctuary for refugees and a centre for international merchants, so 'there is no one in the whole of Italy who does not consider himself to possess double citizenship, the one of the city of which he naturally belongs, the other to the city of Florence'.[40]

If these things were not always carried out in practice, at least they gave an ideal to aspire to. The humanists emphasized *libertas* both for the city and the individual. The value of tolerance and the freedom to think and write came naturally to thinkers and writers. Petrarch wrote that 'many can be forced to confess, but not to believe. No liberty is greater than the liberty to think. As I claim it for myself, so I do not deny it for others.'[41]

Erasmus of Rotterdam (1466–1536), the great Dutch humanist defender of tolerance, would eventually take this Renaissance libertarianism to its logical conclusion, by declaring that the eagle is the symbol of kings because it is carnivorous and rapacious:

> Do we not see that noble cities are erected by the people and destroyed by the princes? That a state grows rich by the industry of its citizens and is plundered by the rapacity of its rulers? That good laws are enacted by representatives of the people and violated by kings? That the commons love peace and the monarchs foment war?[42]

Renaissance scholars supplied the confident Italian cities with a new, secular ideology. Previous generations had glorified spiritual withdrawal, and even Petrarch thought that traditional rural life was ideal. Now instead scholars spoke up for a civic form of humanism. The good citizen was actively involved in the life of the city and in politics, and could find honour in this activity.

Many humanists even started championing entrepreneurship and wealth creation. Alberti talked about the virtue of record keeping and said that as the merchant 'watches over the enterprise, he should almost always have a pen in his hand'. Salutati praised merchants as 'a most honest breed of men whose activities beautify cities and make available to everyone the bounties of nature', and Bruni declared: 'As health is the goal of medicine, so riches are the goal of the household.'[43]

Poggio Bracciolini, who served four popes, went so far as to praise avarice under the cover of a philosophical dialogue. After having heard all the arguments against greed, Bracciolini's spokesman declared that 'avarice is not only natural, it is useful and necessary'. He argued that the desire for gain spurs achievement and risk-taking, in terms that reminds one of Abbasid Baghdad. If people produced only what they needed for themselves, there would be nothing left over for economic exchange, culture or charity. 'If we were to remove that profit, all business and work would entirely cease, for whoever undertakes anything without hope of it?', he asks, 'Every splendor, every refinement, every ornament would be lacking.'[44]

Inclusivity had its limits. The question of whether women had a Renaissance has been much debated. The answer is mostly negative. While there were prominent Renaissance women like the sculptor Properzia de' Rossi and Cassandra Fedele from Padua, who even performed public orations, women were mostly excluded from the public realm. Women had no political rights, were the legal subjects of fathers and husbands, and had mostly no independent property rights.

Preachers warned women, regarded as the source of temptation and sin, to stay out of sight. They should not be visible in doorways or windows and should step outdoors only to go to church. Even there, women were often segregated from men. Disappointingly, male humanists rarely had a better attitude to women. Alberti said that even he had to admit that men needed women – in order to give birth to sons. When the bookseller Vespasiano, who got grumpier with the years, decided to write about role models for virtuous women, he mentioned the saint who plucked out her eyes when a suitor admired them, and the Roman woman who, on hearing about the death of her husband, rushed to the fire and swallowed pieces of coal.[45]

Catherine Fletcher argues that, counterintuitively, women often had less power in republics than in monarchies. When a king was away leading troops or inspecting other cities, or suddenly died, there were mothers, wives or daughters who could take his place. In a republic, however, where kinship was not the decisive factor, there were always many other elected men who could step in.[46]

Nevertheless, wealthier and more literate societies still presented opportunities for some women. After having lost her husband to the plague, Christine de Pizan (1364–1430) from Venice supported her family by becoming a professional writer, eventually at the French court. She actively criticized popular but humiliating stereotypes of women. In her book *The City of Ladies*, she had allegorical figures like Lady Reason and real historical women refute the idea that women were inferior to men.

Another Italian humanist, Laura Cereta (1469–1499), is sometimes described as the first feminist since she wrote persistently about why women should not be denied education and should not have to be enslaved in marriage. Women might not have had much of a Renaissance, but some pioneers definitely argued their right to have one.

The spread of humanism

As it suddenly seemed possible to exchange learning and literature for prosperity and power, other rulers wanted to follow suit. Florence's new prominent status encouraged other states to also hire humanists for important roles.

Milan had tried to defeat Florence militarily, but also hired scholars who could challenge the rival city in literary feuds. King Alfonso of Aragon and Naples had plenty of scholars in his court and didn't take a break from his learning when he was away at war. On military campaigns he brought his library in a tent next to his own, and had a scholar read Livy aloud to him and his soldiers. In 1437, he recruited the famous humanist Valla as his secretary.

Federico da Montefeltro, lord of Urbino, was the greatest warrior of his time, who would send his army on a killing mission for the highest bidder. But he was also a lover of humanism and literature, interestingly nicknamed 'the Light of Italy'. He was said to have hired five men to read aloud to him during his meals, on philosophy, history and warfare. And he carried a lavishly decorated copy of Aristotle's *Nicomachean Ethics* with him everywhere, even into battles. The bookseller Vespasiano claimed that Federico put together the world's finest collection of books, always keeping thirty to forty scribes busy copying scripts.

Such were the times. Even the great enemy of Christendom, the Ottoman Sultan Mehmed II who conquered Constantinople in 1453, hired Italian and Greek scholars and artists at his court, who spoke to him in Latin and Greek, and built a library filled with such literature. However, his invasion also meant that many scholars fled from Constantinople to Italy, thereby giving a boost to Greek learning there.

Meanwhile, Rome was being rebuilt as a Renaissance city. In 1378, the pope had finally given up on Avignon and its bad wine and returned the papacy to Rome. When the University of Rome was restored, Leonardo Bruni wrote the statues, calling for a full programme of studies including the teaching of Greek. The humanist Alberti inspired the architectural plans for the city.

In 1447, Rome elected a pope who was sympathetic to the humanist programme: Nicholas V, who had worked as a private tutor in Florence. He laid the ground for the Vatican library, expanding its collection from 340 volumes to 1,160, and expanding it further with books gained from Constantinople after its fall.[47] The library included many Greek texts and pagan classics. It would have seemed embarrassingly tiny to contemporary rulers in the east (Mehmed II was said to have a library of 8,000 books) but it established Rome as a centre of learning in the West.

There was even stronger confirmation of the status of humanists when one of their own was elected pope in 1459. Pius II was unusual. He had studied civil law, written erotic literature and was a friend of many of the great humanists. He was also the author of the only published papal autobiography. When he was elected, an appalled French cardinal asked whether they would now 'let the Church be governed on pagan principles'.[48]

That was not the plan, but the restoration of pagan art and philosophy to a prominent place in European history was underway, and in 1511 it got its most conspicuous embodiment in the heart of the Vatican. Raphael from Urbino (1483–1520) was commissioned to paint frescos for the reception rooms of the Apostolic Palace. On the east wall of the Room of the Signatura, Raphael painted an exceptional scene now known as *The School of Athens*. Under statues of Apollo and Athena, ancient philosophers and scientists are gathered. At the centre are the two giants of Athens, Plato and Aristotle. On the left, the aged Plato is pointing upwards to the world of forms. On the right and slightly ahead of him, a younger Aristotle holds his hand in front of himself, horizontally, to show that the real, material world holds the answers. They are surrounded by a multitude of philosophers and scientists from ancient Greece, such as Socrates, Pythagoras and Archimedes, but also the Iranian prophet Zoroaster and the Muslim Aristotelian Averroes. The humanist influence was now evident even on the walls of the Apostolic Palace.

The humanist school would have a lasting impact on the education system. New schools and universities sprang up all over Europe, and the language and literature of pagan antiquity became the foundation of the new curriculum, which was based on a view of humanity and its capacity that had undergone a radical shift.

In the late twelfth century, the future pope Innocent III had written his influential *On the Wretchedness of the Human Condition*, perhaps the most depressing book ever published. He wrote at length about how the human body is disgusting, ambitions are futile and the end of human life is horrible. According to this much quoted text, man's origin is in sin, slime and filthy sperm, and 'the soul that later flows in from them picks up the stain of sin, the blemish of guilt and the filth of wickedness'. When the newborn cries, it is 'noises of pain and complaint to express our nature's real misery'. Human beings are even worse than plants, claimed Innocent III, since plants exude oil and wine, 'while your discharges are spit, piss and shit'.[49]

This was the most authoritative formulation of the version of Christianity that despises the world and the human body; many Renaissance scholars argued against it and considered ways of refuting it. The most famous expression of a more optimistic view of mankind is a short 1486 text by Pico della Mirandola (1463–1494) that was given the title *Oration on the Dignity of Man* by an early editor. Pico argued that man was in fact the most impressive of creatures. God had given a fixed role to both beasts and the highest spiritual beings. But he gave human beings no static nature or defined place, so that he might instead find it himself:

> We have made you a creature neither of heaven nor of earth, neither mortal nor immortal, in order that you may, as the free and proud shaper of your own being, fashion yourself in the form you may prefer. It will be in your power to descend to the lower, brutish forms of life; you will be able, through your own decision, to rise again to the superior orders whose life is divine.[50]

Pico's oration was poetically written, but his mystical approach and blending of incompatible traditions made his case for humanity mostly reliant on its rhetorical power. A more detailed empirical case was provided by the Florentine scholar and diplomat Giannozzo Manetti. His 1452 work *On Human Worth and Excellence* was an explicit refutation of the misanthropy of Innocent III, sponsored by King Alfonso of Naples.

Manetti built his case on the pagan philosophers Cicero and Aristotle: 'everybody's teacher' and 'prince of true philosophers', respectively. But as a staunch Christian he considered the excellence of the human being and potential for pleasure in this life as a testament to God's greatness.

He started by describing at length the complexity and beauty of the human body, and the wonderful fact that it lacked superfluous parts. He talked about the functionality of the senses, breathing and blood flow. He even praised the great skill it took God to create our private parts: sexual pleasure is not shameful, but a great divine plan for procreation. Manetti argued against the pope's insistence that the act of conception makes humans vile and rotten from birth. He added mischievously that as a bonus it provided the saintly with a great delight in resistance.

The body is a 'fitting vessel for the rational soul', concluded Manetti, and went on to describe the intelligence and achievements of a creature created in God's image. 'The mind is so great and remarkable that all later discoveries – after the first creation of a world fresh and wild – have evidently been products of ourselves, coming from that special, singular shrewdness of human thinking.' He thought this was visible in art, sculpture and poetry, and in language and in shipbuilding. Proof of human thought in action was found in the construction of all the houses and cities, which are so great that they 'might well be judged the works of angels rather than men'.[51]

Manetti's book is one of the most splendid expressions of Renaissance optimism, and daring in its explicit rebuttal of a celebrated pope. However, as a Christian, he found the greatest cause for joy in the perpetual happiness of seeing God in the eternal life. The fact that the 56-year-old author was convinced that the blessed would rise again at an age of 30, with bodies without disease, weakness or ugliness, must surely have added to his optimism.

In one of the most memorable examples of the Renaissance's strange blend of beauty and brutality, he adds that when the blessed see that the damned will go on being punished forever, 'they will surely be full, beyond measure, of the greatest jubilation'.[52]

Renaissance men

The dynamic culture of Renaissance Italy was a result of the economic development and social mobility of the period. Rapid growth and ideals of meritocracy were upsetting traditional hierarchies. The aristocracy of blood was to some extent replaced by an aristocracy of wealth. Successful Florentine merchants and even shopkeepers were ennobled, and the old nobility was not ashamed of engaging in lucrative commerce. They often entered into family relationships with the rich bourgeoisie. In such a dynamic economy, people had to claim their status in a new way, and many used the language of art, architecture and literature to ascend the social hierarchy. Guilds, fraternities and individuals started commissioning works of art on a large scale. 'Culture became, in part, a form of competitive, common, and conspicuous consumption.'[53]

For some, patronage functioned as a letter of indulgence. Especially for those who acquired wealth in a questionable way, large donations to charity, churches and art was a way to redeem themselves. The fact that banking seemed dangerously close to the usury banned by Christianity no doubt encouraged the Medici family to become one of the most generous donors to the Church. When Cosimo Medici once spoke to Pope Eugenius about his worries for his soul, he was told that a donation of 10,000 florins could not hurt.[54]

In seeming contradiction of the romantic idea of great Renaissance geniuses, Italian art was a branch of commerce, often a collaborative effort in workshops, with masters, assistants and apprentices cooperating on paintings, cross-fertilizing styles and techniques. By 1478, Florence had forty painters' shops and fifty-four sculptors' shops. Painters belonged to the guild of physicians and pharmacists because they dealt with chemicals, while most sculptors belonged to the guild of goldsmiths. Artworks were commissioned, and the motive, materials and colours were strictly defined in contracts. If an artist was inspired to add a few small angels that weren't in the contract, he was quickly ordered to turn them into puffy clouds.

But somewhere along the way, with this fierce competition for patrons, commissions and fame, some artists developed a strong self-awareness and pride. Some began to be considered almost superhuman: Michelangelo came to be called 'the divine one'.

And there certainly were geniuses. In the early fourteenth century, the Florentine painter Giotto di Bondone (1267–1337) had started a revolution against the conventions of classical Christian art. Byzantine art was rigid and repetitive not because the painters were bad, but because they had been deprived of creative freedom. After a long and violent debate in the eighth and ninth centuries, in which the most radical theologians wanted to destroy all religious images, the emerging compromise was that artists could paint things that had actually happened, like events in the life of Christ, but looks and events could not be varied, and nothing added. Scale and perspective were ignored, since that was not the point. Mary was always bigger than Joseph simply because she was more important. The only thing left to the imagination were colours, which explains the lavish and radiant colours in Byzantine art.

Giotto, who was a successful entrepreneur with as many as six notaries handling his business, broke with such proscriptions. He began drawing lifelike characters, with depth, solidity and motion, and his use of colours gave the impression of distance. His art came alive. At the same moment that Chinese artists abandoned their pioneering representational art, Giotto inspired European artists to observe life and nature and make drawing more realistic. It was stimulated by the invention of oil painting. Oil colours could be mixed to achieve more subtle effects. Oil paint also dried slowly, so thoughtful painters could take the time to achieve better results, more nuanced emotions, and even change their minds, correct and alter their paintings.

One of the greatest innovations was Brunelleschi's (1377–1446) use of the linear perspective around 1413, to imitate a three-dimensional scene on a flat surface. Inspiration seems to have come from the Arab father of optics, Ibn al-Haytham, who had defined how rays are observed by the eye. This was most beautifully utilized by Lorenzo Ghiberti in his lively bronze scenes on the door of the Florence baptistry, the *Gates of Paradise*.

Brunelleschi had been bitter about losing the competition for the commission for those doors, but he soon secured a more important job to build the monumental octagonal dome for Florence Cathedral next to the baptistry. This was also a much more complex task. It was to be wider than the biggest dome in the world, the ancient Pantheon in Rome, and it could not use a wooden frame since there was no timber of that length. Furthermore, its base was more than 50 metres above the ground, so 37,000 tons of material had to be hauled up there even to begin construction.

Rival cities ridiculed the arrogance of the Florentines in devising such an ambitious project but, through a series of innovative solutions and novel techniques, Brunelleschi and his collaborators managed to raise the dome by one foot per month, until in 1436, it was there for all to see, as the proudest architectural accomplishment of the Renaissance. 'To Florentine ingenuity, nothing is difficult', as a local goldsmith put it.[55]

Meanwhile, other art forms flourished. A few years later, Donatello finished his statue of *David*, slayer of Goliath. It was the first free-standing bronze statue since antiquity, as well as the first nude. It had been commissioned by Cosimo Medici, who cleverly hid his own ambitions to manipulate the city's politics by adding text stating that it represented the city's resistance against tyranny. *David* would be a potent symbol for the city's liberties, sometimes even against the Medici. In 1504, an even more awe-inspiring *David* was unveiled by Michelangelo (1475–1564), who was not yet thirty. More than 5 metres tall, the heroic, muscular nude was carved from a single colossal block of marble. According to his own famous description, Michelangelo had merely liberated a figure that he had already seen existing in the stone.

His next major project was to paint the ceiling of the Sistine Chapel. For four years, Michelangelo lay on his back, with paint dripping on his face, painting more than 500 square metres of ceiling. The result was some of the most iconic versions we have of the biblical story, including the scene where God reaches out with his right arm to impart the spark of life into the first man,

Adam. This might not even be Michelangelo's most visible work. By the end of his life, he worked as chief architect of the St Peter's Basilica in the Vatican, and he was the principal designer of much of the building we see there today.

The only artist who can compete with Michelangelo for fame was his older rival, the painter, sculptor, architect, engineer, musician and scientist Leonardo da Vinci (1452–1519), the very symbol of the Renaissance Man, the universal genius. Michelangelo mocked Leonardo for not finishing most of his works, whereas Leonardo thought that Michelangelo's overly muscular figures looked more like sacks of walnuts than real humans. They both had a point.

Leonardo, the illegitimate son of a Florentine notary and an orphan, was the master of observation. He studied nature, life, materials and constructions and filled his notebooks with cascades of observations and drawings. He dissected humans and animals to understand every single detail perfectly: the bones, veins, muscles and organs. He described how to draw a foot in ten different ways, each of which reveals the structure in a unique way.

By studying light and vision, and the nature of painting materials, Leonardo invented techniques to create depth and mimic how some things are in focus and out of focus to the human mind. The result was some of the greatest paintings of all time, like the *Mona Lisa* and *The Last Supper*. 'He knew how to perspective the fuck out of things', as the Netflix series *Cunk on Earth* recently referred to the latter painting: 'You almost feel like you can crawl inside it and betray Jesus yourself.'

Leonardo did not go to all this trouble just to paint more realistically than Michelangelo and everybody else, but also to satisfy his own curiosity. Leonardo was, in Kenneth Clark's words, 'The most relentlessly curious man in history. Everything he saw made him ask why and how', echoing the question in Athenian drama: 'Why is this so? What do we mean by that?'[56] Leonardo was obsessed with every problem he came across: how birds fly, how sound travels, how rivers flow, why we find petrified seashells on mountains, how friction affects machines, how light radiates from mirrors, how they build locks in Flanders. He tried to find out, wrote it down, made drawings and constantly asked new questions about it. And he famously came up with designs for helicopters, flying machines, armoured vehicles, scuba gear, parachutes, a giant crossbow, a robotic knight and many, many things besides. It is exhausting just to look at his notebooks.

This obsessive curiosity also meant that Michelangelo was correct: Leonardo started many more projects than he completed. He often got bored once he knew how to solve a problem, and rather than finishing a painting or design, he was distracted by a new fascinating problem and moved on. But this also makes him an excellent representative of the Renaissance. This was not an era of fixed answers and closed systems, but of curiosity and questions.

This spirit of curiosity and experiment would translate into an explosion of creativity. It has been argued that modern music was invented between 1470 and 1590, as music was taken out of the Church and turned into a secular experience.[57] The first orchestras were set up and the idea of designating specific instruments for different parts was born. The art of printing meant that people could keep notes on paper and not just in their heads. In Florence in the 1580s, a group of musicians and a poet came up with the idea that drama could be sung in a impassioned manner, and so opera was born.

Not much later, in Spain and England, respectively, Cervantes (1547–1616) and Shakespeare (1564–1616) invented the novel and the modern drama. They abandoned the didactic storytelling of both the Church and the humanists for an exploration of the human psyche. Here we have characters who are alive, who think, doubt and change, and not necessarily for the sake of salvation. Perhaps this is the moment that we can talk about the birth of man for real. It took a while.

The three great imports

In his work *On Human Worth and Excellence*, Manetti mentioned modern painters and sculptors as equals to the masters of antiquity, and the late fifteenth century was when Europeans for the first time started to think that they had reached the level of the ancients and perhaps even surpassed them. Despite his admiration for Roman architecture, Alberti thought that Brunelleschi's engineering for the dome in Florence was probably 'unknown and unimaginable among the ancients'.[58] Ptolemy's old maps were being redrawn by sailors, and when the physician Andreas Vesalius dissected human bodies, he found things that the Greek physician Galen had not seen.

In 1492, Marsilio Ficino, the Italian scholar who founded the Florentine Academy in honour of Plato's Academy, wrote: 'For this century, like a golden age, has restored to light the liberal arts, which were almost extinct: grammar, poetry, rhetoric, painting, sculpture, architecture, music, the ancient singing of songs to the Orphic lyre'.[59] It is 'as if upon a given signal, men of genius are arising and conspiring together to restore the best literature', claimed Erasmus in 1517.[60] 'Oh age! oh letters! It is a joy to be alive!' cheered the German poet and knight Ulrich von Hutten a year later.[61]

When the French scholar Loys Le Roy looked back at the previous 200 years from the year 1575, he argued that this era had recovered learning, art and sciences so that 'this our age can be compared to the most learned times that ever were'. But he also made the case that three innovations that we had previously seen in China now ushered in a completely new episode in European history: the printing press, the compass and gunpowder.[62]

In the 1440s, the German goldsmith Johannes Gutenberg managed to combine heavy presses for crushing olives and grapes, the oil-based ink of painters, his own skills in carving punches for coins, and a little bit of inspiration from Asia, to create the first European movable-type printing press. Thanks to this, wrote Le Roy, 'more work is accomplished in one day than many diligent scribes could do in a year'. It also made books affordable. Some scholars, such as Antonio Beccadelli, had sold a farm to afford to buy a copy of Livy's history of Rome, but it was printing that made books accessible for the middle classes. In the last half of the fifteenth century, more books were printed than the total number of hand-copied books since the fall of Rome.

Printing would not have been possible had it not been for the arrival of paper. At first paper was imported from Arabs, but by the thirteenth century there was a domestic Italian paper industry. At this time, paper was not made from trees, but from old rags. For all the wrong reasons, after the disastrous plague, Europe had an excess supply of those.

When printed books started appearing in Italy in the early 1470s, many feared them. 'Now the most stupid ideas can, in a moment, be transferred into a thousand volumes and spread abroad', warned the Medici's librarian.[63] Many complained that it would make scribes unemployed, but in fact the mass of books now printed often left space for illustrations and illuminated capitals, so scribes and illuminators still had a lot of work.

Others worried that the lower classes would not read great works but stupid and erotic literature – or, worse, *read* the great works and so undermine class differences. Among the most popular first print runs were pre-packaged papal indulgencies – expensive forgiveness for one's sins – and soon even more popular were the condemnations of these indulgencies by a certain priest from Wittenberg named Martin Luther.

Aldus Martinus decided to use the invention of the printing press to save classical wisdom from ever being lost again. His print shop in Venice, by now the capital of printing, published rare manuscripts in large editions. He also invented the forerunner to both the paperback and italic type. Between 1495 and 1498, he printed Aristotle's five-volume collected works in Greek: 1,000 copies, perhaps as many as had ever been copied by hand. New standardized editions of classics, with the same pagination, revolutionized not just accessibility but also the ability to research, communicate and criticize.

Navigating the oceans

The second innovation Le Roy mentioned was the marine compass. Thanks to this, whole oceans could be navigated and 'a great part of terra firma discovered in the West and the South, unknown to the ancients, and therefore called "the new world"'. Here again, Europe's fragmentation of power made it possible to seek alternative patrons. The great Chinese maritime adventures were terminated because the emperor changed his mind about ocean travel. In Europe, the Genoese mariner Christopher Columbus also faced problems setting out to sea. He was turned down by various rulers when he put forward proposals to search for a westward route to Asia. The Portuguese, English and

French kings all declined his request to fund the expedition, as did the dukes of Medina-Sidonia and Medinaceli. Columbus spent twenty years trying to get a sponsor, but that is how Western Europe was different from China – he could keep looking for alternatives. And, eventually, the Spanish court said yes, and in 1492 his expedition accidentally discovered America.

Four years earlier, the Portuguese sailor Bartolomeu Dias had managed to navigate around the southern tip of Africa, proving that it was possible to reach the Indian Ocean. In 1497, Vasco da Gama would take the same route and make it all the way to India. In just a few years, a new continent to the west and another route to Asia had been discovered. Both had the effect of reducing the Middle East's central position in world trade and, by extension, some of the importance and wealth of the Italian trading powers.

It also shook an intellectual world that had treated the Bible and ancient thinkers as authorities. Suddenly there was a whole new continent that God had forgotten to tell us about. Ptolemy had been wrong in thinking that it was not possible to sail south of Africa to the Indian Ocean. Pliny's *Natural History* had not covered any of the strange creatures now discovered. And no one had ever seen potatoes, tomatoes, pineapple, cocoa, chocolate, maize, cassava or tobacco before. 'In that hemisphere I saw things incompatible with the opinions of philosophers,' wrote Amerigo Vespucci in 1503 about the continent that would be named after him.[64]

Aristotle and the other ancients thought that life was not possible in the 'torrid zone' of the tropics. If someone held on to such assumptions after the new discoveries, wrote the Italian physician Giovanni Manardi, 'there is no way of arguing with them other than that by which Aristotle himself disputed with those who denied that fire was really hot, namely for such a one to navigate with astrolabe and abacus to seek out the matter for himself.'⁶⁵ At last, Aristotle's method started to overcome his own conclusions.

Much later, in 1620, Francis Bacon would express the sentiment that started growing during this age of discovery: 'it would be disgraceful, in a time when the regions of the material globe, that is, of the earth, the sea and the stars, have been opened far and wide for us to see, if the limits of our intellectual world were restricted to the narrow discoveries of the ancients'.⁶⁶

The Spanish and Portuguese discoveries kicked off a new era of colonialism, where European sea powers would eventually rule over large parts of the rest of the world. This was also the first step towards the creation of the transatlantic slave trade. Slavery had of course never gone away. The Church now condemned the enslavement of other Christians but upheld the right to enslave non-Christians. Augustine had defended slavery as God's punishment for human sin, and the biblical story of how Ham's son Canaan was cursed by his grandfather Noah for his father's sin was often invoked to justify it. The archbishop of Florence declared that slavery was 'instituted by divine law',⁶⁷ and Venetians and especially Genoese prospered from trade with slaves, first from around the Black Sea, and later from the Balkans and West Africa. Renaissance thinkers rarely objected and some of them owned slaves themselves. Pope Nicholas V was sympathetic to humanist ideas, yet he issued a papal bull in 1455 that gave Portugal the right to capture Muslims and pagans and hold them in perpetual slavery.

With the conquest of America, a whole continent of non-Christians, some saw a perfect chance to expand the practice. The crown granted conquerors land with a certain number of native serfs. In 1495, Columbus had 500 natives sent to Spain as slaves, and in 1518, the Holy Roman Emperor and Spanish

King Charles V licensed the importation of African slaves into Spanish colonies.

However, this appalling expansion also resulted in the first great anti-slavery debate in history. In Spain, a group of thinkers influenced by Thomas Aquinas, now known as the School of Salamanca after the university there, developed advanced proto-liberal ideas about individual rights, economic freedom and rule of law. Controversially, some of them argued that the king was only hired by people to protect their rights, and if he abused these rights, they were entitled to depose him. 'If for our welfare, we need someone to govern us, we are the ones who must grant him the power, rather than him imposing it upon us with his sword,' wrote Juan de Mariana.[68]

When adapting these ideas to the Americas, these scholars argued that Indians could not be seen as brute animals and natural slaves, because they had reason and organized societies. The founder of the Salamanca tradition, the Dominican thinker Francisco de Vitoria (1483–1546) declared gutsily that 'the emperor is not master of the whole world'. Instead, the natives 'undoubtedly possessed as true dominion, both public and private, as any Christian. That is to say, they could not be robbed of their property either as private citizens or as princes.'[69] Therefore, it was a crime to enslave Indians, steal their property or land, or force them to convert. The capture of Aztec and Inca treasures was simple robbery and these valuables should be returned to their rightful owners.

Another important Spanish Dominican was Bartolomé de las Casas (1484–1566), who was an early settler on the island of Hispaniola, but came to devote his life to documenting the atrocities against the indigenous, and combatting them. At first, he thought that local slaves could be replaced by Africans taken in 'just wars', but he came to oppose this as well. Eventually, he concluded that 'the same law applies equally to the Negro as to the Indians', thus expressing an idea of equal rights, regardless of ethnicity.[70]

De las Casas' persistent agitation was so influential that emperor Charles V suspended military activities in America until a debate had been held about the conquest, and a group of jurists and theologians ruled on its legitimacy. The debate began in the Spanish city of Valladolid in August 1550 and another session was held in 1551. The main protagonists were de las Casas and the pro-slavery humanist (yes, that was a thing) Juan Ginés de Sepúlveda. It was an astonishing moment in history, when a superior power began to question if it had the moral right to conquest.

The judges were split, and the outcome was inconclusive. The Dominicans had influenced both the pope and the emperor, but the colonial interests were powerful and the conquistadors were far away from home. The conquest eventually continued. Nevertheless, the Valladolid debate was a watershed moment. An idea of human rights had been developed and presented for Europe, even though it would still be honoured mostly in the breach.

The Orson Welles hypothesis

The third innovation on Loys Le Roy's list was the cannonry, which had surpassed all previous weapons in force of motion, violence and speed. This was the technology that broke through walls and castles and allowed centralized states to sweep away independent cities and autonomous lords. By the end of the Renaissance, absolutist monarchies started to divide Europe between themselves. They grew so confident that they tried to forget that the idea of law had recently been rediscovered. Some talked about the divine rights of kings, thinking that whatever pleases the prince has the force of law. James I of England and Ireland and VI of Scotland wrote that 'The king is above the law, as both author and giver of strength thereunto' and is 'not bound thereto but of his good will'. He even told parliament in 1610 that 'Kings are justly called gods for that they exercise a manner… of divine power upon earth.' He was, he boasted, 'accountable to none but God only'.[71]

Le Roy was hesitant to include gunpowder among the great innovations, since 'it seems invented rather for the ruin than the utility of mankind'. The brutality of the new firearms was an important background to the fear Le Roy had about the future of sectarianism, war and destruction. He wrote ominously that he wished that good men could preserve as many as possible of the fine things restored and new ones invented in this era, to transmit them to future generations, since we could not afford to lose civilization again.

Le Roy's foreboding was related to his mystical beliefs. He thought that God had a plan for this apocalypse, but he did not need much divine revelation to make his prediction. He had already seen that his continent was being torn apart and that the great powers had let slip the dogs of war.

In the climactic scene of the phenomenal 1949 movie *The Third Man*, the character played by Orson Welles defends his villainy with a memorable historical reference:

> When Italy came under the Borgias, there were thirty years of warfare, terror, murder and bloodshed but they produced Michelangelo, Leonardo da Vinci and the Renaissance. Switzerland has had 500 years of democracy and peace and what did that produce? The cuckoo clock.

Apparently, the line was not in Graham Greene's script, but added by Orson Welles himself, when more dialogue was needed during filming. It is haunting because it suggests an uncomfortable truth: that tyranny and conflict can stimulate art and progress, and great sacrifices must sometimes be made for development. However, this does not mean that Welles got it right. The cuckoo clock, after all, comes from Bavaria, not Switzerland. And the Swiss were not known for peace in the Renaissance era; on the contrary, they won their de facto independence from the Holy Roman Empire through fierce combat. The Swiss were some of the most sought-after and feared mercenaries in Europe: the pope did not recruit the Swiss Guard as his armed force because he admired their colourful uniforms.

Similarly, a case can be made that the Borgias did not produce the Renaissance, but ended it, by unleashing a long series of wars that shattered Italy. The scheming Rodrigo Borgia got himself elected pope in 1492. As Pope Alexander VI, he constantly made and broke alliances to secure as much power and land for his family as possible.

The most fatal alliance was the pact with the French king Charles VII to invade Naples, to secure a principality for the youngest Borgia son within that realm. In 1494, Charles VII started an invasion of Italy that would drag Spain and the Holy Roman Empire into war and destabilize the whole peninsula for more than six decades. This ended forty years of territorial stability after the Peace of Lodi, which had given Italian states space to prosper.

The French stunned everybody by making the new gunpowder technology truly mobile. They used handheld guns and mounted lighter cannons on horse carriages. Instead of cannonballs of stone that often shattered on impact, they now made cannonballs of iron. This made it possible for the French artillery to move quickly through Italy, and castle walls that used to withstand sieges for months were now levelled in hours.

Shocked by the speed of the French army, the Borgia pope switched sides and joined a new league of Italian states against the French. This was just one of a dizzyingly long number of constellations in constant flux. At times, even England and the Ottoman Empire became involved. The Borgias soon switched back to the French side again, and then against them, with the Spanish. The brutal realpolitik of the period became the background to *The Prince*, the famous amoral instruction manual for political power, written around 1513 by Niccolò Machiavelli, a senior Florentine official.

As the historian Francesco Guicciardini wrote later, in a much less sympathetic interpretation than Orson Welles', the Italian Wars were 'the seeds of innumerable disasters, terrible events and changes in almost everything... subversions of kingdoms, devastation of the countryside, slaughter of cities'.[72]

As Rowan Atkinson's Blackadder once put it, some in the Renaissance era thought that 'the Renaissance was just something that happened to other people'.

The only extenuating circumstance about the war is that the foreign armies were stupefied by the splendour and beauty of the Italian cities. It was as if two ages, two different centuries, suddenly clashed, as Jules Michelet described it, and foreign armies brought some of that Renaissance spirit back home. That – and syphilis, soon known as French disease to the Italians and the Italian disease to the French (it probably originated with Spanish sailors from America). Wigs soon became the court fashion to hide the patchy hair loss often caused by the disease.

Far from creating Michelangelo and Leonardo, the wars diverted efforts from the arts to arms. Great artists still found the time to create timeless masterpieces, in between flights from affected cities, but Michelangelo also had to build fortifications for Florence and was sentenced to death by the pope for it (until the pope realized that he needed the great artist to continue work in the Sistine Chapel). Leonardo designed killing machines and defensive systems for several leading families, even though he told himself that he did it against the greater evil: 'When besieged by ambitious tyrants I find means of offence and defense in order to preserve the chief gift of nature, which is liberty.'[73]

Having surrendered territory to the French invader, the Medici family lost support and were driven out of Florence. During this chaotic time, the ruling council empowered the charismatic Dominican friar Savonarola in 1495. During his three-year rule, he turned Florence into a radical theocracy.

Preaching the need for moral purification, like so many others in times of crisis, Savonarola organized bands of young men into a morality police. They patrolled the streets in search of sodomites, adulterers and drunkards and they entered buildings to seize secular texts and art, musical instruments, tapestries and elegant dresses. At a huge 'bonfire of the vanities', topped by the figure of Satan, he burned these symbols of wealth, luxury and paganism in the main square in 1497 and again in 1498.

But he overreached. After preaching against the pope, Savonarola was condemned for heresy by the Church and hanged in the same main square. At the time, Savonarola seemed like a bizarre fanatic. People were blissfully unaware that he was a portent of things to come.

Florence returned to a more secular form of republicanism for a while, but the Medici family plotted their comeback. They made a deal with the Spanish, who sacked the city in 1512 and returned the family to power. In 1527, however, the Florentines drove out the Medici again and established a new Florentine Republic. It was to be the last. A large imperial and Spanish army, allied with the Medici pope Clement VII, besieged the city for almost ten months. After the death of perhaps 30,000 Florentines, the city surrendered. This time, the conquerors took no chances with the unruly republicans. The government, elected by the guilds, was dissolved and Alessandro de Medici was made hereditary duke by the Holy Roman emperor. For 200 years, the Medici would rule Florence as unelected monarchs.

Few areas were spared fighting during the Italian Wars, but the calamity that would have the deepest impact on the collective psyche was the new sack of Rome. In 1527, Roman imperial troops, holy but angry at being unpaid, surprisingly attacked Rome, which had for the moment switched its allegiance to the French. The soldiers, many of them Germans fired up by Lutheran hostility to the pope, murdered, raped and ransomed civilians, priests and nuns in an orgy of violence. They looted and destroyed churches, palaces and homes. Libraries were torched, tombs were broken and the holy bones of saints were thrown to the dogs. This terror continued for eight months, until the soldiers ran out of food, and decomposing bodies in the streets started a plague. It has been estimated that Rome's population declined after the sack from around 55,000 to just 10,000.

This is often described as the moment the Renaissance ended. I am tempted to agree, although not because Rome was destroyed, but because of how it was rebuilt. Renaissance humanist popes had worldly priorities like art, law, literature, sometimes feasting and corruption. After the sack of Rome, popes were more eager to establish intellectual control and clerical discipline, and the powers of the Inquisition grew.

Papal Rome was now no longer a separate realm, but subservient to Spain, the Holy Roman Empire and the Habsburg forces, which between 1519 and 1556 happened to be controlled by just one man. History's greatest multi-tasker, Charles V (1500–1558), was head of the House of Habsburg, King of Spain and Holy Roman Emperor. The military–religious alliance constructed in the Middle East by the Abbasids and the Seljuks was now erected in Europe too, in the character of a single man.

The Counter-Reformation

The reaction against Renaissance humanism would never have been so sharp if it wasn't for another momentous development in northern Europe. The growing interest in the critical study of texts (and of how the Church lived up to them) and the printing press combined to turn Martin Luther's 1517 protest against the pope into a continent-wide Reformation movement. Erasmus, whose long-standing calls for reform of the Church had inspired Luther, blamed him for 'the irremediable confusion of everything'.[74]

This is the kind of rift within a religion that often sparks panic, since heretics are usually seen as worse than heathens. Both Catholics and Protestants even expressed the idea that their Christian rivals were more wicked than the Muslim Ottomans. The Catholic Church reacted to this existential challenge to its authority in much the same way as the Sunni Abbasids reacted to divisions within Islam, by trying to renew what they saw as a more pure, original doctrine. With military force and inquisitions, they enforced a religious orthodoxy and quashed the unruly debates and independent thinking that we associate with the Renaissance.

The Council of Trent, which sat on and off between 1545 and 1563, drew up the lines of this Counter-Reformation. It reasserted Catholic doctrine, but it did so by turning against the writers and artists who had opened European minds. The Church defined the role of art in the future and laid down rigid rules for artists. The scriptures had to be strictly adhered to and biblical descriptions of age, dress and expressions followed. The paintings had to be realistic and should induce piety. So, for example, in depictions of Jesus on the cross he should be shown wounded, bleeding, with his skin torn. But nothing could be so realistic as to reveal genitals. Much like Adam and Eve had, the Church suddenly became ashamed of nakedness. Had such rules been in place previously, many of the masterpieces of the Renaissance could never have been made; indeed, some now had to be edited retroactively.

Michelangelo's majestic *Last Judgement* fresco in the Sistine Chapel was threatened with destruction unless the massive nudity on display could be hidden. Another painter was brought in, an accomplished artist in his own right, but whose future claim to fame was having spent his days covering genitalia with drapery and fig leaves. Another controversial painting, Veronese's *Last Supper*, was attacked by the Inquisition for including 'buffoons, drunkards, Germans, dwarfs and similar vulgarities'. Veronese cleverly dealt with the order for a correction within three months by changing the title to the less sensitive *The Feast in the House of Levi*.[75] Hilariously, the pope put fig leaves on his large collection of antique statues.

In 1559, an Index of Prohibited Books was drawn up indicating literature that Catholics were banned from printing or reading, including many enjoyed by and sometimes even published by previous popes. The list of banned books would be expanded and regularly updated until 1966. Eventually it read like a who's who of the greatest European writers, with entries like Grotius, Montaigne, Spinoza, Bacon, Locke, Montesquieu and Voltaire.

By 1600, most of the works of the Renaissance humanists were out of print, and some of its authors were in prison. Almost three-quarters of all books printed in Europe were now banned.

The Renaissance classic *The Decameron* was banned and could not be published again until 1573 in an edition where all ridiculous clergymen had been replaced with secular people, since the Church now insisted that the text 'in no way speak ill or scandalously of priests, abbots, abbesses, monks, nuns, bishops and other sacred matters'.[76]

Erasmus had been declared the leader of all heretics, and his books were burned. The archbishop of Toledo was forced to spend almost eighteen years in a dungeon for having leaned towards the opinions of Erasmus. Merely possessing a book listed in the Index was punishable by death in Spain. In France, informers who exposed someone who owned or promulgated Protestant literature received a third of the condemned heretic's estate.[77] Where strange and controversial theories about the world could usually be discussed during the Renaissance, writers like Giordano Bruno, Lucilio Vanini and Ferrante Pallavicino suffered the fate of Socrates and Cicero: executed by the societies they had helped to thrive.

Through its emphasis on the personal relationship to God, Protestantism would come to play an important role in the development of individualist attitudes, but at this moment in time, and especially through its embrace of state power, it was a force for intolerance. Local populations were forcibly converted, and expressions of their spirituality, such as shrines, art and relics, were destroyed. Luther reinforced Augustinian pessimism, declaring reason 'a whore' and condemning the 'damned, conceited, rascally heathen' Aristotle.[78] John Calvin's Geneva was a police state, where church attendance was mandatory and heretics were tortured and burned.

This was rapidly becoming 'an age of competing fanaticisms' in Stephen Davies' formulation, and the European air was being filled with smoke from burned books.[79] After 1570, even Venice started to cooperate with the Pope's censors and local officials prohibited the printing of books that were listed in the Index. A continent that was previously separated between Church and state was now becoming divided between rival Church–state alliances that clamped down on freedom within their domains. Hundreds of thousands, perhaps millions, were forcibly relocated because of their beliefs.

As so often in European history, Jews suffered disproportionately from a growing climate of intolerance. After Ferdinand and Isabella united Spain in 1492, they forced the Jews to leave the country. Anti-semitism was always a part of Christian tradition and most of the humanists shared it at least to some extent. Now it took an uglier turn. In pamphlets and sermons in the 1540s, Luther sanctioned violence against Jews and tried to get them expelled. Just a few years later, popes enacted anti-Jewish legislation and ordered the burning of Talmud books throughout Italy.

The Galileo affair has become the symbol of Catholic intolerance. At first, the Church was not concerned about Copernicus's (1473–1543) theory that the earth revolved around the sun (which was possibly inspired by Arab astronomy). But Luther attacked that 'fool', and his collaborator Melanchthon thought that 'wise rulers should have curbed such light-mindedness'.[80] In England, Thomas Harriot made innovative astronomical discoveries but never published them because 'he preferred life to fame', as the literary historian Stephen Greenblatt put it.[81]

The Catholic Church felt it had to step up its persecution game, not to lose out in the competition between fanaticisms. In 1616, when Copernicus was long dead and his book on heliocentrism had been in print for more than seventy years, the Catholic Church suddenly found it heretical and burned it. The great polymath Galileo Galilei (1564–1642) was warned not to hold such a position or to uncover such evidence with his improved telescopes. He could of course not help himself, and in 1633 he was dragged in front of the Inquisition and threatened with torture. After recanting, he was sentenced to house arrest for life, and publication of his books was banned, including books not yet written.

Five years later, the English poet John Milton visited Galileo in his villa outside Florence, and deplored that the repression against him and others had strangled inquiry and 'dampened the glory of Italian wits'.[82]

At that time, however, Europe had more immediate problems to concern itself with. In 1524, Erasmus of Rotterdam had begged the Duke of Saxony to see reason: 'Tolerating the sects may appear a great evil to you, but it is still much better than a religious war. If the clergy once succeed in entangling the rulers, it will be a catastrophe for Germany and the church... ruin and misery everywhere, and destruction under the false pretext of religion.'[83]

Europe took a long, hard look at the alternatives of toleration and religious war, and decided to take its chances with ruin and misery everywhere. For more than a century, the continent stumbled from one inquisition and massacre to the next. Both Catholics and Protestants started finding witches everywhere, troubled by lingering customs and beliefs where they tried to impose strict orthodoxies. Thousands of women were tortured until they confessed consorting with the devil, so that they could be properly burned. The wars of fanaticism culminated in the Thirty Years' War 1618–1648, which devastated Germany and killed perhaps as many as a third of the population.

No one was more mercilessly downcast by Europe's sudden lapse into insanity than that pre-eminent proponent of toleration and cosmopolitanism, Erasmus. In 1517, the peace-loving Christian had written 'I congratulate this our age – which bids fair to be an age of gold'. By 1536, fenced in by terror and torture on all sides, he began to fear that he was instead living in 'the worst age of history'.[84]

Summary

The Italian Renaissance is remembered as the rebirth of Europe after a long era of stagnation during the early Middle Ages. From innovative art and new finance and business models to the journeys of discovery, here we find many of the factors that would set Europe on a new trajectory towards the modern era.

This was made possible by typical golden-age conditions. There was an increased openness to the rest of the world, led by the north Italian trade centres who thought that trade should be free, even into the gates of Hell. European merchants and adventurers were stupefied to find advanced goods, technologies, scientific knowledge, financial institutions and Arabic numerals on their journeys to the Byzantines, the Middle East and Asia.

Islamic learning helped Europeans to reconnect with a Greek and Roman world that had been lost for almost a millennium, especially a more worldly philosophy that stimulated an interest in nature, science and economics.

However, unlike in these societies, openness was not the result of an enlightened despot deciding that this would benefit the empire. In Europe, an opening for eccentrics and experiments appeared as a result of the competition between a multitude of polities and rivalry between the Church and the emperor. In these gaps, princes, universities and republican city-states began to stake a claim to independence. It looked less like the Roman, Abbasid and Chinese empires, and more like the classical Greek abundance of competing city-states, always fighting but also constantly learning and trading.

This was incredibly important because radical ideas and innovations had by now been repressed in China, Byzantium and the Islamic world, where new rulers had simply changed their mind. In a more fragmented Europe, new ideas could always survive somewhere, and innovators could always find refuge elsewhere. It started to look like this godforsaken continent could finally get its act together.

Relationships between individuals, groups and states were also increasingly guided by rule of law, as a result of the rediscovery and re-interpretation of Roman Law. Just as the Abbasids had found they needed educated scholars to run a large imperial administration, cities and a new worldly Church discovered that they needed scholars to handle bureaucracy, debate law and taunt rivals, thereby stimulating literacy and social mobility.

Characteristically, economic freedom during the Renaissance was brought about not by a political initiative, but because rebellious cities and serfs fought to engage in it. When markets began to break down feudalism, new careers and opportunities emerged. Social mobility in rapidly growing cities and the glass mirror contributed to the familiar golden-age phenomena of curiosity, self-examination and individualism, reflected in literature and a flourishing of painting and sculpture.

Unfortunately, the same tendency towards absolutism and orthodoxy in troubled times that weakened the great empires began to make themselves felt in Europe as well. In the early 1500s, the new iron cannonballs levelled city walls and made it possible for despots to suppress the independent-minded. Destructive wars began to tear down the peaceful exchange of ideas and books. People who used to venture out for adventure and profit started to hide for safety.

Even more fateful was the Catholic panic over the Reformation. In a close parallel to how the Sunni Abbasids had reacted when challenged by other interpretations of the Islamic faith, the Church decided to shut down open debates and the humanist school that it had previously sponsored. The old, constructive division between Church and state was replaced by mutually hostile state–Church alliances and their competing fanaticisms. As John Milton had lamented, repression and religious wars 'dampened the glory of Italian wits'. Instead of inquiry, we got Inquisitions.

Charles V, head of the House of Habsburg, king of Spain and Holy Roman Emperor, even started pursuing a dream of unifying Europe under one man, one army and one orthodoxy. For a time, it looked like the continent would have gone the way of the stagnant empires, terminating the diversity and fragmentation that set it apart. If it weren't for the Dutch, he might very well have succeeded.

6

THE DUTCH REPUBLIC

Trade, Toleration and Other Treasures of the Shore

God created the earth, but the Dutch made their place on it with their own hands.

LUDVIG HOLBERG, 1745

The United Provinces, after a prodigious growth in Riches, Beauty, extent of Commerce... As made them the Envy of some, the Fear of others, and the Wonder of all their Neighbours.

SIR WILLIAM TEMPLE, ENGLAND'S AMBASSADOR ON THE DUTCH REPUBLIC, 1673[1]

Where there is an embedded history of left and right and profoundly different attitudes to the past, I think it's difficult to settle on a consensus, which is why I think that the last period that you can legitimately say was a golden age was the seventeenth century in the Netherlands. Because it's not really political. It's about Vermeer and canals and tolerance and liberation and all this kind of stuff, and who could object to that? Everyone loves a canal and tolerance.

TOM HOLLAND, 2021[2]

In many short history books, the Renaissance is followed by the scientific revolution, the Enlightenment and, ta-da, the modern world! Well, it didn't seem so at the time. The Renaissance was not followed by individual liberty and scientific inquiry, but by state oppression and religious war. And, for a moment, it even seemed as though one single power was on its way to take control of most of Europe, for the first time in a thousand years.

Through an astonishing series of conquests, marriages and dumb luck, the Habsburg dynasty, originally from the Tyrol, had quickly expanded from its power base in Austria and Germany. In 1519, when Charles V was crowned emperor of the Holy Roman Empire, he also inherited Spain, most of the Low Countries (modern Netherlands, Belgium and Luxembourg) and Franche-Comté in eastern France. In 1526, Charles also inherited Hungary and Bohemia. After the Italian Wars, Spain had taken Milan, Naples and Sicily, and was the dominant power on the peninsula. In 1580, Portugal was annexed.

The Spanish army had become the best in Europe with a superior logistics and support system, and with control of the wealthy trade centres in the Low Countries and Italy, the Habsburgs gained access to financial expertise and maritime power. The Habsburg dynasty was also a global empire. From the new colonies in America silver flowed into state coffers and, after the journeys to the east, it controlled access to the Indian Ocean. It even had a colony in the Far East, the Philippines, named after Charles' son Philip, soon to be King Philip II (1527–1598).

The Habsburg family adopted the double-headed eagle as its symbol, looking both east and west. And north! In 1554, Philip, became King of England and Ireland after marrying Queen Mary I (1516–1558). The Habsburg ambition was nothing less than the establishment of a universal empire, something that would have made it possible to coordinate orthodoxy and repression all over the European continent, and so put an end to intellectual openness and economic experimentation, just like Ming China and the Islamic empires had.

The historian Stephen Davies argues that this was a close-run affair and that the critical moment in European history, perhaps in world history, was the decade of the 1580s.[3] France, Spain's last serious rival on the continent, had by then been tearing itself apart in religious wars for decades, and the monarchy had lost control of most of the country. Habsburg forces surrounded the country on all sides, and Philip II of Spain made an alliance with the Catholic faction.

If Philip II had moved in to dismember France at this point or reduced it to client status, Davies thinks that the Habsburgs would have achieved dominance in Europe with no power able to check them. After Mary I of England died, her half-sister Elizabeth I (1533–1603) reversed her pro-Catholic policies, but England was not a major power. Spain was more of a threat to England than England was to Spain. Rumours of a gigantic Spanish armada being prepared for a crusade with papal blessing against the heretic queen terrified the English.

If I pitched what happened next to Netflix as a multiple-season historical drama series, I am sure it would be rejected for being absurdly unrealistic. Spain's universal ambitions would be frustrated, but not by a powerful, rival monarchy. Just as the Habsburgs were on the cusp of domination, one of the smallest and most unlikely parts of the empire rebelled: a group of maverick merchants and radical Calvinists in the waterlogged Low Countries on the north-western periphery, the strange place where banned books like Galileo's were still published.

The Dutch of all people! There were few people living in the region, with no unified church or powerful aristocracy, few natural resources, no army and no navy. They had no monarch, no state and no constitution, just sovereign provinces that mostly fought internally. They didn't even have much land on which to live and grow food; they had to reclaim it from the ocean and had to be on their guard against the perennial threat of devastating floods. When the desperate Dutch, in the middle of their rebellion, offered their throne to the French King Henry III and then to the English Queen Elizabeth, neither was interested.

This 'indigested vomit of the sea' (as an English satirist called the region) was up against the mightiest empire on the planet. And brought it to its knees.

At the end of the Eighty Years' War between Spain and the United Provinces of the Netherlands, it was the Spanish empire that was depleted and impoverished, having declared state bankruptcy *five times*. The sodden Dutch periphery, on the other hand, had become a strong, independent country and a military superpower. The band of rebels had become the world's richest people, and in just two generations they built a world empire.

And, most astonishingly, while this brutal and costly war against the Spanish was going on, through an unprecedentedly open intellectual climate, the Dutch developed an extraordinary efflorescence, with world-leading artists like Vermeer and Rembrandt, merchants and financiers who created the world's first modern economy, and printing houses, scientists and philosophers who kickstarted the Enlightenment.

But, all the while, there were tensions within the Dutch Republic, between those who wanted a more decentralized system and the semi-monarchist Orangist party that repeatedly tried to take power. One of the leading men behind the Dutch miracle was beheaded for treason. Another was lynched and eaten by rioters.

There is no lack of books and documentaries claiming that this or that country or event created the modern world, but by reassembling all the conditions for a true golden age, its trailblazing record on tolerance, trade, finance, philosophy and science, and the influence it had on Europe and the world, this 'indigested vomit of the sea' has a better claim than anyone else.

Free farmers

The case can be made that the Dutch did not become successful *despite* lacking land, people and authoritative traditions, but *because* they did. It meant that they had to find ingenious workarounds to develop institutions and incentives that made them uniquely successful. With little agricultural land, they had to develop international trade. Because they had a small population, they became open to immigration of workers and scholars. The lack of a scientific tradition and a state church meant that they were tolerant to unconventional ideas and innovations.

In other words: the sea takes, and the sea gives. The rule of law, economic freedom and meritocracy that were deliberately fostered by authorities in many previous golden ages seemed to be the default in the Low Countries, flowing from its particular environmental circumstances. Other European counts and bishops could govern ancient lands and immobile peasantry, but the ones in the waterlogged, marshy lands of Holland, Zeeland, Friesland, Groningen, Utrecht and parts of Flanders were not so lucky. The land was difficult to farm, and the recurring threat of floods sometimes took what was left. South Holland and the western half of what is now the province of Utrecht was a vast peat bog, mostly used for fishing, grazing and collecting peat.

Rulers had to try something different to attract people to these regions. In the eleventh century, they started giving farmers who settled the region the right to their land (similar to what the Song court had done in China), and only forced them to hand over a tithe of the resulting production. In the thirteenth century, the Dutch began to reclaim land from the sea on a large scale. They surrounded bays with dykes and pumped out the water. Eventually they used windmills to power water pumps.

These communities built and maintained sea defences themselves. It took constant vigilance. The resulting polders, low-lying tracts of reclaimed land protected by embankments, had to be maintained when water seeped back in, and when a protective dyke burst, a messenger was sent to drum up support from other citizens – literally. Rushing through the community, he beat his drum to call men and women out to repair it. It was easy for later generations to surmise that the Dutch culture of thrift and cooperation derived from the urgent need to stand together when nature was trying to kill them.

They had local drainage and polder boards with elected water guardians and taxed themselves for hydraulic needs. By default, they became real-life expressions of the ideals of some law scholars for how government power is conferred from below and not devolved from the top. Feudalism was weak to begin with in these areas, and as farmers turned to fishing, river traffic and ocean trade, a system of control created for stationary peasants on land seemed even less appropriate.

Land reclamation, performed by local communities, merchants and eventually real-estate speculators, was a source of tremendous pride. In their national mythology, the Dutch wrote about how the ancient Batavian immigrants had found an uninhabited and dangerous country in the north-east of Europe, and their frugality and hard work enabled them to create and maintain this land. Therefore they had a natural right to their property and owed no allegiance to any sovereign. God made the earth, but the Dutch created the Netherlands.

At least according to later Dutch historiography, their lords traditionally respected the limits to their power. The provinces governed themselves through their own assemblies, the States, and all of them met in a large assembly called the States General, and claimed the right to meet when they so chose. They guarded their independence jealously, as the Habsburgs would find out. The Dutch humanist Hugo Grotius declared the local ethos: 'The old customs and laws shall remain unbreakable. Should the Prince ever take a decision which violates them, no man shall be bound to that act.'[4]

The old kingdoms mocked the Dutch for their peculiarities. They had no ancient land, no dynasty, no history of conquests and not even a central power. They were amphibian, slippery, built on silt. The Netherlands was not a real country, but a collection of shit and mud, said a French aristocrat. And their self-reliance made them disturbingly indifferent to rank and honour. A popular English propaganda poem sneered:

> To make a bank was a great plot of state;
> Invent a shov'l and be a magistrate[5]

Another English observer of the Netherlands, Owen Feltham, noticed that anyone who thought they had done something important seemed to get himself a weapons shield: 'Escutcheons are as plentiful as Gentry is scarce; every man is his own herald.' But Feltham also admitted that this spirit of enterprise and meritocracy had made the Dutch 'in some sort Gods, for they set the bounds to the Ocean and allow it to come and go as they wish'.[6]

Free markets

The Dutch did not just create their land; they also made it prosper. The inhabitants had pivoted towards markets and trade two centuries before the revolt against Spain because of the shortage of agricultural land in the west of the Netherlands. Techniques of land reclamation constantly improved, and projects increased in size. But with the technology available in the fourteenth century, reclamation had for the moment reached its limits, and land that had previously been reclaimed sank and became vulnerable to flooding again. A series of disastrous floods led to a sudden loss of arable land.

Affected farmers could have tried to recreate self-sufficiency at a lower level, but instead most of them decided to specialize on what the land could sustain better: livestock, cheese and butter, and crops like hops and flax. They relied on imports for their supply of grain, increasingly from the Baltic region, especially Poland.

Flanders and Brabant regions in the southern Netherlands, most of which would eventually become parts of Belgium, had become important commercial regions early on. An extended trade network with Italian merchants had made them prolific in textiles, spices, metals and sugar. But now bulk freightage and herring fishery also started to turn Holland, in the west of the Netherlands, into an important commercial player. Amsterdam started to develop as an important depot for Baltic grain and timber. With this also came a shipbuilding industry with a multitude of companies making ropes, sails, casks and sacks. By 1560, Holland alone had some 1,800 seagoing ships, of which 500 were in Amsterdam, compared with around 300 seagoing ships in Venice when it was at its peak in the fifteenth century.[7] As Fernand Braudel observed, 'for the Dutch, commerce was king'.[8]

Just as ancient Athens had once done, the Dutch decided to trust international markets for their food supply because of a lack of farmable land, and therefore they could make more productive use of their local resources. This transformed the economy in several ways. It established a tradition of free trade and it thoroughly commercialized the countryside. In 1514, more than half of the work done in rural areas was performed by wage labourers, who were active in fishing, the merchant fleet, spinning for the textile production, peat digging and water management.[9]

Since livestock farming is much less labour intense than cereal production, this reduced the need for workers. The workforce moved to towns and cities in large numbers, making this the most urbanized region in the world. In 1500, the Netherlands had twenty-one cities with more than 10,000 inhabitants, while England had no more than five.[10]

By the early sixteenth century, the Netherlands had already become a highly urbanized market economy, with markets for labour, goods and capital, and where goods and services were produced for internal and international markets. High productivity and technological progress made rapid economic growth possible. In the words of Ad van der Woude and Jan de Vries, the Netherlands was 'the first modern economy', even though we are familiar with the pattern from Athens, the Abbasids, Song China and northern Italy.[11]

The English writer John Evelyn used the Netherlands as his example of the magical machinery of trade, into which you put whatever you have and take out whatever you need. Their lands, he wrote, produced 'neither grain, wine, oyle, timber, metal, stone, wool, hemp, pitch, nor almost any other commodity of use; and yet we find there is hardly a nation in the world which enjoys all these things in greater affluence; and all this from commerce alone'.[12]

Suddenly, without really thinking it through or having any contemporary models to follow, the Dutch had developed a free-market capitalist economy. It wasn't laissez-faire in every respect. The town guilds still controlled crafts and fought to restrict competition to benefit existing members. However, even there they were more open to entry from outsiders than other countries.

As Maarten Prak and Jan Luiten van Zanden point out in their economic history of the Netherlands, the Dutch experience shoots big holes in the Marxist story that capitalism began as a project of violent oppression. Karl Marx claimed, for example, that peasants in Britain and elsewhere were forcibly ejected from communal agricultural land, so that they would be forced to sell their labour on the market. But the creation of the first modern capitalist economy was not an orgy of violence, but the result of a peaceful transition, where farmers chose to rely on markets, since this made their labour more productive and bought them a better supply of food than they could have grown themselves.[13]

Foreign observers often commented that the Dutch had so much to eat and that they seemed to be always eating. Even the labouring classes could afford meals considered luxuries for the elite elsewhere: fish, meat, eggs, butter and fresh fruit and vegetables. The English naturalist John Ray found too much of everything on his visit, except sadly the Dutch had no boiled pudding, 'either not knowing the goodness of the dish, or not having the skill to make them'.[14]

This long pre-history of the Dutch free market also causes problems for Max Weber's thesis that Protestantism, especially Calvin's version of it, was important in unleashing the capitalist spirit in the Netherlands and elsewhere. It might be easy to assume this in retrospect, since the Dutch were so quick to throw off Catholicism. But Luther did not initiate the Reformation until around 1517 and, by then, Calvin was just eight years old. The Netherlands was a market economy with a passionate capitalist spirit decades before the Reformation was even a glint in Luther's or Calvin's eye. It is more accurate to say that Calvinism took the specific form it did in the Netherlands because the region already had a strong capitalist spirit. Even then, the association was rarely cordial. In 1581, the Dutch Calvinist Church banned bankers from communion and their wives were welcome only if they publicly declared that their husband's usury was immoral.

Capitalist Netherlands was also in the process of becoming a bourgeois society. Trends and tones were not set by the aristocracy, but by the urban and merchant elite. The feudal obsession with land, honour and war was replaced by a preoccupation with calculation, commerce and cleanliness in one's modest home. 'It is there unfashionable not to be a man of business', observed Adam Smith about the Dutch.[15]

A culture where everybody traded with everybody else contributed to a tolerant and relaxed climate that surprised foreign visitors. The English ambassador William Temple noticed that there was a 'general Liberty and Ease, not only in point of Conscience, but all others that serve to the commodiousness and quiet of life; Every man following his own way, minding his own business, and little enquiring into other men's'.[16]

Many foreigners considered it 'a seedbed of theological, intellectual, and social promiscuity', writes Jonathan Israel in his monumental history of the Dutch Republic. They were appalled to see the diversity of churches and the relaxed, open discussion of sensitive subjects. A foreign nobleman complained that ordinary people engaged him in conversation without respect for rank. One visitor was disconcerted to find that servant girls dressed and behaved in such a manner that it was impossible to set them apart from their mistresses.[17]

And most surprising of all was the role of women. It seemed to outsiders that Dutch women were free to come and go as they liked, unaccompanied, and to conduct business and speak candidly. Some even feasted through the night in taverns. Many visitors were embarrassed to see Dutch couples freely caressing each other publicly, and even saluting each other with a kiss. One French observer concluded that this could only be because Dutch women were dead to the passions.

A German visitor wrote that, back home, husbands walked together to church, talking, while their wives followed behind in silence and tended to the children. In Holland, however, women accompanied each other, gossiping loudly. And, most absurdly, husbands even took care of the children, 'for here the hen crows and the cock merely cackles'.[18]

There was formal discrimination against women in the Netherlands. They were banned from political offices, excluded from most guilds and were legally subjected to their husbands. But marriage was mostly based on consensus, and women could own property, inherit and make commercial contracts. If the husband died and there were no children, the widow usually had the right both to the property she had acquired and half of the common estate. Women could even appeal to the law if they thought the husband had squandered their estate, and often won.

Market forces slowly undermined discrimination. As Elise van Nederveen Meerkerk has shown for seventeenth-century textile spinners, women were paid the same wages as men when they did the same work. This was not because the men in charge were less biased than other managers, but because there was ruthless competition and labour was scarce, so businesses that discriminated against half its potential workforce hurt themselves financially.[19] The well-developed capital markets were accessible to women, who borrowed and saved on a large scale, and this made it possible for them to participate in the economy. In 1742, 15 per cent of all taxable enterprises in Amsterdam and 24 per cent in Leiden were owned by women.[20]

Foreigners also remarked that Dutch servants were better treated and afforded more dignity. One remarked that it seemed unacceptable to slap servants in Holland as was usual elsewhere.[21] An obvious reason was that, in a commercialized society, even servants could turn to an alternative labour market if they were mistreated.

The Dutch revolt

There was never a chance that the libertarian attitudes of the Dutch would not clash with the high-handed Habsburg emperors. In 1506, when Charles V, the future Holy Roman Emperor and King of Spain, was six years old, he became Duke of Burgundy and Lord of the Netherlands. The reason was that his paternal grandmother was Mary of Burgundy, heiress to the Burgundy Netherlands. When Charles grew up, he would become the archetypal modern monarch of the late Renaissance, who wanted to centralize authority to make it function more efficiently. However, the Netherlands combined the world's first modern economy with one of its least modern political systems. It was more like a medieval jumble of cities and provinces, assemblies and guilds, who governed themselves and had a hard time agreeing on anything substantial.

In line with his ideology, Charles instituted a more centralized bureaucracy and staffed it with university-educated administrators instead of local nobles. This inflamed resistance from large segments of the population. The Dutch did not just complain that outsiders could not possibly understand local needs, but also that this was an attempt to wrest powers of taxation and administration from them. They said it was a threat to their ancient rights and privileges, confirming Charles' fear that they were stuck in the past. The different philosophies created a mutual suspicion that would turn into hostility and, after Charles' abdication, revolt.

When the gout-afflicted emperor publicly announced his resignation to the States General of the Netherlands in October 1555, he physically had to lean on the shoulder of his loyal advisor William, a native of Nassau in Germany and prince of Orange in France, with large estates in the Netherlands. Charles's successor as ruler of Spain and the Netherlands was his son, Philip II (while Charles' brother Ferdinand succeeded him as head of the Austrian Habsburgs and as Holy Roman Emperor). The clash between Philip II (1527–1598) and William of Orange (1533–1584) would decide the fate of the realm.

Philip took his duties very seriously. He seems to have been a pious man with some control issues. The fact that he was not, like his father, born in the Netherlands, but in distant Spain (where he resided) inflamed local suspicion. The Dutch revolt started when Philip tried to force two things on the tolerant and thrifty Dutch that were anathema to them: higher taxes and the Inquisition. The old economic centres of Brabant and Flanders, and the rapidly growing Holland, were treated as cash cows by the Spanish, who wanted to fund their military adventures and imperial ambitions more than ever.

Habsburg ambitions to stomp out the Reformation with force were even more deeply resented in the Low Countries. In 1522, the Netherlands Inquisition was created and, the following year, two men were burned in the Grand Place in Brussels, the first Protestant martyrs in Europe. Between 1523 and 1565, around 1,300 people were executed. However, locals were reluctant to cooperate, so in 1550 the Spanish Crown clarified its position with the 'eternal edict'. Heresy or the distribution of heretical literature was punishable by death and confiscation of property, which meant that the families were punished as well. Men who confessed were beheaded, women buried alive. Those who refused to confess were burned alive.[22]

The Dutch loathed the edict, especially as Calvinism spread after the 1550s. Crowds sometimes attacked Inquisition staff and released prisoners. Traditional church attendance plummeted. Philip II decided that the only response was increased repression, so he initiated a radical re-organization of the episcopal structure to make the Inquisition ruthlessly efficient.

This alienated even non-Calvinists, because the Dutch commercial ethos abhorred intolerance. The merchant community was international and multi-religious. Goods, services and capital constantly crossed religious boundaries. William of Orange complained in vain to Philip, who had given William more power by appointing him as stadtholder, the highest executive official, of Holland, Zeeland and Utrecht. When the Inquisition was coming to Brabant, there was angry opposition from the magistrates of Antwerp, who complained that 'so many heretics came to Antwerp to trade that its prosperity would be ruined if a resident inquisition were introduced'.[23]

All these tensions spilled out into the open in 1566. It was a time of crisis, when war had disturbed trade and had increased unemployment and grain prices. Many nobles decided that the cautious actions against the Inquisition by William – now mocked as William the Silent – were not enough, so they started public protests. In this intoxicating atmosphere, many Calvinists showed their beliefs openly, with large prayer meetings.

When rioters attacked Catholic properties and destroyed images they considered as icon worship, Philip sent a huge Spanish army to the Low Countries and set up a Council of Troubles to prosecute and execute enemies. It made little distinction between apostates and dissidents and came to be known as the Council of Blood.

William of Orange felt it safest to flee to Germany, but the Count of Egmont, a devout Catholic who despised the iconoclasm, remained, still considering himself loyal to king and Church and thinking he had nothing to fear. This made his fate all the more distressing. Egmont was charged with treason, and even though calls for an amnesty came from many rulers, including the Habsburg emperor, Egmont was beheaded on Brussels' main square in June 1568. His composed dignity during the execution inspired Dutch rebels everywhere, as well as Goethe and Beethoven, who would compose great art to this martyr for liberty: 'It was my blood, and the blood of many brave hearts. No! It shall not be shed in vain! Forward! Brave people! The goddess of liberty leads you on!'[24]

When William the Silent openly declared his defiance, the rebellion gained a figurehead who was a master of propaganda and could raise funds from German Protestant princes. But, at first, the rebels were still just local militia, sailors and fishermen. The Dutch navy started out as refitted grain ships and fishing boats. The Spanish army was clearly superior as long as it could mobilize overwhelming numbers. The problem was that it could not afford to do this over a longer period. Philip II could handle weapons of destruction, but not money. His constant warfare indebted the Crown and, without the Dutch skill in growing the economy, he could not afford to repay the debts. In 1575, he had to declare state bankruptcy, and unpaid Spanish troops started plundering towns frenziedly, pushing the whole of the Netherlands and the States General into open revolt.

In January 1579, the northern provinces took the initiative to form the Union of Utrecht, which would become the foundation of the future republic. Important parts of the south also joined, such as Bruges, Ghent, Brussels and Antwerp. They united mostly to raise an army, and listed all the separate rights and privileges of cities and provinces that would not be affected.

The next logical step was a Dutch declaration of independence: on 26 July 1581, the States General proclaimed the Act of Abjuration, where they revoked their obedience to Philip II. Anyone who has read the American Declaration of 1776 will find themselves in familiar territory. The act states that people are not made to be slaves of princes, but that the prince gets his powers from the people, for the purpose of protecting them and their rights. If instead he oppresses them and their ancient liberties, then he is no longer a prince, but a tyrant, and the people may disallow his authority. And it goes on with a long list of the king's crimes against Dutch lives, liberties and properties, including illegal taxation.

It was probably not much of a comfort to Philip II, but it is in fact a testament to Spain's great intellectual tradition that the Dutch States declared their independence from Spain based on a constitutional theory developed by Spanish scholastics at the School of Salamanca.

Hugo Grotius (1583–1645) built on such theories when he developed ideas of international law and freedom of the seas (*mare liberum*) to make wars less likely and less brutal when they took place. He argued that 'the actions of each individual and the use of his possessions were made subject not to another's will but to his own', and the only basis for political power over someone is *pacta sunt servanda* – that contracts are binding on parties (or, in this case, their representatives) that entered into it. Force was acceptable only in self-defence.[25]

Grotius took a brave and important step in intellectual history when he pointed out that 'what I have said would be relevant even if we were to suppose... that there is no God, or that human affairs are of no concern to him'.[26] These principles derive from human nature and not God's views, and we discover them through reason, not revelation. Grotius made ideas of natural rights and social contracts fashionable in seventeenth-century Europe, and thinkers like Hobbes, Locke and Rousseau were in his debt.

In 1584, the revolt lost its leading figure, when William of Orange was assassinated by a Catholic fanatic. It also started losing the south, including Antwerp. The nobility had always been more powerful there and more reluctant to break with Spain. There were more Catholics and they were horrified by the common sight of Calvinist intolerance. Holland, on the other hand, had always had to be a more united province because of the historical need to protect its merchant fleet and herring fishery. The leadership of the rebellion was moving there.

Refugees were moving there too, when southern Protestants who refused to reconvert were exiled. The exodus of perhaps half the population of Antwerp was a ruinous blow to the hitherto largest and richest city of the Low Countries, paving the way for Amsterdam to become the leading city. Ghent and Bruges also lost almost half their populations. Soon almost the whole eastern side of the northern Netherlands was also under Spanish occupation.

With the revolution hanging in the balance, the Dutch sought outside alliances. First they offered the throne to the French king's brother, who accepted but became exasperated by the limits to his power and left. Then they turned to the French king himself and then the English queen, who both rejected it. They might have thought the Dutch were just too difficult for a monarch or that their struggle was unfeasible. Probably a little bit of both. However, Queen Elizabeth I decided to send military assistance to the Dutch, out of fear that a Spanish triumph could threaten England and encourage Catholics back home.

The most important effect was that Philip's attention became divided. In 1588, Spain spent a fortune trying to invade England with an Invincible Armada, which was in fact not invincible. In 1590, the Spanish commander was sent to France to support the Catholics in the civil war. Spain involved itself in too many theatres of war and raised armies and built fortifications with money that it did not have. Economic laws once again proved to be Spain's most difficult opponent. Despite the American silver that constantly refilled his coffers, Philip II had to declare state bankruptcy again in 1596.

The Dutch Republic, on the other hand, was amazingly getting richer while it was fighting for its survival. During the 1590s another economic transformation in the northern

Netherlands helped to turn the tide in their favour. In effect, free trade and immigration won the war.

The economy saves the revolution

The influx of possibly as many as 150,000 southern refugees to mostly Holland and Zeeland in a short period of time stretched housing capacity to the limit. The population of cities like Amsterdam, Leiden and Haarlem doubled. But integration was breathtakingly quick. New large reclamation projects created more land, and confiscated monasteries were used for housing and enterprises. Importantly, merchant guild restrictions were relaxed, entry was broadened, and fees were set much lower. Where other countries and parts of the Netherlands restricted membership by family and religion, Holland increasingly opened it up to all citizens who could prove professional competence.[27]

Through the refugees, the provinces obtained a massive new supply of labour and ideas. The combination of northern shipping and southern knowhow set off an explosion of ingenuity and entrepreneurship. New industries like paper and textile manufacturing sprang up. Intuitively we assume that more labour reduces wages and vice versa, but the opposite happened. After 1585, wages stagnated in the southern Netherlands, while they continued to increase rapidly in the north especially before 1620. The deepened division of labour that migrants made possible, and the ensuing productivity, raised living standards in the north, while depopulation in the south was followed by despecialization and decline.

The benefits that immigrants brought even started a competition between cities. Kampen announced that, for eighteen months, any newcomer would be granted free and immediate citizenship, wherever they were from. Zutphen offered migrants tax and guild-entry incentives. Eventually, some cities even advertised in French-language newspapers to get as large a share as possible of the Huguenots who had fled from French prosecution.

The Netherlands became a republic of refugees, a word we take from the Huguenot exodus and the associated French word for hiding place (*refuge*). It has even led some to question how 'Dutch' the Dutch golden age really was. The French philosopher Pierre Bayle, who fled to the Netherlands himself, called it 'the great ark of the refugees'.[28] Jews fled there from the Inquisition, Huguenots from French repression, and Germans from the Thirty Years' War, and in the next generation, migrants were attracted by economic opportunities. In the mid-seventeenth century, Amsterdam marriage records show that around every third citizen was an immigrant, which probably underestimates their share of the population. Around 44 per cent of men who married in Leiden were immigrants, some of whom were responsible for its resurgent textile industry.[29]

Non-Christians were also welcomed, although at first they had to pretend to be Christians. Amsterdam offered Spanish and Portuguese Jews citizenship in 1598, 'trusting that they are good Christians'. It wasn't long before even migrants who openly professed the Jewish faith were allowed to become citizens. The economic potential that Haarlem saw in their skills and trading connections was revealed by the invitation to what they thought were 'merchants from Portugal, called Jews'.[30]

The other big change in the 1590s was an expansion of trade. Holland had thrived on trade with commodities of low value, but now Spain felt that it had to open its harbours to Dutch trade to survive. The Dutch instantly moved into the 'rich trades' in the Mediterranean, and started carrying fruit, wine, spices, sugar, silks and dye in a trade network from the Levant to Archangel on the White Sea. It brought large profits to the merchants who had often fled from Antwerp, and spurred the local economy. The network of export industries attracted immigrants and skills from all over Europe, and soon the Dutch moved into sectors like copper production, chemical processing, tapestry weaving, sugar refining, cloth processing, and diamond-cutting and polishing.

The invention of a new ship, the 'fluyt', was a great boon. It had a larger cargo space, a flat bottom and a shallow draught, which made it easy to carry more goods over shallow rivers. It could also be manned by a smaller crew. To construct these ships, the Dutch used wind-driven sawmills that reduced the time to cut beams by more than 95 per cent and made it much cheaper. This was the innovation that made it possible for Dutch ships to carry more cargo in 1670 than the combined Spanish, Portuguese, French, British and German fleets.[31]

The emergence of money markets and new financial instruments in Amsterdam made it possible to finance the voyages. Investors raised short-term loans at fixed rates and pooled them to fund risky ventures. Substantial private savings, combined with markets that trusted the republic more than monarchs, drove down the Dutch interest rate compared with that of its neighbours. Partnerships and shares gave investors the chance to own a little piece of several ships, rather than stake everything on the fortune of a single ship.

Spain was taken aback by the speed with which the Dutch moved into almost every trade, and in 1598, when Philip III succeeded his father, it once again blocked all trade with the Dutch. This was an even greater mistake. Dutch merchants decided that they had to bypass the Iberian Peninsula and go straight to Africa and the East Indies if they were not to lose this trade. It was the beginning of this small republic's global ambitions and its colonial empire. With a huge merchant fleet and deep financial markets, the Dutch soon ruled the waves. Until this time, the Dutch had not passed the Cape of Good Hope. In the seventeenth century, more ships from the Dutch Republic passed the Cape than from all other European countries combined.

The Dutch were off to a flying start when a large number of companies immediately sent their own ships east. This created a problem for the merchants, though, since fierce competition rapidly reduced the price of their imports, so in a sharp break with their free-market ideals, they lobbied Holland and Zeeland to monopolize the traffic. The result was the formation of the East India Company of 1602, a joint-stock corporation with shares tradeable on the Amsterdam stock market. The revolution of this, the world's first official stock market, was that anyone could now raise money on a market rather than having to rely on a few powerful, wealthy people. This broad capital base made the Dutch East India Company more successful than the English version that had been founded two years earlier, which had to raise separate funds for every journey. In the Royal Exchange of London, on the other hand, only goods were exchanged. Stockbrokers were not allowed because of their perceived rude manner.

The Dutch East India Company was not just a company, but also a war machine, with its eyes set on Portugal's colonial empire. Unlike other colonial powers, it did not have an ambition to capture and rule vast territories, but to establish trading posts and coastal forts needed to control shipping routes. The Dutch raided Spanish and Portuguese vessels and conquered the Moluccas 'Spice Islands', Malacca, Ceylon and the Malabar Coast on the Indian subcontinent.

As the Dutch started to conquer distant lands, they left their liberalism back home. It was disturbingly easy for the Dutch, who fought for freedom in Europe, to adapt to being oppressors abroad. Unusually in human history, slavery was frowned upon in the Low Countries and the law did not recognize the institution. Slaves who were brought or fled there had to be set free. But Dutch merchants now came across slavery wherever they went, in India, Indonesia, Thailand, Ceylon, China and the Banda Islands. Some of them concluded, self-servingly, that slavery was proper in Asia, just as freedom was proper in the Netherlands. The Dutch colonizers had few qualms over starting to use slaves to solve local labour shortages, and after 1630, when a new Dutch West India Company took northeastern Brazil, they expanded their involvement in slave trade to man their sugar plantations. The Dutch role in the slave trade was nowhere close to that of the Iberians or English, but during the seventeenth century, they shipped at least 220,000 slaves over the Atlantic.[32]

Their crimes did not even enrich the perpetrators. The slave trade with Brazil was clearly a loss-making venture, writes Maarten Prak, and its only role was that it 'saved the plantations from complete bankruptcy'.[33] It was difficult to attract Dutch colonists, so most of the settlers were often hostile Portuguese. They also had constant border skirmishes with the parts of Brazil colonized by Portugal. In 1654, the last Dutch were pushed out. Twenty years later, the Dutch West India Company was dissolved. The share price had dropped by 90 per cent since the start.

The worst atrocity of the Dutch colonists was the Banda massacre of 1621. Promptly ditching their own loudly proclaimed principles of free trade, the Dutch tried to force the Banda Islands to sell nutmeg only to them. This created a deep rift and a long conflict, and to enforce the monopoly, a Dutch force with Japanese mercenaries massacred thousands. Most of the rest of the population was enslaved or deported.

The Dutch cat

Despite the hypocrisy that would soon become apparent and the occasional economic fiasco, the struggle for freedom back in the Netherlands was going well in the 1590s, on the back of rapid economic growth. Two individuals were of crucial importance. Johan van Oldenbarnevelt (1547–1619) was nominally a legal official of the States of Holland, but he used his role so cleverly that he came to dominate the whole republic, almost as a prime minister. By outmanoeuvring both separatist provinces and the English, who had become a state within the state, he created an efficient republic, dominated by Holland. He also worked to empower Maurice of Orange (1567–1625), William's son, who was selected stadtholder (governor) of most of the provinces. While Oldenbarnevelt modernized the political institutions, Maurice modernized the army. Their excellent relationship made their eventual falling out all the more dramatic and tragic.

Increased resources made it possible to develop the first large Dutch field armies. In two decades, the army grew from 20,000 to more than 50,000 men, but Maurice also revolutionized training, transportation methods and siege techniques, just as Dutch entrepreneurs revolutionized all aspects of manufacturing. He also used similar economic incentives. He offered an extra day's wage to men who dug entrenchments quickly, and a bonus for those who dug in exposed locations.

The reforms turned the Dutch military into a leading European force, with methods eventually imitated all over the continent. Interestingly, many of the new ideas came from studying ancient Rome, which fascinated intellectuals during the revolt. Maurice had studied with the humanist Justus Lipsius, who wrote *De Militia Romana*, which became an unlikely manual for modern warfare.

In quick succession, Dutch forces now took back the territories in the east and some in the south. The country began to take the shape of modern-day Netherlands. A tiny strip of rebel land by the sea was quickly turning into a unified republic and a great military power, with a booming economy and great confidence.

Like the first Song emperor in China, the Dutch closely supervised the behaviour of soldiers in relation to civilians, partly to win hearts and minds and not just battles. Troops were paid regularly in small instalments to avoid the temptation to live off the land and pillage conquered cities. When churches were stripped of images, it was done under supervision of commanders. Soldiers were often hanged for rape.

In Europe, the Dutch became known for a gentlemanly manner quite contrary to their behaviour in the colonies. In 1620, the Venetian ambassador noticed to his astonishment that the Dutch, unlike other Europeans, actually wanted to have garrisons stationed in their towns for the business it provided, and did not seem to be afraid of a destabilizing effect. They were not even worried about having wives and daughters in close proximity to these troops.[34] Neither did men have to be anxious about being enrolled against their will. Other countries pressganged recruits into service, and hungover men often woke up on board a battleship heading for enemy lines. When seamen were in short supply in the Netherlands, their wages were raised, and generous compensation was paid to the wounded.

When the Dutch attacked Medway during the second Anglo-Dutch war, the English diarist Samuel Pepys reported that locals said that 'they kill'd none of our people nor plunder'd their houses'. Pepys was embarrassed to hear them saying 'that our own soldiers are far more terrible to those people of the country-towns than the Dutch themselfs'.[35]

One of the most astonishing facts about the eighty years of revolt and war was that the Netherlands never became a militarized society. The Dutch Republic fought a global war, from Brazil to the Far East, and it often faced threats to its very existence. And yet the martial ethos never came to dominate and the Dutch did not fill their town squares with metal men on horseback. Even though the Dutch constantly fought, often brutally, they saw it as a necessary evil, not the source of identity and the highest status. The Netherlands was a bourgeois society that wanted to make money, not war.

There is a superb (if perhaps zoologically dubious) section about this in Pieter de la Court's *The Interest of Holland* of 1662, an influential book that credited the golden age with republicanism, free trade, tolerance and immigration. There he suggested that the lion on the Dutch coat of arms should be replaced with a cat. Lions are symbols of monarchs, de la Court wrote, since they are aggressive and predatory, whereas the cat is self-reliant, meddling with none and shy of war. However, if the cat is attacked, she is more fierce than a lion, fighting tooth and nail. Therefore cats are not feared, 'enjoy more quiet every where, live longer, are more acceptable, and in greater number than lions'. Just like cats, de la Court concludes, the Dutch will fight when needed, but 'we who are naturally merchants, cannot be turned into soldiers'.[36]

While the Dutch cat became increasingly powerful, the Spanish lion fought fruitlessly against economic realities. The Spanish Crown was so financially exhausted by its many wars that it seemed at times close to collapse. Between 1590 and 1607, unpaid Spanish troops mutinied no fewer than forty times. The government paid for deficits by minting increasingly worthless coins. In November 1607, Philip III announced that, once again, Spain was bankrupt.

Meanwhile, the Dutch were also war-weary and the taxes to pay for war were at painful levels. The war was at a stalemate, so hostilities ceased and negotiations started. The parties failed to agree on peace but signed a Twelve Years' Truce 1609–1621. This did not mean that Spain recognized Dutch independence, but major powers like France, England, Venice and the Ottoman Empire did. This was the moment when the Dutch Republic, or the Republic of the Seven United Netherlands as it was officially known, went from hope to fact.

The war began anew in 1621, but this final phase was more of a side theatre to the wider Thirty Years' War. Spain's attention was diverted and once again it overextended itself. Sweden, building on Dutch infantry tactics, intervened successfully in Germany, a resurgent France declared war on Spain in 1635, and in 1640 Portugal rebelled.

The end came about for reasons familiar by now – Spain ran out of money and the Dutch were frustrated seeing their funds diverted to war. In 1627 Spain cancelled payment on its public debt, and in 1647 had to do it again. Five times during the war against the Dutch, the world's greatest empire, with the greatest supply of precious metals in history, had gone bankrupt. On 15 May 1648 a sufficient number of Dutch provinces, led by Holland, ratified the Peace of Münster, over the objections of the stadtholder. Spain finally recognized the independence of the rebellious Dutch.

The Count of Egmont, who had been beheaded in Brussels' Grand Place in 1568, posthumously got the last word. In Goethe's 1788 play *Egmont*, his ultimate sacrifice is also a victory that forebodes the eventual triumph of liberty:

And as the sea breaks through and destroys the barriers that would oppose its fury, so do ye overwhelm the bulwark of tyranny, and with your impetuous flood sweep it away from the land which it usurps.[37]

A continuous fair

Dutch independence, and the fact that the Netherlands became the world's richest region while fighting off the Spanish, injected a new idea in the European debate. The rest of the world marvelled at how the Dutch had transformed the region from morass and slime to pearls and gold. Apparently great wealth does not come from land and natural resources, but from trade, finance and innovation, and that did not require centralized governments and territorial conquest, but private property, free trade and toleration.

The physiocrat economists in France eventually used the Dutch Republic as their primary example of the power of free markets. In Turgot's article about Europe's occasional fairs and markets for the key Enlightenment reference work, the *Encyclopédie*, he quoted an associate saying 'In Holland there are no fairs at all, but the whole extent of the State and the whole year are, as it were, a continuous fair.'[38]

The Rotterdam physician Bernard de Mandeville presented a scandalous explanation for the wealth he saw around him in his 1714 poem *Fable of the Bees*, suggesting that private vice can create a public paradise. His bees are immoral and greedy, yet this is exactly what makes them work hard for profit, employ people and engage in trade: 'Envy itself, and vanity, Were Ministers of Industry.' He went on to explain that when the hive becomes moral and content, it falls into passivity and poverty.[39]

He explicitly made the point that the Dutch might want to ascribe their prosperity to their ancestors, virtue and frugality, but in reality it was just the result of letting everybody follow their own interests.

Karl Marx, faced with the worrying implication for his theories that the first modern capitalist economy was also the richest and freest, dismissed it with a casual put-down, claiming that by the mid-seventeenth century 'the people of Holland were more overworked, poorer and more brutally oppressed than those of all the rest of Europe put together'.[40]

Marx had a Dutch-born mother and should have known better. But, for political reasons, he stood reality on its head. The republic was an island of plenty in a sea of want, and its workers and farmers 'enjoyed higher incomes, better diets and safer livelihoods than anywhere else on the continent', as foreign visitors at the time attested to.[41] Wages were 'extremely high' compared with neighbouring countries, according to a modern estimate.[42]

Jan de Vries and Ad van der Woude's detailed research on wages, living costs and diet show that the seventeenth-century Dutch 'enjoyed a standard of living and a relative security unknown elsewhere in Europe'. Interestingly, the advantage for unskilled workers was much greater than for skilled. In the period 1650–79, skilled workers in Germany, England and the southern Netherlands earned around 60, 75 and 99 per cent of what they did in the western Netherlands. Unskilled workers made only 48, 65 and 74 per cent, respectively.[43]

The Dutch accomplishment was all the more impressive given that this was the middle of the Little Ice Age, a period of regional cooling when harvests often failed and wages declined all over Europe. The Netherlands was one of few regions that did not suffer regular famines and had few food riots. It was in fact the only part of the continent where wages kept pace with the rise in prices.

Another indication of superior working conditions was that it was close to impossible to get Dutch workers to apply for the hard and dangerous work on long-distance shipping or to settle colonies, while these opportunities were a pull factor for French, German, Swiss and Portuguese immigrants to the republic.

Great wealth and the search for profitable investment could misfire, of course. Tulips were a recent import from Turkey, and unique colours and flamed patterns rapidly became status symbols. Tulips increased in price in the 1630s and more people were drawn to the market, thinking prices would rise even further. We don't have detailed price data, but it seems as though prices increased twenty-fold over the winter of 1637, and a rare bulb could command prices equivalent to the value of a luxury house in Amsterdam, just before the market collapsed.

However, this tulip bubble was not merely the outburst of madness that ensuing generations would claim. It was inflated by a long-debated regulation that retroactively changed future contracts into options. Buyers were relieved from the obligation to buy the tulips they had bid for if they paid a small fixed percentage of the contract price. Offering huge sums seemed like a one-way bet. If prices rose, speculators could make a profit and, if not, they could escape the contract.[44] The tulip mania was exaggerated by Calvinist preachers, who used it as an indictment against an immoral economy driven by self-interest and profit, but the economic damage was much smaller in reality than in popular imagination (and it was not followed by the righteous plague that preachers had promised). Long-term, the greatest effect was that Dutch farmers learned to grow the attractive bulbs and turned the republic into a tulip superpower.

True freedom

To some, the political framework of the United Provinces seemed as unlikely as Marx found its economy. It was famously described as a constitutional monstrosity by one historian. Every Dutch polity could be divided into smaller polities, and they all wanted a say: republics within republics. Cities were governed by town councils made up of the urban merchant elite. These 'regents' appointed new members to the council and also elected representatives to the seven provincial assemblies, 'the States', where the nobility was also represented. Representatives of each province met in the States General in the Hague, which directed foreign policy and military affairs, handled shipping and the national budget, but most affairs were left to the provinces, and not even taxation was standardized.

The stadtholder was originally the local representative of a feudal lord, but the office was left intact as a province's highest executive official after the revolt. Provinces chose their own stadtholder, but most of them held the office in many provinces simultaneously, increasing their power. Often they had the right to choose members of regent councils from shortlists.

The balance of power was not precisely defined and there were constant tensions. It seemed like a miracle that the provinces managed to stick together during their long struggle, especially during the seventeenth century when the centralized states of England, France, Germany and Spain broke apart in upheavals and civil war. As Simon Schama puts it, 'the Dutch republic was the great Seventeenth Century exception'.[45]

This does not mean that the Netherlands was tranquil. There was a constant tug of war between the republican States' Party, which argued that political sovereignty belonged to the provinces, and the Orangists, who wanted a centralized state led by a stadtholder, and as indicated by their name, preferably a prince of Orange.

The tension between these two parties, one led by Holland, regents and the urban bourgeoisie, and the other allied with nobles, farmers and militant Calvinists, was a recurring theme throughout the republic's history, and several times it threatened to break down into civil war. Since 1588 the Netherlands had been a fully fledged republic, but both parties had ambitions that challenged the status quo. Holland was happy to accept majority decisions in the States General as long as these went their way, but insisted on going it alone when it was in the minority. The Orangists claimed that they were loyal to the republic but wanted to add a semi-monarchical element with the right to interfere in the provinces and control regent councils.

The first dramatic clash was stadtholder Maurice's coup in 1618 after a struggle about the Reformed Church, during a period when the truce with Spain meant that the common enemy was out of sight and out of mind. Groups led by Holland's Oldenbarnevelt and Hugo Grotius tried to impose moderation and toleration on the Church with heavy-handed means. Maurice of Orange privately admitted that he understood nothing about the theological debate, but traditionally allied with hardline Calvinists and used their grievances to build his base.

When anger against Oldenbarnevelt's ambitions resulted in riots and violent attacks, Holland took the fateful step of raising special troops and declaring that their units of the regular army were loyal to their province and not to the States General. This bordered on secession, and the stadtholder used this and substantial intimidation to rally other provinces and towns against them. Maurice's army disbanded the new troops and imprisoned his enemies. After a lengthy trial, Oldenbarnevelt was beheaded for treason and Grotius and several others were imprisoned for life.

Holland's dominance was ended for the moment and executive power concentrated in the hands of the stadtholder, who put his own men in charge of political assemblies and the Church. With a group of trusted nobles he made all important decisions, and manipulated provinces and the States General. But Maurice died in 1625, and his successor and half-brother, Frederik Hendrik, was more moderate.

Furthermore, it was difficult to keep Holland down for long. The province's economic and intellectual power soon allowed it to float back up to a leading role in the republic. It was not even possible to keep Grotius in prison for long. He was held in Loevestein Castle, but was allowed a large supply of books and papers to continue his writing. In March 1621, he managed to hide in one of the book chests with the help of his wife and servants. He escaped and fled to Paris, where he continued to write some of the most important works of the Dutch era, which inspired republicans everywhere.

The second major crisis came in 1650 under Frederik Hendrik's son, William II, who had opposed the peace of Münster in 1648 and now rejected calls to reduce the size and cost of the army. As both sides refused further compromise, Holland decided, according to its insistence of being a sovereign province, to unilaterally disband army units it paid for. This was the opportunity William II had been looking for. Arguing that Holland was in revolt, he marched with his army to Amsterdam in the summer of 1650 and had leading regents arrested. William II was now in charge, and the Church looked forward to a new era of order and of orthodoxy. But then, a few months later, the prince died of smallpox, at just twenty-four years old. It was a complete shock and a devastating one for many Calvinists who believed in divine intervention.

The States of Holland rejected the whole idea of having a stadtholder after the sudden death of one who had tried to subject them, and started to take over all the political and military functions of the stadtholderate. The Great Assembly in the Hague agreed that it was not obligatory for a province to appoint a stadtholder, and five of the seven provinces now refused to do so. This was the start of the First Stadtholderless Era, when the provinces governed themselves, through war and peace, negotiations and compromise, with the position of highest executive official left vacant.

The leading man of the era was Johan de Witt (1625–1672), who was elected grand pensionary of Holland, its highest official, at twenty-seven years of age. With astute statesmanship, de Witt managed to get the provinces to follow Holland's lead for two decades, as well as divide both Orangists and foreign adversaries. He was an advanced mathematician and sometimes appeared with an abacus in the States General to explain complex economic relationships. His diplomatic and political skills owed something to his works on probability. He always examined the interests and choices of others before plotting his own course. If he had a weakness, it was that he, like Athens' Pericles, sometimes overestimated how much others understood their own rational interest.

De Witt's State Party developed a republican ideology called *de Ware Vrijheid*, 'True Freedom', an ideology of free markets and toleration at home and 'Free Ship, Free Goods' abroad, rejecting ideas of territorial expansion. They denied not just the institution of stadtholder, but any 'eminent head' of the republic or its provinces. Princes stoked wars only to further their own ambitions, but foreign policy could be rational and focus on trade and security, as long as it did not have to heed dynastic interests. De Witt warned the Dutch against the example of Florence under the Medici, where high positions became hereditary and freedom was lost.

The republicans were not democrats. Power was to be kept in the hands of the regional merchants and regents. However, around this time, some of the first modern ideas of democracy were developed by the radical Enlightenment philosopher Baruch Spinoza (1632–1677) and his circle.

Amsterdam's magnificent new city hall, completed in 1655 (now the Royal Palace), was a splendid symbol of this new urban self-confidence. One of the largest buildings in Europe, it made the palaces of nobles, including the House of Orange, seem modest. On the top of the building Artus Quellinus' colossal statue *Pax* presides. Weighing 8,000 lb, this goddess of peace holds Mercury's staff, symbolizing commerce, and an olive branch, invoking the famous peace-loving Athenian olive growers. The consequence of commerce and peace are visible in her third attribute, the cornucopia, representing abundance.

Contemporary royalists and subsequent historians have disdained the republic's chaotic way of governing a state, without a king or even a centralized government, but it coincides with the period when the Dutch Republic was most economically superior and militarily safe. It prevailed in battles that were usually fought to defend its trade against jealous rivals, including two wars against England. Most famously, in 1667, the Dutch fleet under Michiel de Ruyter broke the English defences, sailed up the Thames estuary into the river Medway, where they burned many vessels, and spectacularly captured and towed away the flagship of the Royal Navy, HMS *Royal Charles*, as a trophy. The Dutch fleet was in so many places that one exasperated English officer memorably cried out: 'I think the Devil shits Dutchmen.'

In the peace agreement, the Dutch got what they wanted. As long as they kept the important nutmeg-producing colony of Surinam, they could gladly surrender less valuable parts of the American continent to the English, such as Nieuw Amsterdam, which was renamed New York after the next English king, James II, when he was the Duke of York. So the Dutch traded New York, New Jersey, Pennsylvania, Massachusetts, Connecticut and Delaware for nutmeg, and most thought they got the better deal.

The plan for the raid on the Medway was conceived by Johan de Witt, and his brother Cornelis de Witt joined the fleet to supervise it. This was the moment of de Witt's greatest triumph, and he used it to push through the Perpetual Edict, which abolished the stadtholderate in Holland forever.

At the same time, however, the war gave the humiliated King Charles of England a deep thirst for revenge and made the Orangists even more jealous of the de Witt brothers, who seemed to succeed in their every effort while being determined to keep the sixteen-year-old William of Orange, the son of William II, away from power forever. These two factors would eventually seal the de Witt brothers' ghastly fate. But, for now, they were riding high and the republic was stronger than ever.

Enlightening the world

The Dutch Republic was a melting pot of thoughts and cultures, with a tolerant approach to most ideas and different groups. Hugo Grotius summarized this: 'there are several Ways of living, some better than others, and every one may chuse what he pleases of all those Sorts.'[46]

The United Provinces were much less gripped by the witch craze than other countries, strengthening the theory that this persecution was spillover of a desperate search for orthodoxy. In the 1590s, when the witch trials were about to reach their most active phase in the rest of Europe, they were already being phased out in the Netherlands.

Many outsiders were offended by the toleration they witnessed in the republic: 'sometimes seven religions are found in one family', complained one.[47] And so were some Dutch. Aernt van Buchell, a Catholic canon who became a Calvinist, despaired that: 'In confusion they run in so many different directions that truth can hardly be distinguished from falsehood, nor Christ from the devil, and nothing in the world is certain.'[48]

The Calvinist Church constantly pressured towns and provinces to restrict this confusion, and repress not just alternative churches and secular philosophy, but also smoking, drinking, adultery, dolls, theatre, dancing, organs in churches, the violation of the Sabbath and the popular and blasphemous St Nicholas Day feast in December. In some towns and in some periods the Calvinists managed to regulate social life harshly, and the Netherlands was never a free-for-all. But liberal cities like Amsterdam and Rotterdam left them frustrated, and in most other towns regents allowed the Church to impose ecclesiastical forms of punishment only (for example, exclusion from communion) against misbehaving members.

It was difficult to impose an intellectual monopoly anywhere when only around half of the population was Calvinist; the closest thing to an orthodoxy was to do business with anyone, no matter who he was or what he believed. 'We declare to you that you have no right to trouble yourselves with any man's conscience,' William of Orange had proclaimed, 'so long as nothing is done to cause private harm or public scandal.'

Formally, Catholic services were forbidden, but even allowing people to remain Catholic in private was progress compared with countries that interfered with private beliefs. But the Dutch went further. They allowed clandestine churches, where minorities could have communal sermons as long as they were not conducted publicly.

If you stand in front of Oudezijds Voorburgwal 40 in central Amsterdam, it looks like an ordinary seventeenth-century canal house, but if you walk up to the top three floors, you suddenly find a beautiful Catholic church, complete with decorations and a confessional. The city set rules for these private churches, which was a form of official sanction: for example, hours of operations were set so that Catholics worshipping there would not run into Calvinists going to work, and Catholics were not allowed to carry prayer books in the streets.

Amsterdam also had underground synagogues, and their services were overlooked in the same way. In 1642, the year that Rembrandt painted *The Night Watch*, the stadtholder even visited a synagogue with his wife, giving them an official blessing. A generation later they could be built openly, despite complaints from the reformed church.

The wild combination of people and traditions made the republic fruitful ground for eccentric and innovative ideas. The debate about the revolt and the Reformation had also accustomed large segments of the population to take intellectual issues seriously, discuss right and wrong and find principles and worldviews on which to build their cases. In 1575, the republic built the first of several universities in Leiden, and since the Church's demand for control was rejected by authorities, it was one of the freest universities in Europe, as well as one of the largest. It played an important role in the study of medieval Arabic texts and their relation to ancient Greek thought.

The university was also extremely international. While English and German universities almost exclusively catered to their own countrymen, half of Leiden's students came from another country in the first half of the seventeenth century. The university's reach can be traced in the fact that half of the professors in Uppsala, Sweden, had studied in Leiden. Almost all Danish scientists had studied in the republic.[49]

Toleration and literacy, combined with printers from Antwerp and Huguenot papermakers from France, turned the United Provinces into the printing house of Europe. By 1650, thirty-four Dutch cities had at least one printer or publisher, and Amsterdam had ninety-one. More than 100,000 titles were produced in the republic during the seventeenth century, in many languages and often for export.[50] What was censored in one Dutch city could usually be printed somewhere else, and when something was deemed heretical everywhere, clever entrepreneurs just named a foreign city as the place of publication. In this way, 'the central city of the Republic of Letters moved from Venice to Amsterdam', writes the American historian Elizabeth L. Eisenstein.[51]

The Republic of Letters was a spontaneously organized and rapidly growing transnational network of intellectuals, with roots in Erasmus's network of fellow thinkers in Renaissance Europe. They corresponded across national borders on philosophy, politics and science, to share, test and criticize new ideas and to stay up to date with what the others were doing. Their principles of free entry and contestability turned it into a community of thousands of members, of great importance to scientific innovation and technological advances.

The French philosopher Pierre Bayle (1647–1706), who had fled to Rotterdam and was a leading member of the Republic of Letters, explained the network's ethos:

> This commonwealth is a State extremely Free. The Empire of Truth and Reason is only acknowledged in it; and under

their protection an innocent War is waged against any one whatever. ... Every body, there, is both Sovereign and under every-body's Jurisdiction.[52]

The Republic of Letters was not formally established or designed, it had no statutes, no list of members and no annual meetings, but it came to be 'the main institution behind the meteoric takeoff of useful knowledge in Europe during the Scientific Revolution and the Enlightenment', according to economic historian Joel Mokyr.[53]

If British cafés and French salons would eventually become known as the schools of the Enlightenment, the United Provinces was its cradle. It hosted many of the pioneers of a secular worldview, with a universe that can be explained better by mechanistic and mathematical principles than by miracles and religious texts. In such a world, knowledge comes from the evidence of the senses and human reason, not authorities and divine revelation. And, quite possibly, the goal of life is not to sacrifice one's interests for kin, tribe or afterlife, but to improve the human condition and achieve happiness in this life.

Such ideas had emerged many times and in many places before: as we have seen, Thales and other Greeks pioneered it, and it was the starting point of philosophers in Abbasid and Song times, but as long as authorities and churches controlled thought and speech, these thinkers were soon suppressed. This is why the Dutch Republic became a magnet for independent thinkers opposed to the 'children of darkness', as one professor in Groningen controversially put it.[54] This was the one place where they could debate heretical ideas, print banned books and argue that miracles, angels, witches and demons were just superstition. Maarten Prak points out that, before 1600, hardly any scientific work had been carried out in the northern Netherlands, and precisely this lack of entrenched beliefs and traditions offered ample opportunity for disruptive scientific and philosophical innovation.[55]

Jonathan Israel, a historian of the Enlightenment, has nominated six founding philosophers of the movement: Descartes, Spinoza, Hobbes, Locke, Bayle and Leibniz. Of those six, no fewer than four lived in the Dutch Republic, at least for a while, but perhaps it says even more about the country's openness that only one of them was actually born there, Spinoza, and he was the son of Portuguese Jews who had fled there. Both the French Catholic Descartes and the Huguenot Bayle found the Netherlands more hospitable to radical ideas. 'In what other country could you find such complete freedom', asked Descartes, whose books were put on the Catholic Church's index of forbidden books in 1663.[56] John Locke fled to the republic from Stuart England in 1683, suspected of involvement in plots against the king. He settled in Amsterdam, where he wrote some of his most important works.

Even the last two founding fathers of the Enlightenment, Hobbes and Leibniz, had important connections to the republic. Hobbes published several of his controversial books in Amsterdam because he couldn't get the English censor's licence, and Leibniz developed his ideas under the influence of Spinoza and another Dutchman, physicist and mathematician Christiaan Huygens.

Huygens' search for the mechanistic principles of the universe, his invention of the pendulum clock and the improved telescope with which he discovered the rings of Saturn are a great example of the Enlightenment's combination of theory and practical experiment. Another example is the Delft draper Antonie van Leeuwenhoek, whose interest in lens making led him to discover and experiment with microorganisms. The

Dutch ambition to improve constantly, refining technologies for production and travel, supplied plenty of instruments for this scientific revolution, such as the microscope and the thermometer, just as Dutch trade provided scientists with exotic flora, fauna, fossils and minerals to study and categorize. In medicine, anatomy and botany, the republic led Europe.

Furthermore, the example of the Netherlands itself inspired ideas about the possibility of human freedom. Traditionally, religious and intellectual homogeneity had been seen as the precondition for social peace. But now, to everyone's surprise, the country with the most toleration and most diverse sects turned out to be the most peaceful and well functioning, whereas the insistence on unity in the rest of Europe led countries to tear themselves apart in seemingly endless wars and massacres.

Spinoza argued that toleration explained both Amsterdam's peace and its success:

> In this flourishing state, this city without a peer, men of every race and sect live in greatest harmony, and before entrusting their property to some person they will want to know no more than this, whether he is rich or poor and whether he has been honest or dishonest in his dealings. As for religion or sect, that is of no account.[57]

As Bayle argued: 'As to that monstrous Medly of Sects disgracing Religion, and which they pretend is the Result of Toleration; I answer, That this is still a smaller Evil, and less shameful to Christianity, than Massacres, Gibbets, Dragooning, and all the bloody Executions.'[58]

In 1684, Bayle started publishing *Nouvelles de la République des Lettres* (News from the Republic of Letters). It was probably the first journal of book reviews. It critically examined new publications, compared new ideas to known facts and so created a platform for Enlightenment ideals of open debate and contestability. He was motivated by a passion for progress, claiming that 'History, properly speaking, is nothing but a list of the crimes and misfortunes of the human race.'[59] Bayle and other Huguenot refugees wrote in French, integrating their work in a broader European context.

John Locke (1632–1704) wrote *A Letter on Toleration* in the republic and spent a lot of time with minority groups there. In all likelihood, it informed his conclusion that 'neither pagan, nor Mahometan, nor Jew, ought to be excluded from the civil rights of the commonwealth, because of his religion'.[60] Locke had probably begun his towering 1689 work *Two Treatises of Government* before he left England, but it's not far-fetched to assume that the Dutch example and the Act of Abjuration inspired his argument that governments exist only to defend individual rights, and if the king instead violates those rights, he 'unkings' himself, and the people have the right to rebel.

Symbolically well timed, Amsterdam at this time also became the first real city of light in a literal sense. Towns had previously been dark and dangerous. Travellers often hired a lantern-bearer to make their way safely through dark, winding and uneven streets. In the 1660s, the Dutch painter and engineer Jan van der Heyden invented the first efficient oil-lamp with shielded air-holes that let out smoke without letting in too much wind. Amsterdam patricians financed a city-wide plan and, in January 1670, 1,800 public lamps suddenly lit up the whole city. Admiring the spectacle, a German student commented that 'in the evening the entire city is illuminated with lanterns, so that one can pass through the crowds of people just as in broad daylight'.[61]

The rise and fall of Dutch art

Another area where the Dutch led the world was art. According to the historian Peter Gay, 'Never in history has one country – and so small a country! – produced so many painters of such high calibre in such short time.'[62] This was another consequence of a market-based society. When traditional art centres like Bruges, Ghent and Antwerp fell to the Spanish, many artists and painters fled to the north. There they faced a very different situation, without traditional patrons. The new Reformed Church disliked images, and the nobility was weakened – many of them had migrated in the opposite direction, to the south. On the other hand, there was a large middle class with growing purchasing power, especially after the 1590s, and this is where they turned.

This change in patron also changed the objects of art. The urban bourgeois household did not have room for large-scale historical or mythological paintings but enjoyed smaller paintings of everyday life. Therefore artists pivoted away from religious and martial subjects to portraits, interiors, landscapes, townscapes and genre paintings. Meanwhile, foreign trade provided new inspiration as well as new materials and colours.

The large concentration of artists resulted at first in the proliferation of cheap print, mass-produced etching and temporary decoration. This whetted the public's appetite for art and broadened the market. Fierce competition between artists, combined with the fact that they now assembled in cities like Utrecht and Haarlem without artistic traditions, led to experiments in techniques and concepts.

It also led to a hitherto unknown specialization. Some painters specialized in still lifes, others in sunlit forests or winter landscapes. Frans van Mieris focused on the 'merry companies' of small groups involved in an activity like making music, and Aelbert Cuyp became the master of painting cows. Hendrick Cornelisz Vroom, the pioneer of seascape painting, even sailed into a storm to improve his ability to render rough sea conditions. Frans Hals developed the difficult and almost impressionist technique of capturing fleeting expressions of playfulness and laughter, which models could not keep up for any length of time.

Through this innovation and specialization, all art genres received an injection of creativity and increasing sophistication. The large market also meant that artists started to paint without having commissions, giving potential buyers more to choose from, and they also produced for export. It has been estimated that at least 5 million paintings were produced in the republic during the seventeenth century, an incredible number for a population of roughly 2 million, even though many of the paintings were copies or imitations with only small modifications. Foreigners were amazed to see that even ordinary households had one or two paintings on their walls.[63]

The master of genre painting was Johannes Vermeer (1632–1675), from a Flanders family who had moved to Delft. His subjects are usually placed in a corner of a room, engaged in conversation, or alone, reading or writing a letter, making bobbing lace, pouring milk, playing the lute or measuring distance on a map. Or she is just gazing towards us, wearing a pearl earring. These are intimate situations, where movement is suspended for a moment to let the viewer participate and almost intrude. The scenes are bathed in light, and even the shadows are alive with colours. Only thirty-four of Vermeer's paintings have survived, and he probably did not make many more, suggesting that he worked carefully and slowly, using very expensive pigments.

Rembrandt (1606–1669), the son of a Calvinist father and a Catholic mother in Leiden, was very different in his refusal to specialize. He was an innovator and master of many different styles and subjects, producing hundreds of paintings and drawings and around two thousand etchings. His combination of different techniques breathed fresh air into old genres: for example, his dramatic lightning to create contrasts and capture gesture and posture enlivened his many historical and biblical paintings.

The great Dutch masters were an expression of the republic's strengths, and therefore their decline was a symptom that something was going seriously wrong. A more insular and traditionalist atmosphere became obvious after 1672. Painters dropped their previous eagerness to experiment and became more repetitive, in a development similar to what happened to Chinese art towards the end of the Song era. Consumers no longer looked for novelty and excitement, but old styles and old works.

In private Amsterdam collections, living artists were responsible for more than half of all paintings in the 1660s, but this reduced to 42 per cent in the 1670s and to just 14 per cent in the 1680s.[64] By the end of his life, Vermeer could no longer earn a living from his masterpieces. After his death, his works were auctioned off at ridiculously low prices. Artists who had previously flocked to the republic now started to emigrate. During the eighteenth century, the Dutch upper class often hired French artists to make their portraits instead.

The golden age and its art scene had been set in motion by the republic's openness and curiosity, but these traits were subverted by a more fearful culture towards the end of the seventeenth century. It started in 1672, a year still remembered in Dutch history as the *Rampjaar*, the Disaster Year.

The Disaster Year

France had recovered after the wars of religion ended and Spain's powers waned. Under the long rule of the absolute monarch Louis XIV, its military had become the strongest in Europe. His threats against the Spanish Netherlands stirred up trouble.

De Witt preferred to stay allied with such a strong power, which could also pose the greatest threat, but a strong anti-French, Orangist view in the republic was more tempted by English overtures in 1668 for a Triple Alliance with the Netherlands and Sweden to keep both France and Spain in check. The young William III of Orange was the son of the English king's sister, and this made an alliance between the two maritime powers seem natural to most people, except de Witt, who thought that the English were sore losers in trade and war, and would always come back for more. But he had to yield to pressure.

Even though Louis XIV had promised not to go further northwards than a red line drawn by the Triple Alliance, he was furious about the implied threat of force. He felt betrayed by the Dutch and started laying plans to attack the republic from all sides.

As the war drums beat louder, the Dutch became stuck in political squabbles. De Witt tried to acquire funds for fortifications and soldiers, but Orangists refused unless the young William III was made commander-in-chief, which happened in February 1672. The next month, it became obvious that the very existence of the republic was at stake. To the surprise of his own parliament, King Charles II of England betrayed the alliance he had initiated. In secret he had agreed with France's Louis XIV to join him in dismembering the Dutch Republic. De Witt had been right to mistrust him.

Without warning, the English navy attacked a Dutch merchant fleet, and in May a French army invaded from the south, four times bigger than the Dutch army. Through an agreement with the bishop of Münster and the elector of Cologne, Louis XIV could avoid the Spanish Netherlands, where Dutch defences were strong, and move through the Bishopric of Liège before attacking the republic from the east. Simultaneously, Münster and Cologne also unleashed their forces on the United Provinces.

While the Dutch fleet managed to prevent a seaborne invasion, the French offensive on land was dizzyingly quick: panicked towns surrendered en masse. Within months almost the whole of the republic was occupied by enemy forces. Holland was saved only by the Dutch Water Line, a defence system that relied on opening flood gates to inundate the territory between them and the enemy. It was Holland's version of the long walls of Athens, closing it off from all directions but the sea, where they were the strongest.

But the sense of defeat was immense. Even though Johan de Witt had read the situation better than the opposition, his States' Party was in power and got the blame for the disaster. Preachers, militiamen and Orangist pamphleteers began to stir up unrest against the republicans, claiming that they had left the Dutch defenceless and that the English king was attacking only because they had kept his nephew, William III of Orange, out of power. Angry crowds accused the republicans of being traitors, friends of France and defenders of toleration for Catholics. Others called for repentance and fasting at the end of days. Demonstrators and violent mobs soon ruled the streets and overthrew local assemblies. The intimidated States of Holland finally agreed to make the 21-year-old William stadtholder. The Perpetual Edict had not even lasted five years.

Johan de Witt was severely stabbed in an assassination attempt and resigned as grand pensionary on 4 August, seeing all his plans for the republic in ruin. Meanwhile, his brother Cornelis had been imprisoned and tortured on trumped-up charges of plotting against William. On 20 August, Johan came to the prison to escort Cornelis away. They were attacked by an Orangist mob, beaten, stabbed and shot to death. Their naked, mutilated bodies were pulled up by the feet on a gibbet for all to see. Most sickeningly, the rioters disembowelled the corpses, and roasted and ate parts of them. The fact that the new ruler, William of Orange, never prosecuted the perpetrators has always been one of the strongest indications that the lynching was not entirely spontaneous.

Against all odds, the Dutch Republic did not suffer the same gruesome fate. The Water Line held, and interventions from the old enemies, the Holy Roman Emperor and Spain, forced France to divert men south. The naval commander De Ruyter, who had been accused by Orangists of treachery, was the real hero of the war when he managed to defeat both the French and English at sea three times in 1673, with a much smaller fleet.

For now, the Netherlands was a republic in name only. William of Orange tried to rule as a military dictator at first. He purged regent assemblies throughout the country, and changed their electoral procedures to secure his control. He took personal command of military affairs and handled foreign policy in private. In 1675, the States General declared that the office of commander-in-chief would from now on be hereditary in the male line of the Prince of Orange.

Since all of this smacked of monarchical ambitions, for safety, the States General banned anyone from arguing that the stadtholder aspired to sovereignty over the provinces. Blasphemy and attacks on the Church had often been outlawed before. Even in Holland, books denying God or the divinity of Christ were outlawed (although regents moderated the impact by often warning booksellers in advance that a raid was coming). But this was the first time political debate had been censored by the States.

The spectrum of acceptable opinion was generally more circumscribed in the tense climate after 1672. Traditionalist Calvinists took this opportunity to attack the ideas of Descartes and Spinoza, especially their notion that religious scriptures had to be critically examined and re-interpreted if found inconsistent with natural laws. Such ideas, especially in a popularized Spinozist version, inspired anti-Christian writings of French Enlightenment thinkers, but they were now proscribed at Dutch universities. In 1674, the States of Holland banned books by several troublemakers. Spinoza was considered especially dangerous, for his denial that the Bible was divine revelation, and after having described God in a way that many interpreted as atheism. Long despised by hardline Calvinists, Pierre Bayle was deprived of his Rotterdam professorship in 1693. The only major exception to this repressive trend was that William III presented himself as religiously tolerant and protected Catholics, Jews and Protestant minorities.

In the 1690s, there were violent riots against a ban on public smoking in Haarlem and against taxes in Amsterdam. The economy suffered not just from high taxes. As many regents left the Netherlands, they took their capital with them. Others now invested more in the growing public debt, which seemed to offer a risk-free return, but this deprived businesses of funds. Conflicts and a new era of protectionism began to impair Dutch maritime commerce substantially. At the same time, countries like Britain, France, Prussia and Sweden finally began learning the republic's tricks and offered them serious competition in both overseas trade and local industrial activity.

In London it was reported that the Dutch began to 'look back with compassion on De Witt's fate, they begin to lament his losse, and consider his principles beyond what could be expected'.[65]

There was a slow decline in several different areas, which accumulated. In the winter of 1715, the Dutch Republic had run out of money to pay the interest on its public debt. The union treasury was closed and, when it reopened, creditors had to accept lower interest rates. Humiliatingly, it was time for the financial superpower to declare state bankruptcy.

From then on, there was a disastrous slump in foreign trade, and the processing and manufacturing that used to sustain it. Unemployment increased and there was a dramatic reversal in urbanization. Cities like Leiden, Haarlem and Delft lost roughly half their population between 1688 and 1749.[66] What were once the most impressive cities in Europe began to seem small and quaint. Immigration declined noticeably. The proportion of those marrying in Amsterdam who had migrated there declined from 40 per cent in the 1640s to 25 per cent by the end of the century.[67] Foreign students started to leave Dutch universities.

The group from which the urban elite was chosen also shrank. In a process of aristocratization, the number of new family names among regents declined, and their places were increasingly taken by the sons, sons-in-law, brothers or brothers-in-law of previous regents. The Dutch began to tighten their guild system again, and eventually even imposed their own trade barriers. While the republic remained richer than its neighbours, it had lost the openness and energy that had given it leadership in growth and innovation. Compared with what it had been during the golden age, it was a sad spectacle.

By the mid-eighteenth century the Scottish writer James Boswell studied in Utrecht, having been sent there by his father, who constantly talked about the beauty of the Dutch cities. Boswell wrote disappointedly to a friend that taxes and the loss of trade had ended the Dutch golden age before he made it there:

> this trading nation must be in a very bad way. Most of their principal towns are sadly decayed, and instead of finding every mortal employed, you meet with multitudes of poor creatures who are starving in idleness. Utrecht is remarkably ruined. ... Were Sir William Temple to revisit these Provinces, he would scarcely believe the amazing alteration which they have undergone.[68]

Summary

The history of the Dutch Republic is one of the most sensational. A small group of rebels without much of what constituted a state, and without even much land on which to live and grow food, took on the world's mightiest empire. The Dutch not only roundly defeated the Spanish but emerged from the eighty-year struggle as the world's leading economy, empire and culture.

The Dutch had to perfect the art of openness precisely because they had so little to begin with. Everything had to be created, built, developed and imported. Like the Athenians, their lack of farmable land led them to embrace international trade and specialization, and like the Song Chinese, they gave farmers who broke new ground property rights. Like Romans, they populated their new republic with immigrants who were often persecuted for their beliefs back home. Like the Abbasids, they invited writers and scientists from different countries and traditions to come up with novel ideas and discoveries. And, like Renaissance Italians, Dutch artists constantly experimented with new materials and themes in art, and ways of examining themselves, their identities and behaviours.

The Dutch took ideals of inclusivity and meritocracy and radicalized them. The economy and the guilds were opened for outsiders, women had more freedoms, and even servants were treated better than elsewhere, since free labour markets gave them bargaining power. People of other beliefs were allowed to participate in society and contribute their creativity to the mix.

This resulted in an explosion of innovation, in everything from shipbuilding and financial instruments to intellectual debate and military organization. The republic's success was a challenge to traditional perceptions. Europeans who used to think that wealth came from land and conquest and that stability came from one unifying faith noticed that the one country without land and religious oppression became the richest in the world and stayed stable when other great powers tore themselves apart in religious war. The republic's openness to refugees and debate made it the epicentre of the European Scientific Revolution and the Enlightenment.

This wealth and constant improvement of all spheres of life made the Dutch superior in battle as well. However, even in the Dutch Republic, there were constant attempts from the Church and from the stadtholder party to undermine this openness. Three different princes of Orange conspired to sweep away republican institutions. The third attempt succeeded, when the country panicked during an Anglo-French invasion in 1672 and called out for a strongman to protect them. Johan de Witt, the man who had done the most for the success of the republic, met a fate as ungrateful and unjust as those of Socrates, Cicero and the advisor Jafar in the Abbasid Caliphate. He was lynched by rioters.

Like so many other golden ages, the Dutch decline started with despotic ambitions, political centralization and censorship. The country that had led the world in open debate started tightening the noose. The Church started imposing a Calvinist orthodoxy, books were banned and universities purged of secular ideas. Immigration declined and foreign students started to leave the formerly leading Dutch universities. The group from which the urban elite was chosen shrank, and soon the cities themselves shrank.

The Spanish could not destroy the Dutch miracle, but the Dutch could. However, before everything was lost, the Dutch Republic made one last, desperate and incredibly costly effort to save its ideals of open seas and open minds, a plan so risky as to seem totally unbelievable. They were going to try to transplant their whole political and economic system to their old enemy, the English.

7

THE ANGLOSPHERE

Industry, Individualism and Impertinence

England expects that every man will do his duty.

      LORD NELSON SIGNALLING HIS FLEET BEFORE THE
BATTLE OF TRAFALGAR, 21 OCTOBER 1805

I wish Nelson would make no more signals; we all understand what we have to do.

      ADMIRAL CUTHBERT COLLINGWOOD[1]

What Athens was in miniature, America will be in magnitude. The one is the wonder of the ancient world, the other is becoming the admiration, the model of the present.

      THOMAS PAINE, 1791[2]

The Anglosphere is alive and well, but I wonder whether it needs a better name.

      DANIEL HANNAN, 2014[3]

Of all the economic and cultural transformations in all the golden ages, none is more momentous than the Industrial Revolution that started in Britain at the end of the eighteenth century.

The Industrial Revolution? Dark Satanic mills, child labour and ruthless exploitation in a book about golden ages?! That will seem bewildering to many.

Those of you who saw the opening ceremony of the 2012 London Olympics probably still remember the powerful portrayal of 'the chaos and the noise of the Industrial Revolution, the brutal uprooting of rural Britain', as the BBC presenter put it. At the centre of the stadium, arrogant men in high hats are smoking cigars while they are uprooting farmers and ordering them to erect towering, sinister smokestacks.

Ferocious drummers and frantic actors were 'conveying the thrill and the destruction and the fear of the Industrial Revolution'. Leaving little to imagination, this part of the programme, following 'Green and Pleasant Land', in which happy peasants danced in the fields, was called 'Pandemonium', the capital of hell in John Milton's *Paradise Lost*.

It is a kind of historical amnesia that a post-industrial society can afford to put on such a magnificent display at a budget that could have bought them a handful of English towns 300 years ago. Because the Industrial Revolution was the moment that mankind began – in historical terms – its stunningly rapid rise out of the poverty it had always suffered from. An index of the real wages of English construction workers reveals that they were roughly the same in the late 1700s as they had been at the time of the Magna Carta.[4] There was never any lasting improvement in living standards. The economic historian David Landes famously stated: 'the Englishman of 1750 was closer in material things to Caesar's legionaries than to his own great-grandchildren'.[5]

The problem was that, before the Industrial Revolution, mankind was stuck in a devilish Malthusian trap: since population in a pre-industrial world tended to increase faster than resources could, good times created a larger population and this created bad times, and a catastrophic collapse in population, through famine, plague or war. As we have seen, there were great efflorescences where the lives of many improved, but humanity as a whole never got to see lasting improvements. Until now.

The cleric and economist Thomas Robert Malthus published his theory as *An Essay on the Principle of Population* in 1798, the worst timed book in the history of publishing. This was the moment when mankind started to break free from Malthusian shackles by enlisting technology in the struggle to produce more resources. Labour was increasingly performed by machines and power supplied by coal and steam, thereby revolutionizing every aspect of the economy, from mining and agriculture to manufacturing and transportation. For the first time in history, a rapidly growing population could sustainably acquire much higher living standards. Between 1700 and 1850, the population of England and Wales tripled, from around 5 million to more than 15 million, and incredibly it got richer, and then *much* richer.

Steam power and textile machines have become the great symbols of the era, but there were innovations in almost every sphere, not always related to the others. Suspension bridges, the selective breeding of farm animals, the steam hammer, food canning, smallpox vaccination, railways, techniques for draining rainwater with ditches, gas lighting, the seed drill, the telegraph, anaesthesia during surgery and the turnpike road system did not have much in common except curiosity about the world and a conviction that it could be improved upon. This is why Deirdre McCloskey is spot on when she says: 'The Industrial Revolution was neither the age of steam, nor the age of cotton, nor the age of iron. It was the age of progress.'[6]

Britain's progress after 1700 was incredible. Having been a fairly peripheral European power, it soon became the leading one (despite at the outset having a population just a quarter of that of France). It ushered in industrial progress, became the richest country in the world and took the first steps towards liberal democracy.

Colonial offshoots that retained the English language and common law, like the United States, Canada, Ireland, Australia and New Zealand, are some of the freest and richest countries on the planet. This Anglosphere (as Neal Stephenson called it in his 1995 science fiction novel *The Diamond Age*) is made up of half a billion people and is responsible for almost a third of the world's production and military spending. And this of course underestimates its cultural influence elsewhere, since its democratic and market-based system has spread around the world. Bad English is the world's most common language.

But it is highly unlikely that Britain would ever have become the birthplace of this age of progress if it weren't for the fact that in the late seventeenth century it had been defeated and fundamentally transformed by a colossal Dutch invasion.

The Glorious Revolution

In 1685, the Dutch Republic feared that a new Anglo-French alliance would finish the job of 1672, tearing the republic apart. In February 1685, the English king, Charles II, died and his brother succeeded him as King James II of England and VII of Scotland. This worried the Dutch, since James had converted to Catholicism. Later the same year, the French king Louis XIV revoked the Edict of Nantes, and French Protestants were once again intensely persecuted. Soon a battery of French tariffs paralysed Dutch commerce, breaking their previous peace treaty. And then the French king seized more than a hundred Dutch ships in French harbours. It seemed the Dutch would once again suffer from encirclement and war.

The one consolation was that James II had no legitimate son and would be succeeded by his daughter from his first marriage, the Protestant Mary. In 1677, Mary had married her cousin, none other than William III, Prince of Orange. Any anti-Dutch policy would therefore probably not outlast the king. But those hopes were dashed in late 1687, when James' second wife, a Catholic, was surprisingly reported pregnant after fifteen years of marriage. It was a boy. There would after all be a Catholic dynasty, consolidating whatever policies and alliances James came up with.

Worry turned to panic both among the Dutch and in large sections of English society. James' policies had actually mostly focused on increasing toleration, but many associated Catholicism with absolutism and feared that it was the first step towards persecution of Protestants. The fact that the king ignored parliament and tried to pack it full of supporters to achieve his goals confirmed their fears. Mary I's ('Bloody Mary') brutal attempt to re-impose Catholicism was still fresh in memory and was often used in propaganda. The common folks hate 'popery', wrote Daniel Defoe, even if they 'do not know whether it be a man or a horse'.[7]

But the Dutch Republic was saved. In November 1688, the English rose up to depose King James II. 'The Glorious Revolution' ended the potential for Catholic absolutism, restored parliament's powers and protected the rights of the people. In foreign policy, England started to align with the Dutch. By the end of 1689, England joined the Grand Alliance against Louis XIV and declared war on France.

For the Whig politician and essayist Thomas Babbington Macaulay, writing in the mid-nineteenth century, this revolution, 'of all revolutions the least violent, has been of all revolutions the most beneficent'. Not because it established a new order, but because it prevented one. It was a vindication of 'ancient rights' against a tyrannical monarch who tried to overturn all institutions that protected life, liberty and property. In 1688, it was finally decided whether 'the popular element... should be destroyed by the monarchical element, or should be suffered to develop itself freely and to become dominant'.[8]

At least, that is how the English like to remember it. But if there is glory in the revolution of 1688, it mostly belongs to the Dutch. Because this was not a popular uprising, but a bold Dutch seaborne invasion that stunned Europe – four times larger than the famous Spanish Armada one hundred years earlier. This costly and complicated invasion was organized by all sections of the Dutch Republic in order to 'make this state secure against all external danger', as the Haarlem deputies justified it.[9]

The Dutch, who could never agree on anything according to critics, were able to cooperate on one of the most complex and risky operations ever undertaken because the dynastic ambitions of William III, Prince of Orange, were in alignment with Holland's defence of its commerce and the whole republic's fear of encirclement. If war was coming, a defensive response could be as disastrous as 1672. It was better to strike now against England, which was relatively weak and divided, with strong forces in parliament opposed to the king. They had been promised support by the liberal Whig party, who made sure William of Orange received an invitation from six English nobles and a bishop, 'the Immortal Seven', asking him to come and defend them against their despotic king, James II.

William had 60,000 copies produced of a pamphlet justifying his invasion, which were secretly printed and distributed, an incredible number in an era when best-selling pamphlets were rarely printed in more than a few thousand copies. The pamphlet claimed that the king had subjected the people's 'consciences, liberties, and properties to arbitrary government'. It also talked about the Queen's 'pretended bigness', playing on rumours that she had never been pregnant and that a boy had been smuggled into the royal cradle to steal the throne from Mary.

The Dutch gambled everything on the invasion: their wealth, fleet, best troops and artillery. Had the ships been lost in the stormy late autumn, the republic would have been financially devastated and militarily exposed, and it would of course have earned eternal enmity of the English king. It was the mother of all Hail Marys.

But one reason for the success was the very decentralization of the republic, even after William's 1672 coup. For decades, provinces, towns, companies, the navy and the army had each perfected their respective skills in training, material, finance, shipping, logistics and propaganda according to their local knowledge of how best to do it. And when they combined all this power, they built one of history's greatest war machines at record speed.

The fleet was stuck south of Rotterdam for a month because of adverse winds, but in early November they caught a 'Protestant wind', and the English Channel was crossed by an immense Dutch fleet of roughly 400 transport and supply vessels and 53 warships. On board were the best Dutch troops and English, Scottish and Huguenot volunteers, at least 21,000 men. They also carried 5,000 horses and massive artillery.

The vast fleet stretched out in the Strait of Dover, in a formation twenty-five ships deep, to the awe of the many spectators. On either flank they were surrounded by warships giving threatening salutes. On deck, the regiments stood under arms in parade formations. The flourish of trumpets, the clash of cymbals and the rolling of drums were heard on both English and French shores. It was 'the most magnificent and affecting spectacle ever seen by human eye', said one observer.[10]

The Dutch landed in Brixham (on the 'English Riviera' if you know your *Fawlty Towers*) and quickly took Exeter. On paper, James had a bigger army, but his support quickly slipped away and many deserted his army. Instead of meeting William in battle, the king fled and threw the Royal Seal into the Thames. On 18 December, a triumphant William entered London with his army. All English soldiers had been ordered to withdraw, and Dutch soldiers secured every major institution. The invasion had succeeded and was quickly rebranded as a revolution.

On 12 February 1689, the soon-to-be-Queen Mary arrived on English soil. On board her ship was the philosopher John Locke. He saw the revolution as a golden opportunity to 'set up a constitution that may be lasting for the security of civil rights and the liberty and property of all the subjects of the nation',[11] and proceeded to publish the revolutionary manuscripts that he had kept hidden until then. While the settlement did not go as far as he wished, it had many similarities with the Lockean revolution envisaged in his *Two Treatises of Government*. Parliament declared that the king had broken 'the original contract between king and people', and the new monarch had to adhere to those rights and be under the control of a free parliament.[12]

On 13 February, William and Mary were offered the Crown of England as dual monarchs, after first having had a Declaration of Rights read to them, which protected parliamentary powers and included the 'right to bear arms' and prohibition of 'cruel and unusual punishments', now familiar from the American Constitution. It was written into law as the Bill of Rights, and even though William disliked being bound by it, he assented to it. It is often seen as the birth of rule of law in England.

By an amazing turn of events and because of the circumstances of him being invited to take the throne, William of Orange, the Dutch schemer who always worked to rid himself of constraints to personal rule, became a symbol of British liberalism and a new era of limited government. While the man now known as William III of England was the personal victor, it was, in fact, the principles of his old enemy Johan de Witt that were now being transplanted into a larger body politic, with a bigger population and more resources.

Because of its geographical position, the Netherlands was always vulnerable. It could never stay as far from Europe's intrigues and wars as it would have liked. As an island, Britain was at a safer distance, where these seeds of liberalism could find the space and time to take root, grow and spread even further, eventually to the other side of the Atlantic.

The historian John Lothrop Motley began his history on the rise of the Dutch Republic by declaring that it was 'one of the leading events of modern times', without which the liberty and wealth of the modern era would not have been possible:

> The maintenance of the right by the little provinces of Holland and Zeeland in the sixteenth, by Holland and England united in the seventeenth, and by the United States of America in the eighteenth centuries, forms but a single chapter in the great volume of human fate; for the so-called revolutions of Holland, England, and America, are all links of one chain.[13]

Open Britain

Lord Macaulay was slightly ahead of events when he wrote that the Glorious Revolution of 1688 contained the germ of the rule of law, free speech, religious freedom, and the end of the slavery. The slave trade and repression of Catholicism actually got worse before they got better. But there is no doubt that the new settlement between the Dutch prince and the British parliament emphasized and deepened a local heritage of individual rights and equality under the law that could be used to set the isles on a new trajectory after the dreaded menace of absolute monarchy.

Parliament and the Whigs prided themselves on ancient liberties and the common law, which did not rely on a powerful executive but on courts discovering a law that people had already created. They often claimed that absolutism and aristocracy were alien concepts, forced upon the English by the Norman Conquest of 1066. After the British Civil War (1642–51), revolutionary liberal ideas, as articulated by the Levellers, John Milton and Algernon Sidney, had been very much in vogue, but the war itself had ended in a dictatorship under Oliver

Cromwell and then royal restoration. After 1688, such ideas could finally be realized, albeit in the moderate, sensible form the English loved to think they embodied.

The strongest restriction on personal rule was that the Crown was deprived of independent sources of revenue, like certain taxes and customs or the sale of monopolies and offices. Whatever kings and queens wanted in the future, they had to go to parliament and ask for it nicely. Increasingly they had to choose ministers who could deal with the majority (which made one of William's successors complain that 'ministers are kings in this country').

Whigs had always wanted to control the powers of the monarchy more tightly, but now the Tories also began to share their suspicions after first feeling betrayed by James and then getting a Dutch monarch that many of them saw as a usurper. At times, William III must have felt like he was back in the Dutch Republic, quarrelling with troublesome provinces and pensionaries.

The old Roman principle 'What concerns everyone ought to be considered and approved by everyone' had finally triumphed over the monarchical 'What pleases the prince has the force of law.' It also bestowed on one of Europe's most tumultuous countries institutions that would make it one of the most stable, precisely because they were more open to change.

In 1689, an Act of Toleration was passed that extended the right of religious nonconformism substantially. Alternative places of worship were legalized, and the Church lost its monopoly on education. In 1695, parliament refused to renew the Licensing of the Press Act, censorship ended and the political and philosophical debate became more lively. Other laws deprived the king of the right to dismiss judges and gave the accused the right to a counsel and a copy of the indictment.

After 1707, it was not England alone, but Great Britain. Scotland and England had shared a monarch since 1603, but now they joined together in a union. This was an important further step towards British openness, not just because people and ideas could now move freely all over the island, but because Scotland was a more literate and cosmopolitan culture than England, which helps explain the emergence of the exciting eighteenth-century period known as the Scottish Enlightenment.

At this time, English universities were insular, sleepy institutions. The professors at Oxford had 'given up altogether even the pretence of learning', complained Adam Smith.[14] Scottish universities, on the other hand, were at the intellectual frontier, with new subjects like science, medicine and economics, and teaching Newton's theories before his own University of Cambridge did. Unlike English universities, Scottish universities did not require an oath of religious allegiance, so they were open to novel ideas and attracted students from far away.

'Only London and Paris could compete with Edinburgh as an intellectual center', writes the historian Arthur Herman about the city that is often called the 'Athens of the North'. 'But unlike those two world capitals, Edinburgh's cultural life was not dominated by state institutions and aristocratic salons and patrons. It depended instead on a circle of tough-minded, self-directed intellectuals and men of letters.'[15] Some of the most important thinkers of the era, such as David Hume, Francis Hutcheson and Adam Smith, were Scottish, as well as a disproportionate number of inventors, mathematicians and scientists.

Just as the Netherlands was becoming slightly less Dutch in spirit, England was going Dutch. After 1688 there was increased immigration, not least by Dutch merchants and artisans, Huguenots and Jews. Migrants of other ethnicities and religions were given citizenship with full rights apart from standing for public office and attending the old universities, so they were drawn towards commercial sectors.

Some provided England with superior skills in clock and instrument making, which would be central to the ensuing industrialization. Others used their knowledge and connections to help turn London into the new centre of finance. In 1744, when the City of London declared its loyalty to King George II, of 542 merchant signatories, at least a third were of foreign descent, over a hundred were Huguenot, forty Jewish and thirty-seven Dutch.[16]

In the 1720s, Voltaire praised the openness of British capitalism in words strikingly similar to what Spinoza had said about Amsterdam just half a century earlier:

> Go into the London Stock Exchange – a more respectable place than many a court – and you will see representatives from all nations gathered together for the utility of men. Here Jew, Mohammedan and Christian deal with each other as though they were all of the same faith, and only apply the word infidel to people who go bankrupt.[17]

Combined with a commercialization of society and the sudden rapid expansion of international trade, it is not difficult to see why some Dutch thought that England, after William's invasion, had plundered the republic's glory.[18]

State incapacity

A common explanation for Great Britain's success is that after 1688 it became an effective state, with capacity to accomplish its goals, enforce its laws and provide infrastructure and other public goods. In some respects, this is correct, especially the government's ability to raise taxes (even from the aristocracy) and debt on capital markets. But, in other ways, this is a retrospective attempt to fit eighteenth-century Britain into a now fashionable paradigm about state capacity. What struck foreign observers back in the 1700s was that the British government, whether or not it had the capacity to provide public goods, lacked the will to do it. Almost all the taxes and debt raised were used to maintain the navy and make war. Individuals, civil society and private business had to do almost everything else themselves.

Entrepreneurs and local notables built private roads and canals, and trusts established and improved turnpike roads paid by the users. The railways were built and funded by private businesses. Harbours, bridges, lighthouses, drainage works and gas lighting were funded with private subscriptions. Voluntary associations took the first initiatives for public health projects.

Even one of the pioneers of socialism, Friedrich Engels, recognized the achievement:

> The whole British Empire, and especially England, which, sixty years ago, had as bad roads as Germany or France then had, is now covered by a network of the finest roadways; and these, too, like almost everything else in England, are the work of private enterprise, the State having done very little in this direction.[19]

He described the same private development of canals and railways.

There was an official monetary system but, surprisingly for such a commercial society, there was a chronic lack of small-denomination coins. Therefore many businesses had to pay their employees in goods or in 'company stores'. Trade relied on credit, which made a good reputation absolutely essential for anyone engaged in business. In the 1780s, the market provided a fascinating solution, as George Selgin documents in *Good Money*. Copper tycoons and industrialists started to issue hundreds of tons of their own private coins, which solved the shortage and became the most widely used currency for wages and retail in Britain.[20]

The government didn't even have a bureaucracy that permeated the country. In large parts of the country, no one upheld the laws; in others it was done by amateurs, part-time constables, volunteers and vigilantes. Local Justices of the Peace were unpaid and selected from wealthy locals, who were not always competent and sometimes corrupt. Often it was difficult to find someone willing to carry out the duties. Contracts were usually informal handshakes rather than formally sealed documents. While the letter of the law defended property, property owners often had to pay private security forces to protect them. Most prosecutions had to be carried out by the victims of crime. London's first police force was set up in 1829 – and the city was an early adopter.[21]

Formal institutions came later, when a larger and more anonymous economy made it more complicated to rely on reputation and trust. Taking all these things into consideration, the economic historian Joel Mokyr, who has written the standard work on Britain's Industrial Revolution, *An Enlightened Economy*, concludes: 'we cannot really place the efficiency of the state at the center of the stage of institutional explanations of the British miracle'.[22]

The British government provided something else, which was more important: benign neglect. Compared with all other European countries except the Dutch Republic, it provided more toleration and economic freedom. When the state stepped back, citizens stepped up. In a way, the discretion of local magistrates helped, because they often refused to uphold official rules and regulations if they no longer saw the need for them. This made British institutions more adaptable when times changed. Laws against usury and limited liability companies were neglected, guilds were deprived of their power to coerce, and monopolies lost their dominance. Smuggling was often seen locally as a legitimate exercise of free trade.

This does not mean that Britain was a completely free market. The government intervened in many ways, especially with indirect taxes on everything that was not seen as essential, including a window tax that was in effect a tax on light and air. Sometimes tariffs were imposed to protect certain interests, most infamously the corn laws of the early nineteenth century, which increased the price of bread. One intervention often led to another. In return for protection against French wine in the 1690s, the beer industry agreed to be heavily taxed. But since it was difficult to raise taxes from decentralized brewers, the government restricted entry to concentrate the industry, thus raising consumer prices further. Britons adapted by turning to more potent drinks and the result was the Gin Craze in the early eighteenth century.

Overall, though, markets became much more important, with an advanced division of labour locally, but also an integrated national economy, without the internal toll barriers of the continent. In 1706, a French visitor remarked that ancient Rome had not 'the Fourth part of Shops, Arts and Handicrafts as we have in London'.[23] International trade also grew in importance and the country began to rely more on grain from other parts of Europe, which smoothed price fluctuations and ended the famines that used to be frequent during crop failures. Trade further exposed the British to new ideas and methods.

This was a country in the midst of rapid urbanization. Between 1700 and 1850, the share of the British population who lived in cities of more than 5,000 people increased from 17 to 45 per cent. Growing cities and market exchange led to a society of status being replaced by a society of contract. The old aristocracy complained about the nouveaux riches, and that landed wealth suddenly did not seem to be the only way to respectability. Upper classes noted that previously subservient tradesmen and workers were becoming 'impertinent' as they suddenly found a diversity of customers on markets. In 1703, Daniel Defoe described a strange new mentality: 'Wealth, however got, in England makes lords of mechanics, gentlemen of rakes; Antiquity and birth are needless here; 'Tis impudence and money makes a peer.'[24] Just like a shovel was said to make a magistrate in the Dutch Republic.

Deirdre McCloskey has argued that this bourgeois transformation was one of the most fundamental shifts in economic history. First in the Netherlands and then in Britain, people began to change the conversation and their attitude to others. The ancient prejudice against those 'who descended from persons that *did* anything' (to quote Steele's 1722 play *The Conscious Lovers*) gave way to a new admiration for entrepreneurs and traders. While money-making merchants had once been seen as greedy sinners, growing numbers thought they were 'as honorable, and almost as useful, as you landed folks that have always thought your selves so much above us' (Steele again).[25]

McCloskey points to how the word 'honesty' in the mid-eighteenth century shifted its traditional meaning away from the honourable, which had always meant dignified and aristocratic.

The emerging merchants and their observers started talking about 'honest' dealing in trade, which signalled someone who was not lying or deceiving. 'Honest' changed from being a matter of inherent status to one of character and behaviour. The same had happened to the Dutch equivalent *eerlijk*.[26] The German sociologist Norbert Elias had previously traced a similar shift in the meaning of 'courteous'. What had once meant membership of a royal court eventually took on the meaning of good table manners among rich and poor alike.

Adam Smith thought that 'Of all the nations in Europe, the Dutch, the most commercial, are the most faithfull to their word.'[27] A contemporary, judge William Blackstone, talked of the British as a 'Polite and Commercial People'.

In the 1700s, Dutch and British intellectuals and writers started talking as if people who manufactured things and traded goods for a profit were respectable people (almost as if they were in Abbasid Baghdad). This boosted the growing self-confidence of this class and reduced the hesitation to aspire to such a career. Deirdre McCloskey thinks that this change in rhetoric, of the 'habits of the lip', was the required background for the millions of inventions, experiments and transactions that spurred arguably the greatest transformation in economic history, the Industrial Revolution.

Merchants of light

Before there could be a revolution, there had to be what Joel Mokyr has called the 'Industrial Enlightenment', something he describes as 'the logical continuation of the Scientific Revolution by other means'.[28] Through constant correspondence, collaboration and competition, thousands of scientists and philosophers in the Republic of Letters systematized knowledge about nature and showed its usefulness to solve practical problems.

The more successful the scientists became, the more rulers realized that they also had use for this knowledge, and if they sometimes banned the witchcraft and blasphemy of the scientists, these scholars would just pack their bags and leave to enrich a rival country. Europe's fragmentation meant that troublemakers could always go somewhere else and prove their usefulness there. Doing science and developing technology began to seem desirable, even something that a gentleman could talk about without being disgraced.

Much of the inspiration had been provided by Francis Bacon (1561–1626), who convincingly expressed the idea that material progress could be achieved through scientific understanding, experimentation and technology. One group of scholars developed such ideas in an 'invisible college' and in 1660 they founded the Royal Society in London, which despite its name was a bottom-up initiative and not a government body. It was influenced by Bacon's fictional idea of an academy called Salomon's House, which collected the world's knowledge to solve practical problems. The motto of the Royal Society was a tribute to the rejection of authority and openness to contestability that drives science: *Nullius in verba*, 'Take nobody's word for it.'

For many years the society was led by Isaac Newton, whose laws of motion and description of gravitation made him a symbol of human ability to unlock the mysteries of nature. But the Royal Society was open to anyone who was interested in, and contributed to, new insights and inventions. This did not just mean 'real' scientists: more often they were physicians, merchants and lawyers. Francis Bacon had encouraged cooperation and sharing of knowledge between *savants* and *fabricants* – between those who know things and those who make things.

This was the kind of inclusivity that was specific to the Industrial Enlightenment of the eighteenth century. Scientists started visiting workshops, engineers and chemists were hired by businesses, entrepreneurs and craftsmen studied scientific papers, and they all met in coffee shops to hear the latest gossip and debate new theories. These were far more useful than the old English universities that catered to the clergy or the military; they were called 'penny universities' since the price of a coffee provided anyone with access to the latest debates and discoveries. A contemporary cheered: 'for here an inquisitive man, that aims at good learning, may get more in one evening than he shall by books in a month'.[29]

In provincial centres of industry, private societies sprang up, where men listened to lectures and debated natural sciences and technical matters. The most famous was the Birmingham Lunar Society, where scientists like Joseph Priestley and Erasmus Darwin (Charles' paternal grandfather) regularly met industrialists and engineers to learn from one another. The Spitalfields Mathematical Society even institutionalized a mutual support system, with nominal fines for members who did not look for an answer when another had a question.

Priestley observed that 'the politeness of the times has brought the learned and the unlearned into more familiar intercourse than they had before'.[30] Such intermingling had previously been frowned upon. Separated by class and legal status from artisans, workers and peasants, the upper class previously had little natural connection to the practical economy. In feudal and slave societies, they were above mundane matters such as farming, textiles and ironworking. When they dealt with ideas, it was pure ideas, without much relationship to everyday problems and production. Without accumulated knowledge from the practical world that could speed up the process of innovation, mankind had been lucky to stumble on breakthroughs at widely dispersed intervals.

With the elite interest in practical matters during the Industrial Enlightenment, knowledge was being systematized in mechanics, metallurgy, geology, chemistry, soil science and materials science, and then it became possible to consciously manipulate methods, materials and machines, debug them and adapt them to changing needs. Available knowledge pointed to which kinds of experiments could be fruitful, and resulting trial-and-error approaches were used to inform and improve the state of knowledge, and then the process began anew. A wave of periodicals, dictionaries and compendia flowed from the printers announcing new methods and insights, from water pumps to blood circulation. In 1777, London had seventy-two bookshops, more than any other European city.[31]

Intriguingly, Francis Bacon's utopia described an important group who travelled to foreign countries to find new books and knowledge to speed up progress. They were called merchants of light. Now Britain had them everywhere.

The perpetual revolution

The Republic of Letters and the Industrial Enlightenment were pan-European phenomena – 'the sciences are never at war', as the French chemist Antoine Lavoisier famously said – but Britain was a much more hospitable place than most for those who wanted to put new ideas into practice, for two reasons. First, it had more freedom than other countries to experiment with strange innovations and business models. Rather than banning new labour-saving technologies as the British government (and others) had once done, the post-1688 state became pro-innovation.

After the Glorious Revolution, Britain had a legal system with strong property rights that actively encouraged innovation and business. 'That security which the laws in Great Britain give to every man that he shall enjoy the fruits of his own labour is alone sufficient to make any country flourish', wrote Adam Smith in 1776.[32] The patent system also encouraged surprises. Countries like France and the Netherlands gave patent officials the task of evaluating an invention's contribution to society. In Britain any innovation was protected, whether bureaucrats predicted its usefulness or not.

Second, skilled workers also turned to the market because of a lack of other options. On the continent, engineers were normally expected to work for the government: in the civil service, teaching or the army. Partly because Britain looked to the navy rather than the army, partly because of ideology, people with technical competence had to look to the private sector for employment.

Some entrepreneurs and engineers made huge fortunes on technical breakthroughs, such as Richard Arkwright's spinning frame, James Watt's improved steam engine and Josiah Wedgwood's pottery. They became what today we would call 'superstars', notable public figures who made industrial innovation fashionable and inspired others to try it. Famous innovators constructed textile machines and steam engines that transformed whole sectors, but all sorts of people from humble backgrounds also started to scrutinize their own activities and think of ways of improving them. The number of patents for agricultural tools rose from five or six per decade before 1760 to eighty per decade in the 1830s.[33] 'The age is running mad after innovation; and all the business of the world is to be done in a new way', complained Samuel Johnson.[34]

The innovations weren't always complex. Anton Howes points to John Kay's flying shuttle, which made weaving much more productive. Howes points out that it was extraordinary in its simplicity, it required no special knowledge and only took some string and two wooden boxes on either side to catch the shuttle. And yet, for 5,000 years, no weaver had thought of doing it.[35]

It simply never occurs to most people to innovate. Something must inspire them to do so, and nothing does that like seeing people around them doing it and thriving as a result. A culture of possibility and of improvement inspires more people to try, which strengthens this culture and is one reason why golden ages often become self-reinforcing.

Furthermore, it is not enough to come up with an invention, as many countries discovered when they imported British inventions and subsequently had to import British workers. You also have to find ways to keep it running, supply it with parts and repair it when it breaks down. Britain was crowded with mechanics, millwrights, toolmakers, metalworkers and carpenters who travelled around the country and assembled and maintained machines and equipment.

Guilds had become much less powerful than on the continent. Most of them had been replaced by associations that tried to uphold rules and standards by voluntary means. This meant that growing sectors could quickly attract more labour, and these workers were free to move between sectors and regions. Unlike on the continent, where local guilds could stop outsiders, those who had completed an apprenticeship anywhere in Britain were free to practise their trade anywhere in the country.

This openness made it possible for outsiders to contribute new knowledge and creativity to old industries. Many breakthroughs were made by people who combined ideas and methods from diverse fields. Adam Smith talked about how many innovations were done by a new group, 'whose trade it is, not to do anything, but to observe every thing; and who, upon that account, are often capable of combining together the powers of the most distant and dissimilar objects'.[36] Roughly half of all patented inventions in the textile industry between 1790 and 1830 were made by people who did not work in the textile industry.[37] A clockmaker, a barber and a clergyman were responsible for the three big cotton innovations.

With such a broad base of workers who could maintain and refine things, Britain often counterintuitively imported inventions and contributed tweaks and micro-inventions that made them more operational and effective. Acknowledging this British openness to ideas, the philosopher David Hume even claimed that 'every improvement we have since made, has arisen from our imitation of foreigners'.[38] When other countries wanted to imitate Britain's success they sometimes found that they had in fact imported their own ideas back, but vastly improved.

What is most significant about the Industrial Revolution is that it did not run out of steam. As we have seen, other societies had experienced dramatic innovations before, and their economies underwent major changes. But, after a while, their limited knowledge base was exhausted and they lost their innovative power. They fizzled out and became one of history's glorious but temporary efflorescences. This did not happen in the nineteenth century. Once old problems had been solved, scientists, technicians and entrepreneurs set about working on new problems in other areas and, one by one, they revolutionized every sector of the economy. New innovations gave more knowledge, and this in turn created new breakthroughs, in a spiral of 'continuously emergent novelty', as historian of technology A. P. Usher has called it.[39]

This continuous process was a result of the ideology of progress and spirit of optimism that had been initiated by the

Industrial Enlightenment and reinforced by the evidence of what technology could achieve. Therefore the Industrial Revolution is the first revolution that has not ended.

Winners and losers

The 2012 London Olympics narrative is that the transformative Industrial Revolution was instead a continuously emerging disaster, starting with the enclosures of the countryside throwing people off their land and creating a proletariat that had no choice but to work in Blake's 'dark Satanic mills'. This interpretation borrows from the revolution's fiercest critics. In *The Condition of the Working Class in England* of 1845, Friedrich Engels described industrialization in Manchester as a period of unbearable misery and oppression of the working classes. The social historians John and Barbara Hammond formed the views of generations of readers with a bestselling trilogy of books in the early twentieth century, which featured disinherited peasants, exploited factory workers and villages sinking into poverty as its main characters.

Enclosures had at first been voluntary and those who lost rights to land were compensated, but by the end of the eighteenth century, government compulsion finished the process. Smallholders who had customary, informal rights to common fields lost them without compensation. On the one hand, those who lost suffered very real damage; on the other, increasingly efficient farms grew in size and were often run by professional managers using wage labour.

Traditionally, higher productivity has been interpreted as the result of the enclosures, but recent research has shown that open-field agriculture was also capable of innovation.

In fact, the biggest productivity push had already arrived in the seventeenth century, as farmers adopted new methods from the Netherlands. In any case, the result was that more mouths could be fed with fewer hands. This does not, however, mean that the brutal-uprooting hypothesis is correct overall. Surprisingly, the number of workers in British agriculture in 1850 was almost exactly the same as it was in 1700, at around 1.5 million, because more land was cultivated.[40] The growing masses employed in industry were not made up of uprooted peasants but resulted from an increase in the birth rate and a decrease in the death rate.

As the Austrian economist Friedrich Hayek wrote:

> The proletariat which capitalism can be said to have 'created' was thus not a proportion of the population which would have existed without it and which it had degraded to a lower level; it was an additional population which was enabled to grow up by the new opportunities for employment that capitalism provided.[41]

In 1688, a statistical report classed around half of the population in England's green and pleasant land as cottagers, paupers and vagrants, even by the abysmal economic standards of the time. In 1820, it is estimated that more than 40 per cent of Britain's population still lived in extreme poverty. In 1900, after going through the 'pandemonium' of the Industrial Revolution, this had declined to just 10 per cent and was on its way to disappear completely. Britain was the first country in the world to achieve this, matched only by its Anglosphere peers.[42]

This does not mean that there were no losers. No major economic transition takes place without leaving anyone worse off, especially if its modus operandi is to replace every previous form of economic operation with new ones. The decline of the cottage industry, the small manufacturing operations in people's homes, is one example. In the long run, they had no chance of competing with automation and factories, and it left many with no option but to look for employment elsewhere.

However, weaving and knitting at home was not as romantic as it was presented in retrospect by poets and writers. Demand fluctuated widely and jobs were precarious and low-paid. Many tended a cottage garden simultaneously, not because it was a spare-time activity or a hobby but because it was a survival strategy. Industrial companies tended to pay a higher wage and often tried to protect workers during downturns so that they would be more loyal. Furthermore, as feminists have reminded us, we can't take for granted that a woman's industrial work was more appealing when it was directed by a husband rather than a formal employer.[43]

There are examples of well-paid cottage workers who lost jobs, but sometimes a previous privileged position had been only a temporary phenomenon. The 'Luddites' who destroyed textile machines in the early 1810s were brutally suppressed by the government. History has seen them either as reactionary enemies of technological progress or as unfortunate workers who protested against being made redundant in the only way they could. None of these versions captures the complex story.

In *The Fabric of Civilization*, Virginia Postrel explains that the Luddites were elite craftspeople, handloom weavers who enjoyed a golden heyday of plenty of job opportunities at high pay. Ironically, this had been made possible by a previous wave of disruptive automation. Machines that mechanized spinning in the late eighteenth century had made many workers redundant, but it also supplied weavers with an abundant supply of once-scarce weaving yarn to weave cloth with. Since it took time to educate skilled weavers, those who already had the skills temporarily got very enviable working conditions.[44]

A generation later, much of their work could in turn be automated by the new power looms, and this is the moment when they protested, sometimes by smashing machines. In other words, the Luddites were not principled enemies of technology but defenders of a privileged livelihood owed to an earlier and more disruptive technology. From this we learn that disruption always hurts some groups of workers and benefits others, and that the best way to get the benefits is to ride the wave of innovation. Luddites actually managed to delay wool-shearing technology in much of the West Country (England's southwest). For anyone thinking that we should deal with AI in a similar way, for example, it is worth considering that the result was that this sector collapsed and moved to Yorkshire.

The most important consequence was something else entirely, that more people could for the first time afford a large supply of clothes, bedlinen, sails and sacks, and the resulting increase in purchasing power employed many more workers in completely different sectors.

The new jobs provided by factories were awful, by today's standards. The work was repetitive and physically exhausting, often in dusty, noisy and smelly premises. The heavy, fast-working machines provided new dangers. The workers had to submit to discipline and often they had to walk a long way for the commute to work. The days were long, and the workers did not have the flexibility of hours or ability to multitask as they often did in agriculture or at home.

Most disturbingly, there were many children in the new factories. They were often employed – some of them as young as eight – to repair breaks in the threads in spinning machines. Some of them crawled beneath the machines to remove dirt and dust, others to remove bobbins and replace them with empty ones. Even worse, some children worked in mines, guarding trapdoors or pushing trolleys. They were deprived of time for education and play, and often they were also damaged physically, for life, in unhealthy and hazardous conditions.

Life in congested cities before modern water supply, sanitation and garbage-disposal had always been associated with worse health and shorter lives. Until the modern era, most cities had higher death rates than birth rates, something demographers talk about as the 'urban penalty'. If cities grew it was because of migration. It was to be expected that this urban explosion would lead to overcrowding, disease, epidemics and higher mortality, at least in the short run.

However, we must not let ourselves be deceived by the eloquent nostalgia for agriculture from romantic poets and writers in an era when they were exposed to the dirt and dust of crowded cities and industries. If factory work was so awful, it speaks volumes about the even worse alternatives that people chose to leave behind. Pre-industrial rural life always looks better in poetry and Olympic opening ceremonies than in the autobiographies of those who lived through it. For them, rural roots were rarely something to celebrate, but something to escape. They did not write about how healthy and wholesome agricultural labour was, but about backbreaking work and oppressive rural poverty.

One man scoffed in his autobiography at the notion that agricultural labourers were happier in his youth, when one 'was merely a Serf' with 'an Empty Pocket'. One boy left the countryside as soon as he could, after having learned early on to 'look forward with humble submission to a life of rustic serfdom'.[45] They associated moving to towns, despite all its problems, with opportunity and freedom.

Child labour must be seen in the same light. It was not an industrial phenomenon. Even at the peak of the Industrial Revolution, more children worked in farms and in services than in factories. Children had always worked, for the simple reason that families could not do without their income, and idleness was seen as a terrible scourge. If children didn't work it was because they could not find work, and this was a source of much worry in a family. When Daniel Defoe observed Lancashire's cotton industry in 1726, he was delighted to report that children as young as four had found useful employment.[46]

When they were young, children worked at home, but as they grew older they were often sent to toil in the homes of other families, as domestic servants or agricultural labourers, living under their master's roof and subjected to his will. The desperate circumstances that led them there are clear from the fact that parents rarely removed their children from an employer when they were treated cruelly with overwork, scanty food rations and violence. In autobiographies one can read about children who fled when they were flogged but were sent back by their parents.[47] After the Great Fire of London of 1666, when fire regulations made chimneys angular and narrow, small children were often used for the nasty and dangerous work of climbing the chimneys to clear soot.

So, even though the Industrial Revolution did see many unpleasant examples of the use of child labour, it was not the start but the end of it. In urban industries, working children became more visible than they had been in rural areas, and the whole practice was beginning to seem morally repugnant. Within a generation it was banned. After the 1830s, more automation and large-scale use of steam power could substitute for children's work and increased the need for a skilled workforce. Higher wages made it possible for parents to forgo the work of their children, and instead invest in their education and a better life. In 1803, the first mechanical sweeper was invented, and even though it was resisted at first, it was the beginning of the end of the horrendous use of children as chimney sweeps.

Ugly and unhealthy cities slowly improved as growing wealth and better technologies created new opportunities to deal with ancient problems. The invention of iron pipes finally solved the problem of living in cities without having sewers mixed with drinking water. Amazingly, despite the growth of cities and the urban penalty, life expectancy in England and Wales increased from roughly thirty-five in the mid-eighteenth century to forty in 1800, probably mostly because of the smallpox vaccine. In 1900, it had reached the unprecedented length of forty-six years.

Voices of the workers

The debate about the social consequences of the Industrial Revolution has been long and at times bitter. One reason why it has been difficult to reach a consensus is that scholars have looked at different things. A crude measure of real wages shows stagnation during the early period, 1760–1830 (although even this would have been an achievement since a period of war and a rapidly growing population would traditionally have reduced living standards sharply). However, when weighted by population, the average wage increased by as much as 50 per cent.

But this is still an underestimate of the impact of the Industrial Revolution, since it had a major impact in some regions and didn't make much of an inroad in many others. In agricultural regions wages rose no more than 15 to 25 per cent during this period, while they rose by an incredible 80 to 90 per cent in industrializing counties. By the end of this period, a manufacturing wage was almost twice as high as an agricultural wage.[48] And this was before the period when progress and wages really took off, after 1850.

And this was a visible transformation. Suddenly, even common people could afford comfortable cotton clothes and could change their underwear when dirty. Paper, glass and candles became better and more accessible. Books, newspapers, upholstered furniture, ceramics and mirrors were no longer only for the very wealthiest. The rapid growth of professions like teachers and physicians reveals that a market for their services had emerged. At the same time, trains made it possible for the working class to travel rapidly and cheaply, and often see something other than their hometown for the first time.

In the end, even critics had a hard time denying that the Industrial Revolution resulted in higher living standards. Engels eventually wrote a new preface to his book about proletarians in Manchester, confessing that 'The state of things described in this book belongs to-day, in many respects, to the past', accepting that the workers now 'are undoubtedly better off'.[49]

The Romantic Luddite Thomas Carlyle admitted that 'how much better fed, clothed, lodged and, in all outward respected, accommodated men now are… is a grateful reflection which forces itself on every one', while his complaint remained: this was just material progress and 'not the divine and spiritual'.[50]

In a late revision to their influential anti-industrial work, John and Barbara Hammond admitted that statisticians had showed that 'earnings increased and that most men and women were less poor' after the Industrial Revolution. But, like Carlyle, they insisted that it was still bad, it was just that explanations for the discontent 'must be sought outside the sphere of strictly economic conditions'.[51]

This makes the debate even more problematic, since we leave the world of statistics and turn to subjective evaluations about what is dignified or degrading, beautiful or ugly. How, in that case, can we ever come to any conclusions, when we are heavily biased by our own political, moral and aesthetic ideas about what people back then should have thought?

The British historian Emma Griffin, President of the Royal Historical Society, has come up with an ingenious and unconventional idea of asking those who actually lived through it. Scouring the archives, she has found over 350 autobiographical sketches published after 1760, often written for relatives without any intention to publish. The writers are a representative group of workers, skilled and unskilled, in agriculture and manufacturing, often from very poor backgrounds.

These accounts have rarely been consulted by writers on the Industrial Revolution, perhaps because they 'simply refuse to tell the story we expect to hear'. Griffin writes: '[N]o matter how we try, it is not possible to frame the autobiographical literature within the dark interpretation without imposing a wilful distortion upon the messages our writers are seeking to communicate.'[52]

The consistent impression from these first-hand stories is that they found themselves in an era of rapid progress and opportunity. A miner wrote that wages used to be 'so much lower… Life was very hard for the poor then.' Someone else agreed that some things might have been better in the past, 'but it certainly does not apply to the hours of labour, and the opportunities for rest and recreation. The working classes never had better times than now.' A carpenter had a similar message for his children: 'Look back and see what troublesome times we had during my bringing up… the working classes in my opinion, was never so well off.' The son of an itinerant beggar who became a hatter wrote that 'as a nation we have much cause to feel grateful'.[53]

One returned to the childhood village that he had left, and was 'glad to say things are much better there now'. 'He is a misanthrope indeed who would wish the old days or customs back again', thought another. A third writer concluded that if their ancestors came back and saw the progress, they would not 'believe their own eyes'. 'I only wish [my parents] had each lived to enjoy and to see the improvements I see', wrote a fourth.[54]

According to Griffin, 'The only writers to voice consistent dissatisfaction with the transition were the poets and writers, and they perhaps had rather different concerns to the run-of-the-mill early industrial worker.' In the words of one of those workers: 'When I hear people talk of the good old days, they must be ignorant of what did happen in those days. I know it was hard times where I was…'[55]

When reading this massive collection of mostly laudatory assessments of the Industrial Revolution, it is tempting to assume that there is a selection bias. People who write their life stories, even if only for their children, are usually those who have achieved something, and this might have resulted in a more favourable perspective on the world. But, as Emma Griffin points out, this was the case before industrialization as well, and those autobiographical writers did not make the case that their own personal progress was reflected in the society around them. They did not say that people in general led better lives than ever before, that opportunities were growing and poverty declining. But suddenly, in this era, they did. One of the most common sentiments in these texts was relief that their children and grandchildren would not have to experience the kind of life they themselves had when growing up. 'Society', wrote Thomas Jackson, 'is in a state of constant progress.'[56]

After having spent so much time seeing through the eyes of these forgotten people from the beginning of industrial civilization, Emma Griffin deduces that, no matter how difficult life was for them, what trumped everything was their sense that they belonged to the first generation that had won the ancient battle against hunger. Griffin is not entirely comfortable with her own interpretation, since she thinks that the British government could have done so much more for people than the laissez-faire policy it followed:

> Yet even with a government that did nothing, there is an uncomfortable truth we should confront: industrialisation had remarkable power to put food on the table. And for that first generation, that generation which had expected the hunger of their own childhood to be experienced once more by their children and grandchildren, food on the table was all that mattered. Autobiographers were not romantic about the old days when their children went hungry. And whatever our views on the rights and wrongs of capitalism, nor should anyone else be.[57]

Some reported that children even started to fuss over the kind of food they would and would not eat, which was incomprehensible to generations that had been grateful to get anything, whatever it was, to feed the pangs of hunger.

Ireland, simultaneously, suffered a terrible famine when the potato crops were infected by blight. Around a million people died between 1845 and 1852. The historian T. S. Ashton thought that this was the horrible fate that awaited countries where populations grow without industrialization, and that England would have suffered the same if it had remained a nation of cultivators and artisans.[58] The fact that the industrialized south of Scotland managed to prevent mass starvation in the hungry Highlands supports Ashton's case. Others claim that the great famine was the result of British refusal to help out, or a policy of actively exporting food from Ireland despite starvation. However, the first explanation comes close to accepting that it couldn't be prevented domestically and therefore supports Ashton's claim, while the other is plain wrong, since Ireland imported more food than it exported during the famine.

However, Ireland is a special case since it had been forcibly colonized by the English, who took large chunks of land and hired Irish farmers to manage small plots. Since they had no rights to the land and the landlords resided in England, no one conducted the systematic improvements that had improved yields in the rest of Britain.

Returning to Emma Griffin's study of autobiographies, it's important to note that food on the table was not just food on the table. Poverty had meant that men and women were deprived of room to manoeuvre. Choices about partners and marriage were restricted, as were decisions about careers, education, self-improvement and political activity. As long as options for work were limited, standing up to a controlling or abusive employer meant hunger.

With the abundant work made available by the factories, and the higher wages they offered, it was possible to leave behind not only hunger and poverty, but also servile submission. Suddenly, industrial workers became audacious and might leave employment for what they themselves later described as trivial matters. Some left because they didn't get enough tea breaks. At the same time, workers began to organize themselves in reading clubs, mutual improvement societies, night schools, Sunday schools, campaign groups and trade unions. The flowering of political groups was not the sign of growing discontent that it was often taken to be. Discontent was not new; the freedom to voice it was.

As the chartist Thomas Frost wrote: 'In the towns and villages of the south men's minds seemed to be slumbering, until the puff of the steam-engine should awaken them.'[59] In the end, Emma Griffin decided to title her book *Liberty's Dawn*. Her conclusion is: 'The downbeat narrative of working-class life during the industrial revolution may be cathartic for some. But it is not good history.'[60]

The British Empire

While Great Britain was becoming the industrial engine of the world, it was also in the process of acquiring an empire on which the sun never set. By the end of the nineteenth century, the English historian John Robert Seeley famously remarked: 'We seem, as it were, to have conquered and peopled half the world in a fit of absence of mind.'

There is some truth to that. There was no overall direction or plan for the conquests; often it was done simply to keep other European powers, especially the French, from expanding into a region. During the early seventeenth century, the English captured the West Indian islands as outposts against the Spanish and as way to emulate their overseas empire. Many North American colonies were founded by religious minorities fleeing persecution. India was conquered by the East India Company, a private trade monopoly with its own army; the British Crown took over control only in 1858. Australia was established as a penal colony, and Singapore was created as a British trading outpost on the initiative of Governor-General of the Dutch East Indies, Stamford Raffles, not London. The British built the first forts in Africa to control the slave-trade, but Sierra Leone, the first major African colony, was instead founded to resettle freed slaves (hence the name of its capital: Freetown).

So Britain might not have had an imperial plan, but British privateers, profiteers, settlers and soldiers certainly had their own diverse plans. The fictional cowardly soldier Harry Flashman takes aim at the Seeley hypothesis in George MacDonald Fraser's *Flashman and the Mountain of Light*:

> You'll have heard it said that the British Empire was acquired in a fit of absence of mind – one of those smart Oscarish squibs that sounds well but is thoroughly fat-headed. Presence of mind, if you like – and countless other things, such as greed and Christianity, decency and villainy, policy and lunacy, deep design and blind chance, pride and trade, blunder and curiosity, passion, ignorance, chivalry and expediency, honest pursuit of right, and determination to keep the bloody Frogs out.[61]

The track record of empire is hotly contested. Some object to its bleak reputation by arguing that it also left a legacy of legal systems and infrastructure, and observe that former British colonies have done much better in terms of political, economic and social outcomes than colonies that were run by other powers. However, this selection is distorted by the inclusion of colonies that were settled by large numbers of British, such as the United States, Canada, Australia and New Zealand, and therefore also imported institutions like the rule of law and property rights. Other regions had a disease environment that led to high mortality among settlers, and therefore the British set up more extractive institutions, often aimed at breaking local property rights rather than protecting them. Sure, these people got some roads and railways, but they were also subjected to confiscations, oppressive taxes and trade monopolies.

The most systematic breach of the ideals the British increasingly promoted back home was slavery. Starting in the seventeenth century, Britain imported hundreds of thousands of African slaves to its sugar plantations on Jamaica and Barbados. The conditions for the hard-worked and malnourished slaves were so awful that new slaves had to be brought in so that the high mortality rates did not depopulate the plantations.

Britain soon carved out a powerful position in the Atlantic slave trade and sold slaves everywhere in America, even to other nations. During the seventeenth and eighteenth centuries, British ships carried more than 3.2 million slaves across the Atlantic, more than any other country except Portugal. The conditions on the ships were infamously horrifying, with dehydrated and often shackled men, women and children tightly packed below deck. Those who survived the journey could look forward only to a life as human cattle.

Some defenders of the imperial project talked about it as a humanitarian, civilizing mission; some in the administrative and political elite even believed in it. But, as with so many other times in history, the basic fact of foreign control and military conquest caused a very long record of abuse and atrocities – especially as the imperial ethos was interwoven with a worldview where the British race were natural leaders and saviours of the savages. 'What is Empire but the Predominance of Race?' asked the liberal imperialist Lord Dalmeny, who was briefly prime minister.

The tragic fate of the native Americans when Europeans took their land is well known, even though the microorganisms that colonizers carried with them to the continent took the heaviest toll. After conflicts with Tasmanian aboriginals in 1830, British colonists formed a 'Black Line' over the island, trying to hunt down and forcibly remove every single Tasmanian, resulting in their extermination. During the Boer War, more Boers died in the British concentration camps than in battle.

Protests and mutinies were often put down brutally and with vicious vengeance. After the Indian Rebellion of 1857, British soldiers responded with an orgy of violence. Civilians suspected of supporting the rebellion were massacred and women raped. Captured rebels were tied to the mouths of cannons and blown apart, an old Mughal punishment for rebellion, which makes traditional burial rites impossible. During unrest in Amritsar in 1919, colonial troops fired without warning into a large unarmed crowd for ten minutes. At least 379 people were killed.

There would be a day of reckoning. Britain's open-seas policy and balancing of powers fostered a nineteenth-century Pax Britannica in Europe, but imperialism with its closed colonial markets encouraged a zero-sum game beyond the continent. European nations carved up the world in an increasingly complex and aggressive rivalry that eventually spilled over into Europe and nearly tore it apart.

Anti-imperialism

Much has been made of the hypocrisy of the British, and rightly so. They prided themselves on ideas of individual liberty, limited government and free markets, but in a fit of absence of mind, they suddenly found themselves roaming around the world, enslaving people and blowing them to bits from cannons. But hypocrisy is the compliment vice pays to virtue. If the dominant culture recognizes certain virtues, this can at times rein in its darkest vices.

Almost all of the colonial atrocities were condemned by parts of public opinion back home in Britain; often they led to official investigations and sometimes persecutions. This put limits on colonial repression. Stephen Davies writes that 'liberal imperialism was not just brutal but vulnerable, because its victims could try to hold it to account for violating its own justifications – a path that was impossible with more openly power-based imperialisms'.[62]

A famous example is the campaign against Governor Edward Eyre, after an indiscriminate and blood-soaked response to a revolt on Jamaica in 1865. A who's who of the era's great liberals, including John Stuart Mill, Herbert Spencer and John Bright, publicly campaigned for the arrest and persecution of Eyre for murder, arguing that the skin colour of the victim makes no difference, just as the School of Salamanca argued that native Americans had the same rights as Spaniards, and Cato the Younger proposed that Caesar should be turned over to the Gauls for his crimes against them. Eyre was replaced as governor and legal actions initiated, but he was never convicted.

Interestingly, another campaign was set up to defend Eyre, led by writers and poets like Thomas Carlyle, John Ruskin, Charles Dickens and Alfred Tennyson. The background was not just consideration for public order in the colonies, but a fear that the emerging commercial economy was destroying traditional paternalistic society. Carlyle coined the phrase 'dismal science' for economics, not because the science was boring, but because it meant 'letting men alone', even men of other races. He thought it made for a dreary, dismal world where people didn't know their place. He defended a hierarchical order where 'the black man' is 'compelled to work as he was fit, and to do the Maker's will who had constructed him'.[63]

Revelations of the actions against Boers caused outrage in Britain. The Liberal Party leader Henry Campbell-Bannerman condemned 'methods of barbarism' against the Boers and in 1906 went on to win one of the country's biggest election landslide victories. Furious reactions also followed the Amritsar massacre of 1919. Churchill, then Secretary of State for War and always pro-Empire, denounced it as a 'monstrous event' and MPs voted 247 to 37 against the brigadier general responsible, who was removed from duty.

The Whig politician Thomas Macaulay served on the Supreme Council of India in the 1830s, but he insisted that the goal of British colonialism should be Indian independence. In parliament he argued that 'having been instructed in European knowledge, they may, in some future age, demand European institutions', adding 'Whenever it comes, it will be the proudest day in English history.'[64]

It was a patronizing perspective, but as long as a sufficiently large segment of the British people and its elite held this conviction, it was inevitable that loud calls for autonomy and decolonization would be heard, and that violence to stop it would not in the long run be accepted by popular opinion.

The greatest triumph of the libertarian part of the British psyche was abolitionism. Thomas Carlyle complained that a wedding between the dismal science and 'Exeter Hall Philanthropy' was giving birth to the monstrosity of black emancipation. He was referring to the alliance of free-market economists and Quakers who, starting from different positions, both ended up in the position that all individuals had the same rights and that slavery was an abomination.

In 1787 the Society for Effecting the Abolition of the Slave Trade was founded and turned into one of the first broad social movements. It held anti-slavery rallies, boycotted slave sugar and delivered petitions. Manchester's petition was signed by almost a fifth of its population. The potter and entrepreneur Josiah Wedgwood (Charles Darwin's maternal grandfather) produced thousands of medallions with the society's symbol, a black man in chains, asking 'Am I not a man and a brother?' It was bought to adorn snuff boxes, shoe buckles and hair pins of the supporters of an increasingly popular movement.

Just twenty years later, in 1807, the anti-slavery movement triumphed. Parliament made slave trade illegal throughout the empire. Britain started offering bounties to privateers who pursued slavers for profit and, more substantially, created the West Africa Squadron to suppress the Atlantic slave trade militarily. Sometimes this has been dismissed as a symbolic effort, but to divert warships in the middle of the Napoleonic Wars takes serious devotion to the cause. The fleet constantly grew, and in the 1850s some twenty-five vessels with 2,000 men were protecting the African coast and intercepting slave ships. At its peak, it made up a sixth of the whole Royal Navy. It was active for half a century, and in total freed around 150,000 slaves.

Massive petitioning by the British public even persuaded the government to add slave trade to the agenda of the Congress of Vienna of 1814–15, which marked the end of the Napoleonic Wars. The Duke of Wellington was taken aback by such peculiar demands in an international treaty, but the extent of anti-slavery sentiments is revealed in the warning by his brother Richard Wellesley, the previous foreign minister, that there could be a revolution if they resisted such calls. In February 1815, Britain convinced the representatives of France, Germany, Spain, Portugal, Sweden and Russia to agree to Act XV, which proclaimed an end to the slave trade 'as repugnant to the principles of humanity and universal morality'.[65] It was an incredible moment in human history, though not every state took it as seriously as the British.

The next step for the abolitionists was to ban slavery itself. A new British anti-slavery movement was founded in 1823 and ten years later what had seemed impossible just a few years earlier became reality. Parliament passed the Slavery Abolition Act, which banned the purchase and ownership of slaves by British subjects.

The result of the series of events begun that afternoon in London, wrote French political philosopher Alexis de Tocqueville (1805–1859), was 'absolutely without precedent in history... If you pore over the histories of all peoples, I doubt that you will find anything more extraordinary or more beautiful.'[66]

This historical moment was tainted by the fact that the slave owners were compensated for their loss. British taxpayers had to pay £20 million, a sum equal to 5 per cent of its GDP at the time. That was another injustice. Of course, it should have been the slave holders compensating the slaves instead. On the other hand, as Daniel Hannan has argued, it's easy to object to slavery in theory when it doesn't cost you anything. That the British found this ancient institution so objectionable that they were even willing to pay to abolish it can be described as a source of pride rather than shame.[67]

Did the empire create industry?

A popular narrative has it that Britain prospered not because of the golden-age conditions of openness and rule of law, but because of its imperialism and exploitation. Colonialism and the slave trade have done great harm to regions and populations exposed to it. A legacy of low trust and arbitrary rule has made development more difficult. Furthermore, the extractive institutions set up by European colonizers were often taken over after de-colonization by local rulers who just rebranded them and continued to plunder their populations. However, a corollary of this is not necessarily that empire benefited the imperialists.

The idea that Britain became rich because of its empire has difficulty attracting support from modern economists. Since almost every country until modern times has tried to subject other countries, steal their resources and enslave their people, it was always likely that the one country that eventually broke away from poverty would also have a great many sins to atone for. However, this is not the same as saying that it was those sins that made wealth and industry possible in that country.

After pondering the evidence, Joel Mokyr concludes: 'On the path to a more modern economy driven by technological progress, empire was, on balance, a distraction, not a stimulus to progress… more atavism than path to economic development.'[68]

Stealing treasure from other countries can make a few people immensely rich, and therefore it plays a large role in history books, but it is useless as an explanation for how someone can produce more and more every year. That can only be explained by the fact that knowledge, management and technology make people more productive all the time.

Only after Britain had already become economically successful did it build a world-spanning empire. At the start of the First World War, the British Empire famously ruled over almost 25 per cent of the world's population. One hundred years before that, in 1814, when the Industrial Revolution had been going on for half a century and Britain was already firmly established as the richest country in history, less than 6 per cent of the world population was governed from London. British colonialism does not explain the rise of Britain: the rise of Britain explains British colonialism. Once it attained technological superiority and rule of the seas, it was possible for Great Britain to project its power all over the world.

The empire created huge fortunes, but only for a lucky few. It was a huge rent-seeking project that enriched a small group of imperialists, adventurers and monopolists at the expense of not just the colonial subjects, but also British consumers and taxpayers, who had to fund the infrastructure, the military and colonial wars. One is tempted to ask how much faster the economy would have developed if such incredible amounts of money had not been diverted to building battleships and hiring mercenaries.

This was the argument Britain's anti-imperialists made, from Adam Smith to J. A. Hobson, that the empire benefited aristocrats, administrators, the military and favoured businessmen, but not the majority of Britons. This is why, in 1858, the free-trade champion John Bright called Britain's foreign policy 'a gigantic system of out-door relief for the aristocracy'.[69]

In the eighteenth century, cities like London and Bristol grew as a result of trade (not all of it colonial, of course) and shipbuilding, and while some of those profits were invested in other sectors, including industrialization, this cannot explain why businessmen and mechanics in Birmingham and Manchester suddenly started to innovate. In fact, London's share of the British population actually declined slightly during the Industrial Revolution, because other parts of the country grew so fast. The small town of Birmingham grew from 7,000 people in 1700 to 233,000 in 1851. Manchester expanded from under 10,000 people to an incredible 300,000.

Spain obtained massive resources from its American colonies, but, by spending them unproductively, it made the empire poorer, not richer. It was non-imperial countries like Belgium and Switzerland that first followed Britain's industrializing path, not imperial ones like the Netherlands, Portugal, Spain, Russia and China. Profitable sugar colonies in the West Indies created large revenues for Britain, but they did so for France and Portugal too, and did not help them to industrialize. One of the leading researchers of transatlantic slavery, David Brion Davis, claims that the thesis that profits from slave plantations and the slave trade funded the Industrial Revolution 'has now been wholly discredited'.[70]

Mokyr comments that without colonization the British would not have been sipping Indian tea sweetened with Caribbean sugar when they listened to lectures about science and industry. But it was the lectures that mattered.[71] Slavery mostly gave the British a bad conscience and bad teeth.

The Industrial Revolution came about when entrepreneurs and engineers gained the freedom, knowledge and inspiration to innovate and improve, and this was not dependent on colonial capital. Unlike some early interpretations, it was not a big push of investment that got industry going. Usually businesses started with small sums scraped together from relatives and acquaintances, and then the main source of funding was self-finance – entrepreneurs ploughed their profits back into the business. The revolution 'pulled itself up by its bootstraps'.[72]

Neither did these new industrial ventures depend on demand from foreign markets. The fact that Britain eventually became the world's workshop does not negate the fact that it became so by perfecting new technologies that were initially funded almost exclusively by revenue from the domestic market.

Granted, there was one major colonial market for British exports when industrialization took off in the 1760s, but this happens to be the one part of the empire that it lost around the same time: America.

The Englishman left to himself

When, towards the end of his life, the German 'Iron Chancellor' Otto von Bismarck was asked what the most important political fact of modern times was, he is supposed to have answered: 'that North America speaks English'.

It is tempting to agree, at least if we are allowed a slight adjustment, from 'speaks English' to 'thinks English'. The fact that the British colonized North America in an era when they had begun to be seriously influenced by liberal Enlightenment ideas, and then saw those colonies drift away and make their own future, is the central political fact of modern history.

It was by no means a foregone conclusion that North America would speak the language of the English, who were late to the continent. The Spanish and the French had been there for a long time when the virgin queen Elizabeth in 1585 gave the adventurer Walter Raleigh permission to explore its west coast and to name it Virginia after her. The first colony, on Roanoke Island in 1587, was in a precarious situation, and the governor, John White, returned to England for supplies. Owing to the war with Spain, he was prevented from returning to Roanoke until 1590. By then, the colony had disappeared without trace, including White's wife and young daughter. To this day, what happened to the colonists remains a mystery, but it is likely that they were killed or absorbed by natives.

The historian A. L. Rowse has argued that, counter-intuitively, the terrible fate of Roanoke might be the reason why English colonization triumphed in the long run. Had the colony survived, the Spanish, who claimed the whole continent, would soon have found out about it and easily destroyed it, laid precise claims to the east coast and built forts to prevent more English initiatives. In that case, Queen Elizabeth's successor,

James I, who wanted peace with the Spanish, would have hesitated before allowing more attempts at colonization. In 1588, the Spanish sent a bark along the coast with the intention of building a fort on Chesapeake Bay, but since it did not find any outsiders it was deemed unnecessary.[73]

The destruction of the Spanish armada later that same year, the failures against Dutch rebels and a series of sovereign defaults put the Spanish in a much weaker position when the English returned to found Jamestown in Virginia in 1607 and went on to claim the eastern seaboard. It is one of modern history's biggest *what ifs*.

The royally chartered company that founded Jamestown, named after King James, was disappointed to find no gold, and it was not possible to coerce the dispersed indigenous groups to work for them, as the Spanish had in South America. It tried to force the indentured English settlers to work for subsistence ratios, but the venture was unproductive and some preferred to escape, sometimes to live with the natives, even though this carried the death penalty. As famine gripped the colony, the desperate governor gave in, freed the colonists from their contracts, and gave them their freedom and ownership of a plot of land.

Amazingly, on 30 July 1619, the colonists were also granted a representative assembly, which adapted the governing rules according to the will of the settlers. Polish craftsmen refused to work if they did not get the right to vote like the English, so within a decade of the Jamestown's foundation it had a miniature parliament with voting rights for all adult men. Nothing like this had existed in the Spanish, Portuguese or French American colonies, some of which were more than a century old.

However, in another regard the English colonizers were depressingly similar to the others. Just three weeks after having implemented proto-democracy, Jamestown's governor bought the first African forced labourers from a privateer who had captured them from a Portuguese ship. Thus in 1619 the 'new world' was cursed with multiple personality disorder. At one and the same time, it developed representative institutions, ultimately leading to democratic freedoms, and started using involuntary labour, which would expand into a massive and brutal system of chattel slavery in the American south. The English in America embarked on two incompatible roads, which would cause constant frictions and terrible harm. In the end, the split between the idea of self-ownership and subjection could be resolved only by a horrific civil war.

The French politician and writer Alexis de Tocqueville, one of the sharpest observers of the American character, was certain that slavery would end 'by the deed of the slave or by that of the master'.[74] It just couldn't survive as the ideals of democratic liberty and the Enlightenment gained influence. And Tocqueville was convinced that English America provided particularly fertile ground for those ideals. He thought that just as every man has a special character independent of his social position, every people has a character independent of its political position and interest. Therefore Tocqueville concluded: 'The American is the Englishman left to himself.'[75]

In colonies geographically distant from capitals and mediating institutions, these characters could often develop freely, thought Tocqueville, who noticed that the French colonial administration 'regulates, controls, undertakes everything' as it brought absolute monarchy to its colonies:

> In the United States, on the contrary, the English anti-centralization system was carried to an extreme. Parishes became independent municipalities, almost democratic

republics. The republican element, which forms, so to say, the foundation of the English constitution and English habits, shows itself and develops without hindrance. Government proper does little in England, and individuals do a great deal; in America, government never interferes, so to speak, and individuals do every thing.[76]

The Britons who colonized America did not bring the old institutions of aristocracy, monarchy and state church with them. They had to rely on their own character and power, cultivating the land and organizing their own local government institutions. Such self-reliance co-existed uneasily with aristocratic institutions back in Britain, but here, in the forests of the new world, they were allowed to – and had to – develop freely.

This created what Tocqueville saw as 'the bourgeois and democratic liberty of which the history of the world did not yet offer a complete model'.[77]

It produced a culture that was very sensitive to authority. Britons in America developed a pride in the British constitutional heritage, and the works of John Locke and other Enlightenment liberals figured prominently in libraries and pamphlets. But they also gave this heritage a specific radical slant, emphasizing the dangers to liberty from the authorities and the urgent need to defend it. As Bernard Bailyn discovered when he researched the ideological origins of the American Revolution, one of the most important channels for such ideas was a series of radical essays written by two radical Whigs in the 1720s, the Englishman John Trenchard and the Scot Thomas Gordon. They were called *Cato's Letters*, using the pseudonym of Cato the Younger, Caesar's unforgiving enemy who preferred suicide over submission. A play written by Joseph Addison in 1712, *Cato, a Tragedy*, had turned the republican martyr into a cult figure among the anti-authoritarians.

In colonial America, *Cato's Letters* were published, and republished and quoted, in every newspaper and huge numbers of pamphlets. Bailyn writes: 'the writings of Trenchard and Gordon ranked with the treatises of Locke as the most authoritative statement of the nature of political liberty and above Locke as an exposition of the social sources of the threats it faced'.[78]

It was only a matter of time before this audacious spirit of civil liberty would clash with commands from an ocean away.

The American Revolution

That the greatest controversy would be based on taxes was odd in a way, since the colonies were very lightly taxed, and much less than the British. But, to Americans, it was not the specific sums involved that mattered but the principles. If a parliament in which colonists were not represented could suddenly impose a stamp tax on them, or a tax on tea, it could do anything, they feared. 'No taxation without representation', they said, and when pushed on this, they said that not even representation in London would do, only American representation.

Again and again, British authorities tried to impose new duties and crack down on smuggling (which most merchants engaged in), and they thought this was only fair, since their navy and armies protected the Americas too. Angered colonists responded with boycotts of British goods, civil disobedience and increasingly violent resistance. The more British troops that arrived to control them, the more the locals armed themselves. The breaking point came after the so-called Boston Tea Party in December 1773, when a rebel group calling themselves the

Sons of Liberty threw an entire shipment of tea from the East India Company into the harbour. This displeased many leading colonists too, but the response from London angered them even more. It was similar to the way the sixteenth-century Dutch objected to Calvinist rioters' attacks on Catholic churches but abhorred Spain's retribution even more.

Britain had long seen Boston as a hotbed of resistance, and now they went after the whole colony. Parliament enacted what became known as the Intolerable or Coercive Acts, which closed the port of Boston, ended local self-rule and took control of the courts. It was exactly the kind of despotism that the radical Whigs had always warned about, and it convinced educated colonists well versed in Locke and *Cato's Letters* that the pact between the people and the king had been broken.

A Continental Congress was assembled in Philadelphia in the autumn of 1774, where the colonial delegates agreed to ignore the new acts, refuse payment of taxes and urge every colony to raise militias. All their democratic, republican and constitutional ideals now coalesced into revolutionary fervour. As Americans armed themselves and the British troops came to disarm them, war was drawing close.

When Patrick Henry concluded a fiery speech in Richmond in March 1775 by shouting 'Give me liberty or give me death', he pointed towards his chest menacingly with an ivory paper cutter, to make sure that no one would miss his allusion to Cato the Younger. It was no mere boast: the fifty-six delegates who put their names on the Declaration of Independence at the Second Continental Congress little more than a year later knew that it might very well be their own death sentences they signed.

But to many of the revolutionaries it was probably a much less complex story. In 1842, a young journalist interviewed 91-year-old Levi Preston, the last survivor of the battles of Lexington and Concord (Massachusetts), the first battles of the American Revolutionary War in 1775, and expected to hear stories about unconstitutional government and oppressive taxes.

> **Reporter:** Captain Preston, did you take up arms against intolerable oppressions?
>
> **Preston:** Oppression? I didn't feel them.
>
> R: What, were you not oppressed by the Stamp Act?
>
> P: I never saw one of those stamps. I certainly never paid a penny for one of them.
>
> R: Well, what then about the tea tax?
>
> P: I never drank a drop of the stuff; the boys threw it all overboard.
>
> R: Then I suppose you had been reading Harrington or Sidney or Locke about the eternal principles of liberty?
>
> P. Never heard of 'em. We read only the Bible, the catechism, Watt's Psalms, and the Almanac.
>
> R: Well, then, what was the matter? And what did you mean in going to this fight?
>
> P: Young man, what we meant in going for those redcoats was this: We always had governed ourselves, and we always meant to. They didn't mean we should.[79]

The English in the forests of the new world were simply not used to government, and they did not like when it crossed their paths. This was the first modern anti-colonial uprising, but it was not anti-British. The colonists thought that they were defending traditional English liberties that were being abandoned in London. George Washington's troops fought under the Grand Union flag. It had the familiar thirteen red and white stripes, but in the upper left corner there were no stars, but the red, white and blue Union Jack. (So Emanuel Leutze painted the wrong flag for the famous *Washington Crossing the Delaware*.)

In fact, public opinion about the conflict was quite similar in Britain and the colonies. The House of Commons wanted reconciliation with the Americans but was overruled by the House of Lords. The difference was that the colonial assemblies had a wider franchise and were therefore more representative. The most influential pamphlet-writer for independence, who had the harshest words for the British king, was not a colonist, but Thomas Paine, the son of a corset maker born in Norfolk, England.

It took more than an eight-year-long war to achieve independence. The colonists were underdogs in the eyes of the whole world, much like the Dutch against Spain, but the British had to send troops over an ocean and acted in hostile territory that the enemy knew well. Since this was not a war against another state, but an idea, how could they ever win? It was not enough to take the capital of Philadelphia; the rebels and troops just slipped away and fought on. The British never resorted to the mass terror against cities and civilians that they would have if they were the tyrants of American propaganda. The heart of many of the British commanders was not really in this fight. Some even sympathized with the rebels.

Substantial French military support for independence tipped the scales decisively (and ruined French state finances, contributing to the French Revolution of 1789). The Marquis de Lafayette became a hero of both the American and two French revolutions. In another sign that the revolutionary war was something of a British civil war, the man who convinced Lafayette to support the Americans was the Duke of Gloucester, the estranged younger brother of King George III. At a dinner in 1775, the duke told Lafayette about the growing revolt on the other side of the Atlantic and argued that the colonists had every right to revolt against his brother. Lafayette later said that his heart was enlisted at that very moment, and he thought of nothing but joining the revolution.[80]

Lafayette was there at the siege of Yorktown in October 1781, when a combined force of the continental army and French troops managed to surround the British army, while French ships blocked any escape or reinforcement from the sea. On 17 October, the British commander Charles Cornwallis asked for capitulation terms, marking the end of the last major land battle of the war. Poor Cornwallis was politically aligned with the Whigs, sympathetic to the colonists and one of the few peers who voted against the unpopular royal acts and duties imposed on them.

Cato's revenge

It is matter of immense fascination that when the founding American generation had the chance to begin the world anew, they went back to the past, studying two millennia of lessons about how to succeed, and fail, in protecting the ideals of liberty.

'I have the honor and consolation to be a republican on principle', wrote American Founding Father John Adams to Lafayette in 1782. 'Almost every thing that is estimable in civil life has originated under such governments. Two republican powers, Athens and Rome, have done more honor to our species than all the rest of it. A new country can be planted only by such a government.'[81]

In his study of the influence of the ancients on the founders, Thomas E. Ricks writes 'the thoughts and stories of the ancient Greeks and Romans stood front and center in American political and intellectual life as the founders grappled with the questions of how to gain independence and then how to form a new nation.'[82] The oldest of ideas shaped the most modern of nations.

Knowledge of ancient authors was universal among educated colonists and it was rare for a pamphleteer not to include at least one ancient analogy or quote. They found their inspiration and sometimes their own ideal selves in characters like Brutus, Cicero and Cato. 'Think Cato sees thee' was one of the phrases in Benjamin Franklin's bestselling *Poor Richard's Almanack*.

A descendant of Thomas Jefferson told his biographer that 'the Athenians were, in all respects, his chosen people', and Jefferson exhorted a nephew to read them in the original Greek (though he despised Plato's 'mysticisms incomprehensible to the human mind').[83] John Adams studied law in Massachusetts but claimed that he knew more about Roman law than local law. He read Cicero's speeches to himself aloud at night, and referring to Cicero and his struggles, he remarked 'Change the names and every Anecdote will be applicable to Us.'[84] James Madison, another Founding Father, had a bust of Athena on the mantlepiece of his drawing room and closely studied Greek constitutions before writing the American one.

There is a reason why, today, US 'Republicans' and 'Democrats' in the 'Senate' meet in the 'Capitol', surrounded by buildings that look like Greek and Roman temples. Come to think of it, from afar, the Lincoln Memorial looks suspiciously like the Greek Parthenon, and the Jefferson Memorial like the Roman Pantheon. When the British parliament burned down in 1834 and there was a suggestion to replace it with a neoclassical building with Greek and Roman columns and pediments, it was turned down because it looked too American![85]

The United States and the world should count itself lucky that, when the moment for revolution came, it was led by a group of people who had the audacity to found the new country on the ideals of Enlightenment liberalism and the wisdom to look to ancient lessons about how to do it, including how to stop a new Caesar from vanquishing the republic this time.

It gave us Thomas Jefferson's Declaration of Independence, and its immortal proclamation that all men are created equal, with inalienable rights to life, liberty and the pursuit of happiness. That governments are instituted to protect those rights, and if they become destructive to those ends, it is right to rebel.

The historian Woody Holton points out that the Second Continental Congress actually declared its independence on 2 July 1776, two days before it unanimously adopted the Declaration about it, so in effect 'Americans celebrate the press release rather than the act itself.'[86] But there is much in it to celebrate.

Winston Churchill thought that 'The Declaration was in the main a restatement of the principles which had animated the Whig struggle against the later Stuarts and the English Revolution of 1688.' Yes, but 1688, and the Bill of Rights a year later, were in turn a restatement of the Dutch Act of Abjuration of 1581, which borrowed heavily from the School of Salamanca, who were indebted to Roman law, and so on. Jefferson himself said that he intended the declaration to be an expression of the American mind, along the lines of 'Aristotle, Cicero, Locke, Sidney, etc'.[87]

In 1787, the first constitution had been drafted for the new country. It was unique in several ways. Even in their first sentences, the 1581 and 1689 declarations invoked God. The

US Constitution did not. It did not take its legitimacy from a supreme being, but from 'We the people'. In fact, God and Christianity are not even mentioned, except in the date: 'the Year of our Lord one thousand seven hundred and Eighty seven'. The only mention of religion is in the rejection of religious tests as a condition for holding public office. Opponents were dumbfounded, complaining that the framers had removed God from public life for the first time in history. With such a policy, they feared, a Jew, Muslim or the Pope himself could become the president of the United States – or even a Quaker![88]

This was not an oversight, but a conscious decision by the founders, who mostly considered themselves deists – God created the universe, but all the rest is up to us. In his history of America, Paul Johnson makes the case that had the Constitution been drawn up one hundred years earlier or one hundred years later, it would most likely have had a religious framework and have made provisions to nurture Protestantism as the national religion.[89] (The Pledge of Allegiance was composed by the Christian socialist Francis Bellamy a century later, and the words 'under God' were only added by Congress in 1954.)

The Constitution just happened to be drawn up at the peak of the secular Enlightenment, just before those ideals were tainted by the anti-religious terror of the late French Revolution. The founders managed to get the ideals of complete religious freedom through the door, allowing them to go on to transform the world, just before it was slammed shut.

The lead author of the Constitution, James Madison, had long insisted that a federal government was needed, or the separate states would oppress its citizens or fall like the Greek states fell to Philip of Macedon, the father of Alexander the Great. But this government also had to be strictly limited. The main problem in Greece and Rome, Madison thought, was that different groups and classes took turns to oppress one another. To prevent this, he came up with an ingenious solution to protect liberty by using their power-hunger against them. In a large union, with many layers of government and a division in executive, judicial and bi-cameral legislative powers that constantly check and balance the others, factions will have to fight each other for every ounce of power, and so often cancel each other out.

It was a new version of Aristotle's and Cicero's mixed constitution, but more democratic since the states' various property requirements did not exclude as many in a population of smallholder farmers. By 1790, five states gave all men (white, in some cases) the right to vote for some or all offices, and eventually they all followed.

The Constitution was also more genuinely liberal. The United States swept away the feudal remnants and traditional hierarchies of the old world. There were to be no aristocratic privileges, state church, monopolies, coercive guilds, censorship or political police. Remarkably, the First Amendment to the Constitution said that 'Congress shall make no law respecting an establishment of religion, or prohibiting the free exercise thereof; or abridging the freedom of speech, or of the press; or the right of the people peaceably to assemble.'

Yes, 'a republic, if you can keep it', in Benjamin Franklin's famous phrase. Contrary to proposals from Founding Father Alexander Hamilton to make appointments of presidents and senators for life, Madison and the majority insisted that these had to be changed regularly to prevent the creation of a new monarchy. How extraordinary this decision was came across in the story about how the British king George III reacted to George Washington's career choices. During the revolutionary war, the British king asked his court painter, the American

Benjamin West, what Washington would do if the colonists won their independence. No doubt he expected West to answer that the general would make himself king or become a new Cromwell, but West replied that he believed that Washington would retire to his farm. 'If he did', the incredulous king replied, 'he would be the greatest man in the world.'[90]

So, according to his own old foe, Washington became the greatest character of his age – twice. With his incredible standing with the people after the military triumph, Washington could have done anything, but by the end of the war he chose to lay down his command and returned to Mount Vernon. However, when the office of the president was created, there was a broad consensus that he was the only possible candidate. Many think of him as an old man, but he was only fifty-seven when he became president. After serving two terms, Washington was implored to seek a third term, but refused, setting an important precedent for his young country. Americans compared him to the Roman hero Cincinnatus, who was supposedly elected dictator in 458 BC to fight off an invasion, and after it was averted, relinquished all his powers and returned to his farm.

It may just have been the result of Washington's personal character. Or perhaps it can be explained by him being a man of his (relatively enlightened) age. Who knows, it might have something to do with the fact that *Cato, A Tragedy* was his favourite play.

Some Britons no doubt felt that American independence was a terrible blow, but others saw it as a vindication of its best ideals. 'Strong mother of a Lion-line, / Be proud of those strong sons of thine / Who wrench'd their rights from thee!', Tennyson versified. In his account, the sons of liberty were indeed sons of Britain, who had merely 'Retaught the lesson thou hadst taught'.

Just as 1688 had transplanted liberal Dutch ideas into a larger body with greater resources, 1776 did the same with liberal British ideas. The United States became a deep reservoir of freedom and prosperity on the other side of the Atlantic, in a continent-sized republic protected from potential enemies by two oceans. It would be called upon again and again in the twentieth century, when those ideas were in peril in the old world, from the Kaiser, from national socialism and from communism.

Just as Great Britain was the proudest achievement of the Dutch, the United States was the greatest achievement of the British.

Liberators or enslavers?

But wait, wasn't this just liberty for rich white men? Weren't minorities enslaved and indigenous groups deprived of their lands, freedoms and often lives? Yes, they were, and it is a testament to real progress that we now live in an era where we pay attention to and condemn such grievous crimes. We rarely hear excuses for it, and open celebrations of it would be unthinkable. That is in no small part due to the achievement of the American culture.

'All nations are born in war, conquest, and crime, usually concealed by the obscurity of a distant past', writes the historian Paul Johnson, with one exception:

> The United States, from its earliest colonial times, won its title-deeds in the full blaze of recorded history, and the stains on them are there for all to see and censure: the dispossession of an indigenous people, and the securing of self-sufficiency through the sweat and pain of an enslaved race.[91]

It remains a perplexing and offensive fact that many of the founders of the United States were hypocrites, fighting for freedom while owning slaves, and the system was allowed to go on for many years. Thomas Jefferson dreamed of a nation governed by reason alone but kept many slaves and probably fathered children with one of them. He described slavery as 'the most unremitting despotism on the one part, and degrading submission on the other',[92] yet, because of his large debts, he did not even release most slaves in his will. A historian writes that, his whole life, 'Jefferson wrestled with slavery, even though in the end he "lost".'[93]

To try to understand how such contradictions could exist within the same man takes us to uncomfortable places in human nature. The American Revolution will always be tainted by the crime and the shame of racism and slavery.

In recent years, some have gone much further in their denouncements, even claiming that America itself must be understood as a slave venture. The *New York Times'* 1619 project made the case that the United States' real founding date is not 1776, but 1619, when forced labourers were first brought to North America, and even argued that the revolution was fought to protect slavery against British abolitionism. The founders just hid their true motives by never mentioning slavery explicitly in the documents: 'Our founding ideals of liberty and equality were false when they were written.'[94]

That is a revisionist fabrication wrapped in an anachronism. In 1619, slavery was practised everywhere, had always been and almost no one gave it a second thought. That year did not signal a break; 1776 did. By then, there was no British abolitionism to revolt against, just a few eccentric Quakers and free-market economists. 'Few voices were raised against slavery in Britain until the last quarter of the eighteenth century', writes

David Olusoga in his *Black and British: A Forgotten History*. Abolitionism's unpromising beginning was 'a mere rumbling of discontent' among small minority groups.[95]

Anti-slavery sentiment was much stronger in New England than in old England, and this so happened to be the location where the flames of revolution were kindled. The slave-holding West Indian colonies, on the other hand, refused to join the struggle for independence. The meeting of the Pennsylvania Abolition Society in Philadelphia on 14 April 1775 is often taken to be the world's first organized anti-slavery meeting in history. Benjamin Franklin was eventually elected its president. It would take twelve years before the British abolition movement was started and that was partly due to inspiration from America.

Gordon Wood, a centre-left historian who is one of the leading scholars of the American revolution, thinks that 'it is the northern states in 1776 that are the world's leaders in the antislavery cause', with an abolitionist movement that was 'unprecedented in the history of the world'. He dismisses the assertion that the revolution was undertaken to defend slavery completely, 'in fact the contrary is more true to what happened'.[96]

It is a fact that the founders did not know how to ban slavery without losing the south and therefore the revolution, but it is just false to pretend they had some secret wish to prolong the institution. It is crystal clear from both public actions and private correspondence that most of them abhorred slavery and wanted the system to disappear.

Thomas Jefferson publicly called for abolition and managed to convince Virginia to ban the importing of slaves in 1778. In his first draft of the Declaration of Independence, Jefferson called slavery a 'cruel War against human Nature itself, violating its most sacred Rights of Life and Liberty in the Persons of a distant People'. He described holding slaves captive and carrying them to another hemisphere as 'piratical Warfare' and an 'assemblage of Horrors'. He did not get this through Congress, since it would have led slave states to refuse to join the revolt, but you don't write such stirring prose against something if your confidential plan is to save it.

'I am principled against this kind of traffic in the human species', wrote George Washington, and insisted that 'it being among my first wishes to see some plan adopted, by the legislature by which slavery in this Country may be abolished.' In the Federalist Paper no. 42, James Madison wrote that he personally would have preferred an instant end to the 'barbarism' of the transatlantic slave trade, but also that 'It ought to be considered as a great point gained in favor of humanity' that after a period of twenty years his proposed constitution would make it possible to ban forever this 'unnatural traffic', even to the south. And he called on Europeans to follow this landmark decision.[97]

Many restrained their anti-slavery views in public, no doubt sometimes out of shame for owning slaves themselves, and to avoid political splits and a breakdown between states that could give an opening to foreign powers or even civil war. A concerned Jefferson told friends that he worried that persisting publicly in his abolitionism might do the cause more harm than good. However, John Adams went so far as to say that 'foreign War and civil War together at the Same time are preferable to Slavery'.[98]

During the revolutionary war, all northern states except loyalist New York and New Jersey took the first steps for an incremental abolition of slavery. In 1780, Pennsylvania enacted the first emancipation law in US history. Often the decisive push took brave individual action. Also in 1780, Bett, an enslaved woman in Massachusetts, heard that the state constitution now asserted that 'all men are born free and equal' and thought that this should apply to her as well. She filed a suit, the jury ruled in her favour and she won her freedom, taking the name Elizabeth Freeman.

In 1806, as president, Thomas Jefferson told Congress that the US must withdraw from the 'violations of human rights' that the slave trade represented 'which the morality, the reputation, and the best interests of our country have long been eager to proscribe'. Congress complied and on 2 March 1807 declared American participation in the transatlantic slave trade a crime – twenty-three days before Great Britain did the same.

In the battle against the slave trade old adversaries had found a common cause. In 1819, just five years after the British had burned down the White House and Congress (in a conflict ignited by the Napoleonic War), the American government set up the African Slave Trade Patrol, which helped Britain to protect the African coast and chase slave ships. In 1822, the American Colonization Society founded Liberia as a location for freed slaves and named the capital Monrovia in a sign of gratitude for the support of US president James Monroe.

However, domestic slavery was by now so entrenched in the southern plantation economy that it would take the kind of civil war John Adams talked about to root it out completely. The economy and population of the industrial north grew much faster than the agricultural south, and more non-slave states were added. As this would eventually give them the power to end slavery, the southern states saw no way to protect their system of coercion without secession.

It should give the 1619ers pause for thought that during that period it was abolitionists like Abraham Lincoln and Frederick Douglass who sought strength, support and rhetorical figures from the Declaration of Independence and the Constitution.

Meanwhile, the slavery apologist George Fitzhugh raged against 'that bombastic absurdity in our Declaration of Independence about the inalienable rights of man' and described southern secession as 'a solemn protest against the doctrines of natural liberty, human equality and the social contract as taught by Locke and the American sages of 1776'. Similarly, the leading South Carolinian pro-slavery politician John C. Calhoun argued that 'the most false and dangerous of all political errors' was the Lockean/Jeffersonian doctrine that all men are created free and equal. 'For a long time it lay dormant' in the Declaration of Independence, wrote Calhoun, 'but in the process of time it began to germinate, and produce its poisonous fruits.'[99]

Calhoun had it absolutely right. The impact of the radical philosophy embedded in America's founding documents only grew with time, and soon overcame the compromises, timidity and hypocrisy of some of its proponents.

Calhoun was indignant about that, arguing that the principles of individual liberty 'made no necessary part of our justification in separating from the parent country'. But it was indeed necessary for what the United States was to become that it declared its independence along specific principles about inalienable rights and limited government. This is what made it the first state on the planet explicitly based on Enlightenment ideas.

There is a certain futility in fighting over what America's character was 'really' like and quarrelling over its real founding date. A country is not an organism with a particular birth year, but complex communities of millions of people, often conflicted themselves, living through different eras, holding incompatible ideas and acting in contradictory manners. Some are good, some bad, some admirable, some shameful. And just as the commendable actions of some can never atone for the crimes of others, the abuses committed by some do not invalidate heroic efforts of others. Some of our actions originate with our inner demons and others with the better angels of our nature, and no horrors committed by Americans change the fact that the poetic framing of Lockean liberalism in the Declaration of Independence and the republican statecraft of the Constitution belong in the latter group. In fact, these founding documents ended up being better than the men who drafted them.

And they kept bearing fruit over generations. The pioneering Seneca Falls women's rights convention in 1848 patterned its declaration explicitly on the 1776 Declaration, 'We hold these truths to be self-evident: that all men and women are created equal; that they are endowed by their Creator with certain inalienable rights.' The Constitution had used words like 'persons', 'people' and 'electors', making it easier for courts to interpret rights as applicable to women too, but it took until 1848 before New York became the first state to recognize women's independent property rights, and the right to vote on the federal level had to wait until 1920.

Referring to Jefferson's words about equality and freedom, the gay rights activist Harvey Milk insisted 'that's what America is. No matter how hard you try, you cannot erase those words from the Declaration of Independence.'

In the enduring phrasing of Martin Luther King Jr, when he fought against the Jim Crow system by which former slave states tried to make emancipation a chimera: 'When the architects of our republic wrote the magnificent words of the Constitution and the Declaration of Independence, they were signing a promissory note to which every American was to fall heir.' He was convinced that both whites and blacks would soon experience this freedom, 'because the goal of America is freedom'.[100]

When all is said and done, what made the Anglosphere different was not its shameful history of slavery; in this regard they were just like every preceding civilization that had the chance. African slavery did not begin when Europeans started buying slaves from there but had been practised there since ancient times. The number of slaves brought to the Arab world is probably quite similar to the number shipped to the American continent. Of the slaves transported across the Atlantic, the Americans and British were responsible for just over a quarter. Only 5–6 per cent were brought to what is now the United States.[101]

What made the Anglosphere special was not that it engaged in the horrendous scheme of conquest and slavery, but that it decided to stop – and even to bear significant expense to try to prevent others from continuing. That was a first: the first recorded arrival of African slaves in America in 1619 did not change the world; it was just one in an, until then, seemingly inevitable, endless series of crimes against the inalienable right to self-ownership. But the Declaration of American Independence in 1776 did.

Larger than life

The peace negotiations in Paris after the revolutionary war did not go as France and Spain wished. Great Britain was far too generous to the thirteen states that it had supported. It accepted greatly enlarged boundaries for the new United States and fishing rights off Newfoundland. This was not just the consequence of having skilled negotiators like Benjamin Franklin. Once the issue of sovereignty was off the table, the British started to see that they had much in common with the new republic, and they expected close commercial relationships in the future. London also preferred a strong new state in North America that would not be swallowed up by the powerful French and Spanish presence. The Louisiana Purchase of 1803, when the United States doubled its size in exchange for $15 million to Napoleon, showed that they had bet on the right horse.

An exchange between a French guest and the Scottish official Caleb Whitefoord at the celebrations of the Peace of Paris in 1783 foreshadowed the coming Anglo-American Special Relationship. The Frenchman taunted Whitefoord, saying that 'the thirteen United States would make the greatest empire in the world'. Whitefoord replied: 'Yes, Monsieur, and they will all speak English, every one of 'em.'[102]

Little over half a century later, these thirteen states had been joined by another thirteen, and in 1959, there were fifty of them, spanning from coast to coast, and all the way out to Hawaii. The population expanded even more. When the Americans declared their independence, there were fewer than 3 million of them. A hundred years later, there were 50 million, and four decades after that, 100 million. America had been populated by wave after wave of immigrants, searching for freedom, pursuing happiness.

After 1862, several Homestead Acts mirrored the policies of Song China and the Low Countries, giving newly arrived farmers ownership to the land they settled. This policy opened up 160 million acres and established a large class of independent farmers. Most of the immigrants settled in cities, however, contributing to a doubling of the share of Americans in urban areas from 25 to 50 per cent between 1870 and 1920. New York City grew from a few hundred thousand inhabitants to almost 6 million.

When in 1865 Auguste Bartholdi started planning a colossal copper statue as a gift from the French people to the American people, to symbolize the new republic and its abolition of slavery, he chose to portray the ancient Roman goddess of liberty, *Libertas*.

Dressed in robes, she holds in one hand a torch, enlightening the world, in the other, an ancient tablet representing law, and written on it, in Roman numerals, JULY IV MDCCLXXVI, the date of the Declaration of Independence. It's barely visible under her robes, but at her feet lies a broken chain and shackle. This was how Bartholdi wanted to see the new nation, as did Americans. The Statue of Liberty was privately funded and placed on a federally owned island, now called Liberty Island, in New York harbour. At 93 metres high including the pedestal, the world's tallest statue at the time, it became the symbolic welcome to travellers from the sea.

On a bronze plaque inside the pedestal is the famous sonnet by Emma Lazarus, composed to raise funds for the statue. It presents the new colossus as 'Mother of Exiles', a new Romulus, who populates the country by opening its doors to 'your tired, your poor, your huddled masses yearning to breathe free'. As George Washington had stated, 'The bosom of America is open to receive not only the opulent and respectable stranger, but the oppressed and persecuted of all nations and religions.'[103]

The Dutch Republic and Great Britain were countries full of immigrants, but, like ancient Rome, the United States was a country *of* immigrants. On a visit, Charles Dickens found himself on a railway apologizing to the steward for a misunderstanding: 'You see, I am a stranger here.' The steward replied: 'Mister, in America we are all strangers.'[104]

The people of America quickly defied every expectation. The absence of regulations and internal tariffs created a huge free-trade area, and it was soon connected by a deep and broad network of canals, steamboats, railways and financial transactions. The devotion to work and innovation that Tocqueville had observed led to a frenzy of experimentation that stimulated every industry. Young America 'has a great passion – a perfect rage – for the "new"', proclaimed Abraham Lincoln, 'and if there be any thing old which he can endure, it is only old whiskey and old tobacco'.[105]

At first, America imitated and improved. Samuel Slater became known to the British as 'Slater the Traitor' since he memorized the design of textile machines as an apprentice in an English cotton mill before escaping to America in 1789, and kickstarted industrial manufacturing there. But soon Americans were innovating like crazy. The United States became the world's biggest agricultural power, partly because of its plentiful fertile land. At least as important was the fact that farmers innovated more, from the 30–40 improved versions of horseshoes patented every year to the revolutionary mechanical reaper invented by Cyrus McCormick, a Virginia blacksmith.

In Karl Marx's mind, the connection between slavery, cotton and the US economy was so strong that in 1847 he predicted: 'Cause slavery to disappear and you will have wiped America off the map of nations.' His forecast was tested less than two decades later. In the 1870s, sharecroppers and tenant farmers produced 40 per cent more cotton than they had done before the civil war; by 1891, twice as much. But cotton's share of total production and exports steadily declined, since the future of the country was the north's industrial capacity, which now developed freely over the whole country, and the result was a surge of economic activity.

This would go on to have global implications. There were no guarantees that the British Industrial Revolution would continue and accelerate. There was always a risk that progress would peter out, in a similar way to what had happened in other golden ages, and that economies would settle into some kind of steampunk world of steam-, water- and spring-powered technologies. It would no doubt have looked cool, but it would not have had the capacity to lift most of humanity out of poverty. Led by the pushy, ambitious United States of America, an increasingly integrated North Atlantic knowledge and competition economy saved the world from this fate and ushered in what has been called the 'Second Industrial Revolution'.

In a short period of time, there arrived new, broad technological breakthroughs that had an impact on a multitude of sectors and structures, such as electricity, telecommunications, materials science, organic chemistry, the internal combustion engine, the oil industry, the assembly line, the machine-tool industry and mass-produced interchangeable parts. Breakthroughs in one area facilitated them in another – electric motors could run assembly lines, and cheap steel revolutionized every industry – but they also instilled a sense of optimism that pervaded the whole culture. A steady stream of advances convinced people that there was much left to discover and develop, and if you took your chance you could become fabulously wealthy.

The economist J. Bradford DeLong estimates that, every year since 1870, the world has seen as much growth in useful ideas about technology and organization as was realized every sixty years before 1500. The centre-left economist credits this progress, not unreasonably, to three factors: 'the industrial research laboratory, the large modern corporation, and globalization, which made the world one global market economy'.[106] All three were ways of taking the openness and experimentation that has signified progress in past golden eras, and systematizing and institutionalizing it.

Technological breakthroughs reduced the price and hassle of trade, migration and communication. The new telegraph, linked to a global submarine network, ensured that every event and new insight was soon known on other continents. Crew-propellered and iron-hulled steamships, linked to railroads, shipped millions and millions of migrants over the oceans, as well as consumer goods, machine tools and foodstuff.

The modern corporation achieved a sophisticated division of labour in production, where workers and machines could be organized to produce more and faster, and in competition with other corporations trying to develop an even better division of labour. The industrial research laboratory, epitomized by Thomas Alva Edison's Menlo Park, brought scientists with different expertise together in greenhouses for invention, to develop and deploy the new technologies rationally and routinely.

The value of all of this can be illustrated with the Renaissance giant Leonardo da Vinci, the most relentlessly curious man in history. He came up with ideas and sketches for a whole universe of revolutionary technologies, but being a single, slightly isolated genius, he brought very few of these ideas to fruition. Imagine how world history could have been sped up if Leonardo had also had the backing of venture capital, a laboratory of collaborators and a manufacturing operation standing by to turn his inventions into consumer products. Then one can understand why the economic changes in the late nineteenth century accelerated progress to the fastest rate in human history.

By 1870, factories had mostly given people access to things the rich had possessed for centuries, like better clothes, furniture, pottery, cutlery and books. That was no small feat. But, after 1870, mass production provided them with brand-new gadgets that previous generations could not have dreamed of, like telephones, gramophones, typewriters, lightbulbs, cameras, cars, refrigerators, washing machines, flushing toilets and clean running water. As the British economist John Maynard Keynes wrote in 1919, the new economy had managed to provide 'at a low cost and with the least trouble, conveniences, comforts, and amenities beyond the compass of the richest and most powerful monarchs of other ages'.[107]

And they would go on doing so. Taking ideas from wherever they found them, from foreigners, research laboratories, universities, workshops and garages, Americans always looked for ways of converting them into something useful and profitable. That particular genius for turning abstract science and inventions into cheap consumer goods has allowed them to push the frontiers of every industrial breakthrough since, from the automobile and mass media to finance, microelectronics, the world wide web and AI.

This capacity to produce and reduce prices made the American worker the world's richest. That's why Franklin D. Roosevelt, when asked what single book he would put into the hands of a Russian communist to make him reconsider his views, answered 'The Sears Roebuck catalogue', referring to the king of mail-order merchandise.

There is now a revisionist attempt to credit America's late nineteenth-century industrialization with its tariffs. However, as the leading trade scholar Douglas Irwin has discovered, US productivity grew the fastest in non-traded sectors, like services, transportation, utilities and communications, not in manufacturing and agriculture where the tariffs applied. Irwin finds that the tariffs probably acted as a modest drag on growth, by saving inefficient firms and raising the price of inputs and capital goods. Instead he explains fast late-nineteenth-century growth with a deregulated and integrated national economy, large-scale immigration and the development of financial markets with foreign capital – three aspects of openness.[108]

Openness to innovation and surprises also turned the United States into a cultural superpower. Since it became the crossroads for different cultures and immigrants from all over the world, ideas were cross-fertilized and then combined with foreign ideas and new technologies, providing the world with Hollywood, jazz, rock'n'roll, social media and (sadly) celebrity culture.

When Salvador Dalí in 1920 tried to promote his art in New York by walking down Fifth Avenue with a 4-foot loaf under his arm, he grumbled that almost no one took any notice: 'In America, Surrealism is invisible for all is larger than life.'[109]

It is symbolic that just as Abbasid Baghdad was once seen as 'the crossroads of the universe', and the Song capital 'the hub of the universe', Manhattan in general and Times Square in particular has often been called 'the centre of the universe'.

The anti-imperial empire

Leading the only country that still resisted Hitler's conquest of Europe, in June 1940, the British Prime Minister Winston Churchill promised that his countrymen, against all odds, 'would carry on the struggle, until, in God's good time, the New World, with all its power and might, steps forth to the rescue and the liberation of the old'.

America's crushing dominance in economy, science and technology, in combination with its protected geographical position, transformed global geopolitics. As Theodore Roosevelt ascertained in 1900, it meant that the US was becoming 'more and more the balance of power of the whole globe'. If the new world decided to throw its weight behind one side in a military conflict, it tipped the balance, as Germany learned twice during the twentieth century.

The United States 'is a country of machines' declared an impressed Josef Stalin, at the Tehran Conference, after Hitler had betrayed their totalitarian alliance. 'Without the use of these machines, through Lend-Lease, we would lose this war.'[110] Coming from a communist dictator, it was a startling compliment of American capitalism, but it was obvious to anyone that nothing could rival what the man who led the US armament project, the Danish-born auto industry executive Bill Knudsen, called 'the spirit of competition'. Knudsen had convinced Washington not to nationalize or command production, but just to put in the orders and then allow businesses to find the best and cheapest ways of producing, free from control and regulation.

In 1939 the United States had few and mostly outdated tanks and aircraft and a weaker navy than Japan. Between July 1940 and August 1945, American industries converted assembly lines and shipyards to produce a total of 8,800 naval vessels, including 141 aircraft carriers and 203 submarines, 86,000 tanks, 257,000 artillery pieces, 2.4 million trucks, 2.6 million machine guns and 41 billion rounds of ammunition.

When, in 1940, president Franklin D. Roosevelt announced plans for producing 50,000 aircraft a year, the Germans dismissed it as ludicrous propaganda. 'What is America but beauty queens, millionaires, stupid records, and Hollywood?' scoffed Hitler.[111] In fact, they managed 65,000 a year – 180 a day – and the US still managed to supply Russia and Great Britain with enough raw material to become the second and third producers of aeroplanes. All the while, the US diverted less of its economic output to the war effort than the other combatants.

Arthur Herman, who has shed light on this incredible history in his book *Freedom's Forge*, states:

> It was the most powerful and flexible system of wartime production ever devised, because in the end no one devised it. It grew out of the underlying productivity of the American economy. ... Out of what seemed like chaos and disorder to Washington would come an explosion of innovation, and creativity – not to mention hard work – across the country.[112]

What role did this give Britain in the shadow of such American dominance? At Allied Headquarters in North Africa (AFHQ) in 1944, the future prime minister Harold Macmillan told a colleague:

> We, my dear Crossman, are the Greeks in the American empire. You will find the Americans much as the Greeks found the Romans – great big, vulgar bustling people, more vigorous than we are and also more idle, with more unspoiled virtues, but also more corrupt. We must run AFHQ as the Greek slaves ran the operations of the Emperor Claudius.[113]

It was both an admission of impotence and an expression of self-satisfaction. The Greeks were after all a defeated people. At the same time, they had an older and more sophisticated culture than the Romans, and greatly influenced how that power would be wielded.

Every previous major power with the kind of superiority that America came out of the war with has used it to subjugate other countries. Some Americans no doubt felt a similar imperial itch, and the country regularly intervened in Latin America when it suited its national interest (or what economic and military interests could portray as being in its interest). After the short and successful Spanish–American war of 1898, the US annexed the Philippines, as well as Hawaii, Puerto Rico and Guam. Theodore Roosevelt himself was one of the most shameless enthusiasts for empire.

So the Americans had tried to be imperialists, but didn't particularly enjoy it. It never sat comfortably with a population that saw its origin in an anti-colonial struggle. When cheerful stories of liberation of the Philippines from Spanish oppression were substituted with reports of atrocities by American soldiers, support for the war dipped. The Anti-Imperialist League, with prominent members like Mark Twain and Andrew Carnegie, argued that colonial adventures were an abandonment of the principles of the founders. All presidents after Roosevelt felt that they had to present annexation as a way to prepare the Philippines for democratic self-rule. As is well known, this is a country that can always be relied upon to do the right thing, after having exhausted all possible alternatives.

Of course, it is easy to find examples when America has pushed weaker countries around and intervened militarily with odd justifications. That's what hegemons do. But eventually the US turned into a very different superpower. What set it apart from all previous ones was that it stepped back from building an empire of conquest to start seeing the freedom and prosperity of allies not as a threat, but as the very goal of its foreign policy.

Partly this American peculiarity is a result of the influence of its founding principles. The one form of resistance that invading American troops have never been able to break is public opinion back home. The American people might have taken great pride in being able to liberate other countries, build democratic institutions and leave ('Make 'em vote and live by their decisions', as Washington's ambassador in London explained its preferred policy towards Mexico in 1913),[114] but conquest and subjugation, a source of legitimacy for major powers throughout history, has more often been seen as a source of shame in the United States.

Constantly talking about being a city on a hill, with the eyes of all people upon you, is not just about having an exaggerated sense of self-importance; it also means that you are very conscious that others are watching, and they will notice if you don't live up to the principles you loudly proclaim.

America's behaviour also reflects a deep economic and technological shift. In the twentieth century, the United States emerged as the strongest commercial and industrial power the world had ever seen, and that changes the calculus for war. Wealth is no longer best created by acquiring arable land or subjecting peasants to taxation, but by innovating, building more productive capacity and trading with other economies. Unlike pre-industrial, extractive states stuck in a zero-sum game with others, modern, open economies benefit when other countries develop and are able to participate in a broader division of labour and contribute to the development of more knowledge and innovation. Since the destructive potential of industrial warfare is also much greater than could be achieved with spears and cannons, they have more to gain from peace and more to lose from war. On balance, it tends to make richer, industrialized and commercial countries see less gain in war.

This has gradually shifted the United States' interest towards establishing a system of international rules, to protect the kind of world in which it has itself thrived. It has tried to stop attempts to change borders with force, and has repeatedly gathered international coalitions to punish transgressors. It has tended to try to make the world safe for democracy and open seas (even though it has never hesitated to dirty its hands by cooperating with its enemies' enemy in doing so, such as Stalin during the Second World war or third-world dictators during the Cold War).

The problem with you in the old world, Franklin D. Roosevelt teased Churchill, is that 'You have four hundred years of acquisitive instinct in your blood, and you just don't understand why a country might not want to acquire land somewhere if they can get it.'[115]

Pax Americana

After the Second World War, the United States was so preeminent that it could put all these ideals into action. The Americans did many of the things that Athenians, Romans, Abbasids, Song and Dutch had done when they consolidated their victories: they expanded trade in every direction, established a system of rules that allowed for mobility and openness, and built a network of allies and international institutions to help them uphold this system.

This was an explicit attempt to learn from the horrors of nationalism and war, and the American mistake after the First World War of retreating from the world and imposing high trade barriers, which encouraged protectionism and jingoism all around the world. Roosevelt's Secretary of State, Cordell Hull, who would go on to win the Nobel Peace Prize, repeatedly made the case that 'unhampered trade dovetailed with peace; high tariffs, trade barriers and unfair economic competition, with war'. He acknowledged that reviving world trade alone could not guarantee peace, but it was an essential prerequisite. He argued that the only way to rebuild a peaceful and prosperous world was by 'establishing the foundation of an international order in which interdependent nations cooperate freely with each other for their mutual gain':[116] in effect, a Pax Americana.

In 1947, the US helped set up the General Agreement on Tariffs and Trade, the forerunner to the World Trade Organization, which negotiated tariff reductions and stopped participants from discriminating against other members. After several rounds, average manufacturing tariffs had been reduced from 40 per cent to less than 5 per cent in 2000, thereby reassembling an open world economy that had been shattered by the wars.

The sums involved in the US Marshall Plan for Western Europe of 1948 were not huge, but importantly they were conditioned on Europeans balancing their budgets, imposing realistic exchange rates and dismantling trade barriers, providing Western Europe with market-based institutions and the prospect of peaceful cooperation. Eventually these countries formed a European Union, determined that it's better to have goods, services, capital and people (and bottle-cap regulations) cross national borders than tanks and soldiers.

At the same time, the United States designed a series of mutual defence agreements, most notably NATO, and extended its nuclear umbrella over Europe, to stop the expansion of communism. Americans showed in practice, as the Romans had done, that they were willing to expend serious effort to defend threatened allies such as West Berlin and South Korea, thereby building credibility.

In a further development of the strategic tolerance of many of the ancient golden-age cultures, now even vanquished enemies were nurtured back to health. As Japan and West Germany developed stable, democratic market economies and grew much faster than other countries in the decades after their defeat, a popular joke had it that the best economic plan was to be invaded by the United States.

The European Union could very well have developed into a rival to America that tried to create a more multipolar world, and rich Asian democracies could have joined China in trying to revise the international system. Instead we have seen the opposite. They are doing everything they can to keep America in their regions.

The reason is that the incentives for war and peace have changed for all rich and free countries in the same way that they have for the United States. They have become prosperous in a world of international trade and peaceful cooperation, and have an interest in protecting that. They would not prosper from an unravelling of this order, but instead fear destruction, destabilization and flows of refugees. This is why most of these countries have been so eager in recent years to act against piracy at sea, ISIS conquests in Iraq and Syria, and Putin's invasion of Ukraine, even though they did not have any treaty obligations to do so.

One could even say that all rich and free countries of the world are now part of an extended Anglosphere. It is not about language, but mindset, the kind that usually accompanies industrialization and enlightenment. These countries might not be English-speaking (except when they spend time with each other), but they are all inheritors of Anglo-American ideals, borrowed from the Dutch idea of *mare liberum* and the peaceful resolution of conflicts. If the United States abandoned its commitment to this, it is most likely that the remaining countries would work desperately to keep the rest of the order intact. So far it has, together with nuclear deterrence, resulted in the longest period of peace between major powers since the Pax Romana.[117]

Under this Pax Americana, the systems of liberal democracy, open, digital communication, free-market economies, and globalization based on trade and financial flows have thrived. These are four aspects of one and the same open world. Their common denominator is that they are decentralized systems, where new ideas and innovations can emerge anywhere in the network, not just from the top, and they are tested by consumers and competition, not by authorities and elites. These are ideal golden-age conditions, setting the stage for a wealth of experiments and technologies, with the ability for the whole world to benefit from them.

If we measure human prosperity with GDP per capita, adjusted by inflation, then half of the level of wealth that mankind has attained was created during the ten thousand years until 1990. The other half has been created since 1990. Global extreme poverty, at $2.15 per day, adjusted for inflation and local purchasing power, declined from 38 to 9 per cent. And it's not just because China opened its economy when it saw the potential of the global economy. Excluding China, global extreme poverty declined by almost two-thirds. Nothing like this had ever been achieved before then.

But, as we have learned from history, nothing is forever, and fortunes can change suddenly. There is no lack of worrying echoes of the decline of previous golden ages in today's world. From imperial overreach à la Athens and a willingness to live beyond our means, to the rise of revisionist authoritarians like China and Russia, who, like Germanic tribes and the Mongols, have imitated the methods and technologies of the leading powers, and so can now pose a bigger threat to them.

Our world has experienced many of the shocks that rocked other golden-age cultures: a pandemic, climate change, refugee flows, terrorism and geopolitical threats. As usual, the decisive question is how we react to them: whether we deepen the institutions of discovery, experiments and innovation that make it possible for us to stay ahead and adapt to these problems, or whether we retreat into pessimism, protectionism and control, like so many have before us.

In his Lyceum Address in 1838, Abraham Lincoln declared that no transatlantic military giant could ever crush the American experiment. All the armies of the world, with all the treasure of the earth and a Napoleon for commander, could not take by force a drink from the Ohio. But Lincoln cautioned that there was a much more potent force of potential ruin:

> If it ever reach us it must spring up amongst us. It cannot come from abroad. If destruction be our lot, we must ourselves be its author and finisher. As a nation of freemen, we must live through all time, or die by suicide.[118]

Summary

Great Britain was radically opened up to international influences in a very tangible and unusual way – through a successful foreign invasion and then a union with Scotland. The Dutch-initiated Glorious Revolution of 1688 set Britain on a new trajectory, borrowing its invaders' ideals of trade and toleration, but also leaving the monarch's divine right to rule behind and embracing constitutional monarchy with the rule of law, secure property rights and free enterprise.

This gave the British ample opportunity to test new business models and technologies – and they had to, because they had a government that mostly left them to solve their problems on their own. This led to a surge of creativity and collaboration, and of urbanization and commercialization. Britain was rapidly becoming an unusually inclusive society where traditional divisions between regions and professions broke down. Coffee shops, private societies, lecture halls and workshops became scenes for a fluid mixing of savants and fabricants, thinkers and tinkerers. Scientists, engineers, toolmakers and merchants of light met, compared notes and designs, combined ideas from different fields and cooperated on turning them into game-changing technology and products. As happened among the Abbasids and the Dutch, being a profit-seeking entrepreneur or merchant was no longer frowned upon.

The Industrial Revolution was the most progressive change of the economy and the human condition in modern history. By enrolling machines, coal and steam in our fight for survival, mankind finally prevailed. 'Society is in a state of constant progress', as one worker put it in his autobiography. 'I only wish [my mother and father] had each lived to enjoy and to see the improvements I see', wrote another.

Once creativity and competition had been unleashed, this revolution was soon followed by a second one, based on the modern corporation, globalization and broad new technological breakthroughs like electricity, the assembly line and the internal combustion engine, and later the computer age and the digital revolution, and now robotics, biotechnology and artificial intelligence, and on and on, in the revolution that keeps on giving.

By the late nineteenth century, the baton had been taken over by the United States and an integrated north Atlantic economy. The British colonists in the new world had distilled the libertarian part of their heritage and replanted it on a continent that did not have monarchy, aristocracy or a state church. They had the power to begin the world over again, as Thomas Paine phrased it. But when the Founding Fathers did that, they were wise enough not to try to construct it from scratch but to listen to what history had to say about how to build republican institutions, and how not to lose them. Specifically, they were obsessed with the ancient Greeks and the Roman Republic, and how to stop a Macedonian king or a populist Caesar from tearing it down.

The resulting principles of the Declaration of Independence and the laws of the US Constitution created a formidable framework to balance powers and maintain an open society. In combination with its geographical position, its openness to immigration and its innovative free-market economy, the United States quickly turned into the world's leading economic, technological and military power. Because of its intellectual legacy and the circumstances in which it prospered, it became an anti-imperial empire, using its power to establish a liberal world order with open trade and peaceful conflict resolution. In this way, it created the conditions for other countries on different continents to build their own golden ages, many of which are now doing their utmost to uphold the international system in which they have thrived.

In a fitting way, this brings our story full circle. The first golden ages, in Athens and Rome, left us with not only ruins and masterpieces, but also essential lessons that helped to form the present golden age. And their respective trials and errors taught us how to build a system of openness and alliances, innovation and the constant emulation of whatever works best, but this time built on the voluntary involvement of every participant.

When John Lennon was asked why he moved from London to New York, he memorably replied: 'If I'd lived in Roman times, I'd have lived in Rome. Where else?'

A golden age, if we can keep it.

CONCLUSION:

FURTHER RISE OR INEVITABLE DECLINE?

Scipio, when he looked upon [Carthage] as it was utterly perishing and in the last throes of its complete destruction, is said to have shed tears and wept openly for his enemies... realizing that all cities, nations, and authorities must, like men, meet their doom.

APPIAN OF ALEXANDRIA[1]

My daughter recently told me: 'Every time I study history, my reaction is, *wow*, I wouldn't want to live there.' She's right, of course. Prosperity, peace and progress are rare in human history. It has only been a normal state of affairs in some regions, in some eras, and every time it was eventually snuffed out. Don't take it for granted. If we want our culture to thrive, it is necessary to think about what makes that possible and what ruins it.

Ages become golden because they imitate and innovate. They first emerge because of cheating. They didn't come up with all the innovations that made them prosper; instead they borrowed or stole them from others.

Openness to the rest of the world gave these cultures access to the power of other people's brains, habits and skills, and so broadened their ideas of what is possible. They all chose different strategies to achieve this. Athenian, Italian and Dutch merchants picked up new ideas on their business trips. Rome absorbed more methods and peoples by conquest than foreign trade, and the Abbasids actively sponsored a translation project to lay their hands on the world's knowledge.

But they were all heavily reliant on trade, migration and intellectual exchange. International trade, especially, tends to expose cultures to new ways of doing things and breaks down the perception that only one way is possible, even in non-economic areas like politics, art and religion. This explains why so many of these cultures are maritime. They are always going further and seeing more.

The Athenians and the Dutch embraced foreign trade out of weakness. They just couldn't grow enough food, and were delighted to find out that exchange gave them not only all the food they needed but superior wealth besides. The Roman and the Abbasid empires embraced trade out of strength; they had built vast free-trade zones where production and innovations from anywhere rapidly spread all over it. Medieval European cities were reborn through their trade links, and the Anglosphere finally made the world safe for global trade. It was a difficult task to stop local magnates and pirates from disrupting trade, but it paid off spectacularly in each case.

But there is a limit to how far imitation can get you. To make this progress self-propelling and really usher in a golden age, these cultures had to combine these new ideas and inputs with their own thoughts and methods to create innovations, from higher agricultural yields to artistic rebellions. This takes inclusivity back home. People have to be allowed and encouraged to test their own ways of doing things, even when the elite or the majority finds it uncomfortable. You also need lots of people. All of these cultures were highly urbanized.

One prerequisite for inclusivity is the rule of law, so that people are not governed by the whims of individual rulers, but by predictable rules, applied equally to the whole population. No civilization did this perfectly. They all practised slavery and they did not treat women as citizens with equal rights, but, compared with other cultures, earlier and contemporary, they were much more inclusive, and that made a difference.

Athens had its direct democracy, which gave every free man a voice in the rule, and the Anglosphere pioneered a liberal democracy with division of powers. The Roman Republic, the Italian city-states and the Dutch Republic were controlled by the wealthy, but power was dispersed and, compared with contemporaries, their checks and balances played an important role in reining in arbitrary government power. The rulers of the Roman Empire, the Abbasid Caliphate and Song China held the power over every individual's life and death, but even they had a system of laws to adhere to. However, this centralization meant that their systems were more fragile. An enlightened despot could at any time be replaced by an unenlightened one. Some form of division of power has been instrumental in the protection of freedom, as the American founders learned from ancient civilizations.

The other requisites for inclusivity are free markets and free minds. To bring something new into the world, people must be allowed to experiment with and exchange new theories, arguments, goods and services. Every major technological innovation is 'an act of rebellion against conventional wisdom and vested interests', explains the economic historian Joel Mokyr, and if conventional wisdom and vested interest are in positions to command what can and can't be pursued, the result is stagnation.[2]

One reason why these societies were so successful was that an openness for surprises from a larger group of people allowed them to make use of the local knowledge and creativity that is dispersed throughout every society and can never be centralized to a royal palace, a feudal lord or a guild.

The golden eras in this book were unlike one another in this regard, but they all provided a much higher degree of economic freedom and intellectual freedom than other contemporary civilizations. They gave farmers, manufacturers and merchants more space to test new methods and technologies, and philosophers, scientists and artists more freedom to explore knowledge and visions. They simply put more ideas and business models on the table, and therefore had a greater chance to find successful ones.

This progress became self-sustaining because, at a certain point, it started transforming the self-identity of these civilizations. When more people started realizing what could be done, it encouraged a broader culture of optimism, energy and vigour. Many seem to have taken a great pride in being there, at that particular moment, no doubt partly the result of clever use of elite propaganda in creating a narrative of status and accomplishment, but mostly because of proof of concept.

So even poor Athenians understood that they could stand up and argue in the Assembly, just like the mighty. Chinese farmers observed that they didn't have to farm like their ancestors had done. Italian artists realized that they could also test novel materials and motifs. British instrument-makers were inspired by famous innovations to tweak and tinker in their own workshops. It's as if, at some point, a dynamic culture provides people with permission and stimulus to rebel, in

Mokyr's sense. And that creates a tremendous expansion of creative energy.

However, eventually, the Great Status Quo Filter came for all these golden ages. Often the road to decline was paved with war, pandemics and climate-induced famines, but these are constants in human history, and cultures have also often bounced back from such episodes. Yet, in some instances, these crises gave the conventional wisdom and vested interest that Mokyr talked about a chance to fight back and upend the openness to surprises that signified these societies. A crisis often created an urge to retreat to something familiar, like some imagined good old days, fixed economic relations or an unvarnished faith.

All these golden ages experienced a death-to-Socrates moment, when they soured on their previous commitment to open intellectual exchange and abandoned curiosity for control. In the crisis-torn late Roman Empire, pagans started persecuting Christians, and Christians pagans. When Song China faced invasions, it turned Confucianism into state ideology. When the Abbasid Empire started fragmenting, the caliphs built an oppressive alliance between state and Church. The Renaissance ended when embattled Protestants and Counter-Reformation Catholics built their respective state–Church alliances to persecute dissenters and scientists. Even the tolerant Dutch Republic was taken over by Calvinist zealots in the face of destructive invasions and economic downturns.

The new orthodoxies were often upheld by rulers who started centralizing societies and undermining the rule of law. The late Roman emperors became increasingly imposing and authoritarian, the Seljuk strongmen built a system for control of markets and minds, Chinese emperors after the Song dynasty took it upon themselves to regulate everything from farming to hairstyles, and late Renaissance rulers with cannons and gunpowder razed city walls and republican institutions. And even in the liberal Dutch Republic, the prince of Orange dismantled checks and balances and turned himself into a de-facto king. Hard times create strongmen, and strongmen create even harder times.

As free speech was replaced by orthodoxies, free markets were often replaced with increased economic controls towards the end of these periods. When at times states found it difficult to raise taxes, they undermined property rights and voluntary exchange to take as much as they could, just as when Romans, Abbasids and Chinese tried to fix social relations by feudalizing the economy. A recurrent sign of decline was that they raised money by creating more of it. They debased the coinage, unleashing inflation and chaos in the economy.

Disastrously, they also started abandoning the international trade that had provided them with both wealth and creativity. Sometimes trade broke down because war and fragmentation made roads and sea-lanes unsafe, as in Rome and the late Renaissance. Ming China simply banned foreign trade because it upset the status quo. Abbasid militarization of the economy undermined the previously central role of merchants. After having faced tariffs from other countries, the Dutch eventually implemented their own.

Just as openness had made these cultures strong, orthodoxies and oppression made them weak. When just one answer came to be acceptable in politics, religion and economics, experiment and innovation ground to a halt, and mankind returned to its more natural state: stagnation and hunger.

It is heartbreaking to read the accounts of travellers who made it to Rome, Baghdad, Chinese port towns or Dutch cities just a few years too late. These places had just recently been considered the wonders of mankind but were now found to be depopulated and impoverished. The scanty remains of bygone better times.

The pressing question is of course where this leaves us. The golden age that we are in right now is the most extraordinary ever, because a revolution in communication, transportation and trade under the protection of an Anglosphere world order has broken down geographical barriers to the adoption of local breakthroughs. In Roman and Abbasid times, the scientific, technological and cultural innovations of one region could rapidly be adopted in the rest of the empire. Now, for the first time, they can quickly be adopted all around the world. As a result, for the first time in history we do not just have progress constrained to one region and one civilization. The whole of mankind has been touched by it.

Consequently, the early scientific and industrial achievements of Great Britain and the United States, which once seemed so unique, have been repeated in all corners of the world. Since 1820, the share of people in extreme poverty globally has been reduced from roughly 8 out of 10 to fewer than 1 out of 10. Life expectancy has shot up from thirty to seventy-four. Child mortality has declined from almost 50 per cent to less than 4 per cent.

The same era has witnessed some of the greatest libertarian accomplishments, intimately associated with this progress. In most countries, religion has gone from being something imposed by force to a private matter. Legal slavery has been abolished all over the world. Increasingly, women have been set free from laws that treated them as the property of fathers and husbands. Though piecemeal and imperfect, this is quite possibly the greatest advance ever, setting half of mankind free in the blink of an eye, in historical terms. It's as golden as it gets.

But nothing lasts forever. We have had a run of roughly 200 years. Few golden ages last longer than that. What does history tell us about our chances?

Regrettably, many ominous signs of decline are clearly present in our time. Like Athens, the United States experienced its own moment of hubristic overreach in the early twenty-first century, believing it could reshape the entire Middle East with the Afghanistan and Iraq war, squandering lives and resources while alienating world opinion. The financial crash of 2008 at least temporarily deprived America of its role as inspiration to the world, when countries like China decided that they should stop trying to emulate it. Like other major powers, the US has solved present funding problems by burdening future generations with a crippling public debt, which historically has had a tendency to usher in destructive inflation or panic in the markets.

In a pattern that is familiar from the end of many golden ages, a series of crises, such as financial crashes, migration flows, the pandemic and geopolitical tensions, has replaced the confident, exploratory mindset with a sense that the world is dangerous and that we need to protect ourselves from it. In just a few years, we seem to have gone from what Thucydides described as the Athenian mindset of being open to acquire something new to the Spartan mentality of shutting the world out to preserve what one already has.

Like many old and tired societies, we have a tendency to try to fossilize what we have, and a growing number of regulations and standards make it more difficult for rapid adaptation and disruptive innovation. It is increasingly difficult in rich countries to build anything anywhere or for upstarts to repeat what major incumbents once did. As the journalist Alan Beattie has observed, EU officials often seem like the dinosaurs in Jurassic

Park that hunt by movement: 'If part of the economy is growing fast, they're rapidly on its tail.'[3]

Most worryingly, rich countries have experienced a major backlash against globalization and trade, and immigrants have become scapegoats, just as they were in so many other eras of decline, potentially shutting us out from our most potent source of constant revitalization. All around the world there has been a resurgence of ideas of nationalism, repatriation and centralized industrial policy. After the global financial crisis of 2008, international trade has stopped growing, and indicators of progress have slowed down.

Simultaneously, two different reactions against the sprawling diversity of modern society have emerged, which are mirror images of each other: a hard, nationalist right and a radical, illiberal left. They are both obsessed with identity politics and pursue a dream of sameness, where alternative ideas and cultures are cancelled or deported out of their pure, homogenous utopia. As a consequence, some of them storm the stage when they lose a campus debate, and others storm the US Capitol when they lose an election. Their ambition to enforce one idea on everyone is portrayed as a quest for unity, but since it establishes a zero-sum game, it only fuels tensions and conflict.

These factions are not yet in a position to impose stifling orthodoxies on entire societies, but in countries where either of these tribes get lasting power, rule of law usually suffers. Some seem to be longing for a Caesar. Democracies like Turkey, Hungary and Mexico show how quickly an illiberal leader can dismantle checks and balances and centralize societies. There is no lack of cautionary tales even in old democracies.

Another worrying parallel with history is that the rivals of open societies have caught up with many of its achievements. Just like Germanic tribes learned organizational skills and weapons technology from the Romans, and Mongols took from the Chinese the gunpowder and steel that would destroy them, terrorist organizations and China and Russia constantly imitate the methods and technologies of the free world, and so become a greater threat to it than they would otherwise be.

Both China and Russia have recently taken a totalitarian turn and are working hard to devastate neighbours like Hong Kong and Ukraine, partly because they realize that their own models might not stand up to an example of a prosperous, open society on their borders. In cooperation with rogue states like Iran and North Korea, they are threatening whole regions. They are also trying to undermine democracies in Europe and the US, by stoking our divisions via propaganda and social media. As the journalist and historian Anne Appelbaum has warned, these authoritarians have learned to collaborate across traditional ideological divides. They exchange tactics for stealing, repressing and staying in power, while trading the technologies needed to achieve their aims.

Will they succeed? It won't be easy. The military historian Bret Devereaux argues that the Anglosphere moment and the progress it made possible have fundamentally transformed international relations.[4] The traditional conflict pattern in a state system is that countries tend to align against the one that appears strongest for the moment (today, the US), to contain its advance. If this power manages to break out in any case and become the hegemon, these countries have an interest to align with it to survive as a client state, but if the hegemon stumbles, their interest shifts back to balancing and turning on the hegemon all at once, leading to rapid disintegration.

This pattern has suddenly changed. Of the world's thirty largest economies, almost all are allies of the United States, twenty of them formal treaty allies. Just two of the thirty biggest,

Russia and China, try to challenge the Anglosphere-led world order, but they have a hard time finding reliable friends among advanced states. The more they show their revisionist ambitions, and the more they remind others what a world without US leadership would look like, the less others are interested in going along. Instead these countries then lean even more towards America, and seem to be more eager to help countries exposed to Russian or Chinese aggression and trade coercion.

The reason is not that America is such a bully that others feel they have to cosy up to it or else. They do it because it's not. (When at times it is, the interest in alternatives grows.) It is instead seen as the most powerful guarantor of an open world order that they have a common interest in. They would do what they can to uphold it even if America itself disappeared, physically or spiritually.

This is not a Roman empire that countries are forced into, or a Delian League that they cannot leave. It is an informal grouping of countries that have realized that they have a common interest in peace and trade. In fact, many of them are freeriding on the security guarantees supplied by the United States, rather than the other way around.

But even though they should of course pay for their own defence, America also has an interest in such a broad alliance of free countries. It has created an unusual situation where everybody else does not gang up on the dominant power and look for any chance to trip it up. Without the coalition, it is likely that growing regional hegemons would at some point use their power to push America out and sever its trade routes, for example. Historically, the hegemon had to give in to such behaviour or go to war. If it happened today, the US has a network of allies that would punish the perpetrator politically, diplomatically and financially, making it much less likely.

As long as the richest countries, with some 60 per cent of GDP and overwhelming financial and technological muscle, stay united, it is incredibly difficult to upend this international order. It does not mean that it is impossible. Pericles and Johan de Witt found out to their detriment that everyone is not always willing to act according to their own best interest when they are distracted by pride, religion or ideology. Miscalculations or machismo could very well throw the world into tumult. A major war, possibly involving weapons of mass destruction, could upend the world order.

But the biggest threat to an open world does not come from strong opponents, but from weak proponents. Growing fear and nationalism in major democracies could easily lead them to overlook their interest in openness, or lose the stamina to fight for it. There is, for example, nothing inevitable about America consistently taking on the role of defender of peaceful cooperation and open trade. Unfortunately, there is not even a guarantee that liberal democracies will remain liberal democracies. Let's not forget that we usually find our worst enemy in the mirror. As the historian D. C. Sumervell once remarked, societies don't die from natural causes, but from suicide or murder – and it is nearly always the former.

At this point in most books on the long lines of history, the author tells us to prepare to invest in the biggest challenges for the future, whether it be future geopolitical challenges, existential risks of technology, the environment or demographic changes. I won't, because I don't believe as much in dealing with potential weaknesses as I do in building on our strengths.

The reason is that the nature of our problems will have changed completely in a hundred years' time and our arsenal of possible solutions will, if we do things right, have been radically expanded. Some of the worst challenges will come as total surprises, and therefore the solutions will also have to surprise us. While it certainly doesn't hurt to think about which ones they might be, our most important preparation is to have a dynamic culture that helps us to acquire more prosperity, knowledge and technological capacity overall. That will help us to be resilient, no matter what form future problems take.

If we worry about where we will be in a century's time instead of solving problems here and now, it is not very constructive. We might not even make it to those challenges in that case. After all, we are always wrong about the future. Bear in mind that the whole world considered overpopulation a horrible threat to human survival right up until the very moment it started thinking that underpopulation was the real menace. So the solution is never a single Big Solution, but an open culture that allows us to continually adapt and innovate around every challenge the world throws our way.

How do we do this? How do we stay open when the world seems threatening? We do it by learning from history. It tells us that we have a tendency to react quickly and counterproductively to threats, rather than opening up to the broad diversity of millions and millions of answers, and the trial and error that will allow for better solutions to appear. The real solution is not in one idea, but in ten thousand things, as the medieval Chinese knew so well.

Elites who want to protect their status and status quo by rejecting surprises have to learn that this would just allow them to rule over decaying societies. And all of us have to realize that what we now cherish is the result of such processes of experiment and innovation. Everything a reactionary is now trying to preserve from change is something that a previous reactionary failed to stop.

Jason Feifer has the perfect question to help us understand this: 'What did we once fear, that we now love?'[5] The question is so important because almost every innovation, from the novel to the internet, from democracy to the Eiffel Tower, was once seen as bizarre and threatening; at first we could only see what we might lose and not what we could gain. But then we got used to it, started to use it and learned to love it. You probably have many examples of this in your own life; I know I have.

Only by staying open to such surprises, and learning how to benefit from them, can we continue to make progress as individuals and as societies. By understanding that we often learn to love what we once rejected instinctively, we can build a tolerance for unpredictability. Or someone else will.

One difference with previous golden ages is that we now have more eggs in different baskets. Once upon a time, if Athens or Baghdad failed, it was game over. Now we have 200 different states around the world, and roughly fifty of them are prosperous, open societies. They are deeply embedded in networks of communication and trade. A majority of the world's population has access to the accumulated knowledge of mankind. Some of these countries will no doubt make terrible mistakes, falter and fail, but that won't stop others from picking up the torch.

This prompts the question of where the next golden age will come from. A decade ago, many would have said China but, since then, its leaders have re-centralized both the economy and culture, and stifled the creativity and innovation that could have made it prosper. It seems to have got stuck in the Status Quo Filter even before it experienced a golden age, and this shows that progress is never guaranteed, but dependent on particular courses of action.

Great but subdued cultures like Turkey and Iran have the potential of making the opposite journey, if they manage to rid themselves of present political strangleholds. It is easy to see how some other dynamic countries, like Poland, Vietnam and India, have a chance of reaching stages of self-sustaining renewal, and that Africa, with its large, young population and massive resources, should be able to provide us with many thriving examples. We learn from history that it can happen suddenly, even in unexpected places.

But perhaps this is the wrong way of looking at it. What's new in the present era of globalization and digital communication is that we have a truly global civilization – not in terms of values and policies, but in knowledge and skills. This in itself is one of the great achievements of this golden age. Every literate person anywhere in the world now has the chance to access the accumulated knowledge of humanity and to learn skills in any field. We can each decide whether we want to harness this remarkable technological power to enhance our ability to flourish or to bicker with strangers online.

This means that no one country will hold a monopoly on the ideas that will make them prosper. Future golden ages will be more diluted, since everyone else can emulate them instantly. It also means that the divides will increasingly be seen within every society, between cities, regions, businesses and individuals – between those who embrace transformation to grow and adapt and those who cling to the comfort of stagnation; between those who stay open to acquiring something new, and those who seek to shut the world out to protect what they already have.

Every civilization has a bit of the Athenian and of the Spartan within it. So do you and I. We decide who we let out.

ACKNOWLEDGEMENTS

The first rule of golden ages is to surround yourself with people who are smarter than you, who constantly inspire, teach and challenge you to improve. I am blessed with such friends and colleagues, so if this book is not good enough, I have no one but myself to blame.

I owe a great debt of gratitude to Mattias Bengtsson and Stuart Hayashi, who have been kind enough to read this script and provide me with vital comments and suggestions. Thanks also to Mustafa Akyol, Gustav Blix, Fredrik Erixon, Tobias Nielsén, Tom G. Palmer and Fredrik Segerfeldt for ideas and assistance.

My agent, Andrew Gordon, has been incredibly supportive of this project and saw its full potential before I did. My editor, Ed Faulkner, has helped me to improve it substantially. Thanks to everyone at Atlantic Books and David Higham Associates for turning abstract thought into substance, and Mairi Sutherland for careful copyediting. Karoline Kjellstedt at Speakersnet, my agent for events, is a master of logistics, who helps me to navigate the world and still leaves me with the time to write.

I am a Senior Fellow at the Cato Institute in Washington, DC, where I get a regular dose of inspiration from everyone, from energetic interns to living legends like Deirdre McCloskey. I am especially grateful to Peter Goettler and Ian Vasquez for fostering such a critical mass of champions for golden-age conditions, and for encouraging me to take the time for longer-term projects like this book.

The Cato Institute, by the way, takes its name from *Cato's Letters*, the revolutionary 1720s essays that were inspired by Cato the Younger, Caesar's unforgiving foe in the Roman Republic, who preferred to die on his feet rather than living on his knees. Caesar won that round, but no one in their right mind would call their thinktank the 'Caesar Institute', would they?

History casts long shadows, but also light.

My wife, Frida, is the love of my life, my greatest support and best critic. Thank you for your love, your wisdom and for putting up with all those piles of books everywhere. Sansa, our cat, is the perfect writer's cat, always keeping me company, while also instilling the lessons that life will find a way, no matter how authorities try to control it. Our amazing kids, Alexander, Alicia and Nils-Erik, always ask me the most thought-provoking questions about history, and are a constant reminder of what's at stake in the battle for an open future.

When I was their age and younger, my father, Erik Norberg, often entertained me with stories about past civilizations, exotic peoples and momentous battles. Witty, beautiful and ghastly stories. He instilled in me a love of history, which kept me captivated long enough to start seeing its patterns, and eventually finding it useful – and, in the end, essential. This book is dedicated to him. You can't inherit a tradition from your parents, but you can try to earn it.

NOTES

Introduction

1. Joel Mokyr, *The Lever of Riches*, Oxford: Oxford University Press, 1992, p. 304.
2. Harold J. Berman, *Law and Revolution: The Formation of the Western Legal Tradition*, Cambridge, MA: Harvard University Press, 1983, preface.
3. Jack Goldstone, 'Efflorescences and Economic Growth in World History: Rethinking the "Rise of the West and the Industrial Revolution"', *Journal of World History*, vol. 13, no. 2 (2002), pp. 323–89.
4. Joel Mokyr, 'Cardwell's Law and the political economy of technological progress', *Research Policy*, vol. 23, no. 5 (1994), pp. 561–74.
5. Kenneth Clarke, *Civilisation: A Personal View*, New York: Harper & Row, 1969, p. 3f.
6. https://twitter.com/DavidDeutschOxf/status/1711754517077758309/DavidDeutsch/Oxf/.

1 Athens: Democrats, Dreamers and Other Deviants

1. Charles Freeman, *The Greek Achievement*, London: Penguin, 2000, p. 6.
2. Percy Bysshe Shelley, *Essays and Letters by Percy Bysshe Shelley*, London: Walter Scott, 1886, p. 136.

3. John Stuart Mill, *A System of Logic, Book VI*, Indianapolis, IN: Liberty Fund, 2006, p. 938.
4. G. W. F. Hegel, *Lectures on the Philosophy of History*, London: Henry G. Bohn, 1861, p. 268.
5. Myke Cole, *The Bronze Lie*, Oxford: Osprey, 2021.
6. https://acoup.blog/2019/09/27/collections-this-isnt-sparta-part-vii-spartan-ends/ and Bret Devereaux, 'Spartans were Losers', *Foreign Policy*, 22 July 2023.
7. Plutarch, *Parallel Lives*. Peter Green, *The Greco-Persian Wars*, Berkeley, CA: University of California Press, 1996, p. 130.
8. Cole, *Bronze Lie*, p. 158.
9. Plato, *Complete Works*, Indianapolis, IN: Hackett, 1997, p. 1168.
10. Victor Davis Hanson, *The Other Greeks: The Family Farms and the Agrarian Roots of Western Civilization*, Berkeley, CA: University of California Press, 1995.
11. Martin Wolf, *The Crisis of Democratic Capitalism*, London: Allen Lane, 2023.
12. Euripides, *Euripides II*, Chicago, IL: University of Chicago Press, 2012, p. 155.
13. Herodotus, *The Histories*, London: Penguin, 2003, p. 340.
14. Herodotus, *The Histories*, p. 354.
15. John Stuart Mill, 'Grote's "History of Greece"', in *Collected Works of John Stuart Mill*, Vol. 9, Toronto: University of Toronto Press, 1978.
16. Tom Holland, *Persian Fire*, London: Abacus, 2005, p. 268.
17. Tom Holland, 'Mirage in the Movie House', *Arion*, vol. 15, no. 1 (2007), pp. 172–82.
18. Victor Davis Hanson, 'A Stillborn West?', in Philip E. Tetlock, Richard Ned Lebow and Geoffrey Parker (eds),

Unmaking the West: 'What-if?' Scenarios That Rewrite World History, Ann Arbor, MI: University of Michigan Press, 2006, pp. 47–89.
19. Barry Strauss, 'The Resilient West', in Tetlock et al., *Unmaking the West*, pp. 90–118.
20. Tetlock, Lebow and Parker, *Unmaking the West*, p. 90.
21. Aeschylus, *Persians and Other Plays*, Oxford: Oxford University Press, 2008, p. 18.
22. Plato, *Complete Works*, pp. 1394 and 1388.
23. Thucydides, *History of the Peloponnesian War*, London: Penguin, 1972, pp. 145ff.
24. Thucydides, *History of the Peloponnesian War*, p. 75f.
25. Thucydides, *History of the Peloponnesian War*, p. 145.
26. Thucydides, *History of the Peloponnesian War*, p. 522.
27. Plato, *Complete Works*, p. 1168.
28. Friedrich Hayek, *The Constitution of Liberty*, London: Routledge, 2011, p. 237.
29. Andreas Bergh and Carl Hampus Lyttkens, 'Measuring Institutional Quality in Ancient Athens', *Journal of Institutional Economics*, vol. 2 (2014), pp. 279–310. James Gwartney, Robert Lawson and Ryan Murphy, *Economic Freedom of the World: 2023 Annual Report*, Vancouver: Fraser Institute, 2023.
30. Ian Morris, 'Economic Growth in Ancient Greece', *Journal of Institutional and Theoretical Economics*, vol. 160, no. 4 (2004), pp. 709–42. Walter Scheidel, 'Real Wages in Early Economies: Evidence for Living Standards from 1800 BCE to 1300 CE', *Journal of the Economic and Social History of the Orient*, vol. 53, no. 3 (2010).
31. Plato, *Complete Works*, p. 1392f.
32. Freeman, *The Greek Achievement*, p. 121.
33. Peter Watson, *Ideas: A History of Thought and Invention*,

From Fire to Freud, New York: Harper Perennial, 2006, p. 72.
34. Plato, *Complete Works*, p. 1168.
35. Herodotus, *The Histories*, p. 187.
36. Freeman, *The Greek Achievement*, p. 9.
37. Thucydides, *History of the Peloponnesian War*, p. 598.
38. Thucydides, *History of the Peloponnesian War*, pp. 242ff.
39. Thucydides, *History of the Peloponnesian War*, p. 402.
40. Thucydides, *History of the Peloponnesian War*, p. 539.
41. https://acoup.blog/2019/09/05/collections-this-isnt-sparta-part-iv-spartan-wealth/ .
42. Cicero, *The Tusculan Disputations*, Oxford: J. Vincent, Whittaker, 1840, p. 169.
43. Plato, *Complete Works*, p. 1592.
44. Aristotle, *The Complete Works*, Vol. 2, Princeton, NJ: Princeton University Press, 1995, p. 1707.
45. Aristotle, *The Complete Works*, Vol. 1, p. 1178.
46. Diogenes Laertius, *Lives of the Eminent Philosophers*, Oxford: Oxford University Press, 2020, p. 156.
47. Aristotle, *The Complete Works*, Vol. 2, p. 1732.
48. Samuel Taylor Coleridge, *The Collected Works of Samuel Taylor Coleridge, Volume 14, Part 1: Table Talk*, Princeton, NJ: Princeton University Press, 2019, p. 172f.
49. Aristotle, *The Complete Works*, Vol. 2, p. 1554.
50. Thucydides, *History of the Peloponnesian War*, p. 148.

2 Rome: Melting Pot of Marble

1. Johann Wolfgang von Goethe, *Italian Journey: 1786–1788*, Berkeley, CA: North Point Press, 1982, p. 136.
2. Iggy Pop, 'Caesar Lives', *Classics Ireland*, vol. 2 (1995), pp. 94–6.

3. Edward Gibbon, *The History of the Decline and Fall of the Roman Empire*, Vol. 1, New York: Fred de Fau and Co., 1906, p. 99.
4. 'Män som tänker på Romarriket?', Novus poll, 30 September 2023.
5. David Montgomery, 'What Americans Think About the Roman Empire', YouGov poll, 17 September 2024.
6. Edward Gibbon, *Decline and Fall of the Roman Empire*, Vol. 12, p. 213.
7. https://acoup.blog/2022/10/28/fireside-friday-october-28-2022-the-book-project/ .
8. Walter Scheidel, *Escape from Rome*, Princeton, NJ: Princeton University Press, 2021, p. 59.
9. Tim Cornell, *The Beginnings of Rome*, London: Routledge, 2012, p. 367.
10. Charles Freeman, *The Closing of the Western Mind: The Rise of Faith and the Fall of Reason*, New York: Vintage Books, 2005, p. 68.
11. Mary Beard, *SPQR: A History of Ancient Rome*, London: Profile Books, 2016, p. 69.
12. James H. Oliver, 'The Ruling Power: A Study of the Roman Empire in the Second Century after Christ through the Roman Oration of Aelius Aristides', *Transactions of the American Philosophical Society*, vol. 43, no. 4 (1953), pp. 871–1003.
13. Amy Chua, *Day of Empire*, New York: Anchor Books, 2009, p. 33.
14. Josephine Quinn, *How the World Made the West*, London: Bloomsbury, 2024, p. 236.
15. Adrian Goldsworthy, *Pax Romana*, London: Weidenfeld & Nicolson, 2016, p. 25.
16. Montesquieu, *Considerations on the Causes of the Greatness*

of the Romans and their Decline, 1734: https://www.constitution.org/2-Authors/cm/ccgrd_l.htm.
17. Ian Morris and Barry B. Powell, *The Greeks: History, Culture, and Society*, 3rd edition, Oxford: Oxford University Press, 2022, p. 541f.
18. Freeman, *The Greek Achievement*, p. 544.
19. Freeman, *The Greek Achievement*, p. 393.
20. 'The Twelve Tables' in Samuel P. Scott, *The Civil Law I*, Cincinnati: The Central Trust Company, 1932: https://droitromain.univ-grenoble-alpes.fr/Anglica/twelve_Scott.html.
21. Peter Temin, *The Roman Market Economy*, Princeton, NJ: Princeton University Press, 2013, p. 127f.
22. Beard, *SPQR*, p. 68.
23. Beard, *SPQR*, p. 308.
24. Michael C. Hawley, *Natural Law Republicanism: Cicero's Liberal Legacy*, Oxford: Oxford University Press, 2022, p. 34.
25. Marcus Tullius Cicero, *De officiis*, Cambridge, MA: Harvard University Press, 1994, 1.70.
26. Mary Beard, *Emperor of Rome*, London: Profile Books, 2023, p. 225.
27. Plutarch, *The Life of Cicero*, 49.5.
28. Willem M. Jongman, 'Gibbon was Right: the Decline and Fall of the Roman Economy', in Olivier Hekster, Gerda de Kleijn and Daniëlle Slootjes (eds), *Crises and the Roman Empire*, Vol. 7, Leiden: Brill, 2007, pp. 183–99.
29. Evan Gleadow, 'Roman Emperor's Face Reconstructed for the 21st Century and He's "as hot as Daniel Craig"', *Daily Star*, 9 October 2023.
30. Beard, *Emperor of Rome*, p. 52.
31. Goldsworthy, *Pax Romana*, p. 163.

32. Goldsworthy, *Pax Romana*, p. 169.
33. Goldsworthy, *Pax Romana*, p. 87.
34. Andrew Wilson, 'Large-Scale Manufacturing, Standardization, and Trade', in John Peter Oleson (ed.), *The Oxford Handbook of Engineering and Technology in the Classical World*, Oxford: Oxford University Press, 2008, p. 393.
35. Kyle Harper, *The Fate of Rome*, Princeton, NJ: Princeton University Press, 2019, p. 37.
36. Oliver, 'The Ruling Power'.
37. Harper, *The Fate of Rome*, p. 84.
38. Michael Ivanovitch Rostovtzeff, *The Social and Economic History of the Roman Empire*, 2nd edition, Oxford: Clarendon Press, 1957, p. 54.
39. Peter Temin, 'The Economy of the Early Roman Empire', *Journal of Economic Perspectives*, vol. 20, no. 1 (2006), p. 149.
40. Temin, 'The Economy of the Early Roman Empire' and Temin, *The Roman Market Economy*.
41. François de Callataÿ, 'The Greco-Roman Economy in the Super Long Run: Lead, Copper and Shipwrecks', *Journal of Roman Archaeology*, vol. 18 (2005). Jongman, 'Gibbon was Right'.
42. Temin, *The Roman Market Economy*, p. 252.
43. Mokyr, *The Lever of Riches*, p. 20.
44. An excellent summary of the data is Bryan Ward-Perkins, *The Fall of Rome and the End of Civilization*, Oxford: Oxford University Press, 2006.
45. Watson, *Ideas*, p. 237.
46. Ian Morris, *The Measure of Civilization*, Princeton, NJ: Princeton University Press, 2013.
47. Harper, *The Fate of Rome*, p. 115.

48. Harper, *The Fate of Rome*, p. 125.
49. Ludwig von Mises, *Human Action: A Treatise on Economics*, Chicago, IL: Henry Regnery, 1966, p. 768.
50. J. H. W. G. Liebescheutz, *The Decline and Fall of the Roman City*, New York: Oxford University Press, 2003.
51. https://acoup.blog/2022/01/28/collections-rome-decline-and-fall-part-ii-institutions/.
52. Harper, *The Fate of Rome*, p. 192.
53. Charles Freeman, *The Awakening: A History of the Western Mind AD 500–1700*, New York: Apollo, 2020, p. 295.
54. Freeman, *The Closing of the Western Mind*, p. 316.
55. Freeman, *The Closing of the Western Mind*, p. 317.
56. Montesquieu, *Considerations on the Causes of the Greatness of the Romans and their Decline*, 1734: https://www.constitution.org/2-Authors/cm/ccgrd_l.htm.
57. Watson, *Ideas*, p. 246f.
58. Beard, *SPQR*, p. 532.
59. Holland, *The Forge of Christendom*, New York: Anchor, 2010, p. 73.

3 The Abbasid Caliphate: At the Crossroads of the Universe

1. Fernand Braudel, *A History of Civilizations*, London: Penguin, 1995, p. 73.
2. Adam Smith, 'The History of Astronomy', in *Essays on Philosophical Subjects*, Indianapolis, IN: Liberty Fund, 1980, p. 67.
3. Dimitri Gutas, *Greek Thought, Arabic Culture*, London: Routledge, 1998, p. 8.
4. Lord Acton, *The History of Freedom*, Grand Rapids, MI: Acton Institute, 1993, p. 60.
5. Gutas, *Greek Thought, Arabic Culture*, p. 89.

6. Ehsan Masood, *Science and Islam: A History*, London: Icon, 2009, p. 57. Gutas, *Greek Thought, Arabic Culture*, p. 97f.
7. *Empire* podcast, 'The Rise of Islam', 14 December 2023.
8. Ibn Khaldun, *Muqaddimah*, I: 303.
9. Robert G. Hoyland, *In God's Path: The Arab Conquests and the Creation of an Islamic Empire*, New York: Oxford University Press, 2015.
10. Peter Frankopan, *The Silk Roads*, London: Bloomsbury, 2016, p. 82.
11. Bernard Lewis, *What Went Wrong?*, New York: Harper Perennial, 2002, p. 174.
12. Mun'im Sirry, *Controversies over Islamic Origins: An Introduction to Traditionalism and Revisionism*, Newcastle upon Tyne: Cambridge Scholars Publishing, 2021, p. 274.
13. Justin Marozzi, *Baghdad: City of Peace, City of Blood*, London: Penguin, 2015.
14. Gutas, *Greek Thought, Arabic Culture*, p. 19.
15. Frankopan, *The Silk Roads*, p. 101.
16. Nima Sanandaji, *The Birthplace of Capitalism: The Middle East*, Stockholm: Timbro, 2018, p. 63.
17. William J. Bernstein, *A Splendid Exchange*, New York: Grove Press, 2008, p. 81.
18. Bernstein, *A Splendid Exchange*, p. 75.
19. Frankopan, *The Silk Roads*, p. 96.
20. Ahmad Farras Oran and Ghaida Khaznehkatbi, 'The Economic System Under the "Abbasid Dynasty"', in Muhammed Nejatullah Siddiqi (ed.), *The Encyclopaedia of Islamic Economics*, 2009.
21. Mustafa Akyol, *Why, as a Muslim, I Defend Liberty*, Washington, DC: Cato Institute, 2021, pp. 98–101.
22. Shelomo Goitein, *Studies in Islamic History and Institutions*, Leiden: Brill, 1966, pp. 241 and 239.

23. Oran and Khaznehkatbi, 'The Economic System Under the "Abbasid Dynasty"'.
24. Lewis, *What Went Wrong?*, p. 92.
25. Timur Kuran, *The Long Divergence*, Princeton, NJ: Princeton University Press, 2013.
26. Gutas, *Greek Thought, Arabic Culture*, p. 31.
27. Jim Al-Khalili, *Pathfinders: The Golden Age of Arabic Science*, London: Penguin, 2012.
28. Jonathan Lyons, *House of Wisdom*, London: Bloomsbury, 2010, p. 59.
29. Hugh Kennedy, *When Baghdad Ruled the World*, Boston, MA: Da Capo Press, 2006, pp. 251ff.
30. Joseph A. Angelo, *Encyclopedia of Space and Astronomy*, New York: Facts on File, 2006, p. 78.
31. Gutas, *Greek Thought, Arabic Culture*, p. 179.
32. S. Frederick Starr, *Lost Enlightenment*, Princeton, NJ: Princeton University Press, 2013, p. 521.
33. Gutas, *Greek Thought, Arabic Culture*, p. 158f.
34. Gutas, *Greek Thought, Arabic Culture*, p. 159.
35. Lyons, *House of Wisdom*, p. 91.
36. Sidney H. Griffith, 'The Monk in the Emir's Majlis: Reflections on a Popular Genre of Christian Literary Apologetics in Arabic in the Early Islamic Period', in Hava Lazarus-Yafeh (ed.), *The Majlis: Interreligious Encounters in Medieval Islam*, Wiesbaden: Harrassowitz, 1999, p. 42.
37. Hayyim J. Cohen, 'The Economic Background and the Secular Occupations of Muslim Jurisprudents and Traditionists in the Classical Period of Islam (Until the Middle of the Eleventh Century)', *Journal of the Economic and Social History of the Orient*, vol. 13, no. 1 (1970).
38. Al-Khalili, *Pathfinders*, ch. 5.

39. Patricia Crone, 'Ninth-Century Muslim Anarchists', *Past and Present*, no. 167 (2000), pp. 3–28. Mustafa Akyol, *Reopening Muslim Minds*, New York: St Martin's Essentials, 2021.
40. Akyol, *Reopening Muslim Minds*, p. 136f.
41. Ahmet T. Kuru, *Islam, Authoritarianism, and Underdevelopment: A Global and Historical Comparison*, Cambridge: Cambridge University Press, 2019).
42. Kuru, *Islam, Authoritarianism, and Underdevelopment*, p. 81.
43. Kuru, *Islam, Authoritarianism, and Underdevelopment*, p. 9.
44. The Letters of St Augustine, Altenmünster: Jazzybee Verlag, 2015, p. 228. Eric Chaney, 'Religion and the Rise and Fall of Islamic Science', Harvard University, May 2016.
45. Kuru, *Islam, Authoritarianism, and Underdevelopment*, p. 110.
46. Starr, *Lost Enlightenment*, p. 412.
47. *Alberuni's India*, Vol. 1, London: Kegan Paul, Trench & Trübner & Co., 1910, p. 152.
48. Chaney, 'Religion and the Rise and Fall of Islamic Science'.
49. Kuru, *Islam, Authoritarianism, and Underdevelopment*, p. 119.
50. Akyol, *Reopening Muslim Minds*, ch. 8.
51. Akyol, *Reopening Muslim Minds*, p. 139.

4 Song China: On the Threshold of Modernity

1. Voltaire, *The Works of Voltaire, Vol. 4: Philosophical Dictionary Part 2*, Paris: E. R. DuMont, 1901, p. 94.
2. Adam Smith, *An Inquiry into the Nature and Causes of the Wealth of Nations*, Vol. 1, Indianapolis, IN: Liberty Fund, 1981, p. 89.
3. Stephen Davies, *The Wealth Explosion*, Brighton: Edward Everett Root, 2019, p. 85.

4. William Guanglin Liu, *The Chinese Market Economy, 1000–1500*, Albany, NY: SUNY Press, 2015, p. 134.
5. Joseph Needham, *Science and Civilisation in China*, Part 7, Cambridge: Cambridge University Press, 1987, p. xxx.
6. Marx's Economic Manuscripts of 1861–63: https://www.historyisaweapon.com/defcon6/works/1861/economic/ch35.html?utm_source=chatgpt.com .
7. Watson, *Ideas*, p. 297.
8. Joseph Needham and Wang Ling, *Science & Civilisation in China, Vol. 1: Introductory Orientations*, Cambridge: Cambridge University Press, 1954, p. 134.
9. Peter Lorge, *The Reunification of China: Peace Through War Under the Song Dynasty*, Cambridge: Cambridge University Press, 2018, p. 4.
10. Lorge, *The Reunification of China*, p. 29.
11. Dieter Kuhn, *The Age of Confucian Rule*, Cambridge, MA: Harvard University Press, 2011, p. 33.
12. Kuhn, *The Age of Confucian Rule*, p. 276.
13. Kuhn, *The Age of Confucian Rule*, p. 125.
14. Kuhn, *The Age of Confucian Rule*, p. 278.
15. Mark Elvin, *The Pattern of the Chinese Past*, Stanford, CA: Stanford University Press, 1973, p. 71f.
16. Liu, *The Chinese Market Economy*, ch. 6.
17. Shiba Yoshinobu, *Commerce and Society in Sung China*, Ann Arbor, MI: University of Michigan Press, 1970, p. 46.
18. Yoshinobu, *Commerce and Society in Sung China*, p. 212.
19. Elvin, *The Pattern of the Chinese Past*, p. 130.
20. William H. McNeill, 'The Eccentricity of Wheels, or Eurasian Transportation in Historical Perspective', *American Historical Review*, vol. 92, no. 5 (1987), pp. 1111–26.
21. Elvin, *The Pattern of the Chinese Past*, p. 216.

22. Kuhn, *The Age of Confucian Rule*, p. 194.
23. William Guanglin Liu, 'The Making of a Fiscal State in Song China, 960–1279'.
24. Tom G. Palmer, *Realizing Freedom*, Washington DC: Cato Institute, 2009, p. 351.
25. Yoshinobu, *Commerce and Society in Sung China*, p. 48.
26. Kuhn, *The Age of Confucian Rule*, p. 251.
27. Yoshinobu, *Commerce and Society in Sung China*, p. 212f.
28. Kuhn, *The Age of Confucian Rule*, p. 230.
29. Kuhn, *The Age of Confucian Rule*, p. 42.
30. Ronnie Littlejohn, *Confucianism: An Introduction*, London: I. B. Tauris, 2010, p. 126.
31. Ian Morris, *Why the West Rules – For Now*, London: Profile Books, 2010, p. 380.
32. Davies, *The Wealth Explosion*, p. 82.
33. Kuhn, *The Age of Confucian Rule*, p. 208.
34. Kuhn, *The Age of Confucian Rule*, p. 211. Jacques Gernet, *Daily Life in China on the Eve of the Mongol Invasion, 1250–1276*, p. 44.
35. Joseph Needham, *Science and Civilisation in China, Vol. 4: Physics and Physical Technology, Part 3*, New York: Cambridge University Press, 1971, p. 476.
36. Kuhn, *The Age of Confucian Rule*, p. 275.
37. Yoshinobu, *Commerce and Society in Sung China*, p. 205.
38. Yoshinobu, *Commerce and Society in Sung China*, p. 204.
39. Patricia Buckley Ebrey, *Chinese Civilization: A Sourcebook*, New York: Free Press, 1993, 182f.
40. Brian McKnight and Henrika Kuklick, *Law and Order in Sung China*, Cambridge: Cambridge University Press, 1992, pp. 53ff.
41. Needham, *Science and Civilisation in China, Vol. 4, Part 3*, p. 464.

42. Elvin, *The Pattern of the Chinese Past*, p. 197f.
43. Elvin, *The Pattern of the Chinese Past*, p. 198.
44. Elvin, *The Pattern of the Chinese Past*, p. 199.
45. Kuhn, *The Age of Confucian Rule*, p. 98.
46. Max Loehr, 'Some Fundamental Issues in the History of Chinese Painting', *Journal of Asian Studies*, vol. 23, no. 2 (1964), pp. 185–93.
47. Joseph Needham and Wang Ling, *Science and Civilisation in China, vol. 4: Physics and Physical Technology, Part 2*, Cambridge: Cambridge University Press, 1965, p. 508.
48. Liu, *The Chinese Market Economy*, p. 50.
49. Liu, *The Chinese Market Economy*, p. 74.
50. Elvin, *The Pattern of the Chinese Past*, p. 217.
51. Hok-Lam Chan, 'Ming Taizu's "Placards" on Harsh Regulations and Punishments Revealed in Gu Qiyuan's Kezuo zhuiyu', *Asia Major*, vol. 22, no. 1 (2009).
52. Loehr, 'Some Fundamental Issues in the History of Chinese Painting', 1964.
53. Elvin, *The Pattern of the Chinese Past*, p. 233.
54. Liu, *The Chinese Market Economy*, p. 1.
55. Liu, *The Chinese Market Economy*, p. 64.
56. Liu, *The Chinese Market Economy*, p. 5.
57. John Stuart Mill, *On Liberty*, London: Savill and Edwards, 1868, p. 42.

5 Renaissance Italy: The Rebirth of Law, Literature and Libertas

1. Denys Hay (ed.), *The Renaissance Debate*, New York: Holt, Rinehart and Winston, 1965, p. 22.
2. Hay, *The Renaissance Debate*, p. 9.
3. Vaclav Smil, *Creating the Twentieth Century: Technical*

Innovations of 1867–1914 and Their Lasting Impact, Oxford: Oxford University Press, 2005, p. 7f.
4. Felipe Fernandez-Armesto, *The Renaissance Bazaar*, Oxford: Oxford University Press, 2003, p. 195.
5. Irene Bowen Backu, 'Asia Materialized: Perceptions of China in Renaissance Florence', Dissertation, University of Chicago, 2014.
6. Lyons, *House of Wisdom*, p. 156f.
7. Freeman, *The Awakening*, p. 123.
8. Richard Rubenstein, *Aristotle's Children*, Orlando, FL: Harcourt, 2004, p. 125.
9. Pius II, 'A Bleak Prospect', in James Bruce Ross and Mary Martin McLaughlin (eds), *The Portable Renaissance Reader*, London: Penguin, 1977.
10. E. L. Jones, *The European Miracle*, 2nd edition, Cambridge: Cambridge University Press, 1987, p. 91.
11. Acton, *The History of Freedom*, p. 62.
12. Berman, *Law and Revolution*.
13. Berman, *Law and Revolution*, p. 43.
14. Berman, *Law and Revolution*, pp. 145ff.
15. Berman, *Law and Revolution*, p. 282.
16. Hay, *The Renaissance Debate*, p. 13.
17. Freeman, *The Awakening*, p. 134.
18. Frankopan, *The Silk Roads*, p. 149.
19. Fernand Braudel, *Civilization and Capitalism, 15th–18th Century, Vol. 3: The Perspective of the World*, Berkeley, CA: University of California, 1992, p. 559.
20. Freeman, *The Awakening*, p. 148.
21. Braudel, *Civilization and Capitalism*, p. 559.
22. Winston Churchill, *A History of the English-Speaking Peoples, Vol. 2: A New World*, London: Cassell and Co., 1956, p. 9.

23. Giovanni Boccaccio, 'The Return of the Muses', in Ross and McLaughlin, *The Portable Renaissance Reader*.
24. Ross King, *The Bookseller of Florence*, New York: Grove Press, 2022, p. 20.
25. King, *The Bookseller of Florence*, p. 104.
26. King, *The Bookseller of Florence*, p. 17.
27. Stephen Greenblatt, *The Swerve: How the World Became Modern*, New York: W. W. Norton & Co., 2011, pp. 25ff.
28. King, *The Bookseller of Florence*, p. 171.
29. King, *The Bookseller of Florence*, p. 394.
30. Jacob Burckhardt, *The Civilization of the Renaissance in Italy*, London: Penguin Books, 2004, p. 98.
31. Ross and McLaughlin, *The Portable Renaissance Reader*, p. 30.
32. Watson, *Ideas*, p. 404.
33. Watson, *Ideas*, p. 403.
34. Ian Mortimer, *Centuries of Change*, London: Bodley Head, 2014, pp. 120ff.
35. Hay, *The Renaissance Debate*, p. 14.
36. Brian Jeffrey Maxson, *A Short History of Florence*, London: Bloomsbury Academic, 2023, p. 36.
37. Burckhardt, *The Civilization of the Renaissance in Italy*, p. 65.
38. Freeman, *The Awakening*, p. 282.
39. King, *The Bookseller of Florence*, p. 159.
40. Leonardo Bruni, 'Panegyric to the City of Florence', in Mark Jurdjevic, Natasha Piano and John P. McCormick (eds), *Florentine Political Writing from Petrarch to Machiavelli*, Philadelphia, PA: University of Pennsylvania Press, 2019.
41. Freeman, *The Awakening*, p. 276.
42. Jim Powell, *The Triumph of Liberty*, New York: Free Press, 2000, p. 73.

43. King, *The Bookseller of Florence*, p. 55. Mikkel Thorup, *Intellectual History of Economic Normativities*, New York: Palgrave Macmillan, 2016, p. 33.
44. Poggio Bracciolini, 'On Avarice', in Benjamin G. Kohl and Ronald G. Witt (eds), *The Earthly Republic*, Philadelphia, PA: University of Pennsylvania Press, 1978, pp. 257–60.
45. King, *The Bookseller of Florence*, p. 362.
46. Catherine Fletcher, *The Beauty and the Terror*, London: Bodley Head, 2021, p. 155.
47. Anders Bergman, *Humanismens födelse*, Stockholm: Dialogos, 2016, p. 133.
48. King, *The Bookseller of Florence*, p. 208.
49. Gianozzo Manetti, *On Human Worth and Excellence*, Cambridge, MA: Harvard University Press, 2019, pp. xviii, xxxvii and xliii.
50. Giovanni Pico della Mirandola, *Oration on the Dignity of Man*, Chicago, IL: Henry Regnery Company, 1956, p. 7f.
51. Manetti, *On Human Worth and Excellence*, p. 199.
52. Manetti, *On Human Worth and Excellence*, p. 249.
53. Maxson, *A Short History of Florence*, p. 39.
54. King, *The Bookseller of Florence*, p. 57.
55. King, *The Bookseller of Florence*, p. 269.
56. Kenneth Clarke, *Civilisation: A Personal View*, New York: Harper & Row, 1969, p. 135.
57. Watson, *Ideas*, pp. 415ff.
58. Freeman, *The Awakening*, p. 321.
59. Marsilio Ficino, 'The Golden Age in Florence', in Ross and McLaughlin, *The Portable Renaissance Reader*, p. 79.
60. Erasmus, 'Letter to Capito', in Ross and McLaughlin, *The Portable Renaissance Reader*.
61. John Hale, *Civilisation of Europe in the Renaissance*, New York: Simon & Schuster, 1995, p. 586.

62. Loys Le Roy, 'The Excellence of this Age', in Ross and McLaughlin, *The Portable Renaissance Reader*.
63. King, *The Bookseller of Florence*, pp. 272ff.
64. Anthony Gottlieb, *The Dream of Reason*, London: Penguin, 2016, p. 430.
65. William Eamon, *Science and the Secrets of Nature*, Princeton, NJ: Princeton University Press, 1996, p. 272.
66. Freeman, *The Awakening*, p. 519.
67. King, *The Bookseller of Florence*, p. 187.
68. Alejandro A. Chafuen, *Christians for Freedom: Late-Scholastic Economics*, San Francisco, CA: Ignatius Press, 1986, p. 63f.
69. Francisco de Vitoria, *Political Writings*, Cambridge: Cambridge University Press, 1991, pp. 250–3.
70. Bartolomé de Las Casas, *In Defense of the Indians*, DeKalb, IL: Northern Illinois University Press, 1992, p. xvi.
71. Angus Stroud, *Stuart England*, London: Routledge, 2002, p. 27f.
72. Freeman, *The Awakening*, p. 325.
73. Leonardo da Vinci, *Notebooks*, Oxford: Oxford University Press, 2008, p. 267f.
74. Ross and McLaughlin, *The Portable Renaissance Reader*, p. 1.
75. Peter Burke, *The Italian Renaissance: Culture and Society in Italy*, 3rd edition, Princeton, NJ: Princeton University Press, 2014, p. 138.
76. King, *The Bookseller of Florence*, p. 371.
77. Watson, *Ideas*, p. 465f.
78. Freeman, *The Awakening*, p. 525.
79. Davies, *The Wealth Explosion*, p. 172.
80. Czeslaw Milosz, *The History of Polish Literature*, Berkeley, CA: University of California Press, 1983, p. 38f.
81. Greenblatt, *The Swerve*, p. 239.
82. Joel Mokyr, *A Culture of Growth: The Origins of the Modern*

Economy, Princeton, NJ: Princeton University Press, 2017, p. 156.
83. Paul Johnson, *A History of Christianity*, Ann Arbor, MI: Borders Books, 2005, p. 277.
84. Erasmus, 'Letter to pope Leo X', in Ross and McLaughlin, *The Portable Renaissance Reader*. Hale, *Civilisation of Europe in the Renaissance*, p. 585.

6 The Dutch Republic: Trade, Toleration and Other Treasures of the Shore

1. William Temple, *Observations Upon the United Provinces of the Netherlands*, London: Printed by A. Maxwell for Sa. Gellibrand, 1673.
2. No pun intended. In 'Golden Ages', *The Rest is History* podcast, 25 October 2021.
3. Davies, *The Wealth Explosion*, pp. 149ff.
4. Simon Schama, *The Embarrassment of Riches: An Interpretation of Dutch Culture in the Golden Age*, New York: Vintage, 1997, p. 81.
5. Schama, *The Embarrassment of Riches*, p. 266.
6. Schama, *The Embarrassment of Riches*, pp. 266 and 44.
7. Jonathan Israel, *The Dutch Republic: Its Rise, Greatness, and Fall 1477–1806*, Oxford: Clarendon Press, 1998, p. 117.
8. Braudel, *Civilization and Capitalism*, p. 205.
9. Maarten Prak and Jan Luiten van Zanden, *Pioneers of Capitalism: The Netherlands 1000–1800*, Princeton, NJ: Princeton University Press, 2023, p. 67f.
10. Israel, *The Dutch Republic*, p. 115.
11. Jan de Vries and Ad van der Woude, *The first modern economy*, Cambridge: Cambridge University Press, 1997.

12. John Evelyn, *Miscellaneous Writings*, London: Henry Colburn, 1825, p. 631.
13. Prak and van Zanden, *Pioneers of Capitalism*, p. 89.
14. Schama, *The Embarrassment of Riches*, p. 152.
15. Smith, *Wealth of Nations*, Vol. 1, p. 113.
16. Temple, *Observations Upon the United Provinces of the Netherlands*.
17. Israel, *The Dutch Republic*, p. 1f.
18. Israel, *The Dutch Republic*, p. 676.
19. Elise van Nederveen Meerkerk, 'Market Wage or Discrimination? The Remuneration of Male and Female Wool Spinners in the Seventeenth-century Dutch Republic', *Economic History Review*, vol. 63, no. 1 (2010), pp. 165–86.
20. Schama, *The Embarrassment of Riches*, p. 407.
21. Israel, *The Dutch Republic*, p. 678.
22. Israel, *The Dutch Republic*, p. 99f.
23. Geoffrey Parker, *The Dutch Revolt*, London: Penguin Books, 1988, p. 47.
24. Johann Wolfgang von Goethe, *Egmont*, in *Cosimo Classics, Vol. 19: Faust, Part I, Egmont & Hermann, Dorothea, Dr Faustus*, New York: Cosimo, 2010, p. 330.
25. Hugo Grotius, *Commentary on the Law of Prize and Booty*, Indianapolis, IN: Liberty Fund, 2006, p. 33.
26. Hugo Grotius, *The Rights of War and Peace*, Indianapolis, IN: Liberty Fund, 2005, p. xxiv.
27. Prak and van Zanden, *Pioneers of Capitalism*, pp. 156ff.
28. Geert H. Janssen, 'The Republic of the Refugees', *Historical Journal*, vol. 60, no. 1 (2017), pp. 233–52.
29. Maarten Prak, *The Dutch Republic in the Seventeenth Century*, Cambridge: Cambridge University Press, 2005, p. 141.
30. Prak and van Zanden, *Pioneers of Capitalism*, p. 101.
31. Gerard Tellis and Stav Rosenzweig, *How Transformative*

Innovations Shaped the Rise of Nations, London: Anthem Press, 2018, p. 157.
32. Slave Voyages, Trans-Atlantic Slave Trade Estimates: https://www.slavevoyages.org/assessment/estimates/.
33. Prak, *The Dutch Republic in the Seventeenth Century*, p. 112.
34. Israel, *The Dutch Republic*, p. 268.
35. Schama, *The Embarrassment of Riches*, p. 245f.
36. Pieter de la Court, *The True Interest and Political Maxims, of the Republic of Holland*, 1746: https://oll.libertyfund.org/titles/court-the-true-interest-and-political-maxims-of-the-republic-of-holland/.
37. Goethe, *Egmont*, p. 330.
38. David Gordon (ed.), *The Turgot Collection*, Auburn, AL: Ludwig von Mises Institute, 2011, p. 94.
39. Bernard Mandeville, 'The Fable of the Bees', in Henry C. Clark (ed.), *Commerce, Culture, and Liberty: Readings on Capitalism before Adam Smith*, Indianapolis, IN: Liberty Fund, 2003.
40. Karl Marx: *Capital: A Critical Analysis of Capitalist Production*, Berlin: Dietz Verlag, 1990.
41. Schama, *The Embarrassment of Riches*, p. 323.
42. Israel, *The Dutch Republic*, pp. 630ff and 351f.
43. De Vries and van der Woude, *The First Modern Economy*, pp. 647, 620.
44. Earl A. Thompson and Jonathan Treussard, 'The Tulipmania: Fact or Artifact?', *Public Choice*, vol. 130, no. 1 (2007), pp. 99–114.
45. Schama, *The Embarrassment of Riches*, p. 224.
46. Grotius, *The Rights of War and Peace*, p. xvii.
47. Schama, *The Embarrassment of Riches*, p. 266.
48. Prak, *The Dutch Republic in the Seventeenth Century*, p. 201.
49. Israel, *The Dutch Republic*, p. 901f.

50. Prak, *The Dutch Republic in the Seventeenth Century*, p. 226.
51. Elizabeth L. Eisenstein, *The Printing Press as an Agent of Change*, Cambridge: Cambridge University Press, 1980, p. 413.
52. Pierre Bayle, *Historical and Critical Dictionary*, London: J. J. & P. Knapton, 1735, p. 389.
53. Mokyr, *A Culture of Growth*, p. 189.
54. Israel, *The Dutch Republic*, p. 892.
55. Prak, *The Dutch Republic in the Seventeenth Century*, p. 232f.
56. Steven Nadler, *Spinoza: A Life*, Cambridge: Cambridge University Press, 2001, p. 111.
57. Baruch Spinoza, *Complete Works*, Indianapolis, IN: Hackett, 2002, p. 571.
58. Pierre Bayle, *A Philosophical Commentary on These Words of the Gospel, Luke 14.23, 'Compel Them to Come In, That My House May Be Full'*, Indianapolis, IN: Liberty Fund, 2005, p. 148.
59. Ritchie Robertson, *The Enlightenment: The Pursuit of Happiness 1680–1790*, London: Allen Lane, 2020, p. 595.
60. John Locke, *Political Writings*, London: Penguin, 1993, p. 431.
61. Craig Koslofsky, *Evening's Empire: A History of the Night in Early Modern Europe*, Cambridge: Cambridge University Press, 2011, p. 135f.
62. Peter Gay and R. K. Webb, *Modern Europe to 1815*, New York: Harper & Row, 1973, p. 223.
63. Prak, *The Dutch Republic in the Seventeenth Century*, p. 241.
64. Israel, *The Dutch Republic*, p. 882.
65. Israel, *The Dutch Republic*, p. 818.
66. Israel, *The Dutch Republic*, p. 1007.
67. Prak, *The Dutch Republic in the Seventeenth Century*, p. 265.

68. Frederick A. Pottle, *Boswell in Holland 1763–1764*, New York: McGraw-Hill, 1952, p. 281.

7 The Anglosphere: Industry, Individualism and Impertinence

1. John Knox Laughton, *Nelson*, London: Macmillan & Co, 1895, p. 221.
2. Thomas Paine, *Complete Works*, Boston, MA: J. P. Mendum, 1859, p. 174.
3. Daniel Hannan, 'The Anglosphere is Alive and Well, but I Wonder Whether it Needs a Better Name', *Daily Telegraph*, 2 March 2014.
4. Gregory Clark, 'The Condition of the Working Class in England, 1209–2004', *Journal of Political Economy*, vol. 113, no. 6 (2005), pp. 1307–40.
5. David Landes, *The Unbound Prometheus*, Cambridge: Cambridge University Press, 2003, p. 5.
6. Deirdre McCloskey, 'The Industrial Revolution, 1780–1860: A Survey', in Roderick Floud and Deirdre McCloskey (eds), *The Economic History of Britain, 1700–Present*, Cambridge: Cambridge University Press, 1981, p. 118.
7. John Miller, *The Glorious Revolution*, 2nd edition, London: Routledge, 1997, p. 3.
8. Lord Macaulay, *History of England*, Vol. 3, London: Longmans, Green & Co., 1898, p. 285f.
9. Jonathan Israel, 'The Dutch Role in the Glorious Revolution', in Jonathan Israel (ed.), *The Anglo-Dutch Moment: Essays on the Glorious Revolution and its World Impact*, Cambridge: Cambridge University Press, 2003, p. 120.
10. Dawson Massy, *The Secret History of Romanism*, Dublin: Seeleys, 1853, p. 293.

11. Steve Pincus, *1688: The First Modern Revolution*, New Haven, CT: Yale University Press, 2009, p. 283.
12. Miller, *The Glorious Revolution*, p. 3.
13. John Lothrop Motley, *The Rise of the Dutch Republic*, London: Strahan & Co., 1863, p. v.
14. Smith, *Wealth of Nations*, vol. 2, p. 761.
15. Arthur Herman, *How the Scots Invented the Modern World*, New York: Broadway Books, 2001, p. 190.
16. David Ormrod, *The Rise of Commercial Empires: England and the Netherlands in the Age of Mercantilism, 1650–1770*, Cambridge: Cambridge University Press, 2003, p. 92f.
17. Voltaire, *Letters on England*, London: Penguin, 2005, p. 41.
18. Lisa Jardine, *Going Dutch: How England Plundered Holland's Glory*, London: Harper Press, 2008.
19. Friedrich Engels, *The Condition of the Working Class in England in 1844*, New York: John W. Lovell, 1887, p. 11.
20. George Selgin, *Good Money: Birmingham Button Makers, the Royal Mint, and the Beginnings of Modern Coinage, 1775–1821*, Ann Arbor, MI: University of Michigan Press, 2008.
21. David Philips, 'Crime, Law, and Punishment in the Industrial Revolution', in Patrick O'Brien and Roland Quinault (eds), *The Industrial Revolution and British Society*, Cambridge: Cambridge University Press, 1993.
22. Joel Mokyr, *The Enlightened Economy: Britain and the Industrial Revolution 1700–1850*, London: Penguin, 2011, p. 378.
23. Mokyr, *The Enlightened Economy*, p. 200.
24. Mokyr, *The Enlightened Economy*, p. 365.
25. Deirdre McCloskey, *Bourgeois Equality*, Chicago, IL: University of Chicago Press, 2016, p. 265f.
26. McCloskey, *Bourgeois Equality*, chs. 25–26.

27. Adam Smith, *Lectures on Jurisprudence*, Indianapolis, IN: Liberty Fund, 1982, p. 538.
28. Joel Mokyr, *Gifts of Athena*, Princeton, NJ: Princeton University Press, 2005, p. 34f. and Mokyr, *The Enlightened Economy*, p. 46.
29. Mokyr, *A Culture of Growth*, p. 196.
30. Mokyr, *The Enlightened Economy*, p. 57.
31. Mokyr, *The Enlightened Economy*, p. 253.
32. Smith, *Wealth of Nations*, Vol. 1, p. 540.
33. Jack Goldstone, *Why Europe?*, New York: McGraw-Hill, 2009, p. 129.
34. James Boswell, *The Life of Samuel Johnson*, Vol. 5, London: John Murray, 1831, p. 67.
35. Anton Howes, 'Is Innovation in Human Nature?', 22 October 2016: https://www.antonhowes.com/blog/is-innovation-in-human-nature/.
36. Smith, *Wealth of Nations*, Vol. 1, p. 21.
37. Mokyr, *The Enlightened Economy*, p. 94f.
38. David Hume, *Essays: Moral, Political and Literary*, Indianapolis, IN: Liberty Fund, 1987, p. 328.
39. A. P. Usher, 'The Industrialisation of Modern Britain', *Technology and Culture*, vol. 1, no. 2 (1960), pp. 109–27.
40. Mokyr, *The Enlightened Economy*, p. 179.
41. F. A. Hayek (ed), *Capitalism and the Historians*, Chicago, IL: University of Chicago Press, 1963, p. 16.
42. Mokyr, *The Enlightened Economy*, p. 442. Martin Ravaillon, *The Economics of Poverty: History, Measurement and Policy*, Oxford: Oxford University Press, 2016, ch. 1.
43. Amanda Vickery, 'Golden Age to Separate Spheres? A Review of the Categories and Chronology of English Women's History', *Historical Journal*, vol. 36, no. 2 (1993), pp. 383–414.

44. Virginia Postrel, *The Fabric of Civilization*, New York: Basic Books, 2021, p. 66f.
45. Emma Griffin, *Liberty's Dawn: A People's History of the Industrial Revolution*, New Haven, CT: Yale University Press, 2014, pp. 51, 243 and 121.
46. 'Child Labour in Historical Perspective 1800–1985: Case Studies from Europe, Japan and Colombia', UNICEF, 1986.
47. Griffin, *Liberty's Dawn*, pp. 66ff.
48. Morgan Kelly, Joel Mokyr and Cormac Ó Gráda, 'The Mechanics of the Industrial Revolution', *Journal of Political Economy*, vol. 131, no. 4 (2023), pp. 59–94. Emma Griffin, *A Short History of the Industrial Revolution*, 2nd edition, London: Palgrave Macmillan, 2018, p. 151.
49. Friedrich Engels, 'Preface to the English Edition', in *The Condition of the Working Class in England*, Moscow: Progress Publishers, 1977.
50. Mokyr, *The Enlightened Economy*, p. 475.
51. E. P. Thompson, *The Making of the English Working Class*, New York: Pantheon Books, 1964, p. 208.
52. Griffin, *Liberty's Dawn*, pp. 55 and 16.
53. Griffin, *Liberty's Dawn*, pp. 214ff.
54. Griffin, *Liberty's Dawn*, p. 243f.
55. Griffin, *Liberty's Dawn*, pp. 41 and 243.
56. Griffin, *Liberty's Dawn*, p. 243.
57. Griffin, *Liberty's Dawn*, p. 246.
58. T. S. Ashton, *The Industrial Revolution 1760–1830*, Oxford: Oxford University Press, 1948, p. 161.
59. Griffin, *Liberty's Dawn*, p. 212.
60. Griffin, *Liberty's Dawn*, p. 19.
61. George MacDonald Fraser, *Flashman and the Mountain of Light*, London: HarperCollins, 2011, p. 24.

62. Steven Davies, 'The Brutality of British Empire on Display in Legacy of Violence', *Reason Magazine*, November 2022.
63. David M. Levy, *How the Dismal Science Got Its Name*, Ann Arbor, MI: University of Michigan Press, 2002.
64. Zareer Masani, *Macaulay: Britain's Liberal Imperialist*, London: Vintage, 2013, p. 45.
65. https://en.wikisource.org/wiki/Final_Act_of_the_Congress_of_Vienna/Act_XV.
66. Seymour Drescher, *Tocqueville and Beaumont on Social Reform*, New York: Harper Torchbooks, 1968, p. 138.
67. Daniel Hannan, *How We Invented Freedom and Why it Matters*, London: Head of Zeus, 2013, p. 286.
68. Mokyr, *The Enlightened Economy*, p. 160.
69. John Bright, *Selected Speeches of the Rt. Hon. John Bright M.P. on Public Questions*, London: J. M. Dent & Co., 1907, p. 204.
70. David Brion Davis, 'Foreword', in Seymour Drescher, *Econocide: British Slavery in the Era of Abolition*, Chapel Hill, NC: University of North Carolina Press, 2010.
71. Mokyr, *The Enlightened Economy*, p. 163.
72. Mokyr, *The Enlightened Economy*, p. 262f
73. A. L. Rowse, *The Expansion of Elizabethan England*, Madison, WI: University of Wisconsin Press, 2003, ch. 6.
74. Alexis de Tocqueville, *Democracy in America*, Vol. 1, Indianapolis, IN: Liberty Fund, 2012, p. 581.
75. Alexis de Tocqueville, *Journey to America*, London: Faber & Faber, 1959, p. 177.
76. Alexis de Tocqueville, *The Old Regime and the Revolution*, New York: Harper & Brothers, 1856, p. 300.
77. De Tocqueville, *Democracy in America*, Vol. 1, p. 51.
78. Bernard Bailyn, *The Ideological Origins of the American Revolution*, Cambridge, MA: Harvard University Press, 1977, p. 36.

79. George H. Smith, *The American Revolution and the Declaration of Independence*, Washington, DC: Cato Institute, 2017, p. 19f.
80. Mike Duncan, *Hero of Two Worlds: The Marquis de Lafayette in the Age of Revolution*, New York: PublicAffairs, 2021, ch. 2.
81. John Adams, *The Works of John Adams*, Vol. 7, Boston, MA: Little, Brown, 1852, p. 593.
82. Thomas E. Ricks, *First Principles*, New York: Harper Perennial, 2021, p. xxiv.
83. Ricks, *First Principles*, p. 66. Thomas Jefferson, *The Life and Selected Writings of Thomas Jefferson*, New York: Modern Library, 1993, p. 633.
84. Ricks, *First Principles*, p. 255.
85. Fareed Zakaria, *Age of Revolutions*, London: Allen Lane, 2024, p. 126.
86. Woody Holton, *Liberty is Sweet: The Hidden History of the American Revolution*, New York: Simon & Schuster, 2021, ch. 9.
87. Jefferson, *The Life and Selected Writings*, p. 64f.
88. I. Kramnick and R. L. Moore, *The Godless Constitution: A Moral Defence of the Secular State*, New York: W. W. Norton & Co., 2005, ch. 2.
89. Paul Johnson, *A History of the American People*, New York: HarperCollins, 1998, p. 209.
90. *The Farington Diary*, ed. James Greig, London: Hutchinson & Co., 1923, Vol. 1, p. 278.
91. Johnson, *A History of the American People*, p. 3.
92. Jefferson, *The Life and Selected Writings*, p. 257.
93. James Loewen, *Lies Across America: What American Sites Get Wrong*, New York: Simon & Schuster, 2007, p. 312.
94. Nikole Hannah-Jones, 'The 1619 Project', *New York Times Magazine*, 14 August 2019.

95. David Olusoga, *Black and British: A Forgotten History*, London: Pan Macmillan, 2016, pp. 201ff.
96. https://www.wsws.org/en/articles/2019/11/28/wood-n28.html/.
97. Alexander Hamilton, James Madison and John Jay, *The Federalist Papers*, New York: Mentor Books, 1961, p. 266.
98. Ricks, *First Principles*, p. 268.
99. Damon Root, *A Glorious Liberty*, Lincoln, NE: Potomac Books, 2023, pp. 71–4.
100. Andrew Carroll and Robert G. Torricelli (eds), *In Our Own Words*, New York: Atria Books, 2000, p. 235.
101. Dick Harrison, *Slaveri: Forntiden till renässansen*, Lund: Historiska Media, 2006. Fredrik Segerfeldt, *Den svarte mannens börda*, Stockholm: Timbro, 2018. SlaveVoyages Database: https://www.slavevoyages.org/.
102. Johnson, *A History of the American People*, p. 170.
103. T. West, *Vindicating the Founders: Race, Sex, Class, and Justice in the Origins of America*, Lanham, MD: Rowman & Littlefield, 1997, p. 149.
104. Johnson, *A History of the American People*, p. 681.
105. Abraham Lincoln, *Speeches and Writings 1859–1865: Speeches, Letters, and Miscellaneous Writings, Presidential Messages and Proclamations*, New York: Library of America, 1989, p. 3f.
106. J. Bradford DeLong, *Slouching Towards Utopia: An Economic History of the Twentieth Century*, New York: Basic Books, 2022, p. 35.
107. John Maynard Keynes, *The Economic Consequences of the Peace*, New York: Harcourt, Brace & Howe, 1920, p. 11.
108. Douglas Irwin, *Clashing Over Commerce: A History of US Trade Policy*, Chicago, IL: University of Chicago Press, 2017.

109. Johnson, *A History of the American People*, p. 714.
110. Susan Butler, *Roosevelt and Stalin: Portrait of a Partnership*, New York: Vintage, 2015, p. 117.
111. Arthur Herman, *Freedom's Forge*, New York: Random House, 2012, p. 13.
112. Herman, *Freedom's Forge*, p. 154.
113. Nigel Ashton, 'Harold Macmillan and the "Golden Days" of Anglo-American Relations Revisited, 1957–63', *Diplomatic History*, vol. 29, no. 4 (2005), pp. 691–723.
114. Niall Ferguson, *Empire: How Britain Made the Modern World*, London: Penguin, 2004, p. 350.
115. Ferguson, *Empire*, p. 351.
116. Irwin, *Clashing Over Commerce*, pp. 421 and 456.
117. John Mueller, *Retreat from Doomsday: The Obsolescence of Major War*, New York: Basic Books, 2001, p. 18. Steven Pinker, *The Better Angels of Our Nature: The Decline of Violence in History and Its Causes*, London: Allen Lane, 2011.
118. https://www.abrahamlincolnonline.org/lincoln/speeches/lyceum.htm

Conclusion: Further Rise or Inevitable Decline?

1. Polybius, *The Histories*, Vol. 6, Cambridge, MA: Harvard University Press, 2012, p. 489.
2. Joel Mokyr, 'Invention and Rebellion: Why do Innovations Occur at all? An Evolutionary Approach', in E. S. Brezis and P. Temin (eds), *Elites, Minorities, and Economic Growth*, Amsterdam: Elsevier, 1999.
3. Alan Beattie, 'Brussels Setting Rules for AI isn't Pretty, but Someone's got to do it', *Financial Times*, 13 December 2023.

4. https://acoup.blog/2023/07/07/collections-the-status-quo-coalition/.
5. Jason Feifer, *Build for Tomorrow*, New York: Harmony, 2022, p. 37.

INDEX

Abbas, 137
Abbasid Caliphate, 126, 127–72
   army, 156–7
   astrology, 146
   astronomy, 153, 164
   books/literature, 148–9, 165
   decline and fall of, 156–69
   economy, 145, 158
   foundation of, 136–42
   geography, 153
   Greeks and, 131–3, 147–9
   'House of Wisdom', 9, 151, 183
   intellectual wealth, 145–51
   law, 156
   map, 128–9
   mathematics, 146, 152
   medicine, 152, 164
   military power and aggression, 137–8, 148
   Pax Islamica, 140–41, 170
   personal freedom, 142–3
   philosophy, 147–8, 151, 154, 161–2, 164
   religion, 150–51, 154–5, 160–63, 171; *see also* Islam
   Roman Empire and, 131
   schools, 160–61
   science, 148, 151–4, 161, 164–5
   slavery, 139, 143–4, 156–7
   trade, 141–5
   translation movement, 145–9, 151, 225
   women's rights, 144–5, 167, 170
   see also Arabs; Islam; Baghdad
Abd al-Rahman, 138, 166
Abelard, Peter, 226
Abu Muslim, 137–8
Achaean League, 96
Acropolis, Athens, 26, 34, 49, 52–3
Act of Abjuration (Netherlands, 1581), 301, 328
Act of Toleration (England, 1689), 353
Act XV (1815), 385
Acton, Lord (John, Dalberg-Acton, 1st Baron Acton), 131, 229
Adams, John, 398–9, 407–8
Addison, Joseph. 393
Aelius Aristides, 84
Aeneid (Virgil), 82–3, 102
Aeschylus, 40, 50–51
Afghanistan, 136, 438
Akyol, Mustafa, 155
Al Qaeda, 130
Al-Andalus (Muslim Spain), 138, 166

Al-Jabr (al-Khwarizmi), 152
Al-Khalili, Jim, 151
Al-Maqdisi, 150
Alberti, Leon Battista, 244, 250–51, 253, 263
Alcmaeonid family, 25
Alexander the Great, 18, 67–8, 80, 89
Alexander VI, pope, 271–2
Alexandria, Egypt, 67–8, 89, 108
Alfonso, King of Aragon and Naples, 252, 256
Alfonso X, King of Castile, 225
Almagest (Ptolemy), 149
Along the River During the Qingming Festival (painting), 176–7, 194, 195
America
 discovery and conquest of, 265–9
 North America, 389–94
 see also United States
American Revolutionary War (1775–83), 393, 394–8
Amritsar, India, 382
 massacre (1919), 384
Amsterdam, Netherlands, 293, 297, 303, 305–6, 320, 322–4, 326, 328, 331, 335
'Anarchy at Samarra', 156
Anaxagoras, 49
Andronicus of Rhodes, 88–9
Anglo-American Special Relationship, 412
Anglo-Dutch War, Second (1665–7), 310–11, 320–21
Anglosphere, 344–429, 440–41
 map, 342–3
 population, 345
 religion, 347, 352–3
 slavery, 411
 see also British Empire; Glorious Revolution; Great Britain; United States
Anti-Imperialist League, 421
Antigone (Sophocles), 43, 45
Antioch (modern-day Turkey), 108
Antipater, 68
Antonine Plague, 114
Antoninus Pius, Roman Emperor, 87
Antony, Mark, 100
Antwerp (modern day Belgium), 300, 302–3, 306
Apellicon of Teos, 88
Appelbaum, Anne, 440
Appian of Alexandria, 431
Aquinas, Thomas, 66, 226, 239, 241, 268
Arabs, 134, 139–40
 see also Abbasid Caliphate; Islam
Aristides, 85, 106
Aristophanes, 50–51
Aristotle, 1, 11, 48–9, 52, 62, 64–8, 70–71, 84, 88–9, 94–5, 131–2, 142, 147, 154, 166, 167, 225–6, 236, 239, 243, 248, 253, 254, 256, 265, 266–7, 277, 400, 402
Arkwright, Richard, 205, 364
Artaxerxes I, King of Persia, 39
Ashton, T. S., 377–8

INDEX

Assizes of Ariano, Sicily (1140), 233
Athenian League, 60
Athens, ancient Greece, 1, 3, 23–71, 82
  Acropolis, 26, 34, 49, 52–3
  Assembly of citizens, 27, 29–30, 44, 56, 58, 69
  autochthonous, 34, 42
  citizenship, 41–3
  Council of 500, 27–8, 42
  debates, 22, 50–51, 70
  democracy, 26–9, 40–44, 49, 59–60
  fall of, 58–9, 68–9
  fleet, 23, 35–8, 40–41, 53, 56, 58–9
  judiciary and law, 29, 45–6
  military power and aggression, 30–40, 53–8
  monetary system, 46–9
  ostracism, 28
  personal freedom, 43–6
  philosophy, 51–2, 61–6
  plague, 56
  Plato's Academy, 64–5, 123
  religion/gods, 20–21, 44–5, 90
  Rome and, 88–9, 96
  slavery, 21, 23–4, 28, 46, 66
  theatre, 50–51, 89
  trade and commerce, 23–5, 46–9
  women's rights, 21, 28, 46, 66
  see also Greece; Peloponnesian War
Augustine of Hippo, 66, 120, 163, 165
Augustus, Roman Emperor, 89, 94, 100–104, 110, 125
Australia, 346, 379–80
Austria, 286
Averroes, 131, 166–7, 224, 225–6
Avicenna, 131, 152, 162
Avignon, France, 240, 253
Azo of Bologna, 233

Bacon, Francis, 177, 267, 361, 363
Baghdad, Iraq, 136, 139–43, 151, 156, 159, 161, 163, 165, 168–70
Bailyn, Bernard, 393–4
Banda massacre (1621), 308
Barbados, 381
al-Barmaki, Jafar, 140
Barmakid family, 136, 140
Bartholdi, Auguste, 412
Bayle, Pierre, 305, 324, 326–8, 335
Beard, Mary, 9, 94, 97
Beattie, Alan, 438
Beccadelli, Antonio, 264
Beethoven, Ludwig van, 300
Beijing, China, 209
Belgium, 286, 292, 388
Bellamy, Francis, 401
Bergh, Andreas, 46
Berman, Harold, 2, 231–2
Bernstein, William, 141
Bi Sheng, 196
Bing, Song Emperor, 208–9
Birmingham, England, 388
Birmingham Lunar Society, 362
al-Biruni, 153, 164–5
Bismarck, Otto von, 390

Black and British: A Forgotten History (Olusoga), 406
Black Death, 245–7
Blackstone, William, 360
Boer War (1899–1902), 382, 384
Boethius of Daca, 226
Bohemia, 286
Bologna, Italy, 246
  university, 231
Borgia family, 270–72
Borgia, Rodrigo *see* Alexander VI, pope
Boston Tea Party (1773), 394–5
Boswell, James, 336–7
Brabant, 292, 299–300
Bracciolini, Poggio, 250–51
Braudel, Fernand, 4, 127, 237, 293
Brazil, 307–8
Bright, John, 383, 387
Bristol, England, 388
Britain *see* Great Britain
British Civil War (1642–51), 352
British Empire, 346, 356, 379–89
  anti-imperialism, 382–6
  atrocities and violence, 381–3
  North America, 389–93
  slavery, 381, 384–6, 389, 392
  wealth creation and, 386–9
  see also American Revolutionary War
Bruges (modern day Belgium), 303
Brunelleschi, Filippo, 259–60
Bruni, Leonardo, 243, 248–50, 253
Bruno, Giordano, 277
Brutus, Marcus Junius, 99

Buchell, Aernt van, 322
Buddhism, 178, 197–8
Burckhardt, Jacob, 244, 246
Buyid dynasty, 157–9
Byzantine Empire, 121–4, 126, 131–6149, 157, 258–9

Caesar, Julius, Roman General, 85, 89, 98–100, 249, 383
Calhoun, John C., 409
Caligula, Roman Emperor, 104
Calvin, John, 277, 295
Calvinism, 295, 300, 302, 315, 317, 322–3, 335, 339
Campbell-Bannerman, Henry, 384
Canada, 346, 380
Cannae, Battle of (216 BC), 79–80
Canossa, Italy, 229, 235
Cao Bin, 182
capitalism, 294–5, 314, 355
Caracalla, Roman Emperor, 85–6, 115
Cardwell, D. S. L., 6
Carlyle, Thomas, 374, 383–4
Carnegie, Andrew, 421
Carthage, 79, 81, 96
Catalogue of the Inscriptions on Stone and Bronze, 199
Catholic Church, 226, 228–31, 243, 322–3, 347–8, 352
  Counter-Reformation, 275–80, 282
  Inquisition, 274, 276, 279, 299–300
  papacy, 228–30, 240, 248, 254, 274–5

INDEX

Cato the Elder, 90, 99
Cato the Younger, 98–9, 383, 393, 395, 399
Cato, a Tragedy (Addison), 393, 403
Cato's Letters (Trenchard & Gordon), 393–5
Cereta, Laura, 252
Cervantes, Miguel de, 262
Chalcis, Greece, 30
Chang'an, China, 192–3
Charlemagne, King of the Franks, 153, 240, 249
Charles II, King of England, Ireland and Scotland, 332–3, 347
Charles V, Holy Roman Emperor, 269, 275, 282, 286, 297–8
Charles V, King of Spain, 268
Charles VII, King of France, 271
Chen Bridge, coup at (960), 179–82
Cheng Hao, 198
China, 171–2, 176–9, 185–6, 214–15, 217, 222–4, 389, 426, 438, 440–41, 444
  Communist Party, 201
  Five Dynasties and Ten Kingdoms period, 179
  population, 189–90, 199
  see also Ming dynasty; Song dynasty
Christianity, 66, 118, 123–4, 126, 132, 134–5, 144, 222, 224–6, 255
  Christian art, 258–9
Christine de Pizan, 252

Chrysoloras, Manuel, 248
Chrysostom, John, archbishop of Constantinople, 123
Churchill, Winston, 238, 384, 400, 418, 423
Cicero, 9, 62, 84, 94–6, 98, 100, 101, 105, 131, 133, 143, 156, 241–4, 249, 256, 277, 338, 399, 400, 402
Cincinnatus, 403
Ciompi Revolt (Florence, 1378), 246
City of God, The (Augustine of Hippo), 120
City of Ladies, The (Christine de Pizan), 252
Civilization of the Renaissance in Italy, The (Burckhardt), 244
Clark, Kenneth, 6, 261
Clarke, Arthur C., 153
Claudius, Roman Emperor, 85–7, 105
Cleisthenes, 25–7, 41
Clement VII, pope, 274
Cleomenes, King of Sparta, 26
Cleopatra Queen of Egypt, 100
Cole, Myke, 19
Coleridge, Samuel Taylor, 65
Collingwood, Cuthbert, 341
Columbus, Christopher, 265, 267
Commodus, Roman Emperor, 115
Concordance of Discordant Canons, A (Gratian), 233
Condition of the Working Class in England of 1845, The (Engels), 367

Confucius, 180, 194–7
  neo-Confucianism, 197–8, 207, 213
Congress of Vienna (1814–15), 385
Conscious Lovers, The (Steele), 359
Constantine, Roman Emperor, 117–19, 121
Constantinople, 117, 121–2, 124, 131, 133, 253
Constitutions of Melfi (1231), 233
Copernicus 278–9
Corinth, Greece, 16, 38, 43, 55, 59
Cornell, Tim, 81
Cornwallis, Charles, 398
Council of Blood (Netherlands), 300
Council of Trent (Italy), 275
Counter-Reformation, 275–80, 282
  art, 276
  Index of Prohibited Books, 276–8, 326
  Inquisition, 276, 279
Cousins, Norman, 7
Critias, 59, 62
Cromwell, Oliver, 352–3
Crone, Patricia, 154
Crusades, 163, 165–6, 169, 224, 235
Cuyp, Aelbert, 330

da Gama, Vasco, 266
Dalí, Salvador, 418
Dalmeny, Lord (Archibald Primrose, 5th Earl of Rosebery), 381
Dalrymple, William, 133
Damascus (modern-day Syria), 136–7, 141
Daniel of Morley, 225
Dante Alighieri, 131
Darius, King of Persia, 31–2
Darwin, Charles, 64
Darwin, Erasmus, 362
Datini family, 247
David (Donatello), 260
David (Michelangelo), 260
Davies, Stephen, 173, 200, 278, 287, 383
Davis, David Brion, 389
de la Court, Pieter, 311
de las Casas, Bartolomé, 268–9
De Militia Romana (Lipsius), 310
de Ruyter, Michiel, 320, 334
de Witt, Cornelis, 321, 334
de Witt, Johan, 319–21, 332–4, 336, 338, 351, 442
Decameron, The (Boccaccio), 277
Defoe, Daniel, 348, 359, 372
Delian League, 40–41, 53–4
DeLong, J. Bradford, 415
Delphi, Greece, 25
Demandt, Alexander, 78–9
democracy, 26–9, 40–44, 4, 959, 320
Deng Xiaoping, 217
Descartes, René, 326, 335
Deutsch, David, 8
Devereaux, Bret, 16–17, 60, 80, 119, 440
Diamond Age, The (Stephenson) 346
Dias, Bartolomeu, 266

Dickens, Charles, 383, 413
Digest (Roman law), 230–32, 236
Diocletian, Roman Emperor, 117–19
Divine Comedy, The (Dante), 131
Dome of the Rock, Jerusalem, 136
Donatello, 260
Donation of Constantine, 243
Douglass, Frederick, 408
Dutch Act of Abjuration (1581), 400
Dutch East India Company, 307
Dutch Reformed Church, 317, 329
Dutch Republic, 286–339
  agriculture, 290, 292–4
  Anglo-French invasion (1672), 331–7, 338
  army, 309–10
  art, 329–31
  cities, 293, 315, 336
  coat of arms, 311
  colonialism, 307–10
  decline and fall, 331–7, 339
  Disaster Year (1672), 331–7
  Dutch revolt (1556), 297–304
  economy, 293–4, 304–9, 313–15, 338
  Enlightenment and, 325–7, 338
  fairs, 313
  First Stadtholderless Era, 319
  foundation of, 312
  free market, 292–7, 319
  immigration, 304–5, 336, 339
  independence, 301–2, 312–13
  industry, 304, 306
  land reclamation, 290–92
  liberalism, 296–7, 308, 319
  literature, 324, 327–8
  map, 285
  military power and aggression, 309–12, 320–21
  Orangists, 316, 332–4
  Perpetual Edict, 321, 333
  philosophy, 326
  political system/government, 291, 298, 309, 316–21, 332–3
  refugees, 304–5
  religion, 299–300, 305, 317, 322–3, 327–8, 334–5
  science, 325–7, 338
  servants, 297
  shipbuilding, 293, 306
  slavery, 308–9
  social life, 322
  stadtholderate, 309, 316–19, 321, 333, 338
  States General, 291, 298, 301, 316–17, 319, 334–5
  States' Party, 316, 319, 333
  stock market, 307
  tolerance, 327–8, 334–5
  trade and commerce, 289, 292–7, 299, 305–7, 320–21, 336
  'tulip bubble', 315
  universities, 323–4, 335–6
  wealth, 313–15, 338
  witch trials, 279, 321–2
  women's rights, 296–7, 338
  see also Glorious Revolution
Dutch Water Line, 333–4
Dutch West India Company, 308

East India Company, 307, 379, 395
Ebrey, Patricia, 203
Edict of Nantes (1685), 347
Edinburgh, Scotland, 354
Edison, Thomas Alva, 416
'efflorescences', 4–5, 345
Egmont, Count of (Lamoral, Count of Egmont), 300, 312–13
Egmont (Goethe), 312–13
Egypt, 20, 21, 93, 157, 164
Eighty Years' War (*c.*1566–1648), 288
Eisenstein, Elizabeth L., 324
Elias, Norbert, 360
Elizabeth I, Queen of England and Ireland, 287–8, 303, 390
Elvin, Mark, 189, 205–6, 214
Encyclopaedia of Islamic Economics, The, 141
Encyclopédie (Turgot), 313
Engels, Friedrich, 356, 367, 374
England, 287, 316, 320, 332–3
   Peasants' Revolt (1381), 246\
   union with Scotland, 354
   see also Anglosphere; Great Britain
English language, 346, 390
Enlightened Economy, An (Mokyr), 357
Enlightenment, 289, 313, 325–7, 392–3, 401
Ephesus, Turkey, 108
Epicurus, 66
Erasmus of Rotterdam, 249, 263, 275, 277, 279–80, 324

Essay on the Principle of Population, An (Malthus), 345
'eternal edict' (Spain), 299
Euclid, 139
Eugenius, pope, 258
Euripides, 29, 50–51
Europe, 222–7, 424
   agriculture, 234
   Arab influence, 237
   Black Death, 245–7
   cities, 236
   colonialism, 267
   European Union, 424–5, 438–9
   legal systems, 230–34, 281
   Middle Ages, 234–5
   Mongol invasion, 237–8
   polities, 227–30
   religious intolerance, 279–80
   trade and commerce, 234–5, 237
   universities, 230–31
   see also Catholic Church
Eurybiades, Spartan commander, 17–18
Evelyn, John, 294
Eyre, Edward, 383

Fable of the Bees (Mandeville), 313
Fabric of Civilization, The (Postrel), 369
Fancheng, China, 208
Fatimid dynasty, 157–8, 163
Feast in the House of Levi, The (Veronese), 276
Fedele, Cassandra, 251
Federico da Montefeltro, 252–3
Feifer, Jason, 443

Feltham, Owen, 292
Ferdinand and Isabella of Spain, 278
Ferdinand I, Holy Roman Emperor, 298
Fibonacci, Leonardo, 237
Ficino, Marsilio, 263
financial crash (2008), 438–9
Fitzhugh, George, 409
Flanders, 290, 292, 299
Flashman and the Mountain of Light (Fraser), 380
Fletcher, Catherine, 251
Florence, Italy, 234, 242, 246–52, 259–60, 273–4
   cathedral, 259–60, 263
   Ciompi Revolt (1378), 246
   Florentine Academy, 263
fossil fuels, 192, 202, 385
France, 271–3, 277, 286–8, 303, 312–13, 316, 332–4, 347–8
   colonisation, 389–90
   French Revolution (1789), 397
Franche-Comté, France, 286
Franklin, Benjamin, 399, 402, 406, 411
Frankopan, Peter, 140
Fraser, George MacDonald, 380
Frederick I Barbarossa, Holy Roman Emperor, 235–6
Frederick II, Holy Roman Emperor, 224, 233
Frederik Hendrik, Prince of Orange, 318
Freedom's Forge (Herman), 419–20
Freeman, Elizabeth, 407–8
Friesland, 290

Frogs, The (Aristophanes), 51
Frost, Thomas, 379
Full River Dead (film), 201

Gaius Gracchus, 96
Galen, 149, 263
Galileo Galilei, 278–9
Gaozong, Song Emperor, 192, 200
Gates of Paradise, Florence baptistry (Ghiberti), 259
Gay, Peter, 329
Geneva, Switzerland, 277
Genghis Khan, 168, 206–7
Genoa, Italy, 223, 234
George II, King of Great Britain and Ireland, 355
George III, King of the United Kingdom, 398, 402–3
Germany, 227–8, 237, 279, 286, 312, 316, 385, 424
al-Ghazali, 161–3, 165, 167, 169
Ghent (modern day Belgium), 303
Ghiberti, Lorenzo, 259
Gibbon, Edward, 73, 78–9, 112, 114
Giotto di Bondone, 258–9
global poverty, 426, 437
Glorious Revolution (1688), 347–52
Goethe, Johann Wolfgang von, 10, 73, 300, 312
Goitein, Shelomo D., 143
'golden ages', 3–9, 431–8
   decline of, 435–7
   free markets, 433–6
   free minds, 433–5

government, 433
modern-day, 439–44
religion, 437
rule of law, 433
trade, 432, 436
Golden Bull of Hungary (1222), 233
Goldstone, Jack, 4–5, 10
Goldsworthy, Adrian, 86
Good Money (Selgin), 357
Gordon, Thomas, 393–4
Grand Alliance (1689), 348
Gratian, 233
Great Britain, 354–7, 427–8
agriculture, 367–8, 371
cities, 359, 372, 373
class, 359, 362–3
economic freedom, 358
economy, 387–8
employment, 368–72
government, 352–3, 356–8, 377
guilds, 365
immigration, 354–5
innovation, 360–66
law, 357–8, 364
life expectancy, 373
monetary system, 356–7
poverty, 368, 371, 376, 378
powers of the monarchy, 352–3
private enterprise, 356
Royal Navy, 385
science, 360–63
taxes, 358
tolerance, 358
trade, 357–60, 388
union with Scotland, 354
universities, 354, 362
wealth, 359
see also Anglosphere; British Empire; Industrial Revolution
'Great Chain of Being', 244
Great Fire of London (1666), 372
Greece (ancient Greece), 14–70, 81
city-states, 20–21, 32
farming, 21–2
First Persian Invasion of Greece, 32–3
hoplites, 21–2, 33
language, 122
map, 12–13
religion/gods, 20–21, 44–5, 87
Rome and, 87–90
Second Persian Invasion of Greece, 34–40
trade, 22–3
see also Athens; Peloponnesian War; Sparta
Greenblatt, Stephen, 278
Greene, Graham, 271
Gregory VII, pope, 228
Griffin, Emma, 375–9
Groningen, Netherlands, 290
Grotius, Hugo, 276, 291, 302, 317–18, 321
Guangzhou, China, 179
Guicciardini, Francesco, 272
gunpowder, 202, 207
Gutas, Dimitri, 127, 140
Gutenberg, Johannes, 264

Haarlem, Netherlands, 305, 335
Habsburg dynasty, 275, 286–8, 297–9

Hadrian, Roman Emperor, 87, 89
Hadrian's Wall, 105
Hague, Netherlands, 316, 319
Hals, Frans, 330
Hamdanids, 158
Hamilton, Alexander, 402
Hammond, John and Barbara, 367, 374
Hangzhou, China, 200–203, 208, 216, 223
Hannan, Daniel, 341, 386
Hannibal, 79–80, 86
Hanseatic League, 228
Hanson, Victor Davis, 21–2
Harper, Kyle, 109, 115
Harriot, Thomas, 278
Hawley, Michael, 94
Hayek, Friedrich, 45–6, 368
Hegel, Georg Wilhelm Friedrich, 14
Henry III, King of France, 288
Henry IV, Holy Roman Emperor, 229
Henry, Patrick, 395
Herder, Johann Gottfried, 11
Herman, Arthur, 354, 419
Herodotus, 14, 18, 30–31, 49, 51
Hippias, 25
Hitler, Adolf, 418–19
Hobbes, Thomas, 326
Holberg, Ludvig, 283
Holland, 290, 293, 296, 299–300, 302, 304–5, 307, 30, 312, 317–199
Holland, Tom, 35–6, 283
Holton, Woody, 400

Holy Roman Empire, 227–30, 235–6, 271, 274
Homer, 20, 35, 82, 248
hoplites, 21–2
Horace, 90
Howes, Anton, 364
Hugo of Santalla, 222
Huguenots, 305, 324
Hulegu Khan, 168
Hull, Cordell, 423
Hulu, Artur, 76–7
humanism, 238–43, 249–50, 252–7
Hume, David, 354, 366
Hungary, 222, 237, 286
Hutcheson, Francis, 354
Hutten, Ulrich von, 263
Huygens, Christiaan, 326

Ibn Abbad, Sahib, 158
Ibn al-Haytham, 152–3, 259
Ibn al-Nafis, 152
Ibn Hanbal, Ahmad, 155
Ibn Khaldun, 134
Ibn Qutayba, 150
Iliad (Homer), 82
In Praise of Florence (Bruni), 243
Incoherence of the Incoherence, The (Averroes), 167
Incoherence of the Philosophers, The (al-Ghazali), 161, 167
India, 164, 189, 266, 379, 384, 445
Indian Rebellion (1857), 382
Industrial Enlightenment, 360, 362–3, 367
Industrial Revolution, 344–6, 357, 360–79, 387, 389, 414, 428

child labour, 370–73
Luddites, 369–70
wages, 373–5
workers, 373–9
Innocent III, pope, 255–6
Interest of Holland, The (de la Court), 311
Investiture Controversy, 228–30
Iran, 157, 159, 444
Iraq, 130, 157, 159, 438
Ireland, 346
Irish famine, 377–8
Irwin, Douglas, 417
Isagoras, 26–7, 30
Islam, 133–6, 143, 154–5, 158–64
Islamic culture, 143
Islamic law, 146, 156
Islamic scholars, 160–61
Islamists, 130, 150
madrasas, 160
Shia Muslims, 158, 160, 163
Sunni Muslims, 159–60, 163
see also Quran
Islamic State (ISIS), 130, 425
Isocrates, 55
Israel, Jonathan, 296, 326
Italy, 222, 230, 286
city-states, 234–8
Italian Wars, 272–4
see also Rome; Renaissance Italy

Jackson, Thomas, 376
Jacquerie (France, 1358), 246
Jafar (advisor to the caliph), 156
al-Jahiz, 148
Jamaica, 381, 383
James I, King of England and Ireland and VI of Scotland, 270, 390
James II, King of England and Ireland and VII of Scotland, 321, 347–50
Jamestown, Virginia, 391–2
Japan, 424
al-Jazari, 153
Jefferson, Thomas, 399–400, 405–10
Jerusalem, 136, 165
Jesus, 143
Jews/Judaism, 134–5, 305, 323
anti-Semitism, 278
Jin dynasty, 200, 202, 206–7
John, King of England, 233
John of Salisbury, 233
Johnson, Mike, 79
Johnson, Paul, 401, 404
Johnson, Samuel, 364
Jones, Bob, 176
Juan de Mariana, 268
Jurchen people, 200
Justinian I, Byzantine Emperor, 230–33
Juvenal, 83

Kaifeng, China, 179–80, 190, 191–3, 200
Kampen, Netherlands, 304
Kay, John, 364–5
Kazakhstan, 148
Keynes, John Maynard, 416–17
Khayyam, Omar, 153
Khorasan, Persia, 137
al-Khwarizmi 152
Kiev (modern-day Ukraine), 237

al-Kindi, 132, 149–50
King Jr, Martin Luther, 410
Knudsen, Bill, 419
Kublai Khan, 208–10, 222–3
Kuhn, Dieter, 194, 202
Kuran, Timur, 145
Kuru, Ahmet, 160, 166

Lafayette, Gilbert du Motier, Marquis de, 397–8
Landes, David, 345
Last Judgement (Michelangelo), 276
Last Supper, The (Leonardo da Vinci), 261
Lavoisier, Antoine, 363
Law and Revolution (Berman), 231
Lazarus, Emma, 413
Le Roy, Loys, 263–5, 269–70
Legnano, Battle of (1176), 235
Leibniz, Gottfried Wilhelm, 326
Leiden, Netherlands, 297, 305, 323–4
Lennon, John, 429
Leonardo da Vinci, 261–2, 273, 416
Leonidas, King of Sparta, 15, 18, 35–6
Letter on Toleration, A (Locke), 328
Leutze, Emanuel, 3976
Levant, 133
Levellers, 352
Lewis, Bernard, 134–5, 144
Li Qingzhao, 195, 209
Liao dynasty, 185, 200

Liberal Party (Great Britain), 384
Liberia, 408
Libertas (goddess), 90, 413
Liberty's Dawn (Griffin), 379
Licensing of the Press Act (1695), 353
Lincoln, Abraham, 408, 414, 427
Lipsius, Justus, 310
Little Ice Age, 314
Liu, William Guanglin, 188, 211, 214
Livius Andronicus, 89
Lizong, Song Emperor, 207
Locke, John, 276, 302, 326, 328, 350–51, 393–6, 400, 409–10
Loehr, Max, 210, 213
Lombard League, 235
London, England, 350, 355, 357, 363, 388
Long Divergence, The (Kuran), 145
Lorge, Peter, 182
Louis XIV, King of France, 332–3, 347–8
Louisiana Purchase (1803), 412
Low Countries, 286, 288–90
Lu Mengzheng, 184
Lu You, 201
Luddites, 369–70
Luther, Martin, 265, 275, 277–8, 295
Luxembourg, 286
Lyttkens, Carl Hampus, 46

Maastricht, Netherlands, 229
Macaulay, Thomas Babbington, 1st Baron Macaulay, 348, 352, 384

Macedonia, 66–8
Machiavelli, Niccolò, 272
Macmillan, Harold, 420
Madinat as-Salam (Baghdad), 139
Madison, James, 399, 401–2, 407
Magna Carta (1215), 233, 345
Maitland, Fredric William, 231
Malthus, Thomas Robert, 345
Manardi, Giovanni, 266
Manchester, England, 388
Manchuria, China, 200
Mandeville, Bernard de, 313
Manetti, Giannozzo, 256–7, 263
al-Mansur, Abbasid Caliph, 138–9, 146
al-Mamun, Abbasid Caliph, 131–2, 147, 150, 154, 156
Marathon, Battle of (490 BC), 32–3
Marcellus, Roman general, 87–8
Marco Polo, 222–3
Marcus Aurelius, Roman Emperor, 89, 115
Marozzi, Justin, 138
Marshall Plan, 424
Marsilius of Pauda, 233
Martinus, Aldus, 265
Marx, Karl, 177, 294, 313, 414
Mary I, Queen of England and Ireland, 287, 347–8
Mary II, Queen of England, Scotland, and Ireland, 347, 349–51
Mary of Burgundy, 298
Masts, Battle of the (655), 135
al-Masudi, 131
Matilda of Tuscany, 229, 235

Maurice of Orange, 309–10, 317–18
Mauritania, 144
McCloskey, Deirdre, 346, 359–60
McCormick, Cyrus, 414
McNeill, William H., 191
Mecca (modern-day Saudi Arabia), 133
Medici family, 248, 258, 264, 273–4
Medici, Alessandro de, 274
Medici, Cosimo, 258, 260
Medina (modern-day Saudi Arabia), 133
Mehmed II, Ottoman Sultan, 253
Melanchthon, Philip, 278
Menlo Park, California, 416
'merchants of light', 363
Mesopotamia, 20, 21, 138
Michelangelo, 258, 260–62, 273, 276
Michelet, Jules, 219, 242, 272
Middle Ages, 118, 234, 242
Mieris, Frans van, 329–30
Milan, Italy, 252, 286
Milk, Harvey, 410
Mill, John Stuart, 11, 33, 214, 383
Milton, John, 279, 282, 344, 352
Ming dynasty, 185, 210–11, 214–15
Mises, Ludwig von, 116
Mokyr, Joel, 1, 6, 112, 325, 357, 360, 387, 389, 433–5
Mona Lisa (Leonardo da Vinci), 261
Mongols, 168–9, 206–11, 214, 237–8

Monroe, James, 408
Montesquieu, 87, 123, 276
Morris, Ian, 114
Mortimer, Ian, 245
Moscow, Russia, 237
Motley, John Lothrop, 351–2
Mughal Empire, 164
Muhammad, 122, 130, 133, 136–7, 142–3, 158–60, 162, 171
al-Mutasim, Abbasid Caliph, 156
al-Mutawakkil, Abbasid Caliph, 155–6
Mutazilism, 154–5, 159, 162
Mytilene, Lesbos, 58

Naples, Italy, 271, 286
Napoleon Bonaparte, 412
Napoleonic Wars (1803–15), 385
NATO (North Atlantic Treaty Organisation), 424
Natural History (Pliny), 266
Nederveen Meerkerk, Elise van, 297
Needham, James, 178
Needham, Joseph, 202
Nelson, Horatio, 1st Viscount Nelson, 341
Nero, Roman Emperor, 92, 104
Netherlands, 286–92, 310, 351, 389
  see also Dutch Republic
New England, 406
New York Times, 405
New York, 321, 418
New Zealand, 346, 380
Newton, Isaac, 361
Nicholas V, pope, 253, 267

Nicomachean Ethics (Aristotle), 65, 253
Night Watch, The (Rembrandt), 323
Nizam al-Mulk, 159–60
'Nizamiyyas', 160–61, 164
Norman Conquest (1066), 352
Nouvelles de la République des Lettres (Bayle), 327–8

Octavian *see* Augustus, Roman Emperor
Odoacer, 121
Ögedei Khan, 238
Oldenbarnevelt, Johan van, 309, 317–18
Olusoga, David, 406
Olympic Games, 33
  London 2012, 344, 367
On Human Worth and Excellence (Manetti), 256–7, 263
On the Wretchedness of the Human Condition (Pope Innocent III), 255
One Thousand and One Nights, 140, 156
Open: The Story of Human Progress (Norberg), 7
Oration on the Dignity of Man (Pico della Mirandola), 255–6
Oresteia (Aeschylus), 51
Ottoman Empire, 121, 164
'Ozymandias' (Shelley), 1–2

Paine, Thomas, 341, 397, 428
Pallavicino, Ferrante, 277

Palmer, Tom G., 237
Palmieri, Matteo, 219
Pantheon, Rome, 260
paper, production of, 148, 240, 264
Paradise Lost (Milton), 344
Pasion (Athenian slave), 48
Pax (Quellinus), 320
Pax Americana, 423–7
Pax Britannica, 382
Pax Islamica, 140–41, 170
Peace of Lodi (1454), 271
Peace of Münster (1648), 312, 318
Peace of Paris (1783), 412
Peasants' Revolt (England, 1381), 246
Peloponnesian War (431–404 BC), 44, 49, 54–60, 71
Pennsylvania, 407
Pepys, Samuel, 310–11
Pericles, 41–2, 44–5, 49–53, 55–6, 69, 249, 442
Persian Empire, 14–19, 21, 31–40, 58, 60, 116, 123, 133, 146
Persian Fire (Holland), 35
Persian Gate, Battle of the (330 BC), 18
Persians, The (Aeschylus), 40–41
Pertinax, Roman Emperor, 93
Petrarch, Francesco, 240–42, 244, 249–50
Phidias, 49, 52
Philastrius, bishop of Brescia, 123
Philip II, King of Macedonia, 67, 401
Philip II, King of Spain, 287, 298–303

Philip III, King of Spain, 306, 312
Philippines, 286–7, 421
philosophy, 51–2, 61–, 896, 132
Phoenicians, 20
Pico della Mirandola, 255
Piraeus, Athens, 35–6, 55, 68
Pisa, Italy, 224, 234, 248
Pisistratus, 25, 89
Pius II, pope, 227, 254
plague *see* Black Death
Plague of Cyprian, 115–16
Plato, 1, 11, 20, 23, 41, 44, 48–9, 52, 62–6, 89, 94, 95, 120, 123, 131, 248, 254, 399
Plotinus, 120
Plutarch, 99, 101
Poland, 222, 237, 292, 445
poleis, 20, 22
Politics (Aristotle), 236
Polybius, 79, 86, 90
Pompeii, Italy, 107
Pompey, 98–9
Poor Richard's Almanack (Franklin), 399
Pop, Iggy, 73
Portugal, 267, 286, 307–8, 312, 381, 385, 389
Postrel, Virginia, 369
Prak, Maarten, 294, 308, 325
Preston, Levi, 395–6
Priestley, Joseph, 362
Prince, The (Machiavelli), 272
printing
    Renaissance, 264–5
    Song Empire, 196–7
Protagoras of Abdera, 49, 52

Protestantism, 275, 277, 279, 295, 299, 303, 347, 401
Psellus, Michael, 132–3
Ptolemy, 68, 149, 153, 263, 266
Putin, Vladimir, 425

Qadiri Creed (1017), 159
al-Qaim, Abbasid Caliph, 159
Qarmatians, 159
Qing dynasty, 185
Qinzong, Song Emperor, 200
Quellinus, Artus, 320
Quran, 1, 130, 143, 144, 154–5

Raleigh, Walter, 390
Raphael, 131, 254
al-Rashid, Abbasid Caliph, 140, 153, 156
Ray, John, 295
Raymond of Toledo, 225
Red Turbans, 210
Reformation, 275, 282, 295, 299
    see also Counter-Reformation
Rembrandt, 288, 323, 331
Renaissance Italy, 167, 204, 222–82
    Arab influence, 222, 224–6, 237, 280
    architecture, 259–60, 263
    art, 258–62, 272–3, 276
    astronomy, 278–9
    banks, 236
    Black Death, 245–7
    'bonfire of the vanities', 273
    books/literature, 240–44, 253, 264–5, 276–8
    cannonry, 269, 271–2
    Chinese influence, 222–4
    economic freedom, 281
    education system, 254
    end of, 274–5
    exploration, 265–7
    glass mirrors, 245
    Greek influence, 242, 248–9, 253
    human body and, 255–7
    humanism, 238–43, 252–7
    individualism, 243–6
    libertarianism, 249–50
    map, 221
    military power and aggression, 252–3, 269–74
    music, 262
    religion, 239
    'Renaissance Man', 261
    Roman influence, 241, 249
    slavery, 267–9
    social mobility, 257, 281
    trade and commerce, 236–7, 247–8, 257–8
    wealth, 250–51, 257–8
    women's rights, 251–2
    see also Counter-Reformation
Republic of Letters, 324–5, 361, 363
republicanism, 94–5
Ricks, Thomas E., 399
Roanoke Island, US, 390
Rome, Italy (ancient Rome), 9, 14, 76–126
    army, 86, 97–8, 103, 114–15, 116–18
    building construction, 108
    citizenship, 84–5

civil war (49–45 BC), 98–9
Conflict of the Orders, 91–2
consulship, 91
decline and fall, 78–9, 84, 112–21
economy, 109–12, 116, 118–19
education, 89
fleet, 86
founding of, 82–4
government, 90–91, 125
Greek culture and, 87–90
law, 92, 230–33
liberty (*libertas*), 92–5
map, 74–5
military power and aggression, 79–82, 85–6, 96–8, 104, 114–15
Pax Romana, 104–5, 115, 125
philosophy, 89, 120
public health, 108–9, 114, 115–16
religion/gods, 82, 87, 90, 118, 120, 126
res publica, 90–96
Roman Republic, 90–92, 95–101
Roman Warm Period, 103
sack of Rome (410), 120
Senate, 91, 117, 124
slavery, 92–4, 120
taxes, 110–11
theatre, 89
trade, 105–7, 111, 119
Twelve Tables, 92
women's rights, 94, 125
Year of the Five Emperors, 115
Rome, Italy (city), 253
ancient ruins, 239–40
sack of Rome (1527), 274
Romulus and Remus, 83, 105
Romulus Augustus, Roman Emperor, 121
Roosevelt, Franklin D., 417, 419, 423
Roosevelt, Theodore, 418, 421
Rossi, Properzia de', 251
Rostovtzeff, Michael, 109
Rotterdam, Netherlands, 322, 350
Rowse, A. L., 390
Royal Charles, HMS, 320
Royal Exchange, London, 307
Royal Palace, Amsterdam, 320
Royal Society, London, 361
Ruskin, John, 383
Russia, 237, 385, 389, 440–41

Sabians, 134
Sabine women, abduction of the, 83–4
Safavid Empire, 164
al-Saffah, Abbasid Caliph, 137–8
Salamis, Battle of (480 BC), 36–9, 41
Salutati, Coluccio, 248, 250
Samarra, Iraq, 156
Sanandaji, Nima, 140
Sasanian Empire, 122, 133, 162
Saudi Arabia, 144
Savonarola, Girolamo, 273
Schama, Simon, 316
School of Athens, The (Raphael), 131, 254
School of Salamanca, 268, 302, 383, 400

Scot, Michael, 224
Scotland, 354, 378
   Scottish Enlightenment, 354
   union with England, 354
   universities, 354
'Second Industrial Revolution', 415
Seeley, John Robert, 379–80
Selgin, George, 357
Seljuk Empire, 159–60, 163–5, 171
Seneca Falls women's rights convention (1848), 410
Septimius Severus, Roman Emperor, 87, 115
Sepúlveda, Juan Ginés de, 269
serfdom, 80, 187, 232, 246
al-Shahrastani, 159
Shakespeare, William, 89, 236, 262
Shelley, Percy Bysshe, 1–2, 11, 169
Sichuan, China, 207
Sicily, Italy, 56, 60, 224, 286
Sidney, Algernon, 352, 396, 400
Siena, Italy, 234
Sierra Leone, 379
Siger of Brabant, 226
Sima Guang, 199
Singapore, 379
Slater, Samuel, 414
slavery, 9, 16, 352, 437
   Abbasid Caliphate, 139, 143–4
   abolition, 384–5, 405–8
   British Empire, 381, 384–6, 389, 392
   Greece, 21, 23–4, 28, 46, 66
   Jim Crow system, 410
   Renaissance Italy, 267–9
   Rome, 92–4, 120
   Song China, 186
   United States, 404–11, 414
Slavery Abolition Act (UK, 1833), 386
Smil, Vaclav, 219
Smith, Adam, 127, 173, 191, 295, 354, 360, 364–5
Social War (91–88 BC), 85
Society for Effecting the Abolition of the Slave Trade, 384–5
Socrates, 11, 49, 52, 59, 62–3, 68, 71, 131, 156, 254, 277, 338, 435
Solon, 23–4, 92
Song dynasty, China, 176–217
   agriculture, 188–90
   army, 181–2, 186–7, 215
   art, 198–9, 210, 213
   cities, 191–4, 201–3, 210, 215–16, 236
   creative culture, 203–4
   decline and fall, 209–15
   economy, 199–200
   education system, 183–4
   foot binding, 196
   foundation of, 179–82
   free movement, 187, 192
   government, 182–5, 194
   incomes, 177
   industry, 192, 200, 202
   innovation, 177–8, 202, 204–6
   literature, 196–87

map, 175
meritocracy, 183
military power and aggression, 180–82, 185–6
monetary system, 191
Mongol invasion, 206–10, 214
navy, 202, 207–8
neo-Confucianism, 197–8
philosophy, 197–8
population, 199
printing, 196–7–8
property rights, 187–8
religion, 197–8
science, 178, 199
shipping, 190–91, 204
slavery, 186
Southern Song, 201–2
taxes, 192
trade and commerce, 187–8, 191–5, 204
transportation, 190–91
women's rights, 195–6
sophists, 52, 62
Sophocles, 43, 45, 50, 390–91
Spain, 266–8, 271, 273–4, 274, 277–8, 286–8, 299–303, 305–6, 311–12, 316–17, 332, 385
   Al-Andalus, 138, 166, 224–5
   colonisation, 388–90
   'Reconquista', 165
   Spanish Armada, 303, 391
Spanish–American War (1898), 421
Sparta, Greece, 14–19, 25–7, 30–34, 36, 40, 44, 54–61, 70–71, 82

Spencer, Herbert, 383
Spinoza, Baruch, 276, 320, 326–7, 335, 355
Spitalfields Mathematical Society, 362
Ssu-ma Kunag, 189
Stalin, Josef, 419, 422
Stamford Raffles, 379
Starr, Frederick, 149
States of Holland, 309, 319, 333–5
Stephenson, Neal, 346
Stoicism, 66, 89
Strauss, Barry, 39
Su Shi, 194
Suetonius, 102
Sulla, Roman general, 88, 96
Sumervell, D. C., 442
Sun Tzu, 186
Suppliant Women, The (Euripides), 29
Surinam, 321
Sweden, 312, 332, 385
Switzerland, 270–71, 388
syphilis, 272
Syracuse, Sicily, 56, 87
Syria, 157, 159, 164

T'ing-chou, Fukien, China, 202
Taizong, Song Emperor, 183–5, 195–6
Taizu, Song Emperor, 179–85, 193, 215
Taliban, 130
Tang dynasty, 148, 178–9, 185, 187, 192–3, 198
Taoism, 197

Tarquin the Proud, King of Rome, 91
Tasmania, 381–2
Temin, Peter, 109, 111
Temple, William, 283, 295, 337
Tennyson, Alfred, 383, 403
Teutoburg Forest, Battle of the (AD 9), 105
textile industry, 205, 247
Thales of Miletus, 52, 162, 325
Thebes, Greece, 30, 59–61
Themistocles, 34–8, 41–2, 70
Thermopylae, Battle of (480 BC), 14–19, 34, 36
Theseus, 29–30
Third Man, The (film), 270
Thirty Years' War (1618–48), 279, 312
Thucydides, 42–3, 49, 54, 56–8, 60, 71, 438
Tiberius, Roman Emperor, 102–3, 105
Tiberius Gracchus, 96
Tocqueville, Alexis de, 386, 392–3, 413
Toledo, Spain, 165, 225
Tories, 353
Trenchard, John, 393–4
Triple Alliance, 332
triremes, 36, 38
Turgot, Anne Robert Jacques, 313
Turkey, 444
Twain, Mark, 421
Twelve Years' Truce 1609–1621, 312
Two Treatises of Government (Locke), 328, 351

Ukraine, 425
Umayyad Caliphate, 136–8
Union of Utrecht (1579), 301
United States, 78, 346, 380, 394–427, 428–9, 438, 440–42
 agriculture, 414
 American Revolutionary War (1775–83), 393, 394–8, 403, 405, 411
 civil war, 392, 408
 Constitution, 401–2, 408, 410, 429
 Declaration of Independence, 395, 400, 406, 408–11, 429
 Democrats, 399
 First Amendment, 402
 founding of, 398–404, 405, 409
 Homestead Acts, 412
 immigration, 412–13
 influence of the ancients, 398–401
 innovation and industry, 414–18
 international influence, 422–6
 military power and aggression, 419–22
 native Americans, 381, 383, 404
 religion, 401–2
 Republicans, 399
 slavery, 404–11, 414
 Statue of Liberty, 412–13
 technology, 415–18
 trade, 413–14, 423–4
 wealth, 422, 426
 women's rights, 410
 see also America
Usher, A. P., 366

Utica (modern-day Tunisia), 99
Utrecht, Netherlands, 290, 300, 336

Valla, Lorenzo, 243, 252
Valladolid, Spain, 269
van der Heyden, Jan, 328
van der Woude, Ad, 294, 314
van Leeuwenhoek, Antonie, 326
van Zanden, Jan Luiten, 294
Vanini, Lucilio, 277
Vasari, Giorgio, 242, 245
Vatican City
   Apostolic Palace, 254
   library, 253
   Sistine Chapel, 260–61, 273, 276
   St Peter's Basilica, 261
Venice, Italy, 223, 234–5, 245, 247, 265, 278
Vermeer, Johannes, 288, 330–31
Verona, Italy, 241
Veronese, Paolo, 276
Vesalius, Andreas, 263
Vespasian, Roman Emperor, 85
Vespasiano da Bisticci, 242, 251, 253
Vespucci, Amerigo, 266
Vienna, Austria, 238
Vietnam, 445
Virgil, 82–3, 102
Visconti, Duke of Milan, 248
Vitoria, Francisco de, 268
Voltaire, 39, 173, 227, 234, 246, 276, 355
Vries, Jan de, 294, 314
Vroom, Hendrick Cornelisz, 330

Wang Chen, 205
Wang Yangming, 213–14
Washington, George, 396–7, 403, 407, 413
Washington Crossing the Delaware (Leutze), 397
Watson, Peter, 49, 124, 178
Watt, James, 364
Weber, Max, 295
Wedgwood, Josiah, 364, 385
Welles, Orson, 270–71
Wellesley, Arthur, Duke of Wellington, 385
Wellesley, Richard, 385
Wen Tianxiang, 209
West Indies, 389, 406
West, Benjamin, 403
Whigs, 352–3, 395
White, John, 390
Whitefoord, Caleb, 412
Whitehead, Alfred North, 63
William II, Prince of Orange, 318, 321–2
William III, Prince of Orange (later William III, King of England, Scotland, and Ireland), 321, 332–5, 347, 349–51, 353
William Henry, Duke of Gloucester, 397–8
William the Silent, 298–302
Wilson, Andrew, 106
witch trials, 279, 321–2
Wolf, Martin, 29
women's rights, 9, 94, 437
   Abbasid Caliphate, 144–5, 167, 170

Dutch Republic, 296–7
Greece, 21, 28, 46, 66
Renaissance Italy, 251–2
Rome, 94, 125
Song Empire, 195–6
United States, 410
Wood, Gordon, 406
World Trade Organization, 424
World War I, 387, 423
World War II, 419–20
Wu Zimu, 201

Xenophon, 49, 55
Xerxes I, 14–16, 18–19, 34, 36–9
Xiangyang, China, 208

Yangzhou, China, 200
Yaqubi, 139
Yue Fei, 201

Zab, Battle of (750), 137
Zeeland, 290, 300, 304, 307
Zeno of Citium 66
Zhao Kuangyin *see* Taizu, Song Emperor
Zhenzong, Song Emperor, 185
Zhu Xi, 197–8
Zoroastrians, 134, 163–4
Zutphen, Netherlands, 305

A NOTE ABOUT THE AUTHOR

Johan Norberg is a historian, lecturer and commentator. His books, which have been translated into over thirty languages, include *The Capitalist Manifesto*, the international bestseller *Progress*, and *Open*, which was an *Economist* book of the year. Norberg is a senior fellow at the Cato Institute in Washington DC and regularly writes for publications such as *The Wall Street Journal*, *Reason* and *Spectator*.